HISTORY OF AMERICAN THOUGHT

Paul S. Boyer, *General Editor*

Jane Marie Pederson

Between Memory and Reality

*Family and Community in
Rural Wisconsin, 1870–1970*

977.5
P371

The University of Wisconsin Press

The University of Wisconsin Press
114 North Murray Street
Madison, Wisconsin 53715

3 Henrietta Street
London WC2E 8LU, England

5   4   3   2   1

Printed in the United States of America

Library of Congress Cataloging-in-Publication Data
Pederson, Jane Marie.
    Between memory and reality: family and community in rural
    Wisconsin, 1870–1970 / Jane Marie Pederson.
    330 pp.   cm. — (History of American thought and culture)
    Includes bibliographical references and index.
    ISBN 0-299-13280-3   ISBN 0-299-13284-6 (pbk.)
    1. Wisconsin—Rural conditions.   2. Pigeon (Wis.)—Rural
    conditions.   3. Lincoln (Wis.)—Rural conditions.   I. Title.
    II. Series.
    HN79.W6P43   1992
    307.72'09775—dc20   91-45787

Cover illustration: A Wisconsin family in front of their frontier
farm home, ca. 1890–1910 (photo by Charles Van Schaick. Van
Schaick Collection, courtesy of the State Historical Society of
Wisconsin, WHi [V24] 2179) and the Hanson family of Pigeon
Falls, ca. 1940–1950 (courtesy of Eleanor Ackley, Pigeon Falls,
Wisconsin).

For Laila and Spencer

Contents

viii   Contents

Illustrations

Map and Figures

Tables

Acknowledgments

Many individuals and institutions encouraged and assisted in the research, writing, and editing of this book. To begin, I must thank my family, which inspired the topic of this study. My grandparents, aunts and uncles, parents, cousins, and siblings, all must be included. Over the years their stories and conversations entertained, educated, and provided the basis for my interest in this work as a scholar.

I also owe a considerable debt to Dave Wood, who allowed me to have possession of his family's diaries for an extended period of time. Dave supplied family pictures and wonderful hours of conversation. Dave's published works and stories of Whitehall are a treasure trove on the local culture and history. Eleanor Ackley similarly deserves a special thanks for making her mother's diaries and family pictures available to me.

A special debt of gratitude needs to be extended to my advisor at Columbia University, Walter P. Metzger, who provided invaluable direction. His tolerance, knowledge, insightful critiques, and careful editorial assistance influenced all aspects of this book. Other Columbia faculty who offered helpful suggestions include Rosalind Rosenberg and James P. Shenton.

Others who have read the entire manuscript and offered helpful suggestions are Hal Barron, Robert P. Swierenga, and Paul Boyer. My colleagues Robert Gough and James Oberly supplied advice on portions of the content and editorial suggestions.

Several organizations and institutions need to be recognized for their consistent cooperation and assistance. The Trempealeau County Historical Society always found ways to open their records to me, and the staff of the Trempealeau County Courthouse proved interested and helpful in tracking down records and information. Similarly the staff at the State Historical Society of Wisconsin and the Area Research Centers at the University of Wisconsin–Eau Claire and the University of Wisconsin–La

Crosse provided indispensable assistance. Rick Pifer needs especially to be thanked for his guidance through the complex maze of state archives.

I am also appreciative of the financial support offered during the early stages of this research from the Alice E. Smith Fellowship from the State Historical Society of Wisconsin and the Albert J. Beveridge Fellowship from the American Historical Association.

During the final preparation of this book I learned the value of highly skilled and competent editorial assistance from the staff of the University of Wisconsin Press. Barbara Hanrahan, Raphael Kadushin, and most of all Robin Whitaker did the painstaking labor which compensated for any casualness in my writing and organization.

Finally, above all, I wish to thank my husband, Ronald E. Mickel, whose patience, encouragement, advice, ideas, and editorial assistance were invaluable.

Between Memory And Reality

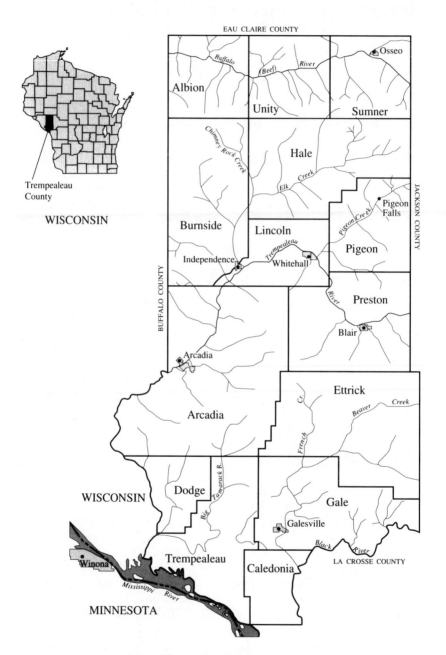

Map of Trempealeau County, Wisconsin

Introduction: Looking at Rural America

The "agrarian myth" is among the most powerful, persistent, and pervasive myths shaping many Americans' sense of their past and national identity. Within our popular culture, romanticized and nostalgic notions of rural life find common expression in literature, film, and music. No doubt, part of the explanation for this preoccupation with life in the countryside is the fact that throughout the nineteenth and into much of this century the rural and small-town world was the birthplace and childhood home of the men and women who would swell the populations of the cities throughout this country. Until quite recently, the majority of Americans grew up in the countryside, even if they did not live most of their lives there. For them, life in rural America was a personal memory, part of their experienced history of a culture which shaped their expectations, values, and behavior. Much of the literature of the last century bears testimony to the reality and significance of such youthful experiences.

While family and community studies have been topics of growing interest to historians, the rural family and community in the late nineteenth and twentieth centuries have not received attention comparable to that of the colonial family in the New England town studies, the black family in slavery, or the family facing the privations and challenges of the frontier. Research on community and family in the late nineteenth century concentrates on the urbanizing and industrializing environments, emphasizing questions of mobility and the adaptation of families to this new social reality. The countryside from which migrant Americans departed in large numbers inspires far less interest among academics than it does in the populous.

This is unfortunate because, unlike the myth and nostalgic imagery of advertising, rural America has not remained static. Like their urban counterparts, men and women in rural families and communities participated in, shaped, and reacted to the many changes of the last century—urbanization, industrialization, the ever-expanding and interconnected market economy, the rise of corporate capitalism, and the growing power of the federal government. But these broad changes impacted upon rural communities in distinctive ways. This distinctiveness has long been a subject of note, if not of systematic analysis, to scholars and creative writers. Recently, historians realized that neither the abundant literature about the frontier nor models for understanding the urban experience are appropriate for understanding the social history of established rural communities in

3

the nineteenth and twentieth centuries. Without careful attention to or research on rural communities, scholars seemingly supposed that rural experience vaguely paralleled that of the frontier in the nineteenth century and then belatedly came to resemble that of the urban communities in the twentieth.[1]

The questions addressed in this study look beyond the frontier period to the transitions brought by the twentieth century to the countryside. What happened after the frontier period? What happened to rural communities after 1920, when the people of this country became overwhelmingly metropolitan in residence and presumably in mentality? What happened to the family and community life after the difficult years of settlement and community building?

The years under consideration here, 1870 to 1970, were years of extraordinary transformations in American society. The majority of Americans ceased to live and make their living on farms and in small towns. In 1890, the director of the census announced that a definable frontier line no longer existed. The anxious and perhaps nostalgic Frederick Jackson Turner eloquently explained the frontier's historical significance and speculated upon the meaning of its demise. Ordinary Americans could no longer look westward for land for opportunities but turned toward the city instead. In 1916 the number of people living on farms peaked at 32.5 million; by then they constituted a minority of 32 percent of the nation's population.[2] Through much of the twentieth century, rural America became a great exporter of people, sending hundreds of thousands of its sons and daughters into the new urban frontier. Also, in these years, the corporate form of capitalism, new ways of organizing work, and the accompanying bureaucratic ethos restructured economic and social relationships.

By the 1920s, rural America stood deeply at odds with the urban America taking shape. The republican ideals of an agrarian America appeared antiquated to many Americans, but not to many who remained in the countryside. The independent yeoman farmer, once the ideal American, became an object of contempt or denigrating concern to more cosmopolitan Americans, whether they employed satire like H. L. Mencken, or the anxious diagnoses of sociologists who "discovered" rural pathology, or the caricature of the anti-small-town novelists. In *Main Street,* Sinclair Lewis's images of youth eager to flee rural tedium, deprivation, and hard work for the bright lights of the city fill the void left by a lack of knowledge. If the frontier tested the mettle and shaped the character of a people, rural life in the twentieth century more often broke the spirit of fictional folk.[3] Whether one reads novelists such as Sherwood Anderson, Sinclair Lewis, and Hamlin Garland, or sociologists such as Arthur Vidich and Joseph Bensman, who wrote *Small Town in Mass Society,* or a historian such as

Richard Hofstadter in his *Age of Reform,* rural communities seem seriously out of step with the rest of American society in regrettable ways.

While the popular media often has romanticized our rural roots, academia and serious writers have rarely done so.[4] As Paul Carter commented over a decade ago, "The historiographic tendency in recent years has been to assume, not merely that the traditional American myth of agrarian virtue pitted against metropolitan vice is untrue, but that the reverse is true: namely, that the city in America has had to fight to sustain its humane values against the onslaughts of mean-spirited and narrow-minded ruralism."[5] But few took pains to test their stereotypes of "country folk" with a close historical study of rural life.

Historical interest in the rural world tends to fade with the frontier as part of "the world we have lost." But the story of rural culture and rural family life does not end with the frontier. Small towns and open-country communities did not grow up to become cities and suburbs. What did become of them is the central question addressed here. This study examines the rural family's and community's fitful birth into the modern world in the postfrontier years. Two neighboring Wisconsin townships in Trempealeau County provide excellent sources on family and community in a rural context, the town of Lincoln,* which surrounds the village of Whitehall, and the town of Pigeon, which includes the village of Pigeon Falls. Here families still live on the farms settled over a century ago, often on the land first tilled by a distant ancestor.

Trempealeau County is in many ways an ideal location for a close study of the rural Midwest. Here popular and academic understanding of the frontier come together. Members of the famed Ingalls family of Laura Ingalls Wilder's "Little House" books appear among the first settlers. Also, two earlier historical studies have focused on this area of Wisconsin, two studies which contrast markedly with each other both in methodology and interpretation. Black River County, of which Trempealeau was once a part, came under the scholarly eye of Michael Lesy in *Wisconsin Death Trip.* In an unforgettably haunting fashion, he documented a life of tragedy, pain, madness, and despair in rural Wisconsin in the years 1885 to 1900 through a selection of photographs and newspaper clippings. *Wisconsin Death Trip* represents the apotheosis of a well-developed tradition documenting rural pathology. Lesy's work is in dramatic contrast to Turner's vision of the frontier.[6]

However, far more important than Lesy's forays into rural social history is the classic study of a frontier community done by the distin-

---

* The terms "town" and "township" are used interchangeably to refer to the same type of political unit.

guished student of Frederick Jackson Turner, Merle Curti. Whitehall is the county seat of Trempealeau County, the locale of Merle Curti's pioneering work in social history, *The Making of an American Community: A Case Study of Democracy in a Frontier County*.[7] Published in 1959, Curti's work is a towering exception to the view of rural America that was propagated following the rejection of Turnerian interpretations.[8]

Curti, of course, studied Trempealeau County to test Frederick Jackson Turner's frontier thesis, and believed he found it substantiated in many respects. Curti's *Making of an American Community* still stands as the outstanding historical study of a midwestern frontier community. Between 1850 and 1880, a generation of pioneers transformed a rugged wilderness into a settled rural community. New Englanders who traced families back to the first Pilgrims at Plymouth Plantation and to the settlers of the Massachusetts Bay Colony reenacted again the drama of building a community in the wilderness. Turner's frontier thesis and Merle Curti's testing of that thesis both raise issues of concern to contemporary historians studying family and community. Anticipating recent directions in social history, Turner and Curti asked questions about "ordinary people." In Turner's poetic and imaginative view of the frontier, democratic institutions and distinctly American ways and values of self-reliance, individualism, egalitarianism, generosity, and neighborliness emerged from the many frontier communities and shaped the American character and an American mind, or what social historians today might call mentalité. Following Turner's lead, Curti's study suggests that the very task of forging a community on the frontier created not only a local mentalité but also a uniquely American one.

Thus, the neglect of the rural social experience, the fine historical work already completed, and the rich sources are no doubt reasons enough for a historian to examine Trempealeau. But there is an additional reason as well which has shaped the questions and direction of this research. If it is true, as has often been noted, that history frequently begins in autobiography, then this research is certainly no exception. I spent my childhood in Wisconsin on a farm owned by my family since the land was first settled by whites, not in Pigeon or Lincoln but in a similar community. From the time I first read Richard Hofstadter's *Age of Reform* and heard my first lecture on the Populist movement as a sophomore in college, I concluded something was amiss with scholars' understanding of rural America. In a review of the treatment of rural history in textbooks by historians, David B. Danbom recently noted, "They ignore it and, at worst, they denigrate it."[9] Like Danbom I have long been troubled by the "gratuitous insults" aimed at rural folk and the aggressive antirural bias that Danbom documented.

My first impressions of what the scholars were saying presented a rather odd picture: Farmers, except for a pathological few, became businessmen, economic individualists, even as they cleared the land of the frontier. Since they produced for national and international markets and worked for profits, survival dictated that they become entrepreneurs on the land. However, the countryside offered little chance of success, and most sensible folk moved to the city, where they found factory jobs—a notable improvement over the isolation, cultural deprivation, tedium, and hard work of the farm. Only the backward-looking, irrational, narrow-minded, bigoted racists remained in the country. Traditional community and family had broken down sometime around 1720 or 1920, depending upon whom one read, and clearly sociologists and historians did not agree with each other or among themselves.

Studying history in graduate school at Columbia University did not quickly dispel my discomfort, but I did eventually encounter historical studies more consistent with my own sense of reality. If my roommate while in graduate school, a woman who had grown up in Scarsdale, New York, experienced recognition of her world when she read Christopher Lasch's *Haven in a Heartless World,* similar responses were stirred in me when I encountered the New England town studies in David Rothman's colloquium on the history of the family and Walter Metzger's colloquium on recent trends in American historiography. I realized that I had grown up in a "community" that had much in common with seventeenth-century Dedham, Massachusetts—as much in common as Scarsdale, which recent sociologists might describe as a life-style enclave. At the same time, I realized that something radical had happened, even during my lifetime, to rural communities similar to the one in which I grew up. And once again the New England town studies with the theme of declension or decline suggested parallels. My first impressions were not, of course, always accurate and they did not go unchallenged. Nevertheless, the confrontations of cultures which my experience represented and the conflict between scholarly analysis and personal experience generated the questions leading to this effort to recapture a portion of the history of rural America.

Rural and small-town life has been carefully analyzed for seventeenth- and eighteenth-century New England. The New England town studies reveal that the first generations on the colonial frontiers set out to re-create traditional corporate peasant communities, and at least for two or three generations were quite successful. By the end of their first century these communities were evolving toward more complex, socially stratified, pluralistic, and individualistic societies. The direction of change has often been described as toward the modern, producing a decline in the traditional community and family relations which had flourished.[10] The evolution of the New England towns fits Ferdinand Tonnies's typology of *Gemeinschaft* to *Gesellschaft*. The theme of breakdown of community and modernization, however, have proved problematic. The timing and nature of the transformations are complex and subject to considerable dispute, as is the concept of modernity.[11]

Recent work of historians suggests that the frontier in the eighteenth and nineteenth centuries, rather than transforming those who made it their home, allowed them to preserve traditional values and traditional family and community relations at least temporarily. The frontier family depended upon a near-subsistence household economy, which supported and depended upon the young and the old. Frontier folk expected hierarchy, authority, and obedience in the well-ordered family and community. The line between public and private life remained vague. Both family and community were inhospitable to individualism and privacy; community and religious leaders presumed to meddle in the private lives of community members, and families continued to bear a wide range of responsibilities later relocated in other institutions.[12]

The recent return to the study of rural Americans raises new questions of the historical experience of the people of Trempealeau. In Curti's analysis of the county, the frontier stage was over by 1880, and if recent scholarship is correct about the inevitable temporary quality of the traditional family and community, the next 50 years should have brought much change. But Trempealeau was not Dedham, Massachusetts, or Oneida County, New York. Before and after 1880, Trempealeau was overrun not only by New Englanders but also by Norwegians, Poles, and a scattering of other nationalities, who introduced into rural Trempealeau an element of diversity absent in New England and many earlier rural American communities. These new arrivals often came directly from Scandinavian and other European peasant communities even more deeply rooted in a traditional society than their American counterparts. This raises obvious questions: What impact did these immigrants make on the evolution of family and community life? Did their traditional ways share a fate similar to that of frontier families in upstate New York? What kinds of conflicts or congruence of values can be found among those who arrived in Trempealeau after 1850? To what extent did the frontier and rural communities sustain or diverge from the traditional cultures dissolving in both Europe and America by the solvents of an urban and industrial order? If one looks back not only to Vermont and New England as Curti did, but also to Norway and Poland, from which most of the county's residents of 1880 had come, will different conclusions result about the dynamics of local communities and cultures? To what extent did ethnic origins shape local traditions, if at all? Did the rural localities quickly melt down the ethnic identities or does an examination of the postfrontier years alter that conclusion?[13]

By 1880 only the bare skeleton of community life and institutions of

Trempealeau County had taken shape. In addition, as Curti discovered, the first 30 years involved a high degree of geographic mobility. Did the early cultural hegemony of those migrant New Englanders, which Curti noted, continue in the postfrontier years? Seemingly, local communities with a highly mobile and ethnically diverse population would hardly have a deeply embedded outlook rooted in a shared community experience in so short a time, unless indeed the frontier was, as Turner described it, a source of perennial "rebirth." Is it possible that many of the virtues, values, and structures which both Curti and Turner associated with the frontier had as much to do with the persistence of Old Country ways as they did with the frontier?

While historians continue to reconsider the frontier legacy, this study is particularly concerned with the postfrontier years and the twentieth-century experience. Here historical literature is even more sparse concerning rural communities than it is for the nineteenth century. It has been argued that by the late nineteenth century local life, even in rural and small-town areas, began to lose the quality of community. Thomas Bender, who cautioned historians about prematurely announcing the breakdown of community, nonetheless concluded that during the late nineteenth century "important economic and political elements of social life were torn from their communal context, reformed into segments of life with their own justification—that is, justification independent of community...."[14] While the nineteenth-century frontier fostered communities and localities which kept alive diverse "little traditions," the twentieth century seemingly did not. Historians have concluded that not only did the diverse traditions dissolve but also the reality of a community's connection to a locality on the whole disappeared.[15] Historians frequently describe farmers as becoming modern individualists and entrepreneurial in their orientation by the 1920s.

Challenging the assumptions of historians is the work of sociologists, anthropologists, and rural sociologists, who offer more ambiguous conclusions. Their ethnographic and quantitative studies document continuities between the past and twentieth-century rural experiences often missed by the historians. While economic and political power lost its base in rural areas, rural Americans nonetheless sustained many traditional ideals and values nurtured in communities of the past.[16] As typical members of what Robert Wiebe identified as the "new middle class," rural sociologists' raison d'être was to foster the modernization of the countryside. As progressive reformers, they sought to bring efficiency and civilization to the farm. Later, modernization theory framed much of their analysis and policy proposals.[17]

While historians may find much to criticize about the assumptions and methodologies of rural sociologists, their work raises questions about and offers insights into rural communities in the twentieth century. First, to their considerable frustration, and despite their reformist goals, rural sociologists documented nothing more clearly than resistance to "progress" and the tenacious grip of tradition on many rural families and communities. Secondly, rural sociologists have been careful to define and document the nature of community in the countryside, especially open-country communities, which are distinct from small towns. Lastly, they have long recognized the diversity that characterizes the rural population.

Throughout most of this century rural sociologists present a rather different picture of the farmer from that of the historian. The farmer who functions as a modern businessman has certainly been the ideal for rural sociologists but not the reality they document. The sociological literature noted a broad division among farmers. Into the decade of the 1960s, rural sociologists lamented the persistence of what some referred to as traditionalists and cheered modern types among farmers. The will as well as the capacity of "traditional" farmers to survive the vicissitudes of the market economy frustrated the experts who saw this as one more of many symptoms of rural pathology. Local control of religious, educational, and political institutions long stood as a protection for the "traditionalists," subverting rural sociologists' ambitions for "reform." Whether rural sociologists work within a framework of modernization theory or Marxism, they do not describe twentieth-century American farmers as modern individualistic entrepreneurs, which historians sometimes suppose them to be.[18]

Colonial historian Darrett Rutman recently bemoaned the difficulties of trying to make historical sense of the diverse findings of community studies spanning American history from the colonial period to the present. He posed an important question: "Will we ultimately be able to sense large patterns in many studies of small places?"[19] Historians studying small communities have sought patterns amid diverse findings. In New England, colonial historians found the basic trend in the town studies to be from homogeneity and consensus toward conflict and pluralism. Hal Barron found the situation reversed in a nineteenth-century New England rural community. In studying the midwestern frontier, Curti identified a pattern of assimilation and growing homogeneity between diverse ethnic groups. Others rely upon the metaphor of a mosaic to describe the complexity of rural cultures. This study of two Trempealeau County townships does not reduce the conceptual conundrums that rural communities present. The Midwest with its ethnic diversity adds another level of complexity. In addition the twentieth century brought an entirely new experience to rural America, which rural sociologists have been careful both to promote and to monitor. Rural economic evolution and cultural patterns in the nineteenth and twentieth centuries simply do not fit the models developed for understanding the New England town or the frontier experience or the urban context. The settled rural communities faced unique challenges and opportunities.

This study explores a local rural culture in the past century, when country folk faced a multitude of changes. One finds a surprising resilience and creative adaptability in the ideals and institutions that migrants and immigrants brought with them to Trempealeau, creating a persistence in custom and commitment which has frustrated the rural sociologist. The cultural heritage of European peasants and American migrants imparted a vital resource for creative adaptation to the situations and opportunities of the frontier and the challenges of the twentieth century. In the way they worked, worshiped, educated the young, and organized and socialized within their communities, the culture from which they originated competed in importance with the midwestern context to which they came.

A word on organization: The following chapters consider a variety of aspects of rural life organized thematically. Each chapter traces the developments of distinct dimensions of the local communities' economy, demographics, politics, and culture during the century from 1870 to 1970. The data revealed roughly three stages of Trempealeau County's history, and each chapter addresses this three-stage development. First, the years 1850 to 1880 represent the frontier or settlement phase, which Merle Curti thoroughly examined. These years featured rapid population growth while land was first claimed and cleared. Among farmers the basic trend of these years was toward economic equality despite the differences in wealth among those who first arrived. Although the farmers produced wheat for a national market, much of the work nonetheless related to a household economy and was local in orientation. The families and the local community depended upon themselves and each other to provide for their own needs economically, socially, and educationally. The early settlers could and often did manage quite independently of the market. Production centered in the household, with much of the exchange being local and frequently based on barter. The household and local economy of the settlers extended well into the decade of the 1880s in the towns of Lincoln and Pigeon. The arrival of the Green Bay and Western Railroad in 1874 in Lincoln signaled an important turning point in the locally oriented economy. By 1880 local trading centers such as Pigeon Falls and Whitehall had established themselves, efficiently linking local markets to a national one.[20]

Much of the focus of this study is on the second phase, or the postfrontier years, of settled and stable community life between 1880 and 1945. While the rural culture of this phase had much in common with the frontier years, it also included distinct characteristics of its own. These years brought population stability, growing ethnic homogeneity, and the shift from wheat cultivation toward dairying as the source of the most important marketable product. A considerable diversification of production on the farm characterized this period, but much of this diversification continued to be oriented toward the household and the local economy. Mechanization increased, complementing family and community systems of labor, which persisted in a position of preeminence. Villages such as Whitehall grew in population and importance as centers of trade, education, and sociability, but open-country neighborhoods flourished as well. Within the rural neighborhoods and towns a variety of locally controlled institutions, cooperatives, and voluntary associations were created to serve educational, cultural, political, social, and economic needs, which earlier had been largely left to families and informal arrangements. The size of the population remained relatively stable, because the county became an exporter of people. The reorientation began slowly in the 1880s and was highly developed by 1910. Until the end of the decade of the 1940s, this basic pattern continued. Phase two, the years of settled rural life, produced relatively autonomous rural cultures that sustained a mentalité and social values deeply rooted in the past. It was a culture and mentalité often in conflict as internal and external challenges were confronted.[21]

The final stage, which began in the mid-1940s and continues to become more pronounced with the passing years, initiated the most dramatic changes to family and local community and culture. In this period the number of farmers progressively declined while the size of the farms increased and became less diversified. More complex commercial farming developed with the accompanying increase in specialization, mechanization, rationalization, and centralization of production. While this happened local families and culture moved into the mainstream of consumer society as never before. When they did so, they became far more dependent upon the market and money for the purchase of consumer goods and cultural definition. Policy makers in Washington, D.C., and an international market became crucial to their survival. While the population increased in villages like Whitehall, such places declined as vital economic centers, since they were unable to compete with the nearby cities for the expanding consumer desires of the locals.

Both the villages and the countryside increasingly looked and perhaps thought more like a suburban America than the country neighborhoods and small towns of the past. Many of the bonds that sustained local communities dissolved when rural dwellers began to lose the battles with diverse bureaucrats and corporations for control over local institutions. Professional educators finally won the struggle to shut down the country schools, a change which was symptomatic of a general decline of local power and control in the face of diverse bureaucracies. Although the developments that are characteristic of the post–World War II years had tentatively intruded during the flush times of World War I, the recession in the countryside of the 1920s, followed by the harsh years of the Great Depression, effectively arrested dramatic change until after 1945.[22]

This study begins with chapters discussing the structural changes which underlay the three phases of local history: demographic development, patterns of land ownership, ethnic composition, and mobility. It then moves on to more subtle expressions of community and culture in religion, work, gender definitions, and other diverse dimensions of local cultural change.

1
On Being "Left Behind"

To the extent that small size, stability, and homogeneity are qualities of localities associated with an earlier age, the communities of Trempealeau County throughout this century are certainly misplaced in time. Even today the small town of Whitehall and the neighboring village of Pigeon Falls leave the impression that these are places that have been left behind or have escaped (depending upon one's point of view) the basic trends in American society. As one approaches Pigeon Falls from the picturesque, winding, hilly roads, a large billboard greets the traveler with these words: "Welcome to Pigeon Falls Where Everyone Is Important." If one notices the population of this unincorporated village—338—one may easily surmise that the billboard's boast is indeed true. In 1980 in the entire township of Pigeon there were only 408 households with a total population of 1,214. No anonymous Americans here!

Actually these seemingly small numbers are the result of a veritable boom in the local population. The decade of the 1970s reversed a 70-year decline in population of Pigeon Township and brought an increase of 26.9 percent. The arrival of a notable number of "outsiders" did not go unnoticed.[1] The neighboring township of Lincoln was saved from a similar earlier loss of population in the countryside by the existence of a county home which accommodated 214 residents in 1970. The village of Whitehall provided almost all the population growth that did occur in the township between 1900 and 1970. The 1980 population of 1,530 was unsurpassed in Whitehall's history (see Table 1.1).

From frontier times until the present, these townships and the entire county of Trempealeau have been exclusively rural. Like many rural areas in the United States, the population of Pigeon and Lincoln townships stagnated after the expansive years of settlement, or in many cases declined in the open countryside in the twentieth century. The nearest urban areas are over 40 miles from these townships, and even those cities—Eau Claire and La Crosse—could hardly be described as major metropolitan centers.

14

Table 1.1. Numerical and Percentage Distributions of Population Growth and Decline in the Study Area, by Township and Village, 1870–1970

	Whitehall		Lincoln		Pigeon[a]		Total	
	N	% change	N	% change	N	% change	N	% change
1870	—		—		—		822	
1880	267		596		793		1,656	+101.0
1890	304	+13.9	633	+6.2	1,038	+30.9	1,975	+19.3
1900	600	+97.0	786	+24.0	1,209	+16.5	2,595	+31.4
1910	703	+17.2	835	+6.2	1,203	−0.5	2,741	+5.6
1920	851	+21.1	789	−5.5	1,194	−0.7	2,834	+3.4
1930	915	+7.5	755	−4.3	1,132	−5.2	2,802	−1.1
1940	1,035	+13.1	746	−1.2	1,067	−5.7	2,848	+1.6
1950	1,379	+33.2	781	+4.7	1,051	−1.5	3,211	+12.7
1960	1,446	+4.9	882	+12.9	975	−7.2	3,303	+2.9
1970	1,486	+2.8	811	−8.0	957	−1.8	3,254	−1.5
1980	1,530	+3.0	935	+15.3	1,214	+26.9	3,679	+13.0

Source: State of Wisconsin, *Blue Books*, 1871–1971 (Madison: State Printer).
[a]These figures include the population of the village of Pigeon Falls.

Unlike the situation three-quarters of a century earlier, few Americans by 1980 would live in small towns and on farms like those of Trempealeau. The stagnant numbers suggest that these country communities were left quietly behind, changing little after 1880, as Americans rushed into the burgeoning cities.[2]

Not only do the population statistics call an earlier era to mind, but the physical appearance does so as well. A mill and mill dam still stand in the same location where Peder Ekern built his original flour and feed mill in 1872. The mill continues to serve the needs of local farmers as it did in the first decades of settlement. As in 1880, today the family farm is still the economic basis of both Whitehall and Pigeon Falls; those villages are country trading centers just as they were a century before. In Pigeon Falls across Highway 53 from the mill is the Ekern Store, long owned by the Ekern Company and originally established in the 1870s. The John Melby Bank dominates Whitehall's main street today much as its creator, John Melby, the paramount patriarch among Norwegian immigrants, commanded the regard of his countrymen. Struggling farmers depended upon Melby to extend credit in the 1880s, and the bank continues to do so today.[3] A 1964 county atlas features pictures of the one- and two-room country schools, which often were built before the turn of the century and which continued to serve their rural communities in the decade of the 1960s. Despite a 45-year effort of "progressive" educators to hasten their

A family in front of their frontier farm home, ca. 1890–1920. Photo by Charles Van Schaick. Van Schaick Collection. Photo courtesy of State Historical Society of Wisconsin, WHi (V24) 2182.

demise, those schools often educated three and four generations of the same family. Only in the 1980s has the school district, influenced by latter-day progressive professionals, begun to close down the last of the two-room country schools.[4]

Just as the public institutions and businesses portray a long continuity, so do the houses show the mark of another time. Between 1900 and 1920 most of the farmers replaced their rough frontier dwellings with spacious farm homes. In 1950, 85 percent of the people of the county outside of the villages lived in homes that had been built before 1920; by that time many of those farmhouses were the homes of the grandchildren and great-grandchildren of the individuals who had built them.[5] In Pigeon Falls one still finds an "upper" and a "lower" church, originally organized because of a schism in the Norwegian Lutheran church in the 1880s. If one enters these churches on week days, one can often find women busy at work in the church basements, making quilts much as one would imagine women working at quilting bees a century earlier.[6]

Perhaps there is something even more striking about the stability of the town: many of the women who are at the present-day quilting bees possess

The Lars Swaim family in front of their elegant new brick home in 1901. Between 1900 and 1920, local farmers replaced the rough cabins of the frontier era with spacious farm homes. Photo courtesy of Arlene Arneson, Whitehall, Wisconsin.

the same surnames as those listed on the 1880 manuscript census of Pigeon Township and in the church records of that decade. Many of the same names that graced the membership rosters of the original churches prevail in the membership lists of the 1980s. While paging through the parish's publications, which provide pictures of the member families, one may imagine without difficulty that these were the solid, alert, weathered, and strong-looking men and women who entered the area as pioneers. The names, the numbers, the appearance of these communities suggest continuities over time.[7]

For the social historian there does seem to be a distinctly anachronistic quality about Lincoln and Pigeon even while they were being settled in the 1850s. The first arrivals cherished the ancient ambition of common folk to establish a claim to the land. While in some places new dreams were being dreamed, new opportunities discovered, and new strategies forged for an urban industrial world, most Trempealeau settlers nurtured notably traditional aspirations. Tilling the soil had been and would continue to be the basis of their livelihood. The peasant's traditional hunger for land created frontier men and women who would clear and cultivate the land, establishing a permanent home for themselves and their children. Others represented the long tradition of the speculator and entrepreneur who would buy cheap and sell dear, moving on when property values went up or when wheat exhausted the soil and easy opportunities. Whether the settlers were transplanted New Englanders, Norwegians, Germans, or Swiss, land tempted them to the Trempealeau frontier. And until the present the land and farming has sustained and retained them in Lincoln and Pigeon.

During the frontier years the steady influx of settlers into the area fueled population growth. Between 1870 and 1880, when immigrants arrived in large numbers, the combined population of Pigeon and Lincoln would more than double as more land was claimed and cleared for the first time.[8] Of those Americans who first broke the sod of Trempealeau, the largest number migrated from rural upstate New York—pushed out by the combined pressures of a too-abundant populous overrunning opportunities on the land, competition from transmountain farmers, and beginnings of urbanization and industrialization. Those who left the developing East behind chose the option of opportunities on the land in the West rather than remaining in New York and becoming part of the growing cities and their emergent middle class. The first settlers of the town of Lincoln joined a several-century flow westward of old-stock Americans.[9] As such, the early settlers of Lincoln Township had closer connections to the past than to the dynamic urban situation at midcentury. For the first few decades these families and communities, in their households' organization and work, in their economy, and in their social institutions, had as much in common with seventeenth- and eighteenth-century New England as with Utica, New York, "the cradle of the middle class."[10]

Of the native born in the 1870 census of the town of Lincoln, New York was the most frequent birthplace of the migrants.[11] Among them were Alvah Wood and his son Dave. Their ancestors for generations had been building homes on the succession of American frontiers and presumably knew a good deal about creating communities and bringing civilization to a rugged wilderness. John Wood first arrived in Lynn, Massachusetts, in 1635 as part of that first wave of nonconformists who left England. By the time of Alvah Wood's birth in 1809, the family had found its way to Van Rensselaerville, New York. Before making his own way to southern Wisconsin, Alvah married Amanda Porter, born in 1813 in Augusta in Oneida County, New York. From southern Wisconsin, he followed his son Dave northward to Trempealeau County in 1856. Widowed in 1854, Alvah wed a second time in 1857, marrying Sally Parsons, a woman of equally venturesome pioneering stock. A descendant of none other than the pioneer governor of Plymouth Plantation, William Bradford, she and her first husband appeared on the Wisconsin frontier in 1844. No doubt the Porter, Parsons, and Wood family histories prepared them well to pass on Yankee ways. The first town meeting of the town of

Lincoln gathered in the home of Deacon Alvah Wood in April of 1860. A few years earlier, Wood's home had served as the first church meeting house, and in 1858 he and a small group of neighbors and kinsman organized the first Baptist church in the area.[12]

Those who left Oneida County and its counterparts elsewhere chose to perpetuate for their families the way of life, "the evanescent frontier identity," as it dissolved in the East.[13] Family relationships in Deacon Alvah Wood's household and that of his son Dave were characterized by the same interdependent family economy, patriarchal authority, and family lineal values of earlier communities. Alvah and Dave owned farms near each other in Lincoln. Their social, economic, and religious activities were intimately interconnected. Year after year they worked their farms, organized their finances, and promoted and participated in the institutions of the community together.

The Wood family's commitment to land, family, and community continued across the generations. When Dave's eldest son married he took over his grandfather's farm after Alvah's death; the youngest son, Ralph, worked Dave's farm much of his life, and another son, with the help of his father, also established himself on a farm in Lincoln. All would remain in the area until their deaths, as would Ralph's son Harold. Alvah Wood's wife spent her years of widowhood in Dave Wood's home. From the

Two generations of the Wood family, ca. 1900–1910: Dave Wood, his wife Mary (*right*), and their son Jim, and his wife Olive (*left*). Photo courtesy of Dave Wood, Minneapolis.

pioneer years in 1850 until the death of Dave Wood in 1927, church, family, and local government were the institutional contexts in which the Wood family's lives unfolded. Dave Wood's children, grandchildren, and great-grandchildren continued to be active members in the community for over a century.[14]

Among those first pioneers meeting to organize the town of Lincoln was a representative of another family with a noteworthy genealogy, Shubal Breed, the future son-in-law of Alvah Wood. The forefathers of this restless early homesteader arrived with the first Puritans of Massachusetts Bay in 1630, and farmed the land which became famous in 1775 as Breed's Hill, site of the bloody battle of Bunker Hill. Similarly, in legend and popular mythology no pioneer community is complete without an Ingalls family, and Lincoln's first town meeting in 1860 did not fall short. In 1856 among the first homesteaders, appropriately named for his task, came Moses Ingalls and his two sons, Francis and Moses D., members of the wide-ranging pioneer kin network of Laura Ingalls Wilder. Since the seventeenth century these families, generation after generation, had remained on the land by moving progressively farther west when the communities they had created developed and became crowded. They had learned in the process much about pioneering in the American wilderness and about community building. From New England to upstate New York, from New York to Ohio, Indiana, and Illinois, and by the 1840s and 1850s on to Wisconsin such families streamed.[15]

Historians such as Mary Ryan, looking back on the developments of the nineteenth century, perceived the rural areas of Oneida County as being left behind by the changes in places like Utica. Those who left Oneida County for Wisconsin's frontier saw the situation rather differently. While to some these communities appear to be the world left behind, those moving on west in the nineteenth century perceived themselves as departing from an older, more decadent world. They continued their independence on the land, escaped the mills and factories that grew up in the East, and avoided the growing inequality and social stratification of eastern cities and the appearance of untoward luxuries and corruption which had unnerved prior generations of New Englanders.

On the Trempealeau frontier a social creed flourished that echoed that of the revolutionary generation's republican moralism. The West with its huge land resources would prevent the development of the extremes of wealth and poverty and the accompanying corruptions of luxury and deprivation. The lands of the West nourished social equality and widespread political participation—to them the essence of democracy. Suspicious of wealth, they lauded the virtues of simplicity of style and manner. In their social and political activities widespread participation was expected. Their creed honored above all the virtues of generosity and helpfulness.[16]

In Pigeon this kind of republican moralism found an eloquent spokesman in New York–born James D. Olds; appropriately enough, he claimed the status of the first real settler in the county. In 1851 this 19-year-old arrived alone in Trempealeau, preceded only by the backwoodsman and fur trader James Reed. During the economic crisis of the post–Civil War years, Olds became a local organizer of first the Greenback party and later the Populist party. As they looked east men such as Olds saw growing inequality, ever-expanding monopolies, and power preying on the liberties of the hardworking and virtuous, and they strove to insure that these vices would not gain a foothold in their West. The generation that settled Trempealeau County carried with it the culture of the New England town and the ideology of republican moralism that evolved earlier in the more egalitarian, homogeneous, and agrarian communities of the past.[17]

The homogeneity so prized in New England towns, however, did not typify Trempealeau's frontier years. Norwegian, Polish, and German neighbors soon surrounded the farms of migrants like J. D. Olds and Alvah Wood. When this happened, many of the first Yankee settlers moved on. Whether they fled when their homogeneity and local control were undercut or in reaction to other stimuli such as the declining productivity and profits from wheat production is unclear. Evidence can be found for both explanations. Whatever the reasons for the behavior of the native born, it is clear that the immigrants introduced a pluralism to frontier communities not present in New England or upstate New York at the time of settlement.[18]

Curti concluded that the influx of the immigrant into the county made little difference: "The good will of the native-born in inviting and accepting the foreigner and the eagerness of the immigrant to accommodate himself to the new conditions made possible the continued dominance of the Old American culture. . . ." Curti also provided another explanation for minimizing the impact of ethnic diversity on the frontier: "There was an absence of any basic cleavages in the value systems of the various peoples."[19] Those who remained in Pigeon and Lincoln such as J. D. Olds and the Wood family may have discovered that they had much in common with their Norwegian and Polish neighbors. It could have been the case that they shared more with each other in their desire to retain their own versions of the traditional family and community than they shared with the urban middle classes in Utica or Oslo.

Norwegian immigrants, like the New York migrants to Trempealeau, left their native lands at a time when population pressure forced them off the land. Rather than remain and adjust to a changing world, they migrated to a country where land was still available, land on which they could continue a way of life and work that was disappearing at home. Frequently Norway's immigrants departed from the more traditional, isolated, mountain, peasant communities; those least affected by the pressures for change supplied the largest numbers of immigrants to America. As one historian of Norwegian migration recently concluded, "The more traditional regions often became the hotbed of America fever."[20] Rather than enter into new kinds of social and economic relationships at home, they chose to go where they could obtain farm land which could support their families in a familiar way of life.

Thus, the decision to emigrate could be a profoundly conservative act. In their commitment to life on the land, there was a real congruence of values among many of those who arrived in Trempealeau after 1850, and particularly among those who stayed there in subsequent years. A higher proportion of Norwegians took up farming than any other group immigrating to the United States in the latter half of the nineteenth century. This preference for life on the land spurred their decision to emigrate despite opportunities for work in Norway in industrial and urban areas.[21] As one historian of German emigration noted, the emigrants "went to America less to build something new than to regain and conserve something old."[22]

In Trempealeau County as a whole and in the towns of Lincoln and Pigeon, the population expanded rapidly in the frontier years. Between 1870 and 1880, when the immigrants arrived in large numbers, the population doubled in the two townships. However, the following decade indicated that the land-man ratio had approached its limit in supporting a farm population at the levels of technology then used. After 1900 almost no further expansion of population was to take place in the countryside. Only the villages grew in subsequent years. In 1880 Whitehall, the county seat, included 267 residents. By 1900 the number more than doubled to 600 and by 1940 totaled 1,051. Like the county as a whole, the townships of Lincoln and Pigeon remained exclusively rural by any definition, including that of the census, until the present. (See Table 1.1.)

Typical of frontier areas, a high degree of turnover in the population took place in Trempealeau before 1880. As the first settlers moved on and new ones arrived, the ethnic mix changed, as did the aspirations and habits of the people.[23] By 1880 the Norwegians claimed the status of the largest ethnic group in Lincoln and Pigeon, and by 1916 an early historian of Trempealeau estimated that about 70 percent of the people of the county were Norwegian.[24] Although it is clear that the immigrants were eager, as Curti discovered, to exploit the opportunities on the land and to use the political institutions to their own advantage, it is less clear that they eagerly sought acculturation. Ethnic identity and traditional ways of thinking and acting became intimately interconnected for the two major immigrant groups in Trempealeau, the Poles and the Norwegians. Norwegian-Americans established and maintained into the second quarter of the twentieth century a flourishing ethnic culture in the Midwest, and Trempealeau County immigrants situated themselves within the mainstream of that Norwegian-American culture (see chapter 2).

When the population became and remained more ethnically homogeneous in rural neighborhoods, it also became more stable. In Trempealeau County as a whole during the frontier years, the old-stock Americans persisted at slightly higher rates than other ethnic groups. This trend ended, however, as the Norwegian immigrants and their children multiplied in numbers. In fact, one of the striking features of the postfrontier years is the extraordinary persistence of Norwegian and Polish families on the land. After 1880, whenever land became available from the families of original Yankee farmers, invariably immigrants or their children purchased it, stayed for decades, and then passed it on to their children.[25]

Because the focus of this research is on families, the question of persistence of individuals across time will not be considered. Rather, family persistence has been analyzed in order to determine to what extent the Norwegian peasant's commitment to sustaining the family line on a particular farmstead continued in Trempealeau. In Norway even today the state protects the family's rights to keep the farm in the family. Although no legal protection sustained Pigeon farmers on their farms, they nonetheless nurtured this traditional commitment in the American environment. Rural communities in Europe and the United States could not absorb the large numbers of children they produced, and the young, perhaps most of them, left the communities of their birth. But in a large portion of those cases they left a brother or sister back home on the farm or in the village. By examining the persistence of families between 1870 and 1970, one can see the basis of the stability which sustained distinct ethnic communities over the years. By tracking the families of Pigeon through manuscript censuses, tax records, farmer directories, and plat maps, one finds almost 80 percent of the families who were present in the town of Pigeon in 1880 continuing to be represented there 20 years later (i.e., just over 20 percent had left by 1900). Eighty years and several generations later, over 40 percent of the families of 1880 still had numerous progeny on the land of Pigeon Township.

Families arriving after 1880 proved somewhat less successful in establishing themselves for an extended period of time. By 1900 another 81 families appeared in the census of Pigeon, at least 18 of which had arrived before 1890. Of all these families, over a third could not be located ten

Table 1.2. Persistence of Families on the Land, Pigeon Township

	N	%
Families Present in the 1880 Census		
1880 only	20	14.3
1880–1890	9	6.4
1880–1900	17	12.1
1880–1905/1910	12	8.6
1880–1920	7	5.0
1880–1930	18	12.9
1880–1954	57	40.7
Households	140	100.0
Families First Appearing in the 1890 Tax Records		
1890–1900	4	22.2
1890–1930	6	33.3
1890–1954	8	44.5
Households	18	100.0
Families First Appearing in the 1900 Census		
1900 only	27	42.9
1900–1910	14	22.2
1900–1930	13	20.6
1900–1954	9	14.3
Households	63	100.0
Families First Appearing in the 1910 Census		
1910 only	23	52.3
1910–1920	2	4.5
1910–1930	13	29.6
1910–1954	6	13.6
Households	44	100.0

Sources: Manuscript Censuses, U.S. Census of Population, Pigeon and Lincoln townships, Trempealeau County, Wisconsin, 1880, 1900, 1920; Tax Records, Pigeon and Lincoln townships, Area Research Center, University of Wisconsin–La Crosse, 1890; *Atlas and Farmers Directory of Trempealeau County, Wisconsin; Triennial Atlas and Plat Book, Trempealeau County, Wisconsin.*

Note: The latter dates indicate that the families are still present on the land, but that they were not present at the time of the next source's publication. These are not exact persistence rates but loose indicators.

years later. Another 22 percent would be gone by 1930, leaving only 44 percent of those who were present in 1900. Only 21 percent of these families could be located on the land or in church records in 1950. Those who arrived after the frontier years apparently found it more and more difficult to become established on the land as the value and cost of the farms increased.

Table 1.3. Summary of the Data in Table 1.2

	N	%
Families staying:		
Less than 20 years	99	37.4
20–30 years	30	11.3
30–50 years	44	16.6
Over 50 years	92	34.7
Total families	265	100.0

The dairy farms that emerged after 1880 required a larger investment and a greater commitment than had the wheat farming of the frontier years and thus depended upon and promoted a more stable farm population. Those who managed to remain on the land for the first 20 years tended to stay. In fact, 48 percent would still be there when the second half of the twentieth century began. Thus, whereas high levels of mobility characterized the frontier years of Trempealeau County's history, the postfrontier years showed more stability, with the immigrants and their children passing their farms from one generation to the next.

Not only did these families persist, but they also expanded their numbers as they replaced the less stable portion of the population. The progeny of the 74 families that were both present in Pigeon in 1900 and persistent through the first half of the twentieth century represented 209 families in the church membership lists of 1964. Of those original 74 families, several had more than one family in the community in each of the generations. Their genealogy can easily be traced in local records. These old families constituted 69 percent of all the church members. Because church membership extends somewhat beyond the boundaries of the town, several of the remaining families resided in the neighboring town of Hale and similarly had a long history of residence in that community. Another six names of those old families can be found among the landowners listed in the atlas of 1964, though they were not listed as local church members. These figures on family persistence are also serious underestimates, because they trace family lineage only through the male line. Many families would no doubt be added if one were to follow the female lineage as well.[26]

The extraordinary persistence of the Norwegian immigrant is further revealed by landownership. Those same immigrant family names which fill the membership lists of the churches in Pigeon owned 75 percent of the land in the town of Pigeon in 1954. If these farmers were not on the original farms owned by their ancestors through the course of two, three, or four generations, they had found land nearby. However striking these statistics

Table 1.4. Family Persistence of Rural Farm Residence, 1900–1964

Families	Pigeon		Lincoln	
	N	%	N	%
Present by 1900	105	59.5	69	54.0
Present by 1930 but not 1900	26	14.5	15	12.0
Present by 1965 but not 1930	46	26.0	44	34.0
Total households	177	100.0	128	100.0

Source: Manuscript Census, U.S. Census of Population, Pigeon and Lincoln townships, Trempealeau County, Wisconsin, 1900; *Atlas and Farmers Directory of Trempealeau County, Wisconsin; Atlas of Trempealeau County, Wisconsin.*

of stability are, they no doubt represent less than the reality. The stability of these rural Pigeon families and the complex and extensive kin networks recall the stability and social arrangements of New England towns and localities in Norway. The high valuation on maintaining the family on the land continued.[27]

Pigeon and Lincoln do not fit models which assume that increasingly complex and economically and socially stratified communities evolved through the course of time. These Trempealeau townships proved to be surprisingly stable through much of their history. Not only was the farm family persistent, but the social structure as revealed in the patterns of ownership of the land also remained stable after 1880. Between the years 1880 and 1940 in Trempealeau County the average farm ranged from 143 to 153 acres. The depression of the 1930s brought some noticeable variations, but the basic structure remained in the number and size of farms. Those under 50 acres were few throughout the years 1880–1940, ranging from 10.7–13.8 percent of the total. For those on farms of 50–99 acres the number is consistently around 19 percent, with a range of 18.2–20.6 percent. Approximately 42 percent steadily owned farms of 100–179 acres and about 19 percent had farms of 180–259 acres. A final 8–10 percent had farms over 260 acres. This distribution differs little from the frontier years, except for an increase in the farms under 50 acres after 1880. While the number of acres owned can be regarded as only a very rough guide to the distribution of wealth in the community, it is suggestive of the structural stability (see Table 1.5).

Noteworthy changes in the distribution of land did not occur until after 1945. In this third historical stage of Trempealeau the trend toward fewer and progressively larger farms is conspicuous. By 1975 the proportion under 10 acres declined only slightly from an average of almost 12 to about 9 percent. The proportion with farms of 50–99 acres dropped from

Table 1.5. Numerical and Percentage Distributions of Land Ownership, by Acreage, 1880–1975

	Total Number of Farms	Average Number of Acres	Number of Farms, by Acreage								Percentage of Farms, by Acreage							
			Under 10	10–49	50–99	100–179	180–259	260–499	500–1,000	Over 1,000	Under 10	10–49	50–99	100–179	180–259	260–499	500–1,000	Over 1,000
1880	2,459	153	7	148	469		1,816[a]		17	2	0.3	6.0	19.1		73.9[a]		0.7	0.08
1890	2,676	—	8	232	569		1,850[a]		16	1	0.3	8.7	21.3		69.1[a]		0.6	0.04
1900	3,138	146	92	310	645	1,275	506	287	21	2	2.9	9.9	20.6	40.6	16.1	9.1	0.7	0.06
1910	3,008	150	62	287	571	1,224	552	297	13	2	2.1	9.5	19.0	40.7	18.4	9.9	0.4	0.07
1920	3,138	147	56	291	631	1,320	560	269	9	1	1.8	9.3	20.1	42.1	17.8	8.6	0.3	0.03
1925	3,204	143	82	316	630	1,357	562	243	13	1	2.6	9.9	19.7	42.4	17.5	7.6	0.4	0.03
1930	3,051	146	61	266	573	1,322	560	259	10	0	2.0	8.7	18.8	43.3	18.4	8.5	0.3	0.00
1935	3,233	143	121	326	589	1,336	580	268	11	2	3.7	10.1	18.2	41.3	17.9	8.3	0.3	0.06
1940	3,040	148	80	249	580	1,303	553	264	12	0	2.6	8.2	19.1	42.9	18.2	8.7	0.4	0.00
1945	3,005	153	71	223	529	1,313	550	299	20	0	2.4	7.4	17.6	43.7	18.3	10.0	0.7	0.00
1950	2,889	158	76	208	488	1,220	547	326	23	1	2.6	7.2	16.9	42.2	18.9	11.3	0.8	0.03
1955	2,689	166	77	186	410	1,053	557	378	26	1	2.9	6.9	15.2	39.2	20.7	14.1	1.0	0.04
1960	2,423	179	52	160	341	903	523	407	36	1	2.1	6.6	14.1	37.3	21.6	16.8	1.5	0.04
1965	2,238	193	46	138	284	798	487	436	45	4	2.0	6.2	12.7	35.7	21.8	19.5	2.0	0.22
1970	1,908	201	49	121	204	648	410	416	54	6	2.6	6.3	10.7	34.0	21.5	21.8	2.8	0.34
1975	1,756	220	57	94	218	529	343	412	90	13	3.2	5.4	12.4	30.1	19.5	23.5	5.1	0.74

Sources: See appendix C.

[a]These numbers and percentages pertain to three categories of farm size combined: 100–499 acres.

an average of 19.1 in 1940 to 12.4 percent in 1975. The proportion of farmers owning 260–499 acres of land increased from 8.7 percent in 1940 to 23.5 percent in 1975. The number of farms with 500–1,000 acres increased from 12 (0.4 percent) to 90 (5.1 percent) in those years. By 1975, 13 farms included what at one time would have been an almost unheard of size of over 1,000 acres. Dramatic changes in the economic structure of Trempealeau are a post–World War II phenomenon best indicated by the increase in inequality that the changing patterns of landownership reveal.

After 1945 as farms became larger they also steadily declined in absolute numbers. While the farms of Trempealeau remained family owned and operated, this shift in size and number signals a revolution in the work of the rural family and in community relationships. An unprecedented concentration of wealth and inequality common elsewhere in the country belatedly loomed upon the horizon of Trempealeau County by 1970. Between 1880 and 1945 the number of farms and their size regularly fluctuated within only a limited range, but after 1940 there has been a steady decline in the number of farms during each five-year period. In this regard, the experience of Lincoln, Pigeon, and Trempealeau County in general have paralleled national trends. Even in the rural county of Trempealeau, farm families were reduced to a minority.[28] Fewer people owned land, and an ever larger proportion of the land ended up in the hands of the farmers with the largest holdings.

Although the changing distribution of landownership and farm size are not a mirror of the social structure in Trempealeau County, they are suggestive of it. There were, no doubt, real differences between the incomes of the 20 percent with 50–99 acres of land and the 19 percent with 180–259 acres, because the former group could produce considerably less for the market. But neither group was radically different from

Table 1.6. Decline in the Number of Farms in Trempealeau County, 1940–1975

	Number of Farms	Decline	
		N	%
1940	3,040		
1945	3,005	35	1.2
1950	2,889	116	3.9
1955	2,689	200	6.9
1960	2,423	266	9.9
1965	2,238	185	7.6
1970	1,908	330	14.7
1975	1,756	152	8.0

Sources: See appendix C.

the 42 percent with 100–179 acres. The work and the way of life of families on these farms varied little from each other prior to 1945. At any rate, locals kept alive a perception of general equality. According to one aging woman, a life-long resident of Pigeon whose family appeared among the first pioneers: "We all had it the same then; no one was any better than anyone else." However, she made clear that this situation contrasted with the present, in which some do have or presume to have it "better" than others.[29]

A final dimension of the local families' relationships and persistence on the land is tenancy; conspicuous trends typify each of the three historical stages. During the frontier years of labor scarcity and cheap or free land, few farmers operated as tenants. And although tenancy never surpassed 27 percent, it nonetheless increased throughout the years between 1880 and 1940. Tenancy varied from community to community perhaps according to the ethnic traditions of the people. For example, in Pigeon with its heavy concentration of Norwegians, the rate of tenancy tended to be somewhat lower than in the county as a whole or in the neighboring town of Lincoln, which included more old-stock Americans. Overall the trend in these years following settlement was toward an ever-increasing number of tenants.

Tenancy functioned in many cases as a family strategy of adjustment. Many of the tenants were actually the sons or other relatives of the owners of the land. Families varied as to how they handled the intergenerational transfer of property. Some sold their farms to their sons when they were ready to retire, whereas others maintained control until their deaths. Dave Wood, one of Lincoln Township's first pioneers, died in 1927. He never sold his farm in Lincoln to his son Ralph, though Ralph farmed and managed it for many years before Dave's death. When Dave died without a will, Ralph lost the property to an heir with a stronger claim to the estate.[30]

Table 1.7. Percentage of Tenant Farmers in Lincoln and Pigeon, 1900–1930

	Lincoln	Pigeon
1900	8.6	7.8
1910	19.0	10.5
1930	22.0	18.6

Sources: The 1900 and 1910 statistics are based on Manuscript Censuses, U.S. Census of Population, Pigeon and Lincoln townships, Trempealeau County, Wisconsin. The 1930 statistics are based upon *Atlas and Farmers' Directory of Trempealeau County, Wisconsin,* pp. 38–42, 54–55.

Rather different strategies prevailed among the Norwegians; studies of inheritance patterns indicate that Norwegian Americans favored the *inter vivos* transfer of property customary in Norway. This method of land transfer has repeatedly been found to be more efficient as a means of maintaining property within the family.[31]

In 1930, of the 24 farmers who rented their farms in the town of Lincoln, 8 were renting from individuals with the same surname as themselves; in Pigeon the number totaled 19 out of 38. So even in 1930, as tenancy approached its peak, 90 percent of the farmers of Pigeon and 85 percent of those in Lincoln worked on farms owned by themselves or by their families, from whom they rented. The increase in tenancy may thus reflect the aging of a generation of farmers and a transitional stage where sons rented from an aging father. It also reflects the economic realities of the 1930s. The number of small farms and tenancy peaked in Trempealeau County at 26.9 percent in 1940 after a decade of depression. Subsistence and marginal farms grew during the depression, representing in part an adaptive strategy for many families whose sons could no longer look elsewhere for a living. Individuals who earlier would have sought jobs and careers outside the local community when the economy offered such opportunities remained in or near the villages, where they at least managed subsistence on a rented farm.

After 1940 the trend toward higher rates of tenancy reversed itself, steadily declining along with the number of farms. Local and national economic innovations explain the new trend. The marginal farmer's land, whether that of a tenant or owner, was gradually incorporated into the

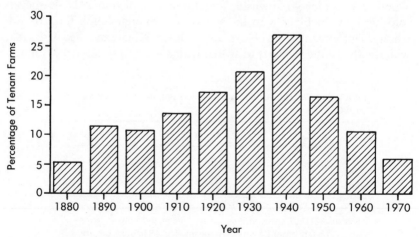

Figure 1.1. Farm tenancy in Trempealeau County, 1880–1970 (compiled from sources given in appendix C; see Table 4.8 for the precise data).

larger, less diversified, and market-oriented farms. The decline in tenancy and the number of farms and the increase in farm size are explained in part by the expansion of alternative opportunities for the children of farmers in the war and postwar years.[32]

High levels of population expansion and mobility characterized the frontier years as the land of Trempealeau was taken up. In terms of the distribution of wealth, Curti found the trend to be toward equality; the least successful perhaps moved on. The postfrontier years brought high levels of stability in both the population on the land and the distribution of that land. Generation after generation, many families passed their farms on to their children and in many instances acquired additional land from their more transient neighbors. Thus, while significant portions of the population continued to leave, particularly the young, there remained a persistent and sizable core to maintain the community and its institutions. The distribution of land and patterns of tenancy also suggest over a half century of stability in the economic structure of the community in the postfrontier years. The post–World War II years brought the most dramatic changes—more changes than an increase in the size of farms and a decline in the number of families making their living on farms. The statistics on landownership barely hint at the changes occurring in family and community life after 1945.

2
Between Memory and Reality

> Ours is a mediating generation. By training and tradition we live in the spiritual and cultural land of our fathers. With our children we are steadily marching into the land of tomorrow. Ours is the riches of two cultures and the poverty of the desert wanderer. We live between memory and reality. Ours is the agony of a divided loyalty and joy in the discovery of a new unity. Like Moses of old we see the new but cannot fully enter in. To us has been given the task of mediating a culture, of preserving and transferring to our children in a new land the cultural and spiritual values bound up in the character, art, music, literature and Christian faith of a generation no longer found even in the land from which our fathers came.
>
> L. W. Boe, 1932

In 1932, L. W. Boe, a second-generation Norwegian American and president of St. Olaf College in Minnesota, expressed the commitment of that immigrant group's leaders to transmitting their cultural heritage.[1] He exposed the sense of marginality of his generation between the Old World and the New, caught "between memory and reality," attempting to preserve a culture and religion lost even in the homeland. Norwegian-American leaders must have felt akin to an earlier immigrant group, the Puritans of Massachusetts Bay Colony, when the raison d'être of their "errand into the wilderness" went astray in the seventeenth century. Like their predecessors in New England, the Norwegian immigrant communities seethed with religious controversy that spawned institutional and cultural creativity. In the defense of their Norwegian identity they resisted cultural assimilation and claimed authority over the local economic context for an extended period of time. In a host of ways they departed from their peasant cultures in Norway, often for the conservative reason of preserving what they esteemed as the essential elements of their heritage. New opportunities, the availability of land, and challenges from within and outside their culture caught them between "memory and reality" in ways that designed a distinct historical experience.

Accompanying the increased population stability and persistence on the land between 1880 and 1945 was a change in the ethnic distribution and culture of the people. By 1880 Scandinavian Americans composed 55

32

percent of the county residents. By 1915 an early historian of Trempealeau County estimated that Norwegian Americans totaled 70 percent of the county's population; German and Polish Americans, 20 percent; and others which included the old-stock Americans, only 10 percent.[2] One of the consequences of the growing numbers of immigrants in the county was the departure and dwindling numbers of Yankees. Seemingly reversing the modern trends in America toward a growing pluralism, Trempealeau communities turned the clock backward and became more rather than less homogeneous with time. Lincoln and Pigeon did not deviate from this trend in the first quarter of the twentieth century (see Table 2.1).

As the first settlers moved on, new arrivals and newborns replaced them, and the new ethnic mix altered the aspirations and habits of the people. Contrary to Merle Curti's expectations, the frontier years did not begin an unrelenting process of acculturation of immigrants. Curti surmised that the basic values of the immigrants were similar to those of the Yankee migrants; however, the cultural forms were not, and each group remained deeply committed to their own. As was true of the Yankee migrants, the household and kinship networks, the neighborhood, and the churches provided the context in which the immigrants spent their lives. But each group had their own church, neighborhood, and kin associations. Small neighborhood school districts became the most important political unit, even more important than the town. The homogeneous neighborhoods shaped the cultural and economic life of these communities for several decades into the twentieth century.[3]

Manuscript censuses and plat maps reveal an unmistakable pattern of ethnic clustering in neighborhoods. From the time the town of Pigeon separated from Lincoln in 1875, it was predominantly Norwegian (nearly 88 percent in 1880) and would remain so throughout its history. This separation of the town allowed the original Yankee groups to maintain control of Lincoln and the village of Whitehall, but eventually they would be outnumbered by immigrants in those places as well. The native-born Yankees and their children declined both in absolute numbers and, more conspicuously, in their proportion of the population. They would be replaced by the foreign-born and their children from Norway, Poland, and to a lesser extent Germany. After the frontier years the ethnic composition of the town of Lincoln was drastically altered. Old-stock Americans dominated the county, villages, and towns during the frontier years, but by 1900 Norwegians were the dominant group. The old-stock Americans, although conspicuous in their leadership of Lincoln during the frontier years, declined to a meager 14 percent in the area by 1910.[4] (See Table 2.1.)

Table 2.1. Numerical and Percentage Distributions of Household Heads, by Ethnicity, 1870–1964

	1870		1880		1900		1910	
	N	%	N	%	N	%	N	%
LINCOLN AND PIGEON TOWNSHIPS AND THE VILLAGE OF WHITEHALL								
American[a]	67	42.9	100	30.9	93	18.9	72	13.9
Norwegian	61	39.1	180	55.6	329	66.7	356	68.6
English[b]	15	9.6	15	4.6	14	2.8	24	4.6
German[c]	11	7.0	29	8.9	29	5.9	30	5.8
Polish[c]					28	5.7	29	5.6
Other	2	1.4	0	0.0	0	0.0	8	1.5
Total	156		324		493		519	
VILLAGE OF WHITEHALL								
American[a]			41	64.0	52	35.8	43	25.9
Norwegian			13	20.3	82	56.6	97	58.4
English[b]			7	10.9	7	4.8	15	9.0
German			3	4.7	4	2.8	8	4.8
Other			0	0.0	0	0.0	3	1.8
Total			64		145		166	

	1880		1900		1910		1930		1964	
	N	%	N	%	N	%	N	%	N	%
LINCOLN TOWNSHIP										
American[a]	46	38.7	30	21.3	25	20.3	12	10.7	9	7.1
Norwegian	43	36.1	57	40.4	43	35.0	38	33.9	37	29.5
English[b]	5	4.2	5	3.5	6	4.9	2	1.8	3	2.4
German[c]	25	21.0	21	14.9	15	12.2	24	21.4	9	7.1
Polish[c]			28	19.9	29	23.6	29	25.9	58	46.0
Other	0	0.0	0	0.0	5	4.0	7	6.3	10	7.9
Total	119		141		123		112		126	
PIGEON TOWNSHIP[d]										
American[a]	13	9.2	11	5.2	4	1.7	4	1.9	3	1.8
Norwegian	124	87.9	190	91.8	216	93.9	204	96.7	142	89.9
English[b]	3	2.1	2	1.0	3	1.3	0	0.0	0	0.0
German	1	0.7	4	1.9	7	3.0	3	1.4	7	4.4
Polish	0	0.0	0	0.0	0	0.0	0	0.0	6	3.8
Total	141		207		230		211		158	

Sources: The statistics for 1870, 1880, 1900, and 1910 are based on the Manuscript Censuses, U.S. Census of Population, Pigeon and Lincoln townships, Trempealeau County, Wisconsin. Those for 1930 and 1964 are based upon farm atlases which provide the names of all rural residents: *Atlas and Farmers Directory of Trempealeau County, Wisconsin; Atlas of Trempealeau County, Wisconsin.*

[a] American = old-stock Americans.

[b] English = immigrants from England, not including those among old-stock Americans.

[c] The figures for the Germans and the Polish are combined for certain years, as indicated by the alignment of entries.

[d] The 1964 figures in the PIGEON TOWNSHIP panel exclude household heads whose ethnic background is uncertain. If one were to include the heads of new families which do not appear in earlier censuses and for which ethnicity cannot be determined with certainty, the number of Norwegians in Pigeon Township would decline to 80 percent instead of the 90 percent indicated, and the percentage of "Other" would jump to 11 percent. Determination of ethnic backgrounds of families becomes increasingly problematic by 1940.

34

The ethnic distribution of Lincoln Township indicates its position on a line dividing three ethnic clusters. North, east, and southeast of Lincoln were three townships in which Scandinavians concentrated, including Pigeon to the east. West of Lincoln, the Polish population concentrated in the town of Burnside, and on the southwest, Lincoln was bordered by the town of Arcadia, in which Polish and German Catholics became the largest population. After 1900 the expansive Polish families of Burnside bought up the farms of both the departing Yankees and the Norwegians on the west side of the town, and by 1964 Polish names were predominant on the farms of Lincoln.

Like the old-stock Americans that preceded them in the village of Whitehall, the Scandinavians continued to dominate village life longer than they did the countryside of Lincoln Township. In 1910 there was not yet a single Polish-American family in the village. However, in 1948 there were enough of them to establish St. John's Catholic Parish in the village with 225 members. By 1964 the parish included 565 members. The frontier period, with the high mobility noted by Curti, appears to have been a time when people began a process of sorting themselves out, of finding communities of like-minded folk of their own cultural background and predispositions.[5]

Besides the immigrant families' persistence on the land through generations, nothing better illustrates the commitment to traditional cultural values than the degree to which language was retained in families and communities. Nothing is more fundamental to a culture than its language, and in the towns of Pigeon and Lincoln both the Polish and Norwegian Americans proved extraordinarily resistant to efforts to replace their mother tongues with English.[6] Not only did the second generation of residents learn the language of their parents but so too did the third and sometimes the fourth generations. Harold Tomter, a third-generation man interviewed by the State Historical Society of Wisconsin in the 1970s, was born and grew up on a farm in Pigeon; he recalled: "We talked Norwegian all the time. I studied the catechism in Norwegian. I can still speak it and have an accent." Harold Tomter is by no means exceptional.[7]

In many instances the young entering elementary school as late as the decade of the 1930s could not speak English. Their parents depended upon the schools to teach it to them. A third-generation woman, born in 1915, had just this experience. She and her five younger siblings spoke only Norwegian when they started elementary school. Norwegian remained the language of her family and many in her community for most of the first half of the twentieth century. Curiously, the 99-year-old mother of this woman did not have the same experience. She and her siblings entered the public schools as bilinguals, though she did not use English at home while rearing her own children. As her daughter noted, "There seemed to have been more people around who spoke English when mother was growing up."[8] As the statistics of the changing ethnic distribution suggest, the older woman growing up in the 1890s experienced a more pluralistic community than her daughter did in the second decade of this century. Although the second and third generations did learn English in the schools, and despite the fact that after 1889 the Bennett Law prohibited the use of any language other than English in the schools, in many neighborhoods Norwegian or Polish remained the language of the people.[9]

The findings of linguist Einar Haugen, author of the two-volume *Norwegian Language in America,* indicate that Pigeon was not an eccentric community. Nearly a million immigrants spoke Norwegian and many of their descendants "had full and active use of the language for over a century." For these people, "English has been the language of the pocket book—the outer shells of life, without warmth or depth."[10] Although most of the immigrants and their children became bilingual, they could, if they chose, live out their lives without learning English and without being unduly burdened by this fact. By 1890, relying solely on Norwegian, they could trade at Peder Ekern's store, grind their flour and feed at his mill, borrow money at John Melby's bank in Whitehall, and get legal advice from Hans Anderson, all of whom were Norwegian immigrants and spoke the mother language.[11] On Sundays their sermons, music, and prayers were in Norwegian into the 1920s, and not until the 1940s did the Norwegian service cease to be regularly scheduled. For news they could buy the *Skandinavian* or the *Decorah Postem.* As late as 1940 there were still almost a hundred subscriptions to the latter Norwegian-language weekly in the townships of Lincoln and Pigeon.[12] Many of the harsher shocks and adjustments that immigrants confronted were mediated by small non-English-speaking communities like those in Pigeon and Lincoln.

The two areas in which the immigrant generally first began to struggle with the new language related to politics and the market.[13] But in Trempealeau County, after Norwegians became the dominant group, even these difficulties diminished. In Pigeon and Lincoln only a small portion of the immigrant community needed to be highly skilled bilinguals—men like the merchant, miller, farmer, and politician Peder Ekern, the banker John Melby, and the lawyer Hans Anderson. Non-Norwegian merchants and politicians like J. D. Olds, who continued to thrive after 1880, often learned the language of their immigrant neighbors.[14] One woman born in 1892 told of an embarrassing moment in her youth while shopping in a local store in the nearby town of Osseo. When her sister commented on the high prices, she responded in Norwegian, expressing a common stereotype, "Ya, the prices are high here. The owner's a Jew, you know." To her humiliation the shopkeeper initiated a chat with her in Norwegian.[15] In many instances Germans, Jews, and others who lived in the Norwegian American communities learned to speak Norwegian as children or as adults.[16] If those seeking to make a living in the town did not learn the language, they often hired clerks who could speak it. In 1918 the *Whitehall Times* still carried ads like the following: "Wanted—Experienced Norwegian sales lady in general store"; "Salesman Wanted—Man with experience in general mercantile store. Norwegian or German preferred."[17]

Not all the early Yankee shopkeepers were quite so acquiescent in the face of the growing local hegemony of the Norwegians. One incident reported in 1883 by the *Whitehall Times* reveals the earlier tensions and the frustration of one Yankee shopkeeper:

D. K. Hagestad assaulted by David Harris

While Dave [the shopkeeper] was trying to make a trade Hagestad was conversing in Norwegian with a customer. Dave who assumed his rights were being abused assaulted Hagestad after ordering him not to speak. Justice Trowbridge, who thought a man has a constitutional right to speak in any language and all known languages, fined Harris $1 and costs of $11.77.

Since Hagestad was one of the county's most respected economic and political leaders among the Norwegians, one can only imagine the consequences of such incidents on the future prospects of that shopkeeper's business.[18] Tension between the growing population of Norwegian immigrants and the Yankee shopkeepers and businessmen may have contributed to the high rates of turnover among the latter in Whitehall and Lincoln after 1880. Without the personal and bilingual skills necessary to win the immigrant's business, chances of success declined as the exclusively English-speaking community shrank. There is abundant evidence that immigrants preferred to take their trade to their own kind when possible. Immigrant businessmen such as John Melby and Peder Ekern shared the immigrants' language, won their trust, and kept their business.[19]

If ignorance of English did not seriously interfere with most community members' activities in the marketplace, neither did it prove to be a major burden to political participation. An inability to speak English did not exclude citizens from voting, understanding the issues, or gaining political office on a local level. As Curti noted, beginning in the mid-1870s the political parties deliberately included Norwegian candidates.[20] The politician with bilingual skills, like the businessman and professional, commanded a definite advantage over a monolingual competitor. Progressive Robert La Follette always won resounding victories in Trempealeau and even more resounding ones in Pigeon and Whitehall. Though he was not

Norwegian, La Follette grew up in a Norwegian-immigrant community and spoke the Norwegian language fluently. In Pigeon and Lincoln, where many of the children and adults spoke Norwegian, both local and state politicians often made their appeals in that language.[21] J. D. Olds, a migrant from upstate New York and one of the first settlers in Pigeon, held political positions in the township throughout his life and was a skillful bilingual. Whitehall lawyer and son of Norwegian immigrants, Herman Ekern was well served by his language skills in Wisconsin politics. After 1902 when he was first elected to the state legislature, his political star would rise and fall with that of the La Follettes. By 1938, when Ekern ran and lost a bid for the United States Senate on the Progressive ticket, he ended a distinguished political career as a Wisconsin Progressive.[22]

The pressures on the old as well as the young to discard the immigrant language were light indeed in Pigeon and Lincoln. During the first quarter of the century the expectation of speaking Norwegian fluently may well have been higher than it had been before 1880. Haugen in his extensive and careful study of language transition found that in 1940 62 percent of the second-generation Norwegian Americans in Wisconsin learned Norwegian. The second-generation Polish Americans achieved an even higher rate of language retention—over 90 percent. With few exceptions, the residents of rural communities clung to their native language more successfully than the immigrants who located in urban areas.[23] In addition, in communities where a neighborhood spirit was strong, the language sustained a longer life. Language serves to set a group apart and to define the perimeters of the neighborhood itself. According to Haugen, the immigrants usually did learn English; the process of learning went on steadily if slowly: "Nonetheless, Norwegian had been established as the language of the family, the church, and the neighborhood, spoken to all who showed any inclination to speak it back. . . . English, on the other hand, was the language spoken to outsiders. . . ." This situation persisted to the turn of the century, and had hardly begun to show important signs of deterioration before the outbreak of World War I.[24] No doubt, over the years English increasingly came into usage in these communities, but it is striking how lengthy a process the transition proved to be. A postcard survey of Trempealeau County in 1946 revealed that Norwegian was still used in preaching sermons and in private conversation and that the generation under 30 years of age was still using Norwegian.[25]

Within the language of a people is embedded much of its culture and values. Keeping theirs alive as long as they did, the residents of Lincoln and Pigeon were able to transmit and sustain that culture for a surprisingly extended period. In homogeneous communities like Pigeon the second generation grew up with a considerable knowledge of and loyalty to their parents' culture. Hans Anderson, immigrant lawyer and county judge, worked tirelessly to transmit to his children and to preserve for the communities of Trempealeau County a knowledge of the culture and character of the Norway he had left as a boy.

Since World War II, the numbers of those who are bilingual has steadily declined among the third and fourth generations. The parents of these first monolingual generations did not experience this change as the wrenching loss and challenge to their cultural identity that the earlier generations might have. The changes in the language came slowly, almost imperceptibly, and, for the most part, painlessly. The language and other expressions of Norwegian culture have steadily retreated into memory in the post–World War II decades. However, as late as the 1970 census 40 percent of the residents of Trempealeau County reported themselves as having a mother tongue other than English.[26]

Despite the growing hegemony of the immigrants, Deacon Alvah Wood's progeny counted themselves among those who remained in the town of Lincoln when most of their Yankee counterparts departed. Economically and politically they continued to participate in the community's development. Socially, too, the Wood family would be in the vanguard of change in the community. In 1907 Wood's grandson Ralph married the daughter of Scandinavian immigrants. Much of his married life and many of his adult activities were anchored among the kin and community of his wife's family.[27]

The consequences of this interethnic marriage can best be illustrated in the writing of Ralph's grandson, Dave Wood, former English professor, author and journalist. He writes with humor and nostalgia about life in Whitehall, about traditions being lost—traditions which often originated in Norway. In 1976 he recalled:

> Twenty years ago, everyone knew about Jule Bokking, or Christmas Fooling. A firmly entrenched Scandinavian tradition in our community, legends had sprung up around this custom in which "foolers" disguise themselves right after Christmas, perform in neighbors kitchens, eat and drink in front of wood cookstoves, then take the neighbors along to "fool" with someone else down the road a piece. Grandma used to tell about Jule Bokking in a horse-drawn sleigh. Pa tells about doing the same in a Model "A" coupe, the rumble seat packed sardine-style with merrymakers. And of course everyone tells about getting to Tollefson's just in time to help with morning milking.[28]

Ironically, in reality Dave Wood traces his family back to the the first generation of Puritans of the Massachusetts Bay Colony, but the memories that he carried with him when he left Whitehall indicate the vitality of a

Ralph Wood (youngest son of Dave Wood), and his wife Martha, ca. 1900–1910. Martha was the daughter of a Swedish immigrant farmer Charles Johnson. Photo courtesy of Dave Wood, Minneapolis.

Martha Wood and her children, Harold and Helen, 1913. Photo courtesy of Dave Wood, Minneapolis.

quite different cultural tradition. He remembers jule bokking, which actually lasted longer in rural Lincoln and Pigeon than in Norway, singing "Helsa" ("The Homecoming Waltz") and "Kann du Glenn Gammel Norge?" ("Can You Remember Old Norway?"), and standing in line for the annual Lutheran church supper in Pigeon Falls with its characteristic Norwegian peasant menu of "Lutefisk—Lefse—Meatballs—Potatoes—Rutabagas—Slaw—Pie." Dave Wood's yarns about village life in Whitehall reveal both the strength of the ethnic traditions of the Norwegians through the first half of the twentieth century and their demise in the third quarter. After 1880 it appears that at least for a time the Americans who remained in Pigeon and Lincoln were as Norwegianized as the Norwegians were Americanized.[29]

By the time Ralph Wood married Martha Johnson such marriages were not uncommon among the few remaining old-stock Americans who matured in the area. In Lincoln and Pigeon between 1880 and 1885, they married outside of their own group in only about 13 percent of the marriages that occurred. But by 1905 at least a third of the marriages of the old-stock Americans were to Norwegian Americans, and by 1930 they totaled 50 percent. Despite this apparent lack of prejudice among Yankee Americans toward marrying the offspring of immigrants, the small numbers of old-stock Americans dictated that such marriages were few of the total. In the 1880s and 1890s only 3—4 percent of the marriages in Lincoln and Pigeon were exogamous. Between 1900 and 1925 only 7 or 8 percent were so. Most interethnic marriages were between the transplanted easterners and second-generation Norwegian Americans and a handful of German Americans.

These statistics are based upon marriage records; however, Merle Curti, using the manuscript census, found somewhat higher rates of intermarriage for the county as a whole by 1888. His analysis of the 1880 census revealed that 29 percent of the marriages took place between men and women of different national origins. This higher rate found in the county as a whole may reflect the larger sample Curti used, or it could also be an indicator of the more pluralistic nature of the earlier years. It also reflects the fact that Curti's statistics include American-born children of immigrants as being of a national origin different from a first-generation immigrant.[30] (See Table 2.2.)

While it is true that a small number of marriages across ethnic lines did crop up in the earliest years of the frontier, far more exceptional were marriages across religious lines. Before 1880 intermarriages between Norwegian Lutherans and Catholic Germans or Poles were almost unknown. The postfrontier years brought little variation from the earlier pattern. According to locals today, 40 years ago the infrequent marriages between a Polish Catholic and a Norwegian, German, or Yankee Protestant in Lincoln and neighboring towns spawned a local scandal and community consternation.[31] Marriage records bear testimony to local prejudice. For the first and second generations, relatively precise information can be assembled, since the birthplaces of the couple and the parents are listed in the marriage records. Before the decade of the Great Depression, no such marriage appeared in the records examined, and between 1930 and 1935 only one couple ventured on such a course.

By 1940 establishing the ethnicity of couples becomes problematic, because many of the parents were born in the United States. Familiarity with the names and the availability of other records do allow for some conclusions. In the years between 1940 and 1945, of the 135 couples who made their way to the altar in Lincoln and Pigeon, only 3 appear to have involved couples that clearly combined Norwegian and Polish names. While proximity always is an important determining factor in marriage choice, it apparently made no difference at all that the neighboring town of Burnside was predominantly Polish and that they were rapidly expanding their numbers into the countryside of Lincoln and the village of Whitehall. Despite the fact that between 1930 and 1964 the Polish Americans became the largest single ethnic group in Lincoln Township, between 1950 and 1955 there were no obvious instances of marriages between Catholic Polish Americans and Norwegian Americans or old-stock Americans. While ethnic background clearly influenced the choice of mates throughout the communities' history, the most rigid barrier against intermarriage was religion. American, German, and Norwegian Protestants did intermarry in small numbers, but the instances in which they married a Catholic Polish American remained exceedingly rare.[32]

While there is ample evidence that people of differing religions—the young particularly, and the adults to a lesser extent—frequently socialized with each other in the continual round of dances, celebrations, and other community events, when it came to courtship and marriage, locals drew a firm line. One 69-year-old Whitehall woman in 1984 recalled as a young woman dating a Catholic after leaving home and while working in a nearby city. But the grapevine of small towns is both long and efficient, and very soon a letter arrived from her mother which firmly and tersely stated, "I hear you're seeing a Catholic. You better stop that." And how did this young woman on her own beyond the constraints of the parental household respond? "And so I did stop!"[33]

The post–World War II years did bring changes. But according to locals, not until the 1960s did the religious division between the young of these neighboring towns clearly begin to crumble. A local Polish American woman who violated this community taboo in the mid-1940s noted a

Table 2.2. Numerical and Percentage Distributions of Ethnic Intermarriages, by Ethnicity, in Pigeon and Lincoln Townships and the Village of Whitehall, 1880–1935

	1880–1885		1890–1895		1900–1905		1910–1915		1920–1925		1930–1935	
	N	%	N	%	N	%	N	%	N	%	N	%
NORWEGIANS												
Norwegian/												
Norwegian	154	95.0	136	96.5	124	91.2	118	93.6	100	90.1	110	84.0
American	6	4.3	3	2.1	9	6.6	3	2.4	8	7.2	11	8.4
German	2	0.7	1	0.7	3	2.2	4	3.2	3	2.7	7	5.3
Pole	0	0.0	0	0.0	0	0.0	0	0.0	0	0.0	1	0.8
Jew	0	0.0	1	0.7	0	0.0	0	0.0	0	0.0	0	0.0
Irish	0	0.0	0	0.0	0	0.0	0	0.0	0	0.0	2	1.5
Canadian	0	0.0	0	0.0	0	0.0	1	0.8	0	0.0	0	0.0
Total	162		141		136		125		111		131	
AMERICANS												
American/												
American	48	87.3	44	91.7	18	66.7	10	66.7	14	58.3	10	45.5
Norwegian	6	10.9	3	6.3	9	33.3	3	20.0	8	33.3	11	50.0
German	1	1.8	0	0.0	0	0.0	2	13.3	2	8.4	1	4.5
Jew	0	0.0	1	2.0	0	0.0	0	0.0	0	0.0	0	0.0
Total	55		48		27		15		24		22	

GERMANS

German/											
German	4	67.1	8	88.9	6	66.7	30	79.3	22	81.5	6	40.0
Norwegian	2	28.6	1	11.1	3	33.3	4	10.5	3	11.1	7	46.7
American	1	14.3	0	0.0	0	0.0	2	5.2	2	7.4	1	6.7
Irish	0	0.0	0	0.0	0	0.0	0	0.0	0	0.0	1	6.6
Total	7		9		9		36		27		15	

POLES

Pole/											
Pole	0	0.0	2	100.0	10	100.0	0	0.0	10	100.0	16	94.1
Norwegian	0	0.0	0	0.0	0	0.0	0	0.0	0	0.0	1	5.9
Total	0		2		10		0		10		17	

INDIVIDUALS MARRYING WITHIN OR OUTSIDE THEIR OWN ETHNIC GROUP

Within	206	95.8	190	96.9	158	92.9	158	92.4	146	91.8	142	86.1
Outside	9	4.2	6	3.1	12	7.1	13	7.6	13	8.2	23	13.9
Total	215		196		170		171		159		165	

Source: Trempealeau County Records, marriage records, Trempealeau County Courthouse, Whitehall, Wisconsin.

Note: The heading "American" refers to old-stock Americans.

The statistics in this table are based on marriages in which one or both of the individuals involved reported their home address as Pigeon, Lincoln, or Whitehall. Marriage records provide information on the birthplaces of the parents of the couple. For those who were third-generation Americans married before 1935, manuscript censuses composed in earlier years can also be used to establish ethnicity. This is workable until 1940, when new names appear which cannot be identified from censuses taken in earlier years. Further, by 1940 a majority of parents are identified in the marriage records simply as born somewhere in the United States, and thus those records become unhelpful. Finally, by 1940 there were more occurrences of marriages which involved an individual from outside Trempealeau County (often from some distance away) or which involved an individual who recently moved into the village of Whitehall. Thus, information on ethnic backgrounds of those marrying after 1935 becomes increasingly incomplete and unreliable.

change since the time of her marriage. In her view, local clergy rather than community members took the lead in promoting a more tolerant social and religious environment.[34] Few residents today any longer perceive religion as a important social division. Once again the Wood family is a useful gauge of Lincoln township's social evolution. Ralph Wood's granddaughter married a man from a Polish Catholic background in the 1960s and appears to be assimilating much of what remains of that group's cultural traditions.[35]

Through much of the history of Trempealeau the local churches and religious affiliations powerfully buttressed cultural traditions. According to Hans Anderson, the immigrant generation and no doubt many of their children equated being Norwegian with being Lutheran. A similar perhaps even stronger connection could have been made between being Polish and being Catholic.[36] To the extent that secularization, Americanization, and modernization are interconnected processes, the marriage statistics alone suggest that these rural communities' long resisted the changes involved in these processes. In much the same way as in other colonial and frontier communities, no institution except the family played a more prominent role in the lives of the immigrants on the frontier than the church. Churches remained vital local institutions in the post–World War II years, though their ethnically distinct identities diminished somewhat.[37]

Before 1880 apparent social divisions along ethnic lines surfaced in the frontier county. As Curti noted, "One does not in general find the names of Norwegians, Germans, and Poles attending social events outside their own group, even when some among these had established themselves as substantial property holders and as leaders among their own people."[38] In the schools, businesses, churches, and cooperative associations each group sustained its own community social life.[39] In the 1880s the *Whitehall Times* carried notices of the activities of the Norwegian community in the Norwegian language as well as reports in English, such as the following: "Our Scandinavian friends enjoyed Christmas tree festivities at Scott's Hall Christmas night."[40] This frontier pattern of ethnic separation continued into the postfrontier years. Between 1880 and 1910 many of the social activities and organizations described in the *Whitehall Times* reveal this. Historian Peter Munch, examining rural Wisconsin communities in the 1940s and 1950s, found patterns of social separation persisting into those decades. In Viroqua, Wisconsin, which included Norwegian and old-stock Americans, Munch discovered:

> . . . an interesting example of a pronounced dual community, with a dualism that can be traced through the whole of the social prestige scale from top to

bottom. The split between the two groups seems to be most pronounced at the top of the scale. The two elites are rather exclusive to each other, although the withdrawal seems to be stronger on the Norwegian side. . . . The Norwegian group is pretty much closed.[41]

Dual social structures emerged in Lincoln and Whitehall during the frontier years and continued for at least another two or three decades, though there was a variety of activities in which individuals of diverse backgrounds cooperated. Central to sustaining this dual structure for a century were the Lutheran church, the intense sense of family loyalty, and a continued social deference to those who represented the traditional Norwegian elite of educated professionals and business leaders. The churches and the kin networks directed much of the sociability, and they remained quite ethnically distinct into the twentieth century.[42]

However, the pattern of dual social structures noted by Munch in Viroqua did not appear to sustain itself as long between the Norwegians and the Yankees in Whitehall and Lincoln. The local newspapers in 1880 attended to the activities of leading Yankee families, but by 1900 and 1910 in the *Whitehall Times* leading Norwegian-American families such as the Ekerns and the Andersons were duly noted as often as the Scotts, the Webbs, and the Woods.[43] The exodus of old-stock Americans and their intermarriage with Norwegians eventually undercut the duality of the social structure and the nature of the reportage of the *Whitehall Times*. The unlikely marriage of John Melby to Jennie Beach in 1875 perhaps set the tone of social relationships in Whitehall and the county. Her brothers edited the *Whitehall Times* beginning in 1880 and then passed the newspaper on to the next generation of Beach editors. By 1900 John and Jennie Melby served as the preeminent leaders of the community, and to the extent that the town and county had an elite they certainly acted as its center.

Jennie Melby, born in Charlotte, Vermont, in 1847, migrated with her family to Trempealeau County in 1866. Her father, Charles G. Beach, and her mother, Caroline Barnes Beach, like so many who claimed the first farms of the county, "descended on both sides of [their] house[s] from a long line of Colonial ancestry." Having been as well educated as a woman was likely to be in the Vermont grammar schools and female seminaries, Jennie took up the task of teaching in the frontier community before she married the Norwegian immigrant John Melby.[44]

Born in 1845, Melby departed from Norway at the age of 24 and worked for a time in the saw mills of Wisconsin. After 1870 he worked as a clerk at a general store owned by Iver Pederson, a Norwegian merchant in Ettrick, Trempealeau County. Along with Pederson he enthusiastically joined the Grange movement, and early won the trust and regard of the

Jennie Melby, ca. 1910–1915. Photo reprinted from Eben Douglas Pierce, ed., *History of Trempealeau County Wisconsin* (Chicago: H. C. Cooper, Jr., & Co., 1917).

John Melby, ca. 1895–1919. Photo reprinted from Eben Douglas Pierce, ed., *History of Trempealeau County Wisconsin* (Chicago: H. C. Cooper, Jr., & Co., 1917).

immigrant Norwegians. In 1876, seven years after coming to the United States, Melby won political office as the register of deeds of the county, one of the first of the Norwegians to be elected to a county office. A year before his election to that post, Melby married Jennie Beach. After winning every annual election until 1887 Melby finally decided to retire from that position to begin his career as a banker in Whitehall in 1888. John Melby and his brother Anton were two of the most financially successful of the Norwegian immigrants. Both married women with roots in Vermont and Massachusetts. By the turn of the century John Melby no doubt stood at the pinnacle of the Norwegian community both in his financial success and in the regard of the community.[45]

The activities and interests of Jennie Melby differed little in kind from the middle-class women of the East. She led the Whitehall women in literary societies and in musical and theatrical performances, was the "leading member" in the Methodist church, and promoted diverse village improvement and fund-raising drives. She organized and was the first president of the local Women's Christian Temperance Union and an active member in the Ivy Chapter, No. 115, Order of the Eastern Star.[46]

Unlike Ralph Wood's family experience, on the surface it appears as though Jennie Melby's marriage to an immigrant had little impact on her way of life. As had been true of Martha Wood, Jennie and her kin network appeared to have set the tone of their social and family life. Much of her energy centered on the declining group of old-stock Americans and a few Norwegian families who like her husband were making their way as merchants, professionals, and businessmen in the town. The Melby's only son was named after her father, and was sent east for his education. After completing his law degree at George Washington University, he practiced in Washington, D.C., before returning to Whitehall. "He was reared with the special end in view of some time assuming control of the extensive Melby holdings." Unlike the Woods, however, Charles Melby's children would not remain in Whitehall.[47]

Although such marriages as the Melby's were rare indeed in 1875, the few that did occur in communities where "everyone is related to everyone else" were important to making Trempealeau a congenial place for immigrant Norwegians. The immigrant Melby became part of his wife's extensive kin network, which included the editors of the local paper. Even though Melby's marriage appears to have had an assimilating impact on him and his family life, both the declining group of old-stock Americans and the immigrants and their children held Melby in high regard.[48]

During World War I and after, when the anti-hyphenate hysteria peaked, the *Whitehall Times* represented a voice of reason and responsibility, defending even the loyalty of Robert La Follette and of German Americans generally.[49] The paper no doubt articulated the beliefs and commitments of many Trempealeau County residents. Before the American entrance into the war, the paper criticized those who would involve the United States in the war. Taking a typically Populist stance and anticipating the conclusions of the Nye committee, the *Times* charged that only the armament producers and the moneyed interests wanted an end to neutrality.[50] By 1917 few of the old-stock Americans remained in the county to launch an anti-hyphenate drive. But also of importance was the kind of social and economic relationships that had been forged between families. The Norwegian-American culture on the defensive elsewhere in these years flourished in homogeneous rural Trempealeau neighborhoods.

The frontier years as recalled by Hans Anderson were the years with the greatest degree of conflict, but in time relations grew more peaceable, more consensual. The response to the war indicated the degree to which this was true.[51] The war brought an outpouring of patriotic sentiment and activity that depended upon highly developed local traditions of association and organization and upon a highly developed sense of local identity which was rooted in the Norwegian-American culture. The war stimulated the first self-conscious effort to link these local identities to the larger American one.[52] This did not, however, overtly challenge the Norwegian American culture. The county depended upon established leaders (mostly Norwegian Americans), institutions, and organizational methods to promote the war. The election of immigrant and county judge Hans Anderson as the chairman of the Trempealeau County Defense League seemingly guaranteed a tone of tolerance.[53] The nature of the appeal was to make Pigeon people proud. Neighborhoods, towns, institutions, and organizations competed with each other to make the most blankets or to send the most volunteers. Nationalism became meaningful when linked with the already highly developed local community identities. The regular reports in the *Whitehall Times* of the comparative contributions to the war effort exposed this dynamic. On March 7, 1918, the *Times* made the following report:

> The campaign for $750,000 for war service on the part of the Lutherans in America has met prodigious success in this county. The amount allotted to Trempealeau County was $7000 and county chairman Urberg of Eau Claire reports that over $10,500 have been subscribed with some districts yet to hear from. The amount will run over $11,000. In Reverend Christophersen's [Pigeon] and Reverend Ork's congregations the subscriptions were $2,425, fifty percent over.

Through these kinds of strategies the deep local loyalties were tapped to promote a national identification. Communities within the county competed with each other in demonstrations of patriotism much as their baseball teams competed.[54]

By the time the war broke out the political orientations of the ethnic groups in Trempealeau were in place. From the beginning localities linked politics and ethnicity. In 1875 by popular vote Pigeon separated from Lincoln, and the Norwegian-American majority in Pigeon elected Peder Ekern as town chairman. By that time the political control of the township of Lincoln by old-stock Americans was clearly at risk. In 1880, 55 percent of the combined population of the divided townships was Norwegian. Pigeon was predominantly Norwegian at the time it was created as a separate township from Lincoln. The division of the township established more homogeneous political units and preserved the position of control of the established old-stock Americans at least for a time in Lincoln Township.

The separation of the town of Pigeon from Lincoln, Curti surmised, revealed the rapid assimilation of democratic ways on the part of the Norwegians and the adaptability of American political institutions. But it also indicated the desire of both Yankee and Norwegian leaders to consolidate their local political positions. While the Norwegians of Pigeon had a distinct fondness for J. D. Olds, with few exceptions Norwegians represented Pigeon on the county board and in the township offices. At the same time Norwegians progressively expanded their numbers in both the village of Whitehall and Lincoln Township in general. The old-stock Americans continued to dominate political leadership in the village of Whitehall, though by the turn of the century they shared offices with Norwegians. In the sections on the east side of the town of Lincoln, another group, the Polish immigrants, turned up in significant numbers after 1880 and crowded out the old-stock Americans as well. Independence, a village located about five miles east of Whitehall, was the focus of that group's political, social, and economic life. As soon as their numbers made it possible, the immigrants became a political force in the local governments and soon would be an important presence in state politics.[55]

In his analysis of the political culture of Trempealeau County, Merle Curti, borrowing from the Turnerian vision, presumed that "Americanization is part of the democratic process." Therefore, Curti, of course, gave much credit to the original Yankee settlers for teaching immigrants democratic ways:

A word here needs to be said about the demonstrated capacity of the Norwegian-Americans, who formed the great majority of the new town of

Pigeon, to come quickly and efficiently to terms with the democratic appara-
tus of the town meeting imported from New England to this frontier. . . .
Property and age qualifications had probably prevented most of Trempealeau's Norwegians from participating in politics in the Old Country. Although they must have learned something by watching in Norway, they
learned more by emulation and practice on the frontier.[56]

In the concluding sentence of his study, Curti wrote, "The story of the
making of this American community is a story of progress toward democracy."[57]

The rapidity with which Pigeon's and Lincoln's immigrants grasped
political leadership may have had more to do with experiences in Norway
than Curti supposed. The organization and responsibilities of the township government in the United States and that of the *herred* in Norway
parallel each other. These small units of government in Norway, like the
New England town, had responsibility for locally maintaining roads,
bridges, and schools, and for the poor. The *herred* served as an important
unit of the economic and political organization of the nineteenth-century
Norwegian peasant. No doubt families of men like Ekern and Melby, who
came from landed families in Norway and who rapidly launched themselves as leaders on the frontier, had had experience with the *herred* in
Norway.[58]

If it was true that the New Englanders were the teachers of democratic ways, it must have been the Populist radicalism of J. D. Olds that
had the deepest and most lasting impact. But the Norwegian Americans of
Pigeon and Lincoln were too much a part of larger patterns of Norwegian
American political behavior for either J. D. Olds's or the frontier's influence to be the explanation of their political behavior. Norwegian Americans, particularly rural ones, generally located themselves "left of center"
on the political horizon, and those in Trempealeau proved to be no exception.[59] While Curti argued that in frontier times the politics of the county
and of Pigeon and Lincoln adapted and assimilated the changing ethnic
population to democratic ways, it might be more appropriate to argue that
Trempealeau and Wisconsin politics were profoundly influenced and
modified by their immigrant population. Pigeon immigrant Peder Ekern
by 1880 sponsored bills to restrain the corrupting influence of the railroads in Wisconsin politics, and later his nephew Herman would be one of
the leading Progressives of the state, winning a national reputation for the
innovative reforms related to insurance, which he introduced in the Wisconsin legislature.[60]

In order not to overstate the shaping power of the Wisconsin context
or the radicalizing influence of Peder Ekern's neighbor, the Greenbacker

and Populist J. D. Olds, the Norwegian political background deserves some attention. In Norway during the nineteenth century the peasantry was coming into its own as a class-conscious political force. The nineteenth century brought political turmoil when isolated, corporate, peasant communities faced a state-imposed enclosure movement and pressure for a more individualized and market-oriented agriculture. In response the Norwegian peasantry forged political and economic strategies of its own. As a Norwegian scholar summarized, "Norwegian peasants developed their own national political strategy, their own coordinated class policy, and finally a distinct agrarian party."[61]

Religion and language became the focus of a symbolic cultural battle. The official language of Norway was Danish, however, the peasants used a wide range of Norwegian dialects. The nineteenth century brought a series of religious revivals which challenged the authority of Norway's official Norwegian Lutheran church. A peasant-organized cooperative movement which began before 1850 was the basis of economic policy. The peasant movement brought a simultaneous national and cultural awakening. A peasantry so politicized and creative as this hardly needed to be instructed in democratic ways and the use of political means to secure their interests.[62]

In fact, these immigrant peasants needed neither J. D. Olds nor the frontier to instruct them in democratic ways. Their recent entrance into the market economy spawned a powerful cooperative movement linked to a political drive for power. Coming from such a context they had little to learn from even the Populists and perhaps much to teach in practical experience in the organization of cooperative efforts. To some extent, Norwegian peasants achieved earlier what American Populists sought in the 1890s. Norwegian immigrants became a driving force behind the successful cooperative efforts in Trempealeau County after 1880 and on into the twentieth century. They succeeded locally where the Grange of their Yankee predecessors had failed. Could it be that their cooperative traditions were stronger than those the frontier fostered?[63]

When Norwegian peasants left Norway they brought their political culture with them. Men such as John Melby and Peder Ekern, like others in the Norwegian American communities, kept close touch with developments in Norway in these years through the Norwegian-language press, continued immigration, and regular visits to Norway. On more than one occasion Herman Ekern's proposals for reform were based on his knowledge of developments in his father's homeland.[64] Quantitative analysis of ethnic voting patterns in Wisconsin illustrates the result of Norwegian immigrants bringing their peasant politics to the American frontier. One

Herman Ekern, Whitehall lawyer and representative to the Wisconsin legislature, 1920. Ekern was the son of immigrants and one of the key figures in Wisconsin's progressive politics from the time of his first election to the state legislature in 1902 until the demise of the Progressive Party in the 1940s. Photo by John Glander. Photo courtesy of State Historical Society of Wisconsin, WHi (X3) 3096.

historian concluded that rural Scandinavians "must rank as one of the most reform bent ethnic groups in American history."[65]

Scandinavians in rural communities like Pigeon surpassed any other group in their support of La Follette and the Progressive reforms that he promoted. Eighty-nine percent of the rural Norwegians voted for La Follette in the gubernatorial election of 1900 (see appendix A for the Lincoln, Pigeon, and Whitehall gubernatorial vote). One analyst argued that the election of La Follette and the rise to power of the Progressives in Wisconsin represented "the mid-Nineteenth Century immigrant groups coming into their own in the political arena."[66] Scandinavians were the second largest ethnic group in Wisconsin; to them, Progressivism in the state did not signal a resurgence of socially displaced Yankees, but rather, as indicated by voting patterns, it signaled the loss of that group's stranglehold on politics. This voting block was central to La Follette's strength and provided the strongest support to Progressivism of any ethnic group in Wisconsin. Within the state 86 percent of the Scandinavian voters supported La Follette in the presidential primary in 1912, and in 1924, 90 percent would support La Follette's third-party presidential bid.[67]

Wisconsin historian Robert C. Nesbit has described the Norwegian vote as one of the three crucial elements in La Follette's original power base, along with the younger members of the Republican party and alienated Republican party leaders such as former governor William D. Hoard. Norwegians were a neglected self-conscious minority who were "also looking homeward to an intensely democratic Norway which was implementing a social service state."[68]

Like rural Scandinavians elsewhere in the state, the Norwegian Americans in Lincoln and Pigeon consistently remained "left of center." From 1900 through the decade of the 1930s they were unwavering in their support of progressive Republicans and of independent progressive parties. Between the two world wars the La Follettes continued to dominate Wisconsin politics. Robert La Follette's sons, Robert M., Jr., and Phillip, took over the leadership after their father's death in 1925. Like Robert, Sr., they would depend upon coalitions of labor organizations, socialists, Progressives, and radical farm groups, in which the two largest ethnic groups, Germans and Norwegians, played a critical role. In 1926, the La Follettes supported the unsuccessful gubernatorial candidacy of Whitehall's Herman Ekern, whom Nesbit describes as "a faithful La Follette follower through thick and thin."[69]

Despite a long history with a few notable exceptions of voting solidly Republican, beginning in 1932 the farmers of Pigeon and Lincoln voted for Democrats in presidential elections (see Figures 2.1 and 2.2). Nevertheless, their Progressive loyalties remained strong, and like many others they

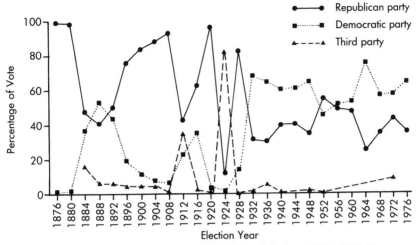

Figure 2.1. Pigeon Township voting patterns in presidential elections, 1876–1976. (See appendix B for the complete data, including a breakdown for the village of Pigeon Falls vote, 1960–1976.)

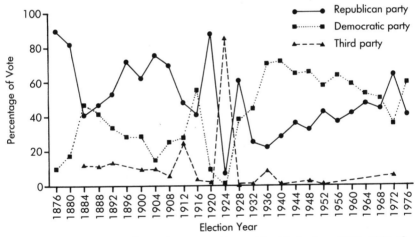

Figure 2.2. Lincoln Township voting patterns in presidential elections, 1876–1976. (See appendix B for the complete data.)

stood solidly behind the La Follettes' third party, the Progressive Party, for gubernatorial candidates (see Figure 2.4). The voting behavior of villagers in Whitehall began to diverge from the farmers at this point. They too supported the Progressives in Wisconsin, but with few exceptions a majority of town folk voted for Republican presidential candidates (see Figure 2.3).

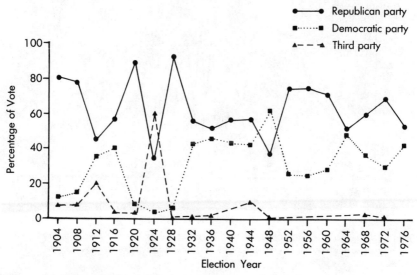

Figure 2.3. Village of Whitehall voting patterns in presidential elections, 1904–1976. (See appendix B for the complete data for 1900–1976.)

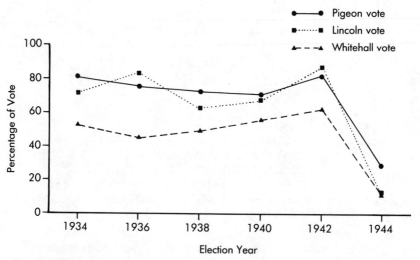

Figure 2.4. The voting patterns of Pigeon, Lincoln, and Whitehall for the Progressive party in gubernatorial elections, 1934–1944. (See appendix A for the complete data for the Progressive, Republican, and Democratic parties, 1876–1976, including a breakdown for the village of Pigeon Falls vote, 1960–1970.)

Phil La Follette's policies as governor in 1930 were in the La Follette tradition, and rather consistently anticipated, paralleled, or sought to go further than those of Franklin Roosevelt's New Deal.[70]

After 1940 the political picture became more complex; elections were closer, but Democrats generally won in Pigeon and Lincoln, while the village of Whitehall usually voted Republican. This pattern of Democratic farmers and Republican villagers typifies the county as a whole. In 1960 when the tiny village of Pigeon Falls was first incorporated, it followed this pattern of Republican majorities in the villages. Presidential election years invariably brought a high voter turnout in the county. (See appendix B for the presidential vote.)

If the migrants from New York and New England were the driving force behind the "making of an American community," the immigrant and ethnic cultures had much to do with the *re*making of that community. By 1926, 75 years after J. D. Olds staked the first claim in Trempealeau, the county's countryside, politics, economy, institutions, and even its language had taken a rather different form from that of a New England town.

For almost 100 years the memory of the Norwegian culture remained vital in the lives of these rural folks. The local hegemony which Norwegian Americans achieved by the time the frontier retreated into memory allowed them to shape their reality to the memory for at least three generations. And although that memory dimmed with each decade, and the institutional and cultural formations which grew out of it eventually disappeared with the language, many individuals still continue to define their community as essentially a Norwegian-American one. This background continues to help locals define who they are in relationship to the larger American society. Whitehall High School's athletic teams are referred to as the Norsemen. The *Whitehall Times* still keeps locals informed about events of interest to Norwegian Americans, just as some families continue to send their children to private colleges originally established by the first generation of Scandinavian immigrants. When members of these communities become world travelers, venturing beyond the borders of this continent, they still are likely to return to Norway, seeking to reacquire memories lost to the attrition of time.

3
The Men and the Mentality
of Main Street

The country town of the great American farming region is the perfect flower of self help and cupidity standardized on the American plan.

Thorstein Veblen, "The Country Town"

Just as the immigrants reshaped the politics and cultural traditions of Trempealeau, they also influenced the beliefs and business activities of main street. Veblen's critique of the merchants of the country town paralleled the perceptions of many of those who shared his Norwegian immigrant background.[1] The power of the traditional attitudes of the immigrants and migrants is revealed in the way they thought about and organized their local economy. During the frontier years farm families labored at clearing the land, breaking the tough sod, and establishing and maintaining a largely subsistence household and local economy. Wheat served as the cash crop upon which almost all depended to create their first homes. But 1873 brought the railroad to Lincoln Township, and its arrival gave birth to main street. The village of Whitehall displaced the earlier frontier trading posts and, although it never became a city, it did become the county seat and the important trading center of the township with efficient connections to the national market. As the frontier wheat production declined in the face of exhausted soil, the chinch bug, and competition from the cultivation of grain on the Great Plains, Trempealeau County farmers turned to dairying and animal husbandry as the basis of their agricultural economy. Whatever hopes the early pioneers of Lincoln nurtured of escaping the kind of commercial economy developed in upstate New York in the early nineteenth century would be short-lived.[2]

The attitude of Trempealeau's farmers to the coming of the railroad did not fit the conventional view that profit-minded western farmers eagerly awaited and generously supported the extension of railroads into their communities. At best, Lincoln farmers exhibited an attitude of indifference; at worst, hostility. Despite the unwillingness of farmers to put up cash for the purpose, the Green Bay and Western Railroad laid its tracks across the wheat fields of Lincoln. Perhaps by purely economic calculation,

60

Lincoln farmers would have been well advised to invest in railroad bonds and to facilitate the growth of a transportation network that would carry their produce to market. Their nearest market was the village of Trempealeau on the Mississippi, over 40 miles away.[3] Dave Wood spent two or three days making such a trip before the railroad came to Lincoln.[4]

But Lincoln's farmers were not eager to invest their own money in order to improve their access to the expansive American economy. In 1873 they twice voted to reject offers that the Green Bay and Pepin Railroad Company made to build a track with bonded support from the township (first by a vote of 110–30 and later 87–82). Merle Curti attributed this refusal of support to their sagacity and tightfistedness; they accurately reckoned that the railroad would come anyway, so why put up the money?[5] But it may well have been that a majority of these pioneers saw neither the need for nor the benefit of the railroad to their household and local economies; rural communities from which most of the pioneers came maintained themselves for centuries in Norway and in the United States without the railroad. Distrust of new technologies and innovation typified peasants of the past and many American farmers as well. Similarly, in 1884 Pigeon's farmers refused to grant aid for a railroad line into their tiny trading post of Pigeon Falls, and a railroad never would cross through their fields.[6]

This less-than-enthusiastic reaction of Pigeon's and Lincoln's farmers to the railroad's arrival anticipated their responses to a growing involvement in the market economy and corporate capitalism in general. Economic development, the changing leadership on main street, local economic institutions, and the way these people and institutions were regarded are aspects of the communities' history necessary to understanding main street and its mentality in Trempealeau. As has often been noted, the intrusion of the market frequently creates a conflict between the values and behaviors expected of the individual in the community and those of the impersonal and competitive marketplace. Pigeon and Lincoln residents were not quick to abandon the ideals of a moral economy found in American republicanism and in the traditional peasant communities of Norway. This is revealed in their conception of the proper behavior of those individuals who played an important role in mediating between themselves and the larger economy, of the local economic and professional elites, and of the organizations that they created in the local community that also mediated between themselves and the larger market.[7]

But the railroad, the great harbinger of change, did come. With it came the corporate power of the late nineteenth century and the ambitious individuals who served that power. T. H. Earle was the first man to step off the first passenger train that wound its way into the Lincoln wheat field that he soon transformed into the village of Whitehall. In 1873, at the age of 33, this Ohio-born businessman embodied the entrepreneurial spirit of the small-town businessman along with many of the qualities that Frederick Jackson Turner associated with the American frontier: restlessness, optimism, ambition, and individualism. As the son-in-law of Henry Ketchum, president and promoter of the new Green Bay and Western Railroad, Earle came to build a town, represent his own and the Green Bay and Western's interests, and make money for both. In essence he created the main street of Lincoln Township. Within a year he platted the village of Whitehall, began selling the lots owned by his father-in-law, built a comfortable home (the first in the village), put up a building to store grain, and established his place of business as a grain buyer adjacent to the railroad. Wheat was king in the decade of the 1870s in Trempealeau, and most profitable businesses depended upon that product.[8]

T. H. Earle, grain buyer and mill, warehouse, and elevator owner, was the undisputed "boss" or the "most commanding citizen" of the town. He dealt in grain, lumber, and farm equipment, selling among other things "the most popular reaper ever sold in that county—the Perry Roys." During his years in Whitehall, Earle led the town as its most conspicuous promoter. His machinations won the county seat for Whitehall when several villages competed for this prize between 1876 and 1878. When they created and promoted the frontier village of Whitehall, Earle and the Green Bay and Western established themselves immediately in an economically advantageous position.[9] Earle and the corporations that he represented were the primary beneficiaries of this frontier town's expansion. Descriptions of his character reveal a man who knew and used his power in the community.[10] While lauding his intelligence and ambition, a local noted that Earle could be:

> . . . brusque and abrupt at times, he had a hair-trigger temper and a tongue like a rapier. When angry he poured out a flood of expletives that are still barred from appearing in standard dictionaries. Generous to a fault with his friends, open and frank in his opinion of those he loved not, he made many friends, warm friends—and bitter enemies.[11]

By 1880 the new village had a busy main street and a population of 267 people in 64 households. Those who had established themselves in the earlier trading centers of Lincoln Township in Coral City and Old Whitehall, located on the Trempealeau River, soon moved to Earle's main street or moved on.[12]

Earle represented a far different kind of Yankee from what Deacon Alvah Wood and J. D. Olds represented, and, significantly, his stay was far briefer. It is not known what Deacon Alvah Wood thought about the coming of the railroad and the making of main street, but it is clear that his son Dave became one of its enthusiastic supporters, one of those who convinced enough of his neighbors of the value of a railroad to increase the number of people supporting the bond from 30 to 82 on the second vote. From the beginning he allied himself with T. H. Earle, a relationship that proved highly beneficial to Dave over the years. He was one of the farmers employed by the railroad during its construction, providing supplies and renting his teams of horses, and later in a partnership with Earle he built a haybarn and set a haypress in operation which shipped hay out of the area.[13] Besides his association with Wood, Earle entered into other business ventures with locals H. E. Getts and C. E. Scott, who ran a milling operation.[14]

In 1885 Earle moved on when better opportunities beckoned and when the businesses he promoted proved less profitable than he wished.[15] Earle's departure signaled the end of the frontier wheat economy and the need for some reassessment by the businessmen of main street. Among those who preceded and followed Earle's departure were a number of farmers and others who had been involved in wheat production, the profits from which were declining steadily. At the time they blamed the flight westward on "hard times" because of low prices, drought, the "cynch bug," and exhausted soil.[16] In 1878 a combination of unfortunate weather conditions and exhausted soil resulted in an almost total loss of the wheat crop.[17] After 1880 wheat production plummeted in the county. In 1895 Pigeon farmers produced less than a third of the number of bushels of wheat that they had in 1885, and Lincoln's production fell even lower. Facing this situation many would join the "rush to the Dakotas."[18]

The unwillingness or inability of businessmen and farmers to meet the challenge of moving into other kinds of production may explain some of the considerable movement out of the county that Merle Curti noted. The *Whitehall Times* in 1879 and 1880 leaves the impression that a genuine exodus occurred in the hard times of those years. Although there was a steady increase in population before 1880, at the same time there was a high degree of turnover. In the frontier years few stayed for any extended period of time.[19] Indeed, at least a third would disappear in any of the 10 years between censuses. In the townships of Lincoln and Pigeon between 1870 and 1880, 55 percent of the families disappeared. In 1870 about 43 percent of the families were transplanted New Yorkers and scattered New Englanders, 39 percent were Norwegian, and the remaining 17 percent were small numbers of Germans, English, Irish, Scots, and Canadians. None of these groups seemed any more inclined to stay than the others. Like the restless frontiersman of mythology and Hamlin Garland's and Abraham Lincoln's fathers, the early settlers of Trempealeau regularly

Table 3.1. Number of Heads Persisting in or Moving from Lincoln and Pigeon Townships, 1870–1880

	Number Persisting	Number Moving	Unattributable	Total	Percent Persisting
Yankee	30	37		67	42.9
Norwegian	26	35		61	39.1
Other	12	14		26	16.7
Illegible			2	2	1.3
Total	68	86	2	156	100.0
Percent	43.6	55.1	1.3	100.0	

Source: Manuscript Censuses, U.S. Census of Population, Lincoln and Pigeon townships, Trempealeau County, Wisconsin, 1870, 1880.

packed up their families and followed the sun west, selling their homesteads and moving where land was still cheap or free for the taking and wheat was still king. A contemporary of Earle in Whitehall noted and explained the restless habits of the frontiersman: "The spirit of the West has a yeast-like effect on most men, for under its magic influence men seem to grow larger and demand more room. They settle in large spaces, but as soon as these spaces fill up they grow restive and move again."[20]

The villagers of Whitehall appear to have been restive indeed. Although the Wood family stayed for five generations and the members of Getts and Scott families were still in the village in 1910, mobility in general was very high between 1870 and 1880. Fifty-five percent of all the household heads present in Lincoln in 1870 were not listed on the 1880 census. Those like T. H. Earle who were engaged in a trade, a craft, or a business left at a rate of 72 percent. The restlessness of town folk contrasted radically with that of the farm-owning families. By 1900 little trace remained of the 64 household heads in the village of Whitehall in 1880. Only four reappeared on the 1900 manuscript schedules: one retired merchant, one merchant named Charles Adams, the upwardly mobile John Melby, who climbed from the position of register of deeds to banker, and a retired laborer. Christopher Scott's and H. E. Getts's sons continued as businessmen in Whitehall in 1900 and 1910. Of the nine merchants listed in the 1880 census, three families continued on main street by 1900. Two other sons of village families of 1880 persisted and became merchants by 1910. Three widows remained in 1900 of the other villagers of 1880. Thus, of the 64 households of 1880 only 11 were still represented to one degree or another in the village by the early twentieth century.[21]

The high mobility between 1880 and 1900 remade main street. In 1880 almost two-thirds of the household heads were old-stock Americans, and only about a fifth of the villagers were of Scandinavian background. All nine professionals and eight of the ten merchants were Yankees; the other two included one English and one Canadian immigrant. Of the elected county and town officials only John Melby was not of old-stock background. By 1900 an entirely different situation prevailed. Main street acquired practically an entirely new group of men and women. Yankee T. H. Earle had been the most commanding citizen in 1880, but immigrant John Melby had laid claim to that position by 1900. Scandinavians competed with old-stock Americans as professionals, merchants, and elected officials. Lawyer Hans Anderson, soon to become county judge, and his partner and son-in-law, Herman Ekern, future Progressive legislator and state political leader, competed with Yankees for the legal business, and by 1910 only one of the four lawyers in town was not from immigrant stock. By that year, half of the 18 professionals were Scandinavian in background, and only a quarter were Yankees. The preceding decade had brought a radical shift in this regard. In 1900, Ekern and Anderson were the only non-Yankees of the 11 professionals in the village. By 1910 eight more had appeared, whereas four of the seven old-stock professionals had departed and only three others had replaced them.[22]

Norwegian Americans similarly steadily expanded their numbers among the businessmen of main street and like their counterparts on the farm became more stable. The merchants of 1900 remained in the community at a much higher rate than those of 1870 and 1880. Seventeen of the 22 merchants of 1900 were still present by 1910; 7 of the 8 old-stock Americans remained, and 7 of the 11 Norwegian Americans continued to do business on main street. But joining the competition with the 17 remaining merchants were another 9 Norwegian Americans who set up shop. By 1910, 62 percent of the village's businessmen were Norwegian Americans. Scandinavians increased from only 24 percent of the skilled workers and artisans in 1880 to 75 percent by 1910. Among the Scandinavians the proportion of household heads who worked as unskilled laborers varied little from 1880 to 1910; in 1880, 57 percent of the unskilled laborers were Scandinavian, and in 1910 the proportion totaled 61 percent.[23]

The new men on Whitehall's main street differed from their predecessors in persistence, ethnic background, and very likely in the way they interacted with the community. The rise to a position of influence by 1900 of one of the new men, Hans Anderson, is worth examining in detail for what it reveals of the experiences and attitudes of those who remade main street. If T. H. Earle arrived with considerable advantages to establish himself, most did not. Many would come to frontier Lincoln without even the pioneer know-how acquired by the Wood and the Ingalls families. In his autobiography Hans A. Anderson told the story of his Norwegian-immigrant family's experiences, which in many respects are representative of the background of the Norwegian-immigrant settlers.

Born in 1855 Anderson spent his childhood in a self-sufficient mountain-top hamlet in the Søndfjord region of Norway. This hamlet, Alværen, included a cluster of three families on 40 acres of land, which the families farmed in a semicommunal fashion. No roads reached this remote peasant home, only footpaths. Alværen had only recently been first cultivated by land-hungry peasants; earlier Alværen had been used as a *stolen,* a mountain summer pasture for animals of peasants from more hospitably located areas. When Norway's population boomed in the nineteenth century, crowding on the land became acute and the most remote and rugged places like Alværen were carefully cultivated.

Ultimately the American frontier provided an irresistible opportunity to Norway's hard-pressed peasants like Anderson's parents. Anderson's mother and stepfather joined the throngs of impoverished peasants leaving Norway for the United States. When rumors of the rich land and resources of the United States reached the Andersons' mountain home, Hans's mother soon determined that the family must go. Unlike Beret in Ole Rolvaag's *Giants in the Earth,* it was Anderson's mother who possessed the strong will and resolve for their move. Many tried to dissuade her with predictions of dire consequences, but she was undaunted. Her husband, seemingly unconcerned about his patriarchal prerogatives, acquiesced to her decision and leadership, as he apparently did in the face of most of life's crises and challenges. To her son Hans, she was the very spirit of the frontier: "Mother had in her make-up all the higher qualities desired in an immigrant, and it was at her initiative that in the spring of 1867 our little place was sold and all personal property which we could not bring with us."[24]

With the assistance of a loan from an uncle they put together enough money to get the family of seven to Milwaukee, Wisconsin. On May 9, 1867, Ole Gunderson, his wife, Berthe, and their five children—15-year-old Ole, 12-year-old Hans, 8-year-old Andre, 6-year-old Julia, and the nursing baby, Hannah—departed from Norway. After a six-week ocean voyage from Bergen to Quebec, they proceeded by train to Milwaukee, where they ran out of money. Leaving their luggage as security for transportation to Winona, Minnesota, when they reached that Mississippi River town they were penniless and depended upon the generosity of Norwegians and Americans to aid them in the downriver trip to the village of Trempealeau. From there, they made their way on foot another 40 miles to Pigeon Creek. Their goal on reaching Pigeon was the home of Mads Knudtson, their only acquaintance on the entire continent and the first immigrant from the Søndfjord region, from which they came. A 12-by-16-foot log cabin constituted Knudtson's home. That small cabin housed the two families for several months.[25]

For most of the impoverished immigrants who came to the wilds of Wisconsin during the frontier years, the first year proved the most difficult. The Anderson family's experience was not an exception. During the first summer and fall Hans's mother and stepfather worked three miles from Knudtson's farm on that of another Norwegian immigrant. Husband and wife did the same work for the same wages, two dollars a day. In addition, his mother would walk back and forth to and from the Knudtson's household to nurse her baby. Twelve-year-old Hans worked for clothes and room and board for a farmer-teamster in the area. The first winter the family spent in Wisconsin Anderson recalled as the most miserable of his life. Relations became strained in the crowded Knudtson cabin, and the family moved into an incomplete cabin abandoned by a homesteader. Most of the money earned during the summer and fall served to redeem the luggage left in Milwaukee, and the family approached starvation. When neighbors discovered this, they acted with the generosity for which the frontier is famed. At a local prayer meeting, neighbors agreed upon a plan to supply the family with food. Hunger did not threaten again.

The next summer Anderson's family began homesteading in the "Big Slough" coulee of Pigeon. With the help of neighbors they constructed their first home in a single day, a 13-foot-square log cabin. In the two years following the move into this humble abode, two more children were born to Anderson's parents. If that were not enough for their small cabin, it also became a stopping place for family and friends who followed Anderson's parents from their Norwegian home community. Anderson's family extended every bit as much frontier hospitality as they had enjoyed. During the summer of 1870 Hans's uncle and family of nine arrived and spent the summer. The next summer another equally large family spent the season with them, and then "the following year came Henry Gunderson and his wife and a young man and lady, all of whom stayed for some time."[26]

In 1877 at the age of 22 Hans married and set out on a 10-year struggle to find a secure means of making a living. He started his own family in the 13-foot-square cabin built nine years earlier. His parents, like so many of the early settlers, moved again in 1877 to a farm elsewhere in the state, and young Anderson bought his parents' farm. Berthe Gunderson had left Norway for the very clear purpose of finding for her children better opportunities on the land than those available in Norway, and this arrangement represented a reasonable beginning.

Unfortunately for Anderson and his young wife, the next year brought the disastrous harvest of 1878. Like many others, the young couple could not survive the bad harvest, and Anderson sold the farm at a "heavy loss." The next few years brought insecurity, hard work, and separation from his wife and children while Anderson sought a means to establish himself. He tried his hand at a variety of occupations from school teaching to laboring in the Dakotas building railroads. Apparently some Norwegian immigrants like Anderson were ill-suited for the discipline of such labor. While working for the railroad company he organized a protest by the crew against their "boss," a "heartless and cruel" Irishman, and recommended his replacement by a "Swede." Unimpressed by the concerns of this Norwegian immigrant and his democratic notions of how work should be organized, the managers promptly fired Anderson and his fellows. After this misadventure Anderson returned to Wisconsin, and worked as a farm hand, janitor, school teacher, law clerk, town clerk, and at whatever odd jobs he could pick up in Pigeon and Whitehall.[27]

When T. H. Earle left Whitehall for better places, Anderson was still without a niche in the new country. By 1887, at age 32, Hans Anderson had five children and was expecting another. His financial circumstances remained precarious at best. At this point he determined on a plan that might bring him the security that had until then eluded him. On the advice of his friend Peder Ekern (Pigeon's most prominent and respected farmer-businessman and politician), Anderson, whose "hope and aim for some years had been to become a missionary," decided, reluctantly it seems, to pursue a career in law. He did so with much ambivalence. He shared his Norwegian neighbors' distrust and disregard for lawyers: "This thought had never entered my mind, in fact, from the general reputation current among the farmers of the rascality, etc., of lawyers, I had little taste for the work. . . . But even the strongest must yield to the inexorable demand for food and shelter." In a single year Anderson completed the two-year law program at the University of Wisconsin in Madison and then returned to Whitehall where he established his practice. Thus, 1890 began his long and respected career as a lawyer, district attorney, county judge, and public figure.[28]

Unlike T. H. Earle, who had arrived on the first train and built a comfortable home on land owned by his father-in-law with supplies arriving by rail, Anderson's family had arrived on foot and depended upon the charity of both friends and strangers as well as their own hard labors to make their small claim on the frontier. In these years, families like Anderson's made Herculean efforts to establish themselves on a farm or in a business or profession. Young men and women "worked out" in the communities where their parents settled, earning a little extra to help the families get established. Until his marriage Anderson worked for a variety of farmers in the area and around the state, as did his wife. Many of the

Hans Alfred Anderson, Whitehall lawyer, district attorney, and county judge, ca. 1925–1935. Photo courtesy of State Historical Society of Wisconsin, WHi (X3) 46447.

immigrants who arrived during the frontier years, like Anderson and his parents, spent several years orienting themselves in the new country. Initially they did what they had to do simply to survive, building a rude log cabin, planting their first harvest, and acquiring the means for a subsistence agriculture. They then more carefully explored their options and exploited the opportunities available. In some instances they desperately pursued an illusive security that did not always meet with Anderson's success. The *Whitehall Times* reported on many who would enter and leave and then on occasion return again to the community, as Anderson did through the course of his life. Sometimes they took temporary jobs or sought better opportunities on the land or in a business or through education. Obituaries of the first generation of Norwegian immigrants to Lincoln and Pigeon reveal a common pattern. After the immigrant first arrived, the family or individual would often make two or three moves during the initial decade before settling permanently in Pigeon or Lincoln. Most worked on their own land or someone else's land, and when they became more familiar with their new homeland many would discover opportunities on main street, as did Anderson.[29]

Even before the coming of the railroad to Trempealeau, corporate America played a central role to the building of frontier farm economics and main street. The lumber industry dominated Wisconsin's economy and politics in the nineteenth century, and its influence penetrated the economy of main street and the lives of frontier farmers. Although they did not play a role in Anderson's struggle to establish himself, "the woods" or the "pineries" competed with the production of wheat in importance both to the local economy and to immigrants trying to establish a foothold in Trempealeau County. During the winter months, farmers and more often their sons worked for the booming lumber companies of the state. Some worked as employees, acquiring some extra cash to make a down payment on a farm or to help pay off their own or their parents' mortgage. Farmers hauled hay or other products to sell or trade for lumber needed for building. Others went with their teams and worked hauling products for the lumber companies. Throughout the decade of the 1880s and into the 1890s the local paper reported on those leaving and returning from work in the woods, on the availability of such work, on the travel conditions to the woods, on what prices were being paid for hay, and on the names and descriptions of what was happening to those who were hauling their produce to the woods. In 1889 a correspondent of the *Times* from the rural community of Elk Creek illustrated the continuing importance of the pineries to the local economy when he complained, "Men used to making up in the winter what they lose in the summer farming are disheartened. Five of our boys went to Chippewa Falls, but have returned unable to find work."[30]

For many of the immigrants and the old-stock Americans, work in the pineries played a crucial role while they established themselves on the farms or on main street. Local merchants buying and selling farm products sent a veritable army of men and animals into the woods, which served as a key market for their produce. While some merchants, like T. H. Earle, relied on the railroad after 1874, others continued driving their stock and produce to nearby markets.[31]

So common was the experience of winter work in the woods that even the social life of the community was organized around it. In 1881 the *Whitehall Times* announced that a dance would be "put on for the benefit of the boys just out of the woods." The *Times* went on to note: "There is quite a sprinkling of well dressed young men on our streets who have but recently returned from the woods. They are quiet and well behaved, and their conduct is in marked contrast with what it was several years ago. It's a good change."[32]

The importance of the lumber industry to the pioneers was apparent when the county's first homesteaders arrived. In 1851, when the young James D. Olds set out alone from his birthplace in Chenango County, New York, to make his claim in Wisconsin's wilderness, he depended upon labor in the pineries to support his frontier claim. Olds explored the countryside alone, staked the first claim in the county of 160 acres, and built a rough log cabin with an axe borrowed from James Reed. Then like hundreds of settlers who followed him, he went to work in the woods. For over two and a half years he worked "at good wages" for a lumber company in Chippewa Falls, Wisconsin, returning briefly during the summer to do a little work on his claim. By 1854, when J. D. Olds returned to his claim, his father and his entire family had followed young James west and settled next to him.[33]

Besides homesteading, J. D. and his brother George opened a store and blacksmith shop at a place then known as McGilvray's Ferry on the Black River. Olds would not again return to wage labor in the woods. True to the free-labor ideals of the republican ideology of the pre–Civil War North, Olds achieved the independence which was so admired as a farmer and small businessman. Wage labor was but a temporary necessity, a means to establishing oneself independently. Such was the perception of both the immigrants and the native-born Americans like J. D. Olds, and so too was it the reality of their experience.[34]

Compared with many of those who settled in Lincoln and Pigeon, Olds's stay in the woods was relatively brief. For the immigrant families the struggle for independence often took much longer. Thurine Oleson, the daughter of Norwegian immigrants, reported that her husband spent seven winters in the woods and gave all his earnings to his widowed mother until he married, so that she might be comfortably established on her own farm.[35] Peder Simonson, who immigrated with his wife and children from Norway in 1871 and settled in Pigeon in 1875, "came here empty-handed" and "spent twenty winters in the pineries, many springs and summers on the rivers, and several more summers" employed by the lumbering industry.[36] Until almost the turn of the century, well after the frontier years, the woods played an important role in the economy and the lives of the people of Lincoln and Pigeon, both as a market for their products and as an employer.[37]

One of the Norwegian immigrants who spent his first year in Wisconsin's pineries was John Melby, the man who replaced T. H. Earle as the dominant figure on Whitehall's main street. His background and experiences, like those of Hans Anderson, his sometime partner and friend, made him a very different kind of business and community leader. Their Norwegian background shaped their perceptions and behavior. Thorstein Veblen, the son of Norwegian-immigrant farmers in Minnesota, may well have been articulating commonly held views of Yankee merchants when he focused his sharp satire on the country town's farmer-businessmen:

> They have been cultivators of the main chance as well as of the fertile soil. . . . American farmers have been footloose, on the whole, more particularly that peculiarly American element among them who derive their traditions from a colonial pedigree. There has been an easy shifting from country to town, and this steady drift into the towns of the great farming sections has in the main been a drift from work into business. And it has been the business of these country towns—what may be called their business as usual—to make the most of the necessities and ignorance of their underlying farm population. . . . But the upshot of it so far has habitually been that the farm population find themselves working for a very modest livelihood and the country towns come in for an inordinately wide margin of net gains.

Veblen went on to note that net gains "go in under the caption, 'Something for Nothing.' . . . It's an idle waste as far as the farm population's well being is concerned. . . . The country town of the great American farming region is the perfect flower of self help and cupidity standardized on the American plan."[38] Such attitudes provided the Norwegian businessman and professional with advantages. The businesses of the middleman of the country towns were distrusted and their legitimacy questioned to the extent that they appeared to be narrowly focused on profit alone.

Whitehall may have been born as the child of the railroad, the corporation, and its entrepreneurial representative, T. H. Earle, but it quickly became the adopted child of a rather different kind of orientation. Immigrants John Melby and Hans Anderson in Whitehall and Peder Ekern in Pigeon Falls became the preeminent community and county leaders. Melby made his way from the pineries to a position of store clerk, to register of deeds, and finally organized the Melby Bank in Whitehall. He and his children spent their lives in the village and were perceived quite differently from T. H. Earle. Hans Anderson expressed what appears to have been a widespread perception of Melby in noting that Melby's political and financial success derived from the respect and trust he had won from his Norwegian neighbors:

> From every section of the county people came to him with their problems and troubles, and this is especially true of those of his own nativity, whose inability to speak the English language or whose lack of knowledge concerning our laws made them hesitate to confide in others. To those he gave his time and the benefit of his intimate business knowledge with a patience and kindly interest that early in life endeared him to all who knew him.

A quarter of a century after his death he continued to be held up in the community as a model businessman and human being. "No more admirable copy for young men to follow has ever been furnished by any citizen of our village than the life of John O. Melby." He was remembered as a man deeply committed to the community's interests and needs, but T. H. Earle was assessed as a man who set out to and did advance primarily his own fortunes.[39]

One incident reveals something of the differences between Earle and Melby. The land in the village area that had not been owned by Earle and his father-in-law, Henry Ketchum, had been tied up in a law suit between the Green Bay and Western Railroad and one of Ketchum's original partners. The law suit had long retarded the town's growth until 1884, when it was finally settled. Few people besides Melby had the wherewithal to buy the land. When he purchased it, Melby insisted on making a partner of the struggling young immigrant Hans Anderson, who admitted that he "didn't have a dollar in the transaction," but received profits "like getting money from home without care or cost" to himself. Hans Anderson further noted:

> An examination of the records of our sales will show that in no town in our county were lands sold so cheaply as in Whitehall. . . . No immigrant to our county ever had greater opportunities to make money through speculation than Melby and it may be said with equal truth that no man more studiously avoided to speculate with funds which came to him in a fiduciary capacity. . . . The fortune he gathered was not the result of big takings, nor big makings, but came to him through the great number of small remunerations received for services during many years.[40]

In 1906 Melby donated over 20 acres of this land to the city as a public park, which exists today as Melby Park. Melby appeared the very model of civic virtue and responsibility.[41]

In Pigeon, Earle's counterpart as merchant, mill-owner, politician, and farmer was the immigrant Peder Ekern. His relationship to Pigeon's residents anticipated Melby's. Like Earle, Ekern platted the village of Pigeon Falls and located himself at the center of the local economy as mill-owner, proprietor, landowner, and farmer. Politically his success surpassed that of Earle, because Ekern from the beginning became Pigeon's most influential figure in town, county, and state. Even before the separation of Lincoln and Pigeon he was elected to leading positions in the township. Pigeon repeatedly elected him to the town and county boards, and eventually he served in the state legislature. Like Melby but unlike Earle he was an immigrant who spent his life in Pigeon, to which he was devoted.

Ekern arrived in this country with financial resources far surpassing those of Anderson and Melby. In 1868, at the age of 31, Ekern, the son of a landowner, had emigrated with his wife and children from Norway and settled on a farm in Pigeon. The name Ekern is one long associated with Norway's elite, and Ekern's rapid acquisition of property and his political savvy suggests that he may have transferred to this country the knowledge and bearing of a person of high status in his native land. In 1872 he purchased a general store in Pigeon Falls and a few years later a mill and

Peder Ekern's Mill, Pigeon Falls, Wisconsin, 1908. Photo courtesy of University of Wisconsin–La Crosse, Murphy Library.

A worker inside the Coral City Mill in Whitehall, ca. 1900–1910. Photo courtesy of Dave Wood, Minneapolis.

280 acres of land. By 1880 he had replaced both the mill and the store, and had equipped the former to handle both feed and flour.

Unlike T. H. Earle, who left once wheat lost its profitability, Ekern placed himself at the center of the development of dairying as he had earlier done in relationship to wheat. His connections and commitments were not to a corporation but to the community, or at least that is the way he was perceived. His progeny continued to dominate the community's leadership until the 1960s. This family was long judged according to the same standards applied to Melby. An anonymous local historian writing sometime shortly after World War II described the Ekern family's role in Pigeon:

> The scope of the influence of Peder Ekern and his descendants in Pigeon Falls can never be measured. The community, learning early of the trustworthy business practices of Peder Ekern, have, during these many years, turned to P. Ekern Co. for service in its many phases. P. Ekern Co. has been loyal to its people, so the people have reciprocated, even when modern travel has made shopping in larger centers easy.
>
> The policy of fair dealing for the honest man was established when the first pioneer pocketed his pride as the cinch bugs destroyed his wheat crop and he had to come to "Per" Ekern, as he was called in the strictly Norwegian community, for aid. The families which Peder Ekern kept from starving during the long winter months when the diphtheria scourge and other catastrophies hit these struggling early-day pioneers, can never be enumerated.
>
> When money wasn't available to repay the debt, farmers were given opportunities to repay in any way they could. Credit was given for the hauling of merchandise from the railroad station at Whitehall, for days labor on the farm, for farm products and many other means of erasing their debts were offered. Much was charged off to advertising. That advertising has paid off big dividends and its influence is still being reflected.[42]

Success in business on the competitive main street of country towns was always precarious. The considerable prestige and comparative wealth achieved by men like Ekern and Melby (Melby's will revealed an estate of $133,520 and Ekern's will an estate of $80,000), in the view of their neighbors and patrons, reflected their responsibility toward and service to the locality. They did not move on when better opportunities beckoned and leave former partners to face financial ruin as T. H. Earle had done. Those who had roots in strong local and communal traditions expected local businessmen whose profits sprang from the community to be willing to assist locals cooperatively through hard times and to have a clear and continued commitment to the community. Ekern and Melby may have been only shrewd businessmen, but their success depended upon being perceived as much more. As one Whitehall woman explained, "In the old days every town seemed to have its leading family."[43] Melby and Ekern set the standards of appropriate behavior for those leading families, whereas frontier entrepreneur T. H. Earle did not.

Despite the corporate and entrepreneurial beginnings of the village of Whitehall, the perception of social and economic relationships took a temporary turn toward the traditional, toward the paternal. Men such as Melby and Ekern commanded a great deal of respect based on the perception of mutual obligation and responsibility. They are best understood, as Curti noted, as local patriarchs.[44] Anthropologist George M. Foster has commented: "Patron-client patterns, in which peasant villagers seek out more powerful people . . . with the power to aid, are a significant element in most peasant societies. . . . Their role is mediating between the peasant and his Little Tradition, and the more powerful elements in his society, who participate in the Great Tradition."[45] Within immigrant and ethnic communities' "Little Tradition," individuals like Melby and Ekern function in mediating roles, mediating between those with lesser skills in the language and the market economy and wider culture. In addition, Pigeon and Lincoln residents perceived the relationship between themselves and the Norwegian-American elites in a fashion that paralleled that of peasant communities; the relationship involved reciprocal obligations and mutual benefits, though clearly the rewards of the patron far outweighed those of the client. Sophistication, education, family, and position set the local elites apart as they had in Norway.

Norwegian Americans did not transport intact the social structure of Norway by any means, but it was not without its impact either. Peter Munch has argued that the importing into this country of deference to traditional educated and professional elites, and presumably the configuration of thought that justified that deference, played an important role in defining group boundaries and in maintaining a distinct sense of ethnic identity. Even a century after immigration, this contributed to maintaining dual social structures in Viroqua. Similarly in Pigeon, the respect still shown for three generations of Ekerns after World War II indicated that the traditional expectations of social responsibility from economic leaders was still alive, though the reality had no doubt been much transformed. The days when every little town had its "leading family" dominated by a notable patriarch have long since passed.[46]

Both the men and the mentality of main street changed, and so too did the products and organizations on which its economy rested. As long as wheat served as the essential cash crop in Lincoln and Pigeon, the mills, warehouses, and elevators and those who owned them and traded in grain stood at the center of economic life. When wheat production and prices declined, T. H. Earle and the corporate presence that he represented moved on. By 1900 dairying became primary, replacing wheat, and an economic localism flourished when farmer cooperatives and associations, which sometimes included businessmen, took over the responsibility for the enterprises connected to processing and marketing. Norwegian peasants had devised such cooperative strategies much earlier. They had structured their local and household economies around dairy products and animal husbandry. When they faced the growing intrusion of a market economy into their subsistence communities, they responded by midcentury by creating a wide range of producer and consumer cooperatives to maintain traditional control in their neighborhoods and to reduce their vulnerability to the market. Pigeon and Lincoln immigrants followed their example.[47]

Initially the immigrant pioneers, like their Yankee counterparts, often had no choice but to turn to wheat production and wage labor because of the need for cash simply to establish themselves.[48] Thus, during the frontier years immigrant farmers rapidly followed Yankees in devoting acreage to wheat. But, once they could afford it, Norwegian farmers in Pigeon and Lincoln acquired livestock and modeled their farms on the Norwegian *gard,* in which animal husbandry was central to the household and local economy. Eventually dairy products replaced wheat in Trempealeau, and, like the Norwegian peasants, Trempealeau's immigrants turned to cooperative organizations as a means of protecting themselves and maintaining control over their products.

Those studying peasant societies which confronted increased involvement in the market find that the peasants' widespread response was to seek communal or cooperative means of protecting their interests. Communal strategies in the interest of self- and community preservation were longstanding peasant traditions and experiences, and they naturally turned to cooperative efforts when confronting new risks and opportunities. No doubt, the Norwegian immigrants who created cooperatives in Trempealeau shared the Norwegian peasants' distrust of the potentially exploitative role of businessmen, as did many American farmers, who also turned to cooperative solutions from time to time. Many were very likely in agreement with Veblen's opinions of the Yankee businessmen. Regardless, no individual rose to dominate the dairy industry as T. H. Earle had done in marketing wheat.[49]

The decade of the 1880s brought the realization that wheat could no longer be relied upon by those who wanted to remain on the land or on main street. An editorial in the *Whitehall Times* in January of 1880 revealed the widespread sense of insecurity, with the editor lecturing the locals about staying out of debt. To survive one must "pay as you go," though the editor noted sympathetically, "Our crops, it is true in this section, for the past two seasons, have compelled many to become involved, but it is our belief that with care, frugality and by turning to account the energy and natural inborn grit which characterize our people, that the tables will be turned and peace and plenty prevail."[50] Others like J. D. Olds adopted a different approach to the problems of indebtedness by organizing and acting as the contentious spokesmen of the Greenback party and the Populist party. Even small debts became impossible to repay and threatened humble homes like that of Hans Anderson's log cabin and 80 acres. The inability to pay off a debt in those years drove many off their farms and out of the community. In 1880 the *Whitehall Times* reported, "Some parties heading for Dakotas were caught up with by their creditors."[51]

And, of course, the crisis on the farm created a crisis on main street. T. H. Earle joined with Olds in supporting a local organization of the Farmers Alliance. The year 1883 brought another disastrous wheat harvest, which the *Times* noted early in 1884: "Farmers are feeling hard up because wind and hail storms damaged their crop in the summer of 83."[52] That year after "feeling hard up" farmers and businessmen seriously sought solutions. Under T. H. Earle's leadership the village of Whitehall sponsored the Farmers' Convention of February 1884. At that convention over 300 farmers listened to professional agriculturists urge them to switch to stock raising for the production of butter, to cultivate clover to counter the effects of the depletion of the soil by wheat, to change their ways in order to keep their boys on the farm, and to find more time for reflection and recreation.

The transition to dairying had already been made in areas of the state settled earlier than Trempealeau. Soon after the convention one of the speakers wrote in the *Western Farmer* that the soil was barren because of spring wheat, and the "blighting influence is visible on every hand." But he also concluded that "the convention in its earnestness showed that the people saw the trouble and were studying how to best help themselves out of it. . . . I predict for no county a more healthful and rapid change from the poverty of spring wheat raising to dairying and stock raising." This prediction proved correct. No doubt, a large portion of the 300 farmers who attended this convention came from Lincoln and Pigeon, although at the time there were fewer than 300 farms in the two towns combined.[53]

The dairying industry developed rapidly after 1880. Trempealeau was part of a "new butter region" notable in the state for its unusual institutional forms and rapid appearance. Elsewhere in the state dairying had developed more slowly while alternatives to wheat were explored. Also the transition was guided first by migrants from New York, who brought entrepreneurial approaches and factory organization of cheese production with them. But cheese factories and their owners discovered the "new butter region" to be inhospitable to their enterprises. In this region, which included Vernon, La Crosse, Monroe, and Trempealeau counties, farmers led the way in creating cooperative creameries very rapidly following the decline of wheat growing. Farmers themselves acted as the leadership in the dairy enterprise, running their own cooperatives. Instead of privately owned businesses, numerous small cooperative creamiers sprang up.[54] By 1895 Trempealeau led the new butter region, producing over 2 million pounds of butter in its several small farmer-owned creameries.

Why this distinct approach to dairying occurred becomes obvious with a careful consideration of the past experience of Trempealeau's immigrants. It was not by accident that the economy took the shape it did. Efforts had been made by New York cheesemakers to duplicate the industrialization of dairying that had taken place in the southern part of Wisconsin. Cheese factories preceded the creameries in the county, but they never approached the importance of butter production. Seemingly, as was true in the building of railroads, the farmers of Trempealeau did not always have a sharp eye on the main chance, though no doubt some did. Efforts made by the county's entrepreneurs to establish cheese factories usually ended in failure. One of the county's wealthiest and most prestigious leaders, Noah Comstock, attempted to operate a cheese factory in the village of Arcadia between 1869 and 1881, but finally gave it up as unprofitable.[55] In 1882 a cheese factory opened in the village of Blair, another Norwegian stronghold located a few miles from Lincoln and Pigeon. But by July of that year, it shut down because of a shortage of milk. The *Times* explained that its failure was due to the indifference of farmers and the lack of proper grasses to feed the animals.[56]

In 1882 a transplanted New York cheesemaker and entrepreneur, Fred Hinkly, established a cheese factory that would be somewhat more successful in Pigeon Falls. The experiments with cheese factories, like the Pigeon cheese factory, were the creations of individual entrepreneurs, typically transplanted New Yorkers like Fred Hinkly.[57] Hinkly and his family spent their summers making cheese in Pigeon and then left for the winters for his home in the city of Sheboygan, Wisconsin. In 1883 the cheese factory produced over 20,670 pounds of cheese, and by June of 1885 the *Times* recorded its growing importance to the farmers of the area: "The Pigeon cheese factory is receiving about 3000 pounds of milk daily, a two-thirds increase over last year." And in 1886 more than 20 tons of cheese were produced by the Pigeon factory.[58] Hinkly and other former New Yorkers were some of the early advocates of dairying in the state, but in Trempealeau County they frequently had troublesome relationships with the farmers, like those in Blair. The cheese factory in Pigeon Falls long remained the only such operation in the county.

Among the Norwegians an important reason for the difficulties may well have been their distrust of the Yankee middleman, who they regarded as being in business for profit but without local loyalties. Cooperatives and farmers' associations attempted to eliminate the middleman altogether. Blair farmers had no problem supplying their cooperative creamery with milk after the demise of the cheese factory. Creameries which made butter were usually cooperatively organized and required less skill than did the cheesemaking process. In Pigeon in 1905, the 16 farmers who supplied the cheese factory with milk represented only a minor portion of the farmers producing milk for market. Even though some of the early efforts to refocus the economy met with indifference, eventually dairying became the mainstay of the local economy, but butter made in cooperative creameries, not cheese in privately owned factories, became the primary product.[59]

The shift from the frontier economy, which had combined subsistence agriculture with the cultivation of wheat, to a primary dependence on dairying did not necessarily come smoothly or easily to many of the farmers of Trempealeau. Although farmers were accustomed to working hard in the clearing, planting, and harvesting necessary to the production of

One of the many local creameries that appeared in the "new butter region" in western Wisconsin, ca. 1890–1910. Photo by Charles Van Schaick. Van Schaick Collection. Photo courtesy of State Historical Society of Wisconsin, WHi (V2) 156.

grains, many were unprepared for the year-round daily discipline that milk production demanded. More prepared than others were the Norwegians. During the frontier years farmers and many villagers as well owned a few cows and other stock. Livestock compared with the kitchen garden in importance, as part of the household and the local economies, providing family and neighborhood with meat and milk. Production for a larger market was peripheral. Farmers on the average kept only about three animals per farm for milk production in 1880.[60]

Domestic butter-making by women did become important to the economies of some families. In 1880 each farm household produced an average of 178 pounds of butter.[61] For some this was a useful supplement to their income. Thurine Oleson's immigrant mother made butter and carefully hoarded it, allowing her family to use none of it during their first precarious years in Wisconsin.[62] Her mother made butter of such quality that it was in some demand, though according to an early local historian of the county most of the locally produced butter did not share a similar reputation. As he explained:

> For the most part the butter made on the farms of the county was of poor quality. Store keepers took butter "in trade," and by charging a good price for the goods sold "in trade" usually came out even on the transaction, though much of the butter which they thus took in was suitable only for lubricating purposes, and was in fact often shipped by the merchants to makers of axle grease in the larger cities.[63]

Despite its poor reputation homemade butter continued for some time. Long after the creameries came into existence women churned butter for use in their own households. In 1925 when numerous creameries dotted the countryside, 340,892 pounds of butter were churned on the county's farms, an average of 106 pounds per farm. According to the agricultural census of 1935, 38 percent of the farms in the county continued to make their butter at home, averaging 173 pounds each.[64]

Even before T. H. Earle organized the Farmers' Convention of 1884, some of the farmers in Pigeon had already been exploring the potential in dairying. In February of 1882, the Pigeon Falls Dairy Association was formed with 18 members, and within a few years the village had both a cheese factory and a creamery. As time passed the immigrants' herds grew to approximate the size they would have been on the Norwegian *gard,* and eventually they became larger in the twentieth century. In Norway peasants faced a scarcity of land, which limited the number of their animals, but the size of Pigeon and Lincoln farms permitted the herds to grow. Within the county the number of cattle used as milk cows rose from 7,481 in 1880 to 17,566 in 1890, a 135 percent increase. After 1890 a steady growth in the number of dairy cows occurred; by 1935 there were 38,674 in the county. Each decade as wheat declined, the hay, oats, and corn needed to sustain the herds of Holsteins increased.[65]

Under the leadership of Norwegian immigrants many of the first creameries in the county were cooperatively organized between 1885 and 1890. H. K. Hagstad, a Norwegian immigrant in the town of Ettrick, was the force behind the construction of the first cooperative creamery in the county. In Norway at the time, a politically active peasantry already had considerable experience with both consumer and producer cooperatives, which had become common for both marketing and purchasing by 1880. In the early nineteenth century Norwegian peasants had faced an aggressive state-sponsored enclosure movement which sought to destroy their communal lands and to bring an end to their subsistence-oriented household economy and communal traditions for the purpose of encouraging a more productive, individualistic, market-oriented farmer. In response to this effort Norwegian peasants created the economic institution of the cooperative, which was organized, owned, and operated by peasants in their local communities. Politically they countered as well with the organization of a powerful political party. When the Norwegian immigrants of Trempealeau shifted to dairy production they quite naturally drew on the institutional forms with which they were familiar in Norway. Almost all the immigrants in Pigeon and many of those in Lincoln came from that turbulent country. Not surprisingly, they were quick to organize themselves locally both politically and economically.[66]

The cooperative creameries included as patrons and members both immigrant farmers and Yankees. Like the immigrant Norwegian farmers, old-stock Americans, although a declining presence in Lincoln and Pigeon after 1880, also had a tradition which included cooperative efforts. Both the Grange and the Alliance movements received active support in Trempealeau County in the 1870s. Leading farmers and businessmen organized Grange stores, which "sought to bypass the middleman and his profit by pooling orders and buying direct from the producer." Collective marketing efforts also appeared and, in at least one instance, when members of the Grange decided that a local mill-owner was prospering unduly, they organized their own mill. However, by the 1880s, the Grange, except as a social organization, appeared to have declined. The farm and business leaders of Trempealeau, most of whom were old-stock Americans, provided the leadership for the Grange organizations. These county leaders, who had earlier been so eager to bring the railroad to Trempealeau, joined the chorus of criticism of the "soulless corporations" once the economic depression of the 1870s set in. One of the problems leading to the demise of the local Granges, in Curti's judgment, was the fact that "too few farmers

participated, usually only or chiefly the best informed men in the country."
The high rate of outward mobility of the old-stock Americans may also
have been a contributing factor. The Grange, which was significantly a
social organization, especially in its later years, appears to have included
very few of the immigrant farmers. Immigrant John Melby, however, did
become active in the Grange, though he was not a farmer.[67]

The later cooperatives did not face these same problems. They included a much broader basis in the population, in that they were less
exclusively based on the county's elite, and they were not limited to a single
ethnic group, though certainly the Norwegians were a large majority. Also,
the later organizations in the postfrontier years rested on a more stable
population than the frontier Grange had.

The Norwegian farmers and merchant-farmers like Ekern appear to
have been better prepared than their Yankee neighbors to make the shift
toward the dairy industry. Dairying and animal husbandry came more
quickly to Pigeon with its homogeneous Norwegian population than it did
to the ethnically mixed Lincoln, in part because the peasants in Norway
had long depended upon dairying and animal husbandry as an important
component in their household economy, and because they had been exposed to the institutional developments of nineteenth-century Norway.
Norwegian immigrants relied on wheat initially to establish themselves,
but once they were in a position to do so they acquired additional animals
and reestablished the dependence on animal husbandry and diversified
farms that typified the peasant *gards* in Norway. Contrary to historian Eric
Lampard's assertion that Trempealeau's farmers were "relatively recent
converts to livestock husbandry," in fact in Norway they had long experience with it and with the farmer cooperative organizations which made
Trempealeau's dairy industry development unique and so rapid in
growth.[68]

Peter Ekern built the first creamery in Pigeon Falls in 1885 and
quickly surpassed Hinkly's cheese factory in attracting local patrons. The
Whitehall Times editor discouraged the competition that Ekern's plans
presented to Hinkly. In February of 1884 the *Times* reported: "It is not
true that Ekern is opening a creamery. The cheese factory leaves no field
open for a creamery. Mr. Ekern while a man of great enterprise is not one
to inaugurate an industry in opposition to one that is already supplying
all the wants of the community."[69] Despite this ingratiating hint, Ekern
proceeded. The Ekern business was an exception in the county in that it
was a privately owned creamery, a fact which obviously caused discontent among Pigeon's farmers. In 1892 under the leadership of
Norwegian-immigrant farmer Nels Hegge, the farmers organized the Pigeon Creamery Association and purchased the creamery. Six months later

this creamery burned down. Apparently the farmers of the cooperative were left "with no salvage and no insurance," were either discouraged or financially unable to rebuild it, and by December Peder Ekern himself built another. The records do not explain why Pigeon farmers remained content with Ekern's ownership of the creamery until 1918, but on March 22 of that year once again the farmers' desire for a cooperative creamery inspired a "mass meeting." The creamery was again bought from Ekern's heirs, and the Pigeon Falls Cooperative Creamery was formed, with Nels Hegge's son Even elected chairman.[70]

In the village of Whitehall, entrepreneurs less prescient than those in Pigeon tried a variety of alternatives to wheat as a basis for their economy. They built a sugar refining factory and encouraged the local farmers to grow sugar cane.[71] They tried other cash crops including sugar beets, sorghum, and tobacco with little success. Whitehall merchants also raised funds to build an improved grain elevator.[72] H. E. Getts, who bought out T. H. Earle's mill and elevator, faced the financial debacle that Earle had avoided by moving on in 1885. After 1880, as the native-born Americans departed and Norwegian immigrants and their children increased in number, dairying expanded. As early as 1882 the *Whitehall Times* editor was calling for a creamery in the village, but it was not until 1887 that one finally appeared.[73] When it did, it was a cooperative. In Pigeon, where the farm population was almost exclusively Scandinavian, dairying quickly matured. For a long time the average number of dairy cows per farm was greater than in the town of Lincoln. In 1905 the figure in Pigeon was 10.2 compared with 7.2 in Lincoln. That year the patrons of Ekern's creamery owned average herds more than twice the size of those of farmers associated with the Whitehall Creamery Association, having 15 animals each as opposed to

Table 3.2. Average Number of Animals per Farm in 1905

	Lincoln	Pigeon
Milk cows	7.2	10.2
Cattle	9.0	21.0
Chickens	61.0	80.0
Pigs	9.5	2.6
Sheep	13.0	7.6

Source: Wisconsin Department of State, *Tabular Statements of Census Enumeration and the Agricultural, Dairying and Manufacturing Interests of Wisconsin* (Madison: State Printer, 1906), p. 171.

6. The farmers of Lincoln, still more ethnically mixed than those in Pigeon, were also somewhat more diversified in their farm operations.[74]

In the first stage of Lincoln's and Pigeon's economic histories, wheat had been the dominant cash crop. Those were years of demographic and economic growth and instability. By 1890 the shift toward dairying was clearly well under way in the county, and by the end of that decade the transition to dairying, with all the accompanying difficulties and adjustments, had been made.[75] After this transition, years of comparative demographic and economic stability followed. The first two decades of the twentieth century brought economic prosperity and growth to the farmers in Lincoln and Pigeon.[76]

In the years that the farmers of Pigeon, Lincoln, and the county at large generally shifted from wheat to dairying, they organized to meet a variety of their needs, using cooperative structures or corporations and associations which included many of the local farmers. These farmer organizations, as much as main street, determined the terms by which the rural folk grappled with the twentieth century. After 1885, when the farmers left the frontier wheat production behind and sought more of the benefits of the expansive economy, such organizations proliferated. Within the next few decades, besides the creameries, farmers put together insurance cooperatives, telephone cooperatives, and oil purchasing and distributing cooperatives, all of which were locally organized and owned. In 1892 when the Pigeon Creamery Association took out articles of incorporation, they sold a total of 150 shares of stock in the company for 10 dollars a share, provided for an annual election of officers by stockholding members, and then added the precaution, "No one not engaged in Agriculture shall be eligible to membership."[77]

Early in 1929, when a battle raged between the corporations distributing milk in the city of Chicago and the farmers' associations in southern Wisconsin and Illinois, the *Whitehall Times* expressed well the farm community's perception of their past and concerns for the future. Corporations, it noted, were steadily expanding their grip on the countryside:

> The powerful Borden Company refused the farmer's demand and is attempting to destroy the dairy organization. . . . The present situation in the Chicago milk war is perhaps the result of farmers permitting outside interests to gain control of marketing their products. This important question is facing dairymen in our home community. Farmers have prospered as a result of cooperative creameries owned and operated by themselves and the manufactured product marketed by them. Conditions are changing. Corporations are entering the dairy field. Gradually control is wrested from

the farmers and when conditions are favorable they are told to take "our terms or go without."

Local farmers organizations should look into the future and prevent, if possible, such serious conditions as now exist throughout the territory in which Chicago Corporations have gained control.[78]

The farmers of Trempealeau long followed that advice. Pigeon farmers several times voted to reject offers by corporations to purchase their creamery cooperative.

The Pigeon Falls Cooperative Creamery, having weathered the farm recession of the 1920s, the Great Depression of the 1930s, unionization of its 26 workers by the AFL–CIO in the 1950s, and many offers of corporate takeover, continued to operate in the 1980s. Through the years the cooperative allied itself with the Farmers Union, which, like the politics of Pigeon, represented the left of the farmers' organizations, continuing the ideals of the Alliances and Populists.[79]

As these farmers became increasingly implicated in the market economy, like their counterparts in Norway and like American farmers who supported the cooperative efforts of the Grange and the Alliance movement, they attempted to take control of as much of that economy as they could. In seeking the benefits of improved technology and standards of living, they long continued to try to maintain local control. Typical examples of this were several telephone cooperatives. In 1905 the Lincoln Telephone Cooperative was organized, and three years later the Pigeon Valley Farmer Telephone Cooperative came into being. The latter lasted until 1966.[80] Such local telephone companies were common in these years. Their demise, like that of many of the institutions organized in the first decades of the century, was bitterly and long resisted. By the end of the second decade of the twentieth century, the pressure for the incorporation of these local telephone companies had begun. In 1929 one local farmer expressed the point of view that kept these local cooperatives alive for another four decades: "Farm relief is necessary but the popular sentiment seems to be [to] relieve the farmers of prosperous business enterprises." He was referring to an attempt to "relieve the farmers of a well organized and paying telephone system which has been operated successfully by the farmers in his community for many years." H. C. Erickson, who owned stock in the local company, argued that it was a good system that paid reasonable dividends. He particularly opposed turning the company over "to the capitalists who have no interest in the community other than realizing a profit."[81]

Another example of the attempt to maintain local control was the Pigeon Mutual Fire Insurance Company. Organized under the leadership of Peder Ekern and Nels F. Hegge in 1882, year after year until well after

World War II, this locally organized insurance company elected its officers, provided insurance to many locals, and once every year elected its directors and published in the local paper its financial status.[82] There were many others, like the Whitehall and Pigeon Trading Association, which was incorporated in 1888 for the purchase and sale of everything farmers needed or produced, the Pigeon Grain and Stock Cooperative, the Cooperative Oil Company, and the Whitehall and Pigeon Cow Testing Association.[83]

All these tended to be organized in a fashion similar to the Pigeon Falls Cooperative Creamery. Membership included the patrons, annual meetings were held in which members reviewed finances and elected directors or officers (usually nine), and the financial transactions and status were published in the local newspaper each year. The officers made most of the management decisions during the year, but controversial or particularly important issues were voted on by the membership.[84] In 1980 the tradition was still alive as revealed by the 23 cooperatives operating in the county, including most recently the first cooperatively owned local cable television network.[85]

There is no indication that anyone became wealthy by owning stock in these companies or as members of cooperatives. No single individual like T. H. Earle concentrated power or profits in the hands of one or two individuals. Nor did these local organizations have expansionist ambitions to increase their territory and profits; the focus remained local until, like the telephone companies, they were purchased by a corporation or went out of business. The cooperatives functioned more as service organizations than as capitalistic profit-making ones. Prestige in and service to the community were the rewards of being elected an official in these enterprises, not lush salaries or profits. "Interest in the community" legitimized the leaders of these enterprises. Community members kept firm democratic control over institutions which mediated between themselves and the market. They had no intention of placing their fate in the hands of "the capitalists who have no interest in the community other than realizing a profit."

Communities, organized as these, kept a tight rein on the merchants of main street and offered few opportunities such as T. H. Earle had once exploited. Success on main street depended upon mastering and conforming to the relentlessly egalitarian mentality and the communal traditions that immigrant peasants and migrant Americans brought with them and adapted as they became farmers on the frontier. Possessive individualism may have flourished on main street, but when it did, public poses of another sort were required.[86]

During the important years of transition in American society from frontier and rural life to a largely urban one, the men and women of Pigeon

Whitehall's main street in 1945. Photo courtesy of University of Wisconsin–La Crosse, Murphy Library.

Inside a general store in rural Trempealeau, ca. 1930–1945. Photo courtesy of Arlene Arneson, Whitehall, Wisconsin.

Whitehall's main street at Christmas, 1950s. Photo courtesy of Arlene Arneson, Whitehall, Wisconsin.

and Lincoln were not being left behind. They were not passively watching or following as life around them took new forms. Rather they were actively engaged in changing their own world, and they were aware of the changes going on elsewhere. They were interested in the possibilities of new methods and technologies and selected those which suited their needs and purposes. At the numerous farmers' institutes and conventions that were organized in the county, hundreds of farmers and businessmen turned up and listened to the agricultural scientists and debated the economic and social issues.[87] Various farmer clubs and associations focused on extending information and seeking solutions to common problems. As individuals and groups they visited other parts of the state and the nation to acquire knowledge of new technologies. In 1887 in a typical *Times* report, a local farmer traveled to a neighboring county to get information on the proper construction of a silo, an important innovation which would enable milk production to increase considerably.[88] Throughout these years farmers visited other farms and cities around the state and took summer courses and extension courses from the University of Wisconsin for the purpose of understanding and acquiring new methods and technologies. But in the end they fashioned institutions and methods most congenial to their values and purposes. They turned out en masse at the farmers' conventions and institutes organized in Whitehall, like the one T. H. Earle promoted in 1884. They recognized the market potential of the developing dairy industry, and then cut the men of main street out, except for those like Ekern, whom they trusted. Rural sociologists found that the midwestern cooperatives remained strong in the 1930s and commanded 55 percent of the business in the rural areas in that decade.[89] In Trempealeau County the proportion may well have been higher.

While rural people aggressively sought out the technologies that would transform agriculture, they were equally cognizant of the potential snares of the economy that they confronted. By organizing locally in a variety of ways, they attempted to educate themselves and to retain for themselves as much control and security as they could. The informal cushion of community that operated in frontier times, the generosity and helpfulness that allowed them to survive the precarious world of the peasant and the frontier, were inadequate in the face of the opportunities and hazards of the market. Frontier generosity and helpfulness were replaced by a host of community cooperatives and organizations, which provided a cushion in relationship to that market economy to which they were becoming increasingly vulnerable. Local insurance companies, telephone companies, creameries, and oil companies preserved the locus of power in the community and did not sacrifice it to entirely impersonal and distant corporations which they did not trust. That would not happen until the second half of the twentieth century.

4

The Home Town and the Home Place: To Leave or Stay?

The discontent of youth with life on the farm and with the constraints of small-town life has often been noted by scholars and writers of fiction. The twentieth century brought a veritable exodus of the young from the countryside to the city. The young, some argue, grew restless and rebellious under a community's intimate and often intolerant scrutiny and with the tedium and hard work of daily life. Thus, they welcomed the life of the city for its economic opportunities, diversity, privacy, and liberation from narrow norms. Rural youth along with immigrants fueled the cities' growth and provided the labor for this country's expanding industrial order.

There has always been some truth to this perception. For many decades the young did take flight from the rural area of Trempealeau for the cities, but not as large a number or over as vast a distance as has sometimes been supposed.[1] A notable number remained to farm and to manage main street as their parents had done. Whether they stayed or left, young men and women faced the challenges of making a living. When they left, where they went, what they did, and what strategies they used are questions of importance in understanding the rural social experience.

Like youth everywhere, those who grew up in Pigeon and Lincoln made decisions about whether to stay or leave and what work to pursue based upon changing opportunities offered within and outside the community. During the frontier stage as settlers poured into Trempealeau County the area offered opportunities on the land and in the creation of small businesses in the villages. But already by 1880 the crisis faced by wheat farmers and the limited local opportunities pushed many out while the promise of better futures elsewhere pulled others away. Cheaper land to the west and related opportunities attracted young and old as long as the frontier existed. In the postfrontier years, like Americans in general, Trempealeau youth had no choice but to look elsewhere for opportunities.

Many of the young did leave as they began their adult lives and sought a way of making a living. The distribution of population by age groups in a

Table 4.1. Percentage Distribution of the Population in Trempealeau County, by Age Group, 1930–1970

Ages	1930	1940	1950	1960	1970
0–14	30.2	26.0	27.5	30.4	29.1
15–29	24.1	25.0	19.5	16.1	18.6
30–44	19.5	18.8	19.5	17.3	14.3
45–64	18.1	20.7	22.0	22.1	22.3
≥65	8.1	9.5	11.5	14.1	15.7

Sources: See appendix C.

rough way indicates trends related to the mobility of the youth (see Table 4.1).

In the nineteenth century and for the first quarter of the twentieth century, among the Norwegian-Americans, childhood symbolically ended when the young boy or girl was confirmed by the church at the age of 14 or 15. By that age, most males and females of the area had acquired the education, strength, and skills which equipped them to function as adult workers. On the farms and in the villages they had by that age long been working with their parents in the fields, barns, and households.[2] During the frontier years and through most of the postfrontier years some continued to work on the family farm or in the family business until the age of 20, when most began to live independently; in a few instances they stayed longer. For most, the ages between 15 and 25 witnessed a move toward work outside the family, with few young men or women continuing to live with their families of origin (see Table 4.2).

By 1930 and the following decades, considerable numbers of young left not only their families of origin but also the county itself by age 25. The lack of local opportunities for them left many with no choice but to depart for other areas. Tracing the changing size of different age cohorts in the county reveals at what ages and in what numbers the young left the area. For example, the age cohort from five to nine in 1930 would be reduced by 37.5 percent by 1950, when they had reached the ages of 25–29. The age cohort that consistently declined most dramatically in any 10-year period was the 10–14-year-olds. Quickest to depart were the females in that age group; from 1930 to 1940 they declined by 37.3 percent, while their male counterparts were reduced by only 20.2 percent (see Table 4.3). Until 1970, females left the county at younger ages and in larger numbers than males.

With the return of prosperity after the Great Depression both men and

Table 4.2. Numerical and Percentage Distributions of Sons and Daughters Living in Their Family Households in Lincoln Township, by Age Group, 1880 and 1910

| | 1880 | | | | 1910 | | | |
| | Sons | | Daughters | | Sons | | Daughters | |
Ages	N	%	N	%	N	%	N	%
0–4	45	26.2	49	35.0	48	24.9	50	27.6
5–9	47	27.3	37	26.4	36	18.7	46	25.4
10–14	42	24.4	36	25.7	52	26.9	41	22.7
15–19	20	11.6	18	12.9	32	16.6	28	15.5
20–24	14	8.1	0	0.0	16	8.3	10	5.5
25–29	2	1.2	0	0.0	6	3.1	4	2.2
30–34	1	0.6	0	0.0	1	0.5	2	1.1
35–39	0	0.0	0	0.0	2	1.0	0	0.0
40–44	1	0.0	0	0.0	0	0.0	0	0.0
Total	172		140		193		181	

Source: Manuscript Censuses, U.S. Census of Population, Lincoln and Pigeon townships, Trempealeau County, Wisconsin, 1880, 1910.

Table 4.3. Percentage of Decline of 10–14-Year-Olds in Trempealeau County, by Decade, 1930–1970

| | | Percent Decline in Original Cohort in: | |
Cohort	Number of 10–14-Year Olds	10 Years	20 Years
1930			
Males	1,346	20.2	35.5
Females	1,287	37.3	45.3
1940			
Males	1,125	36.3	43.2
Females	1,112	43.2	47.1
1950			
Males	984	49.0	45.5
Females	933	52.2	42.6
1960			
Males	1,191	52.4	27.2
Females	1,136	48.2	27.6
1970			
Males	1,286	23.8	—
Females	1,163	24.9	—

Sources: See appendix C.

women left at even higher rates. Of those between 10 and 14 in 1940, 36.3 percent of the males and 43.2 percent of the females would be gone before the age of 24. Between 1950 and 1960 over half of the females (52.2 percent) and 49 percent of the males of that cohort departed before age 24. By 1970 and more clearly by 1980, however, a new pattern of behavior emerged: the decline in the numbers of younger members of the county was lower than it had been since perhaps frontier times. The 10–14-year-old group in 1970 declined by less than a quarter by 1980. In 1960 there were only 969 20–24-year-olds, whereas in 1980 the number had almost doubled, totaling 1,793.

The exact destinations of those who left the communities are difficult to determine with accuracy, although various local sources can provide hints if not precise information. Obituaries of first-generation individuals who settled and remained in Pigeon and Lincoln until their deaths between 1915 and 1930 provide information about the family life and mobility of their children. The obituaries, which were front-page news items in the *Whitehall Times*, invariably mention the location of the children of the deceased. A sample of 26 obituaries between 1915 and 1930 reveals a pattern of persistence and mobility of the children of the first generation of residents in the townships of Lincoln and Pigeon and the village of Whitehall, a pattern that no doubt corresponds to the realities of the time. Based on the obituaries, at the time of their deaths those individuals who had ever had children averaged six children still living. (The census of 1910 reveals that married women of Pigeon and Lincoln between the ages of 45 and 54 averaged 7.3 births.) Usually, two or three offspring would still be in the

Table 4.4. Location of Offspring from the Study Area at Time of Parent's Death, 1915–1930

	N	%
Local (Pigeon, Lincoln, Whitehall)	93	43.0
Nearby (in Trempealeau)	34	15.7
Rural Wisconsin	4	1.9
Nearby city (within 150 miles)	26	12.0
Distant city (in the U.S.)	4	1.9
Midwest (rural)	30	13.9
Far West (rural)	21	9.7
New England	1	0.5
Canada	3	1.4
Total	216	100.0

Source: The *Whitehall Times*, 1915–1930.

immediate vicinity, generally one or two on the "home place" and another in a nearby town.[3]

Having one's children nearby was important to the pioneer generation, as 71-year-old Norwegian immigrant Ole O. Semb commented to Hans Anderson in 1912:

> I couldn't have things better than they are. I have seven good daughters, all married to good men, and I can start from my home in the morning and call on them all in one day, and I have one son who is a good boy, with me at home. I have seen hard times, but God gave me a good wife, and we have had a life together.[4]

Unlike Semb, however, most of the families had at least one child in one of the cities of Wisconsin or an adjacent state, usually Minnesota. Almost a quarter of the offspring lived in Minnesota, the Dakotas, Montana, Washington, Oregon, and California, usually in smaller cities or rural areas. In these years, 70 percent of the offspring had not ranged much beyond a few-hour train ride from home. A majority were within 20 miles of their home community at the time of the death of a parent. Only about 14 percent of this group located in cities. Clearly, most found opportunities in rural or small-town America. How closely these statistics correspond to the broader reality is difficult to determine. The fact that the parents of this group had spent much of their lives in Trempealeau may create biases of behavior distinct from that of more mobile families.

Alumni lists compiled in 1922 and 1938 on Whitehall High School graduates from 1904 through 1935 reveal the nature of the geographic and social mobility of a more educated minority.[5] In 1910, 52.9 percent of the 15–19-year-olds were in school, and in 1920, 36.7 percent of the 16- and 17-year-olds were. Thus, high school graduates represent only a portion of the youth. Many remained in the area or very nearby. Of the men who graduated before 1920, 35.2 percent were living in urban areas by 1938, whereas the women graduating before 1920 were less likely to be found in cities in 1938 (only 19.2 percent). Among the graduates of the 1920s, the situation was nearly reversed, with 19 percent of the men and 29 percent of the women having located in cities by 1938. That trend continued into the decade of the depression, when only 1 percent of the male graduates and 9 percent of the female graduates moved to cities by 1938.

The 1938 figures reveal the consequences of the Great Depression on the opportunities of those who graduated during 1930–1935; it caused a bottleneck for the geographic mobility of the young. Most of the male graduates before and after 1920 either remained in the area or made their livings in rural and small-town communities like the ones in which they had grown up. By the early twentieth century the opportunities on the

Table 4.5. Percentage Distribution of Whitehall High School Graduates, by Location in 1938

	1904–1919		1920–1929		1930–1935	
	Males	Females	Males	Females	Males	Females
IN WISCONSIN						
Original community	20.4	25.2	52.0	33.0	80.0	61.0
Nearby towns	11.1	24.2	14.0	18.0	18.0	26.0
Elsewhere in rural Wisconsin	11.1	16.1	7.0	9.0	0.0	2.0
Urban Wisconsin	13.0	8.1	10.0	17.0	1.0	9.0
IN OTHER STATES						
Cities	22.2	11.1	9.0	12.0	0.1	0.2
Rural/towns	22.2	13.1	8.0	11.0	0.0	0.0

Source: Whitehall High School Alumni Records, assembled in 1922 and 1938, Office of the Superintendent of Schools, Whitehall, Wisconsin.

Note: The above percentages do not include a small number whose location was unknown or who had died.

Of the females graduating in 1904–1919, 2.2 percent were located in other countries.

land, which had long lured the young and other members of the community westward, had disappeared. Nonetheless, the cities absorbed only a small portion of the graduates, ranging from a high of 35.2 percent of the males graduating before 1920 to a low of 1.1 percent for those graduating during 1930–1935, and from a high of 29 percent of the females graduating during 1920–1929 to a low of 9.2 percent for those graduating during 1930–1935.

Like their male counterparts, when women from these two groups left the area, whether married or single, they tended to disperse widely around the state and nation prior to 1930. When graduates left the state, they usually either remained in the Midwest or moved on west. They settled in rural areas of Ohio, Illinois, Iowa, Minnesota, North and South Dakota, Montana, Oregon, Washington, and California, or, when they left rural life behind, they located in cities across the nation including Boston; New York; the area of Washington, D.C.; Chicago and Rockford, Illinois; Los Angeles, Oakland, and San Francisco, California; Seattle and Tacoma, Washington; Madison, La Crosse, River Falls, Superior, Platteville, and other cities in Wisconsin; Grand Forks, North Dakota; and Minneapolis, St. Paul, and Winona, Minnesota. In other words, they ranged widely, moving to both urban and rural environments in this country and also into Canada and Central and South America.

In all these years the number of female high school graudates averaged between 61 and 65 percent of the total number of graduates. Since they attended school in larger numbers, their mobility patterns may be more reflective of the total population, or there may have been significant differences between the sexes in their mobility patterns. If so, these statistics suggest that the behavior of rural men and women changed after 1920, with women more often than men finding the cities attractive. Young women graduates became more geographically mobile and wide-ranging than their male counterparts.

With the disappearance of opportunities on the land and given the local pattern of females achieving higher levels of education than their brothers, women may have been better equipped than men in the 1920s to confront the new economic opportunities of the cities. Growing up on a farm and developing the strength and skills for that life prepared the sons less well than the more educated daughters to make the change to a way of life outside of agriculture. The depression of the 1930s with its lack of opportunities no doubt kept the young men in their home community in those years, but it does not explain the differential between male and female behavior in the 1920s.

Because similar information on the mobility of the less-educated majority of youth is not readily available, the alumni records, like the statistics generated by the obituaries, leave us unable to see to what extent the geographic mobility of high school graduates parallels that of the population as a whole. However, the higher rates of departure of young women surfaced as a trend throughout the county.

One obvious result of the earlier and more frequent departure of women from the county was a consistent imbalance in the gender ratio,

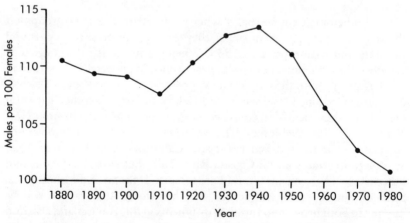

Figure 4.1. Gender ratios in Trempealeau County, 1880–1980 (compiled for sources given in appendix C).

particularly in the countryside. Women left the community at younger ages and as a rule in larger numbers throughout the twentieth century. No doubt the greater demand for male labor on the farm accounts for much of this differential. But there is also evidence of a growing dissatisfaction among young women with life on the farm. The peak decades in the imbalance coincided with a period when farm work increasingly came to be perceived as inappropriate for women.

The expanded role of the educational system and the mass media's growing presence contributed to the dissatisfaction among the generation of women who first attended high school in significant numbers. The number of high school students steadily increased over the years. By 1930, 45.7 percent of the county's youth aged 16 and 17 were in school (see Table 4.7). The biggest increase came in the decade of the 1940s. The proportion of 16- and 17-year-olds attending school increased from 58 percent in 1940 to 78.9 percent in 1950.

The long-established differential in the gender ratio narrowed for several reasons: the gap between life styles on the farm and those in the village lessened; most families became villagers rather than farmers; the

Table 4.6. Numerical Distribution of Males per 100 Females in Trempealeau County, by Age Group, 1930–1980

Ages	1930	1940	1950	1960	1970	1980
0–14	109	102	104	103	107	103
15–29	115	114	110	105	103	108
30–44	113	123	119	108	101	104
45–64	123	117	116	115	106	101
≥65	119	118	110	100	92	86

Sources: See appendix C.

Table 4.7. Percentage Distribution of Those in School in Trempealeau County, by Various Age Groupings, 1910–1970

Ages	1910	1920	1930	1940	1950	1960	1970
14–15		66.4	77.1	82.5	94.0	96.9	98.0
15–17	52.9						
16–17		36.7	45.7	58.0	78.9	88.5	90.7
18–20	13.8	16.4	22.4	21.0	21.2		
18–19						40.0	44.1
20–21						7.9	4.5

Sources: See appendix C.

young family workers on the farm, male and female, were steadily replaced by machines and by farm wives returning to the barns and fields; and the gap between male and female educational levels decreased.[6]

Questions about rural youth that are perhaps even more difficult to answer than when they left home and where they went concern what they did, how they fared, and what strategies they used in establishing themselves. What kinds of opportunities did they find both within their communities and outside of them? However partial and incomplete the statistics on geographic mobility may be, they nonetheless indicate that from frontier times until the present many found opportunities within the locality.

By 1900, the second generation living in the area was taking over and rearing its own families. Accounts such as the following, which were common in the *Whitehall Times,* display one obvious and possibly the most important source of opportunity to be the family:

> Raymond Kersaw Warner was born Jan. 19, 1880, on the old homestead in Hale, being the fourth of a family of five children. Attending the district school and helping with the work on his father's farm, he grew to manhood and on the retirement of his father in 1905, he, together with his younger brother, Rufus, assumed the management of the home farm and successfully carried on the work until 1913, when they decided to sell the farm and purchased the Tubbs implement business in this village, which they have successfully conducted since December of that year.[7]

Many of the young, like Raymond Warner, worked on their parents' farms until the retirement or death of their parents and then took over. Some, like the Warner brothers, moved into nearby villages when opportunities arose, though such moves were not common.

In the villages, businesses too passed from one generation to the next. Charles Melby returned to Whitehall after his education and after working in Washington, D.C., to take over his father's interests as the banker-businessman John Melby aged. In turn, Charles's son William became a local banker as well.[8] H. E. Getts, one of the first merchants in the village of Whitehall, was followed by three generations of descendants who were local merchants. In 1917 the *Whitehall Times* noted, "E. C. Getts, who has been in business here for twenty-five years and his father before him, is doing a big business."[9] The Getts family continues to be represented today as village merchants. Through the years, the *Whitehall Times* frequently recorded the passing of farms and businesses from one generation to the next.

In Pigeon even the religious leadership at times was passed on to the younger generation. Between 1876 and 1963 the two Christophersens,

Emmanuel and son Einar, served as ministers of one of the two Lutheran churches in Pigeon. At the other church in Pigeon, the Reverend A. J. Orke, who arrived there in 1896, was followed at his death in 1934 by his son, H. A. Orke.[10]

As parents aged, both on the farm and in the villages, their sons and daughters often filled their positions. This type of transition between generations was also often noted in the *Whitehall Times:* "Peter Nelson, senior member of the firm Nelson and Larson who has for several years been active about the warehouse and grain elevator is relieved of heavy work. His sons Nels and Oscar are doing it."[11] In a similar instance, the *Times* reported, "Archie Torson succeeded his father, O. C. Torson, as member of the firm of Torson and Libakken-City Meat Market."[12]

Where there was no son to take over the family farm or business, a relative or son-in-law was often available. In 1882, in a not uncommon item, the *Whitehall Times* noted: "Ole Nelson Skar sold his farm to his son-in-law K. S. Knudtson. Ole retains a certain annuity, to be paid him and his wife during their natural lives and out of the proceeds of the farm."[13] Peder Ekern passed much of his estate and position on to his daughter and her husband, Ekern's partner and son-in-law, Ben M. Slettland. Slettland's two sons, Oscar and Earnest, continued as the community's prominent leaders until the 1960s.[14] Within the communities of Lincoln and Pigeon, then, an important source of opportunity was the family.

Not only parents but also an extended and dispersed kin network assisted the young; Ludwig Solsrud's youth is a case in point. Born in 1864 in Norway, Solsrud migrated to the United States in 1883 to the home of an uncle for whom he worked for a time. In 1885 he was encouraged by another uncle whom he was visiting in Whitehall to stay in town with that uncle and go to school. In a year's time he completed the two-room school's program and started to work on local farms. He also spent time working for the railroads and in the pineries. In 1890 while visiting his uncle in Whitehall again, he began to work at that uncle's store, and in 1895, at the age of 34, Solsrud became a partner in the enterprise. Forty-six years later, in 1941, L. L. Solsrud was still a merchant in Whitehall.[15]

Although Solsrud relied upon his uncles to make his way as a young immigrant, those who remained in the community after the first generation more often depended upon parents to assist them in claiming their positions in the community. Many of the youth who remained in Pigeon and Whitehall thus began their adult lives much as peasants in Norway or villagers in New England had done for centuries, following the careers of their fathers and depending upon them for property, skills, and status.

It may have been the case that fewer young people remained in Pigeon and Whitehall than would have liked to stay. Opportunities were limited in the area and depended heavily upon family resources. After completing law school in Madison, Herman Ekern considered himself fortunate in entering into Hans Anderson's law firm.[16] The villages supported a few small businessmen, craftsmen, and professionals, but the area hardly offered a significant outlet for the large number of youths coming of age each year. The departure after 1880 of many of the old-stock Americans from the businesses and professions of main street and the steady growth of the village population indicate some expansion in the structure of opportunity for those who remained.

Between the ages of 15 and 25 many young men worked as farm laborers on parents' or neighbors' farms and a few as day-laborers in the village. As long as the lumbering industry needed large numbers of workers, they could also spend portions of the year in the woods. Sometimes they spent some of the summer months working wheat harvests in the Dakotas. But these jobs were expected to be the work of youth in transition to the adult independence of owning a farm or business and achieving traditional republican goals of independence and self-employment.[17]

In the late nineteenth and early twentieth centuries, farming was by far the occupation of the majority of adult males. According to most accounts, the transfer of farms between generations was smooth. High rates of persistency on the land over generations illustrate the successes in making the transfer of the "home place." Sons who had worked hard on their parents' farms, as many did into their 20s and in some instances even longer, expected and no doubt generally received liberal terms when they became renters or owners. When asked to do an appraisal for a Pigeon farmer named Hans Fremstad, who had decided "to turn his farm over to his boys," Hans Anderson and two other men of the community "agreed upon a moderate price, for we knew the boys had contributed much to the upbuilding and the accumulation of property." The father then even further reduced the price when he sold it to his sons.[18]

The ready availability of land during frontier years and other opportunities in later years perhaps dictated that relations between parents and children be relatively amicable. Parents who were determined to keep too long or too tight control of farms which their sons expected to take over risked the abandonment of farming by the sons or a move to the Dakotas or to some other area where land was still cheap. One local woman reported that her husband had been one such son who was discontented with his father's tight rein. When a conflict relating to the terms of the sale of the farm arose, the young man packed up and moved to the village of Pigeon and never returned to farming. On the other hand her father and her brother always maintained congenial relations as they worked together, and the farm remains in the family in the 1980s.[19]

Fathers, sons, and brothers all cooperated on the farms. In 1929 the *Times* described one family's handling of their farm. The 65-year-old Hans Christian Johnson had turned his farm over to his three sons in 1917. "All work together amiably. No jars, discords, jealousies or tempermental out breaking have marred their pleasant tranquil life."[20] While the intergenerational transfer of property and position was fraught with potential conflict, which occasionally did surface, what is most striking is the apparent reality of family cohesiveness that made these transfers common and generally smooth. High rates of persistency among farm families bear this out.

A sense of equity, mutual responsibility, and cooperation were the expected norms. Deviation from the expectations became cause for comment in the community and sometimes issued in a legal suit. That the farmers sometimes operated on the basis of traditional peasant expectations of familialism rather than contractual relations is revealed by some of the problems that did surface, particularly after the death of a parent. Indifference to legalities and reliance on informal agreements between generations could lead to problems. More than one son who had remained on the family farm, helping the parents as they aged, could find the products of his labors and his parents' promises of little value if there was no will or contract and if siblings demanded an equal share of the estate.

Hans Anderson recalled losing all his respect for one long-time friend who made such a claim on a farm that his brother had built up and improved though his parents retained legal ownership. While legally his claim was unquestionable, eventually the combination of kin and community pressure convinced him to back down, but only after sacrificing much esteem in the eyes of his neighbors. Parents and children would agree on the terms of inheritance and then neglect to write the wills or transfer the deeds that made the arrangement legal. This did not always lead to a problem, since family members often acquiesced in the informal agreements after the death of a parent. However, in a few instances, one of the heirs decided to challenge these arrangements in court. Community and family censure came down heavily on individuals who took such action, which, while legally indisputable, violated the family's and community's sense of seemly family conduct.[21]

In some instances parents treated their children in highly exploitative and manipulative ways. Michael Feuling, who finally went to court to challenge his decreased mother's will, believed himself to be a victim of his mother and brothers. In childhood and as a young man, he had worked hard supporting his family and maintaining their farm after his father was incapacitated. Apparently his sense of responsibility to his mother prevented him for years from establishing himself independently and from protecting himself from his family's exploitation of him. Although he dropped his legal case, he nonetheless cared enough about local opinion to write to Judge Hans Anderson a long letter of explanation as to why he had made the claims:

> In 1880 I was 21. Mother promised to pay me $1100 for my labor if I stayed with her during the summer and most needed help and pay me as soon as her debts were paid . . . we agreed on four year. In 1883 I bought a joining farm of 208 acres for $2750 from John Fluetsch. I wanted mother to let me have this $1100 but she was afraid I would leave her, so she wanted to buy this farm in her name and sign it over to me as soon as all debts were paid. The farm was bought in mother's name. I helped mother in all of her most needy work till I was 34 years old. In 1885 mother promised to pay me $3000 if I helped her in all her most need work. In 1908 mother and I compromised that I had some education and could get along among people much better than her other children and that she will sell this farm, intended for me, to George. At this time it was agreed that I would do her will but she must sell this farm to George for $10,000, and pay me my promised $3000, and all money and mds. I gave her up to this time, which was in all $4000 and over. All of these suggestions were granted and gladly and cheerfully promised and agreed to pay me all of my wages and money and merchandise given her except, George should have the farm for $8000 because he has no money at this time and might lose the farm but, if George gets the farm of $8000 he has nothing to get after mother's dead. This was agreed. In 1892 I got married and in 1893 mother sold me her whole farm of 447 acres for $7500, that, I must keep both parents during their life time and pay this $7500 to my brothers and sisters after their death. No transfer was made and we concluded that it is better for my parents to keep their land, only, sign this 207 acres over to me had mother wanted to wait—so we did. In 1908 George bought this 207 acres from mother.

At last Michael Feuling went to the Dakotas after working for years in his mother's and his less-able brother's interests.

Seemingly, since the family perceived him as more than able to take care of himself, his mother gave him little and instead gave to brother George much that had been earned by and promised to Michael. "From each according to his abilities, to each according to his needs" appears to have been the principle by which Michael's mother managed her struggling family. According to Michael, all he ever received for his years of effort and from all his mother's promises was $505, which she sent him while in the Dakotas. His mother refused to send more "because she feared it might get lost in the mail." The long pattern of Michael subordinating his own interests to his mother's continued: "In 1915 I seen mother and she thought it best to let all moneys in bank while she was alive, for she might need cash at times but she will make up a will in which she will make and set up $3000 to be paid to me for what I had coming and was due me out side of my share of legacy." Although Feuling assisted in the writing of the will, seemingly assuring his claim, the family later argued that the will had been lost by the time of his mother's death, and once again Feuling failed to receive payment.

It is striking that at no point over all the years when Feuling worked for his mother had he taken care to legalize any of the agreements about land and labor until the will was drawn. Instead, he left all in the control of his mother. After her death he finally gave up his claim, because, he concluded, the local lawyers were squeezing the estate with high-fee charges: ". . . these two fellows would have conquered our entire estate and I would never even receive a single dollar as legacy nor claim. Nor would the rest of the heirs ever have received a penny." So even at that point his willingness to act, when his brothers would not, protected the interest of his family if not himself.[22]

Lawyers had a poor reputation among farmers, which may have been deserved; small-town lawyers doubtless fattened on the townspeople's innocence or indifference to legalities that many of the farm families exhibited. Even the responsible and rational Dave Wood neglected to write a will, and his son Ralph would watch the family home in which he had been living for several years and the family lands go on the auction block after his father's death in 1927. Soon after the death of Dave, his son James died without a will and then, James's wife, Olive, as well. After a lengthy search distant relatives of Olive became heirs, and they compelled the sale of the estate. By a predictable set of circumstances the executor of the estate, Hans Anderson, found a buyer in his partner and son-in-law, Herman Ekern, who became the new owner of the land and home which the Wood family had lived on and improved for three generations. While Anderson proceeded in the case entirely according to the dictates of the law, the unhappy results for the Woods cast a shadow on Anderson's integrity in the eyes of the Wood family.[23]

The neglect of legalities in managing the family's economy and in transferring property from one generation to the next was sometimes a source of scandal, conflict, and tragedy. The casualness with which some families entered into agreements about their property also highlights their traditional reliance on face-to-face personal relationships rather than the contractual ones required for the efficient transferal of property in the twentieth century. Whether the reason was trust, ignorance, or indifference, some families depended upon informal agreements which could leave individuals vulnerable despite expectations of good faith. Not everyone, of course, was as casual about legal niceties as were the Feulings, but more estates were settled without wills than with them, and the instances when that led to conflicts, as it did in the case of Michael Feuling's mother, reveal a habit of mind quite different from that which prevailed in urban, capitalistic, and corporate America of the late nineteenth and early twentieth centuries. In fact, as Feuling belatedly perceived, traditional ways left people highly vulnerable to the machinations of lawyers or kinsmen who dissented from the taken-for-granted but legally nonbinding agreements of the family.[24]

The ability of families to provide local opportunities to the young varied as doubtless did the interest of the young in exploiting them. But even in recent times, a good number of the young in Pigeon and Lincoln continued to wish to farm and depended upon their parents to help them do so. Establishing oneself on a farm appears to have become more difficult with time. The later a family arrived in the county, the less successful its members were in sustaining themselves on the land. One young man, Harold Tomter, after serving in the Air Force during World War II, returned to Pigeon with the goal of becoming a farmer in the community as his father had been. His father's small 40-acre farm, worked exclusively by horses, with a tiny house and no indoor plumbing (just the kind of subsistence farm that should have driven an ambitious and able young man to the city), did not dissuade him from seeking to follow in his father's footsteps. He did attempt to work his father's farm, which by local standards in 1945 was small and inadequate. Young Tomter sought but could not obtain financing for larger, better-equipped farms, and so took the parental one. "It was my only opportunity for starting."

By the 1950s Tomter had to sell the farm, as farmers with smaller holdings increasingly had to do. For a while he rented the farm of another, always dreaming, as renters did, that one day he would buy one of his own. It was a dream never to be realized.[25] For years Tomter farmed as a renter from the Pigeon banker Oscar Slettland, grandson of Peder Ekern. The terms of the lease were typical for the few renters of the area, and they were much better than the notorious tenant conditions of some parts of the nation. The owner and Tomter shared expenses and profits jointly with some exceptions. Slettland paid for the fertilizer and Tomter lived rent free in a huge 10-bedroom house with a bath and a half. Slettland paid the real estate taxes and Tomter the personal property taxes. Most of the machinery was owned by Tomter, but they jointly purchased some items such as the bulk tank for milk storage. According to Tomter, the two men had "a good working relationship," though he "had to often be a salesman to convince the landlord to be a part owner" in certain equipment and improvements. Together they created what Tomter regarded as a showcase farm. Despite his tenant status, Tomter lived and worked on an excellent farm and became a respected and active leader in the farm community.

Table 4.8. Percentage Distribution of Farm Ownership and
Tenancy in Trempealeau County, 1880–1975

	Farms Owned	Farms Rented
1880	94.7	5.3
1890	88.6	11.4
1900	89.3	10.7
1910	86.5	13.5
1920	82.8	17.2
1925	81.0	19.0
1930	79.7	20.5
1935	80.4	19.6
1940	73.1	26.9
1945	76.8	23.2
1950	83.5	16.5
1955	86.3	13.7
1960	89.4	10.6
1965	90.5	9.5
1970	94.1	5.9
1975	94.2	5.8

Sources: See appendix C.

After the death of Oscar Slettland, however, Tomter's relationship with the heirs proved less congenial, and he soon joined the ranks of former farmers in Whitehall. Without the assistance of families, becoming securely established on the land increasingly became a practical impossibility even for the most ambitious and able.[26]

One aspect of the passage of farms between generations in the pre–World War II years was the creation of extended-family households. Many households at different stages in the family members' life cycle became extended. Young married couples in some instances shared the household of their parents. Dave Wood's sons, Archie and Ralph, lived for periods of time with him after they married and began their own families. Eventually Archie moved to the "old place," where his grandfather, Deacon Alvah Wood, had farmed.[27] Aging parents and especially widows and widowers lived their final years with one of their children, in many instances on the home farm. Accurate statistics on household composition for the years after 1910 cannot be determined because manuscript censuses are not available. But the situation at the turn of the century is clear. In the 1900 Lincoln census, 10.9 percent of the households of the immigrants and their offspring included one or more of the parents or parents-in-law of the household heads. The smaller number of old-stock American families were similarly extended in 12.6 percent of their households.[28] If families could be traced over their entire life cycle, however, no doubt it would be found that a considerably higher proportion of households than this were extended at some point.

In Norway the elderly were cared for on their farms by their offspring or by the people to whom they sold their farms. Not surprisingly this practice continued, though Hans Anderson declared it a bad arrangement, fraught with potential conflict.[29] In her autobiography, Thurine Oleson reported beginning her marriage living with her husband's family, and she prided herself on the fact that never a harsh word ever passed her lips toward her mother-in-law, whose ways she did not always approve. For the women who entered into the households of their mothers-in-law, a priority was placed on maintaining a harmonious relationship.[30]

In Pigeon in 1900, 21, or 10.1 percent, of the households, were extended upwards, including one or both of the parents of the head or of the mate of the head. Five included the parents of the male head of the family and an equal number included both parents-in-law of the head. Widowed parents distributed themselves between their sons' and daughters' households; five widowed mothers and one father lived in their sons' households, and two widowed mothers and three fathers lived with their daughters' families.[31] In Pigeon Township in 1910, of the 27 widowed women, all but 9 were living with their children; 6 of these women were listed as heads of households themselves, and 11 lived in households headed by their offspring. One widowed woman lived with her grandson's family and another with her brother's family. Of those widowed women 65 and older, 11 of the 12 lived with their children. Widowers 65 and older were more inclined to live alone. Five of the eight males of that age group did so. Some farm couples moved to their own homes in the village during their retirement years, when sons took over or when they sold their farms to someone else. The tendency of retired farm couples to move into the villages accelerated during the course of the twentieth century and was already apparent in the 1910 census, when the number of retired farmers in the village increased.[32]

Those who found little or no opportunities in Trempealeau, whether they were young or old, did not necessarily leave because they were dissatisfied with rural life. In fact, many of those who left Lincoln and Pigeon sought places and positions not unlike the ones left behind. Already in 1880 when settlers were still clearing the land, families were looking westward to locate land for themselves and their sons. As long as cheap land was available in the West the young of Pigeon and Lincoln would look in that direction for their futures—first in Minnesota and the Dakotas, and then in Colorado, Montana, Washington, Oregon, and California. Former Whitehall youth became ranchers in Canada, wheat farmers in the Dakotas, and fruit growers in California. The tie to the land remained strong.[33] Only when the frontier had entirely disappeared did they start looking elsewhere for opportunities.

In this continued preference for farming, the second generation of Norwegian Americans was typical of that ethnic group as a whole in this country. The children of the Norwegian immigrants did not follow the flow to the cities in the early twentieth century. The proportion of second-generation Norwegian Americans who remained on farms was larger than that of any other immigrant group. The 1900 and 1910 censuses indicate that as many as 54.3 percent became farmers.[34]

The Norwegian Americans were not alone in this preference for farming. The movement out of Lincoln and Pigeon of the old-stock Americans did not always break their ties to farming. In 1931 an obituary for Leslie James Stratton, one of Lincoln's old-stock migrants, described family strategies of physical and social mobility involved in maintaining the tie to the land across generations and space. Born in 1871, the son of pioneers, Stratton grew up in Lincoln. When he married in 1892 he built a home for himself and his wife on his father's farm and later bought the home farm when his father moved west. In 1899 he followed his parents and sister's family to Santa Clara County, California. After raising fruit for a time, he bought a large ranch in Meadow Valley, California, which one son was running at the time of Stratton's death. In 1913 he bought a nut ranch, which another son operated.[35] In the nineteenth century, many may have left Lincoln and Pigeon, but they usually were not heading for the growing cities in large numbers; instead, they often sought opportunities and communities not unlike the rural ones they left behind.

The same strategies by which immigrants and migrants discovered and exploited the opportunities offered by frontier Trempealeau served those who left the area. They depended heavily upon the kin networks as a source of information and assistance in locating land and work and in acquiring an education. When parents lived on farms in areas where the education they desired for their children was not available, a relative nearby or the financial assistance of a child's older sibling might determine the opportunities that were available. Young men or women who did not work on the family farm or in the business of a neighbor when they first began to work outside the home very often worked for and lived with a relative. Often the earliest ventures outside the parental home or community were within the context of the kin network, and, as in Ludwig Solsrud's case, one's life's work was often determined by the kin connection.[36] Kin and to a lesser extent community networks which extended across space and time provided the young with information and opportunities.

Just as immigrants like Solsrud looked to America for opportunities and depended upon kin networks to exploit them, the immigrants' children looked westward in the nineteenth century and continued to depend upon kin and community networks to locate opportunities. In the 1880s they frequently set out as individuals, but more often in pairs and groups, "prospecting" for new locations. When Mads Knudtson first left his community in Norway, he led the way for a small colony of neighbors and relatives who received news and information from him about America and a place to stay when they arrived. Similarly, as individuals moved west from Lincoln and Pigeon, they returned to report on and wrote home about the quality of opportunities they found. In letters to friends and relatives or even to the local newspaper, they described in detail the land and climate that would have been of interest to potential followers to the new environments. These extended kin and community networks provided detailed and precise information, a place to go, and familiar faces to see when people left their home communities.[37]

Geographer Robert Ostergren, examining settlement patterns in the Midwest, found an important feature of that settlement to be the "strings of communities that were linked by bonds of kinship. When the population of a community grew beyond the capacity of the land to support it, surplus population left the community in search of land, establishing daughter communities farther west."[38] In the 1880s the sons and daughters of Lincoln and Pigeon were prospecting for farms in Minnesota and the Dakotas and seeking gold in Colorado. The son of Pigeon pioneer Mads Knudtson followed the movement first to North Dakota and eventually to California, where he became a fruit grower. Early in 1881 several local residents including the often restless J. D. Olds were talking of heading for the gold fields of Colorado.[39] In April of that year after the departure of Billy Webb and John and Henry Knudtson "for San Miguel, Colorado—gold is the hope," local residents regularly heard of their progress in letters and through visits.[40] In 1883 John Knudtson was back in town with his "pockets filled with gold, silver and greenbacks."[41] And in October of 1884, the *Times* reported that "Billy Webb formerly of Whitehall according to the *Evening News* in Telluride, Colorado, owns a very valuable claim, an eighteen inch wide gold vein,"[42] Two years later Billy Webb returned to marry a local girl, Ella Lake, before taking her back to Telluride.[43] In 1887 Billy Webb's achievements once again came to the attention of the *Times* when it reported: "We notice in an article taken from the Telluride Journal that our ex-townsman, Will Webb, is highly extolled as a mining superintendent. His many friends here will be pleased to hear that his valued services are appreciated in the mines of Colorado."[44] The local paper and people continued to have connections with those who grew up and left the community.

Several of the old-stock Americans who joined the flight westward established a daughter community in San Jose, California. Nothing illustrates better the connections of the extended community than items such as the following in the *Whitehall Times* in October of 1918:

> Mr. and Mrs. James F. Adams of San Jose, California, are guests at the home of Mrs. Adam's sister, Mrs. H. W. Bishop. Mrs. Adams will be remembered as Florence Stratton. They bring news from the Wisconsin colony in California at San Jose, including Mr. and Mrs. Henry Stratton, Mr. and Mrs. E. A. Warner, Mr. and Mrs. E. A. Webster, Mrs. William Blodgett.[45]

All the couples had been residents in Whitehall in 1880 but were absent by 1900.[46] In 1916 the *Times* had also noted the visit of another member of the "Wisconsin colony in San Jose."[47] The extended community was further illustrated by the *Times* in its report that "Paul Larson of San Springs, Montana, has rented his farm to his son Clemens and has bought a large ranch at Bensien, Montana. There are four hundred head of cattle on the new ranch. Evidently Paul is prospering in the West."[48]

As the twentieth century progressed, the educational system, including both high schools and colleges, supplemented and eventually nearly replaced as the source of opportunity the former far-flung kin and community networks on which the young had depended in the agriculturally oriented nineteenth century. The young women who graduated from Whitehall High School used their education to enter many of the white-collar positions opening up to women after 1900. Of the 59 women who graduated between 1915 and 1921, 73 percent were either working or continuing their education in 1922, and all but 4 of the 47 who were not married were so occupied (see Table 4.9). If married women continued to work, the alumni records do not reveal it. Typically most married women did not in these years. Of the group graduating between 1915 and 1921, by 1922, 20 percent were married, and by 1938, 84 percent of those still alive or about whom information was available would be married. This is a somewhat lower rate of marriage than the graduates in the group that preceded this one. By 1938, 91 percent of the 1904–1914 graduates were married.

Like the women graduates, male graduates of Whitehall High School by 1922 tended to move almost exclusively into professional, business, or other white-collar occupations, with the exception of a few who remained in famring. This was true for the sons of both the old-stock villagers and the immigrant farmers. Whitehall High School thus effectively prepared the sons and daughters of farmers and villagers for pursuing the opportunities offered by the American economy in these years. The graduates dispersed across the physical and social landscape of America. Among them

Table 4.9. Statuses and Occupations of Female Graduates of Whitehall High School, 1904–1921, as Recorded in 1922 and 1938

	Graduated 1904–1914 (N = 56)		Graduated 1915–1921 (N = 59)	
	1922	1938	1922	1938
STATUS				
Married	44	50	12	47
Single	12	5	47	9
Dead or unknown	0	1	0	3
OCCUPATION[a]				
Lawyer	1	1	0	0
Nurse	2	1	6	4
Teacher	3	2	13	3
Clerk	2	0	3	0
Stenographer	0	0	4	1
Bookkeeper	0	0	2	0
Saleslady	0	0	2	0
Milliner	1	0	0	0
Proofreader	0	0	0	1
Student	0	0	13	0
At home	3	1	4	0

Source: Whitehall High School Alumni Records, 1922 and 1938.

[a]The data on occupations pertain only to the single graduates, because the records do not reveal any occupational information about married women; most did not work in these years.

were a banker in Big Timber, Montana, a lawyer in Chicago, a lumber merchant in Garibaldi, Oregon, two decorators in Chicago who attended the Art Institute of Chicago (one the son of a farmer, the other of a drover), a real estate agent in Los Angeles, and a rancher in Alberta, Canada. Contrary to popular conceptions of rural youth flooding to the cities to fill the factories with unskilled laborers, Pigeon and Lincoln youth, or at least all those who took advantage of the local educational institutions, almost exclusively became professionals, businessmen, or other types of white-collar workers. Fewer than 6 percent of the total became either skilled or unskilled workers, and none of the farmers' sons did so. Of the 34 graduates who were sons of farmers, except for those who followed their fathers' occupations (26.5 percent), all of those whose occupations were known became professionals, businessmen, or other white-collar workers.

In the twentieth century the college degree competed in importance with the tours of the West in the nineteenth century as the means of launching the young in their life work. In the nineteenth century a smaller

Table 4.10. Numerical Distribution of Occupations of Male Graduates of Whitehall High School, 1904–1922, by Their Fathers' Occupations

Father's Occupation:	Farmer	Merchant/ Business	Professional	Skilled Labor	Unskilled Labor	Unknown	
Graduate's Occupation:							Total[a]
Farmer	9	0	0	0	0	2	11
Professional	9	2	2	0	1	4	18
Merchant/business	6	2	0	1	2	5	16
Other White-collar	7	2	2	2	0	2	15
Skilled labor	0	0	0	0	1	0	1
Unskilled labor	0	1	0	0	1	1	3
Unknown	3	0	0	0	0	3	6
Total[b]	34	7	4	3	5	17	70

Source: Whitehall High School Alumni Records, 1922 and 1938.
[a]These totals indicate the number of graduates who entered each occupational category.
[b]These totals indicate the number of graduates according to their fathers' occupational categories.

number depended upon a university or college education of some type to establish their position, as did Hans Anderson and Herman Ekern. In the twentieth century the numbers would grow. While no statistically clear information is available on the numbers who pursued degrees after high school, of those who graduated between 1915 and 1922, at least 25 percent did so. Ten of the 41 graduates of those years attended some institution of higher learning in 1922: 6 at the University of Wisconsin in Madison, 1 at the Teachers College in nearby La Crosse, 1 at the University of Chicago, 1 at the Art Institute of Chicago, and 1 at St. Olaf College. Half of these students were sons of farmers, three of professionals, 1 of a drover, and one of a saloon keeper. Others no doubt had completed advanced work by 1922, so at the very least a quarter continued their educations after high school. The *Whitehall Times* regularly reported on the students leaving for school and returning for visits during vacations, and every year their numbers were notable. Whatever the proportion may have been of the young pursuing higher education, it is clear that local farmers and villagers were well aware of the importance and availed themselves of the opportunities for education in the twentieth century.

The regular return of the young and former residents extended the boundaries of the community far beyond the farms or villages. In their local newspapers and perhaps even more carefully in their gossip networks, local communities kept track of their youth when they left the community and for much of their lives thereafter. So while perhaps a majority of those born in the area left, the local newspaper assured that

Whitehall High School, 1907. Photo courtesy of University of Wisconsin–La Crosse, Murphy Library.

their lives and achievements did not go unobserved. Those who were in colleges or in training of various kinds were frequently noted.

Such reports became more common in the twentieth century as opportunities on the land declined. Visits back home by students often resulted in the *Times* noting such information as what fraternity, sorority, or other campus organizations they had joined, or reporting items such as the following: "Joseph Beach Wins in Debate." According to the *Times*, young Beach led his debate team to victory at the University of Wisconsin in Madison. The team also included Robert La Follette's son, Phillip, and was presided over by John R. Commons. Beach, representing his home community's left-of-center politics, led the team opposing the proposition: "Resolved that strikes and lockouts should be made unlawful during the continuance of the war, in government establishments in which the bulk of the product is under contract with the government."[49] One suspects that this continuous back-home audience had its effect on the motivation, ambition, and choices that individuals made long after they had left the community behind.

While rural youth in the nineteenth and twentieth centuries left their farms and small-town homes in large numbers, their choices, opportunities, and strategies varied over time. Local and familial loyalties and commitment to life on the land remained strong. A significant portion would remain in the communities, providing the familial continuity on the land, which is a notable aspect of rural life. Those who did remain in the communities usually depended upon their families to establish themselves. Those who left in the nineteenth and early twentieth centuries frequently chose to locate in rural communities either within the Midwest or farther west. Some did make their way into the cities around the country, but before World War II the proportion is surprisingly small. When they left in the years between 1880 and 1940, wherever they went, the extended kin and community networks usually played a critical role in both social and geographic mobility.

In the twentieth century, information on the occupations of those who left, based on the data presented here, concerns only those who graduated from high school before 1938. What is most striking before the depression decade is the extent to which these farm and small-town youth rather exclusively entered the ranks of white-collar workers and professionals. This was true whether they were the children of immigrants or of old-stock Americans. The educational system played an increasingly critical role in the lives of rural youth in this century and by the post–World War II years may have gone a long way toward replacing the kin and community networks upon which the young earlier depended. Until very recently, more often than men, young women in these rural neighborhoods availed themselves of educational opportunities, which allowed them greater geographic mobility. Local loyalties and local opportunities bound men to the communities more closely than the women.

5
Salvation and Social Rituals of Community

The immigrants and migrants left behind them worlds based on kinship, local community, and church, and these would long be the primary institutions in rural Trempealeau. The dimension of life which the immigrants most successfully shielded from acculturation in the American environment was their religion.[1] Besides the family, the institution which carried much of the responsibility for cultural transmission on the frontier and in rural areas was the church. A sense of peoplehood or ethnicity is deeply tied to a group's religion. This certainly is borne out in the experience of rural Trempealeau.[2] Each group of settlers brought with them their own churches, and with few exceptions those churches continue today to serve the needs of the people in the countryside and the villages.

The diverse groups of pioneers kept their religions alive in their homes in the early years before churches could be built and ministers could be obtained. There they held prayer meetings, observed the various rituals of their church, and occasionally listened to itinerant ministers. The frontier period brought religious revivals and an increased interest in spiritual concerns. Among the Norwegian Americans, religious and social conflicts of the old country surfaced and intensified, stirring doctrinal debate and schism. By 1890 most of those small informal prayer groups had formed congregations, built churches in the community, and located resident ministers for their congregations.[3] By 1900 Pigeon Falls had two congregations, and the village of Whitehall and Lincoln Township combined boasted six.[4]

The old-stock Americans organized churches almost immediately upon arriving in frontier Trempealeau. Deacon Alvah Wood's home served as the first meeting house for the Baptists in 1857, and it was there that the itinerant preachers gave their first sermons in the area. In 1858 this little group of eight, including neighbors and kinsmen of Wood, formed the First Baptist Church of Preston (Lincoln had not yet organized as a separate township and was at this time a part of the town of Preston). In 1860 its membership totaled only 20 souls, and not until 1870 did this church become large enough and rich enough to construct its first building at a cost of $1,100. The mobile New Yorkers also brought with them Methodism as well. Like the Baptists, a small Methodist congregation began meeting in the homes of pioneers in the 1850s. The members of the Methodist Episcopal Church of Whitehall finally completed their first church building in 1875. A latecomer to the village was the Presbyterian Church of Whitehall, established in 1893. While the old-stock Americans were few in number, their commitments to their traditional religions on the frontier were strong; each group maintained its religious identity in the community.[5]

These churches early became the center of the social life among the settlers, and through the years they would sponsor numerous revivals and organize a host of activities in the community ranging from ice cream socials to temperance groups. The diaries of Dave Wood, Alvah's son, clearly illustrate the primary role that the circle of kin and church members held in the lives of these pioneering families. Between 1870 and 1900 Dave Wood's diaries year after year record the continual round of interaction in prayer meetings, social activities, and economic arrangements between those families which Alvah Wood organized into the First Baptist Church.[6]

Among the immigrants, churches played an even more dynamic role as the primary institutions adapting and transmitting ethnic cultures. The immigrant generation and no doubt many of their children equated being Norwegian with being Lutheran. A similar, perhaps even stronger, connection could have been made between being Polish and being Catholic. Within their churches, immigrants preserved their language, their values, their music, and their social traditions. Like their Yankee neighbors, they organized themselves into churches and parishes as soon as they arrived.[7] In 1866, with 40 communicants, the Pigeon Creek Norwegian Evangelical Church was organized with the assistance of one of the early pastors sent by the Church of Norway to the county. Four years later the Whitehall Evangelical Lutheran Church came into being. Both congregations were affiliated with the Church of Norway's American arm, the Norwegian Evangelical Lutheran Synod of America (conventionally and hereafter referred to as the Norwegian Synod).[8]

When the Norwegian immigrants brought their church to their new country, they also brought with it the same tensions and troubles which that Lutheran church faced in Norway. The nineteenth-century Church of Norway confronted the challenges of a series of reformers and revivalists who had a distinctly pietistic and puritanical turn of mind. In the nineteenth century, Norway still maintained an established state church, which the government was prepared to defend by prosecution of dissidents when the occasion required. No doubt, the Norwegian Synod would have continued its imperious ways in the early settlements of the Midwest if it had had available to it the legal powers granted to first-generation Puritans in New England. As it was, members of the Norwegian Synod did what they could to maintain the Norwegian Americans within the Lutheran orthodoxy of the Church of Norway.

The Norwegian clergy that first followed the pioneers to America were members of a self-conscious, educated elite, determined to bring and sustain religion and civilization for Norwegian Americans in the cultural wilderness of America, a wilderness for which they felt a haughty disdain.[9] Educated and ordained in Christiana, Norway, they were sent by and given the economic support of the Church of Norway. Like the Puritans before them, these Norwegian clerics depended upon traditions of deference to their leadership long after the legal and state supports for that deference had collapsed.[10] And as was the case in seventeenth-century New England, they fell prey to conflict over doctrine and institutional schism. These doctrinal battles divided congregations in Norwegian-American communities including those of Pigeon and Whitehall. The doctrinal and social tensions that divided the "high"-church position of the state church in Norway and the "low"-church orientation of the reformers arrived intact and grew in the American frontier communities.[11]

The Norwegian Synod, which organized the first churches in the towns of Lincoln and Pigeon, represented the high-church position. It stressed the authority of the clergy, strict organizational discipline, a doctrinal orthodoxy, and opposition to religious teaching from anyone but properly educated and ordained ministers, who for centuries had come exclusively from the bureaucratic and commercial elite of Norway. The extreme low-church position, which led to a host of splinterings, paralleled that of the Puritans and separatists of the seventeenth century with a similar spectrum of radicalism. Some took the extreme position that only the converted and the saved should be allowed to be members of a congregation. At issue, too, were doctrinal questions of predestination, of God's power versus human choice in the achievement of salvation. Human choice played a critical role in salvation from the perspective of low-church leaders, while the high church reasoned from the omnipotence and omniscience of God to denigrate the individual's ability to will election and salvation.

The low church stressed the role of conversions and salvation by grace following repentance, and forged a pietistic religion which reflected itself in a holy daily life, a life dependent upon the dignity and sanctity of work. Low-church leaders made war on traditional peasant habits of sociability, urged their peasant converts to take advantage of the opportunities of the expanding economy to improve themselves in cooperatives and businesses, and pressed politically for democratic reforms. The emphasis of the low church was on a pietistic and experienced Christianity within the context of Lutheran orthodoxy and, like the Puritans of another time, on work as a Christian calling. Other issues between the reformers and traditional leadership related to the church's authority and the role of the clergy. Low-church leaders made greater claims for congregational autonomy and independence in opposition to the hierarchically structured and liturgical high church.[12]

The Norwegian peasant cooperatives and politics of the nineteenth century were rooted ideologically and organizationally in the low church, inspired by the revivals of Hans Nielson Hauge in Norway early in that century. These revivals gave an important impetus to the political awakening of the peasantry facing a changing economy to raise their sights beyond their local mountain neighborhoods. In the words of one historian, Haugenism laid the "spiritual foundation for a democratic social-political movement."[13]

Until the late nineteenth century, the Lutheranism of the established church in Norway had not profoundly affected the lives of the peasant class, from which most immigrants came. It was the religious revivals of Hauge that began the process of "disciplining the personality" of the Norwegian peasantry. As one scholar analyzing this peasant movement explained: "What Hauge did essentially was to take some concepts of Lutheran religion, give them new meaning, value, and vitality, thus transforming Lutheranism into a religion that achieved exactly the same behavioristic results from slightly different premises as Calvinism did."[14]

And in fact the social realities of nineteenth-century Norway correspond more closely to those of seventeenth-century England than to those of the United States in the nineteenth century. Michael Walzer has argued that the rigors of the Puritan religion, with the psychological tightrope it imposed, corresponded to the harshness of the social reality of seventeenth-century England. It provided an inner psychic discipline sufficient to impose order internally in a dangerous and disordered world, and it sustained the energy which similarly made it possible to transform the social environment. Norwegian peasants of the nineteenth century faced social circumstances similar to those of sixteenth- and seventeenth-century people in England: a population explosion that the economy could not absorb, an enclosure movement, uprootedness, and poverty. Immigration and frontier life did little to diminish the sense of precariousness but, as was true for the Puritans, provided fertile ground for community-building and imposing a new order.[15]

Elling Eilsen, one of the important leaders of the low-church position in Norway, carried the dissenting tradition to the American midwestern frontier. He dismissed the established church leaders as misguided theologians who supposed that religion consisted of "masses, gowns, and dead ceremonies" while they left "the miserable people to tumble about in their unresurrected lives," ignoring their "drunkenness, cursing, swearing, dancing and fiddling and other noisy pleasures."[16] Eilsen zealously sought to end such sinful ways in the immigrant communities, where the Church of Norway's power was easier to challenge. As was true of the "new lights" of the Great Awakening of the eighteenth century, the low church was associated with political radicalism and social reform. The defiance of established religious authority in Norway spilled over into social, political, and economic challenges to the Norwegian elite beginning in the early nineteenth century.[17]

In fact, the divisions in the Norwegian church became even more exaggerated in America. Here the squabbling created major schisms in the Norwegian Synod, divided the Norwegian-American congregations, and spawned several independent Norwegian Lutheran synods. As in Norway these schisms revealed a deep dissatisfaction with the authoritarian, dogmatic, and elitist leadership and with an "objective" and intellectualized religion that discouraged a more emotionally vital and subjective religion. As early as 1878 these conflicts broke out in the Whitehall and Pigeon churches. Before this, some of the early Norwegian settlers had turned to the revivalistic religions that were already thriving on the American frontier, although most of them did affiliate with one of the Norwegian churches. Consequently, whereas once there was one Norwegian Lutheran congregation in each of the two townships, by the end of the decade of the 1880s six different Norwegian Lutheran congregations served the area, each affiliated with one of the splinters of Norwegian Lutheranism.[18]

The most extreme low-church position of Haugenism found few adherents in the area, although they did briefly organize a congregation in Lincoln between 1887 and 1893 with 58 members. Far more important to the communities in Whitehall and Pigeon were the somewhat more moderate critics of the Norwegian Synod; in 1890 these critics came together organizationally and doctrinally in the United Norwegian Lutheran Church of America (hereafter referred to as the United Synod). In 1890 approximately two-thirds of the 924 members of the local Norwegian Lutherans remained loyal to their traditional leadership in the Norwegian Synod, while the remaining one-third turned to the United Synod for leadership. The Pigeon Falls Norwegian Lutheran Congregation (referred to by locals as the lower church, describing both the geographical location of the church and its doctrinal sympathies) began as a minority congregation, under the leadership of Peder Ekern in 1878. Ten years later this dissenting group built a new church on Ekern's property. In 1891 the third dissenting group, Our Saviour's Congregation, which according to local historians "had built a small church on the Tangen property, where the Curtis Anderson property is located today," joined with the lower church.[19]

In Norway the clergy commanded considerable power and authority supported by the state, and they commanded a great deal of deference. They did not hesitate to intrude upon the private lives of their parishioners, whether it be their religious observance, their politics, or the way they ran their farms. The arrival of the first residential minister in 1876 sent by the Norwegian Synod triggered the schism in Pigeon. The Reverend Emmanuel Christophersen, a representative of Norway's privileged social class, had been well educated and had traveled in Europe. He represented a different class and a different culture from that of the typical immigrant. Christopherson solidly defended the traditional social order and the Norwegian Synod's stance in opposition to the church reformers.

The prospering patriarch Peder Ekern concluded that such a presence as Christophersen's added little of value to local leadership. Soon after Christophersen's arrival, Ekern led the revolt against this representative of the old order by organizing a new congregation in 1878. In 1895 the Pigeon Falls Norwegian Lutheran Congregation found a minister more to their tastes, Reverend A. J. Orke from Stavanger, Norway, one of the hotbeds of revivalism in the 1870s and 1880s. Of humble origins and from "a long line of God-fearing people," he acquired his theological training at Augsburg College and Augsburg Seminary after immigrating to this country at the age of 25. Both Christophersen and Orke spent the rest of their lives serving the churches of Trempealeau.[20]

Augsburg College and Augsburg Seminary in Minneapolis were the creations of the Haugean Synod for the purpose of educating a ministry in this country. The selection of Orke thus indicates the pietistic proclivities of many of the Pigeon residents. Pigeon and Lincoln congregations acknowledged their allegiance to the distinct synods of which they were a part by their support of denominational colleges to which they contributed nearly as much as they did to maintaining their local parochial schools.[21] Out of the schism of the Norwegian Lutheran church came an institutional creativity that paralleled the developments of the Great Awakening of the eighteenth century. The conflicting Lutherans spawned several denominational colleges, such as Luther College in Decorah, Iowa, St. Olaf College in Northfield, Minnesota, as well as Augsburg College, in order to educate the leadership and laity of the diverse splinters of the Norwegian Lutheran church.[22] Peder Ekern sent his son to St. Olaf, and others in Pigeon and Lincoln sent theirs to Luther, which the Norwegian Synod established in 1861. Often families established traditions in their choice of schools.[23]

Merle Curti speculated that, in light of the assimilation that had occurred in 1880, the immigrants could look forward to the day when their children or grandchildren would attend, say, Columbia University.[24] What he failed to realize is that in 1880 as in 1980 for many of the families it was far more prestigious to send their children to St. Olaf and Luther colleges than to Ivy League schools in the East. The local elites would long send their children to the Lutheran denominational colleges.

After the arrival of Orke in Pigeon, the lower church quickly grew to become the larger of the two congregations in Pigeon. By 1914 the "upper" church had a mere 395 members, only slightly more than in 1890, while the lower church had grown from 220 members to 820. In Whitehall, where the Norwegian Lutherans were in competition with several denominations, they were less aggressive in their dissent. Only 46 joined the United Synod congregation, but like the Pigeon church it grew rapidly to 190 members by 1900. Nonetheless, the Whitehall Norwegian Evangelical Lutheran Church, which was affiliated with the Norwegian Synod, continued to be the stronger, with 260 members in 1914. As a result of the growth of the United Synod's congregations by 1914, they included over 60 percent of the local Norwegian Lutheran membership of 1,667.[25]

Apparently, the Norwegian Synod's commitment to traditional ways appealed to fewer locals. Until Christophersen's death in 1909 he appeared to hold the line against change. Illustrating this is the different naming practices between the two churches. Until 1909, church records reveal that the upper church membership still used traditional peasant naming practices. Husbands, wives, and children all had different surnames. In Norwegian tradition, the father's first name became the first part of the child's last name; thus a marriage would be recorded in 1866 as between Hans Olson, son of Ole Knudsen and Agnete Pedersdatter, and Karine Olsdatter, daughter of Ole Larson and Ann Olsdatter. By 1880 some had begun to adopt American naming practices, particularly in the United Synod, but the Norwegian pattern can still be found as late as 1909 in the records of the upper church and in county marriage records. After the death of Emmanuel Christophersen, the American pattern of naming became universal in these communities, suggesting Christophersen's influence in encouraging church members to follow the traditional peasant practices that had differentiated classes in Norway. His own family as members of a different class did not follow these patterns.[26]

The United Synod forged a broad consensus among Norwegian-American Lutherans by combining aspects of both the high and the low church traditions. One might say they attempted organizationally and theologically to put together the kinds of thought and traditions that had come apart for other Protestants in the Great Awakening of the 1740s. The new synod retained much of the hierarchical structure, liturgy, and doctrine of the high church but added the pietistic concern for personal salvation and for a faith which expressed itself in one's work and daily life.[27]

In logical rigor, theological hairsplitting, and uncompromising temperaments, these nineteenth- and early-twentieth-century clerics of the Norwegian-Americans' Lutheran synods would have been the equals of the Puritan divines of another time. In 1912 they finally resolved the "election" controversy. The Norwegian Synod earlier began a retreat from its uncompromising authoritarian positions on church polity and doctrine. The high church leadership stood solidly with Jonathan Edwards and Cotton Mather in stressing God's omnipotence and omniscience in contrast with the hopeless corruption and helplessness of men and women in determining their fates. Salvation was God's gift, not human achievement. The United Synod accused the Norwegian Synod of trucking with Calvinism; the Norwegian Synod charged the United Synod with indulging in the sin of eclecticism (called synergism). Both insisted that salvation of the individual soul came only by the grace of God, but the United Synod and more emphatically Haugean Synod claimed a greater role for the individual in determining the fate of his or her soul and insisted on the importance of a conversion experience and a holy daily life which reflected the state of grace. The Norwegian Synod insisted upon the interconnection between election and obedience to the law and church hierarchy, while the United Synod sought to lodge greater authority in the congregation itself than in the hands of the clergy appointed by the synod leadership. Similar to the New England saints of colonial times, the Norwegian Synod's leadership would not tolerate such challenges to their authority over congregations. The authority of the church descended from God; it did not flow upward from the people. The government was properly autocratic, not democratic. Obedience to authority was a prized principle of the church deemed necessary to social order.[28]

In Norway as in America religious rebels aggressively attacked these traditional conceptions of the social order. One concession the Norwegian Synod had to make early in the American environment was to grant a congregation's right to accept or reject ministers. They did, however, continue to insist upon men properly educated and ordained by the church. Lay preaching and ministering of sacraments and rituals was absolutely illegitimate except in cases of extreme emergency.[29]

By 1900 the Norwegian Synod's declining success in competing for membership at last brought a slow retreat toward compromise. In 1917 the somewhat chastened Norwegian Synod itself joined with the United Synod in forming the Norwegian Lutheran Church of America. At the same time the pietism of the low-church tradition had become somewhat tempered as well. The Lutheran churches' leadership and laity of Trempealeau were in the center of these conflicts over doctrine and polity. Ministers and members regularly attended the synodical meetings to engage in doctrinal debates and negotiate compromises. In their own communities they had to choose between the conflicting ideas and leadership. The year after the Norwegian Synod and the United Synod united, the two Lutheran churches in Whitehall merged the two congregations affiliated with those synods into a single congregation. On the other hand, the people of Pigeon went their own way; there the congregations remain separate today against almost 70 years of contrary advice from their ministers and the synod.[30]

The intense involvement in religious issues revealed in revivals, doctrinal battles, and schisms of the Norwegian Lutheran church exposes a dimension of the frontier experience which Turner and Curti neglected, but which since their writings has often been commented upon. According to Timothy L. Smith:

> The acts of uprooting, migration, resettlement, and community-building became for the participants a theologizing experience, not the secularizing process that some historians have pictured. . . . Belief and devotion were powerful impulses to accommodation and innovation; and both helped legitimate the behavior, the perceptions, and the structures of association that sustained the processes of change.[31]

In Pigeon and Lincoln and within the Norwegian-American experience, many turned to their religious traditions as a means of understanding their experience and adapting to it.

Beret Holmes in Ole Rolvaag's *Giants in the Earth* furnishes an excellent literary example of the theologizing impact of the move to the frontier. She sent her husband to a sure death on the strength of her seemingly fanatical religious convictions. Many have read *Giants in the Earth* and concluded that Beret was a woman driven to near madness by the harshness of the frontier. But the rigors of the devout and rigid Lutheranism, which she brought with her from Norway and which intensified on the frontier, had much to do with her anguish on the Dakota prairies. Beret's sanity returned after the arrival of a Norwegian Lutheran prairie minister and after the second, and in her view legitimate, baptism of her son. Beret's own "rebirth" soon followed.[32]

Beret understood her experience in terms of the culture and religion of her home in Norway. As Hauge preached: "Man was by nature sinful and doomed to eternal hell-fire because he had been conceived in sin." Salvation depended upon God's grace and "call" in which one is "born anew" after "deep self-analysis and soul searching."[33] Her inner turmoil was the anguish of a person uncertain of the status of her soul; Beret's lifelong preoccupations were for her own, her husband's, her children's, and her grandchildren's souls. Determined that Per's lifelong friend not die without the comfort of confessing his sins to an ordained minister, she convinced Per to attempt to bring the minister to their frontier settlement. Her husband froze to death in the blizzard because of the strength of her own and their dying friend's religious convictions, not because the prairie was a hard place in which to survive. She was preoccupied far more with her own and others' sinfulness and its consequences than with the harshness and hardships of her environment; the changing Dakota landscape became a metaphor for Beret's internal landscape. What threatened her was the lack of boundaries in both the physical and social landscape—the ways in which the New World loosened the hold of the old faith and traditions on her family and community.[34] Rolvaag was no more eager than Beret to see that happen. It is Beret, the conserver, who survives to build the farm and the community and her irreverent husband who dies.

All the Norwegian synods, despite their squabbling, were culturally conservative and stood firmly against the Protestant liberalism that was permeating many urban American churches at the turn of the century. Adaptation and innovation within their own religious traditions provided the framework in which they coped with the New World.[35]

The religion that Beret and other immigrants brought with them and upon which they depended for understanding their experience bore few similarities to the "sentimentalized" and feminized faith that Ann Douglas found developing in the nineteenth century in the United States. Not all Norwegians in the home country participated in the nineteenth-century revivals, but most of Norway's peasantry had been affected by the spiritual "awakenings."[36] That pietistic strain of Lutheranism came to dominate in America, and for many years it lost little of the "masculine" rigor and intellectual toughness which Ann Douglas found to be dissolving among Americans.[37] God had lost none of his stern power, nor sin its ominous meaning as it had for many of the American urban Protestant churches. The Calvinism of the seventeenth century rather than the late nineteenth-century American religious liberalism more closely resembled the religious framework of the first-, second-, and many of the third-generation Lutherans in the area. Locals who grew up in the 1930s still recall sermons which bring to mind Jonathan Edwards's "Sinners in the Hands of an Angry God." But if they shuddered in response to such sermons then, they often laugh at the memory today; since that time their own Lutheranism has become more liberal.[38]

But such a transition was slow in coming. For Beret, the rigors of her religion equaled or surpassed those of her environment. The same was true for some of the pioneering generation in Wisconsin. Hans Anderson and his mother were early pioneers who turned to a revivalistic religion. Although Anderson's spiritual journey would ultimately be exceptional for the immigrant generation, many of his early experiences were shared by other immigrants. In Norway, Anderson and his mother had already become converts to the Haugean persuasion as they struggled to survive poverty and uprootedness. His parents had "worked out" on a variety of farms and homes during their youth and continued to work separated from each other after their marriage and the arrival of their first children. Hans's father died a year after the couple had acquired sufficient funds to buy a small piece of land from an aging couple whom they were bound by contract to support until the older couple died.

During their difficult early years in Pigeon, Anderson turned to what he later described as the "bleak" religion of the Seventh-day Adventists during a revival that swept through the community in 1872. Later a more secure and established Anderson would write, "Undoubtedly my affiliation with the Adventists darkened several of my years when I needed more cheerful convictions and environments to build up my ruined health." But the "sense of human wickedness and imminent destruction" that the Adventists cultivated in Anderson's mind seemingly corresponded to the disorientation and vulnerability he experienced in those first years after leaving Norway. His conversion came when he was 17.[39] After his arrival in the United States at the age of 12, he had spent much of his time working as a farm laborer, moving from place to place around the state. Eventually he had returned home with broken health after working on the railroad that came through Whitehall. "My health was poor and my mind was very much depressed." During these years he had worked for Seventh-day Adventists, one of whom, a man named Loomis, he described as "very religious and most of the time in doubt about his being acceptable to God. This made him depressed and sometimes irritable. I suffered from dyspepsia and mental depression most of the time." Working on the same farm was another hired man, "a good deal like Mr. Loomis, very uncertain of his future."

Anderson's preoccupation with religious questions came at a time which he associated with ill health, when he did not expect a long life, when he moved from strange household to strange household, and when diphtheria ravaged families and consumption killed youthful friends. Insecurity, mobility, hard work, and ill health characterized Anderson's youth while he tried to make sense out of the country to which his family had brought him. Later, when he was established and successful, he ceased to concern himself deeply with any religious doctrine, refused to be affiliated with any religious denomination, placed his faith in reason and progress, and concerned himself with issues of social responsibility and morality.[40]

During the bleakest, most insecure, and most disorienting years on the frontier, Anderson turned to a religion that mirrored that reality. Eventually, however, he became quite critical of the consequences of religious zealotry on psychic stability. By 1902 his daughter Lily would express a view of religion that had long been common among some of Anderson's less pious Yankee neighbors: "Amanda Scott is quite poorly—mentally unbalanced—Religion being the main trouble."[41] Such a comment suggests that in the course of two generations the Andersons encapsuled changes that had taken over a century to evolve in the families in New England and New York. Lily voiced a point of view frequently expressed in the local press. In the 1880s periodically items like the following appeared in the *Whitehall Times:* "Nels C. Nelson son of Ole N. Skaar was examined by Doctors Floyd and Sonnickson on Monday and pronounced insane. He will be taken to the asylum at once. His derangement of mind is said to be the direct result of religious excitement."[42]

A variety of denominations, including the Baptist and Methodist churches, regularly sponsored revivals in Whitehall. In 1881 the ever-irreverent editor of the *Whitehall Times,* Dan Camp, wrote, "The interest in the Advent meetings is lagging. Our quota at the insane asylum is full."[43] His contempt for the religious enthusiasts continued the next week: "What will the poor boys do for evening sport now that the tent meeting apostles have pulled out."[44] Dan Camp expressed the same contempt and anger for the manipulation of emotions that Hamlin Garland expressed in his short story about a religious revival, "A Day of Grace."[45]

A more educated and acculturated Anderson would look back on his youthful enthusiasm with some discomfort, but would conclude that it had had its benefits. "It made me a student of history, of life, and of the many faiths and doctrines that have both consoled and alarmed mankind through the ages. It kept me morally clean and ambitious. . . ." So, like the secularized "saint" Benjamin Franklin, Anderson abandoned the theology of his predecessors, but salvaged and valued the morality.[46]

In his rapid embracement of modern rationalism during the course of his social mobility, Anderson appears to have been an exception among the immigrants in Pigeon and Lincoln. In 1900 when Anderson's daughter Lily married Herman Ekern, Ekern's family was clearly disturbed by his marriage to a "heathen" (she was not Lutheran) and found reasons not to attend the wedding. A letter to Herman Ekern from his sister Lena after the birth of his and Lily's first child indicates the strength of traditional religious attitudes as well as the pressure put on those who appeared to be leaving traditions behind. When the first child arrived and remained unbaptized, the despair of Herman's mother prompted his sister in October of 1900 to write:

> Oh I wish you only knew how it martyrs your dear old mother. She worries away more moments and sheds more tears over the thought of having a daughter and grandchild who are not christened than you realize. You know how patiently she taught you and brought you up to that better and higher standard than a mere heathen which of course an unchristened person is. Besides it seems to me a great sin to compel her to carry this burden which could so easily be removed, and which would be a blessing for you as parents and the child. Remember it is your duty.[47]

Lena's pressure on her brother proved successful. By December Lena wrote of their mother's happiness upon hearing of the child's christening.[48]

Herman Ekern's connections to the Lutheran church proved to be important to his political and personal career. Church leaders stood firm as influential political allies, and he studiously attended to their opinions. In 1929 he became president of the American Association of Lutheran Brotherhood, an insurance and fraternal organization affiliated with the Norwegian Lutheran church. Norwegian Americans like Ekern continued generation after generation within the Lutheran fold, which closely related to their social identity. For Ekern, as for so many others, their ethnic culture, the church, and its affiliated institutions were primary sources of their social mobility in America.[49]

Whether the Norwegian immigrants were Lutherans, as most were, or converts to one of the revivalist religions, like the youthful Anderson, theological preoccupations and piety declined in importance in time.[50] This decline signaled the onset of the second stage in the history of these townships, the beginning of a long period of stability after frontier life receded into memory. Immigration may have been a theologizing experience stimulating a preoccupation with the salvation of the soul and a holy behavior, but once the communities were established and the churches built, the role of religion and the church in the lives of individuals changed. Herman Ekern, like other second- and third-generation Norwegian-Americans, turned to the church as the strongest institution of the community and of Norwegian American culture. The churches functioned increasingly as social institutions: the symbols of community and ethnic identity, centers of traditional community rituals, and sources of social mobility.

In the early histories of the churches written by members and ministers for the 1917 publication *The History of Trempealeau County* and more recently in histories written as local or church publications, those seeking any sense of the social, ideological, and theological issues that may have engaged the members of these congregations are doomed to disappointment. Instead, what one finds is when and by whom the congregation was organized, when the church was built and how much it cost, when the parsonage was built, what its dimensions were, and how much was spent on it, when the basement was added and at what cost, how much the church paid its minister, how much was spent on parochial schools, how much was contributed to denominational colleges, to missions, and to charities.

At first glance such information seemingly would lend itself to an exuberant quantifier seeking to compare the religiosity of groups based on the hard evidence of the contributions of the believers. But it also provides some insight into the meaning of the churches to the community. The character of the local histories of the churches indicates that the churches had become deeply entrenched, well supported in light of local means, and taken-for-granted institutions of the community with an annual budget and a host of affiliated organizations that consumed a good deal of the time and money of community members.[51]

But a careful accounting of dates and expenses also hints at larger meanings. Like their cabins, barns, and schoolhouses, the pioneer immigrants built their first churches themselves, provided or paid for materials needed, and did the work of maintaining and improving them. However, they did not put up their churches in a day, as they did their own first log cabins. Building and improving upon their churches expressed community solidarity and identity, an indication that they had done more than just survive on the frontier. They were laying the essential building blocks for the preservation in America of the civilization they had left behind them in Norway. Local histories written in the second half of the twentieth century still highlight those who built the local churches, and families still speak with pride about a father, grandfather, or husband who joined the effort. These community churches became sacred places not only because they were built as temples of worship but also because of the real human effort and sacrifice that made them a reality. They stood as a symbol of the local ethnic community and culture.[52]

The importance of church-building to the immigrant community is analogous to the importance of barn-raising to the immigrant farm family. It was momentous in the life of an immigrant farm family when at last they could afford to build the big barn. Between 1880 and 1920 the *Whitehall Times* regularly reported who was building a barn and of what size. Rolvaag's Beret studied, saved, and planned for years the barn that she would build, determined that it would be the best and most efficient around and a tribute to her dead husband—the kind of barn that he would have built.[53]

As Thurine Oleson described it, the big barn stood as a kind of symbol that the family had at last arrived.[54]

For the group the building of a church functioned in the same way. They saved, they planned, they made sacrifices, and finally together they built a church, with an imposing steeple that announced their arrival, their success, and their determination to stay. In 1876, long before the big barns and big houses went up in Pigeon, the Norwegians built the upper church, which continues to serve the congregation today. In 1916 Hans Anderson, writing about the dedication of the nearby, recently completed Elk Creek Lutheran Church, articulated something of the meaning the event held for the communities. It was not the sacred purpose that awed Anderson, but rather it was "the coming of two hundred automobiles and like number of teams, bringing together in the space of three or four hours two-thousand people from nearly every part of our county and surrounding counties." Of the recently completed church building and the other Lutheran churches in the county, he continued: "This represents much sweat and toil, industry, economy and self denial, on the part of thousands. It also represents opportunity and the rich resources of the country around us. But above all it represents the ideals and aspirations without which the race would perish." For Beret, a congregation with a church and a resident minister provided the most essential components of civilized life. Their appearance signaled the retreat of the frontier's rigors and the re-creation of the familiar. In 1916 as Anderson reviewed the history of the communities, he saw a process from "the days of no churches, when straggling processions of men, women and oxen slowly wended their way to some rude cabin or school house to satisfy their spiritual needs, and ending with the grand pageant just witnessed." The churches like the immigrants' big barns and houses fulfilled the purpose of immigration and the years of hard struggle. For Anderson the dedication of the new church symbolized the reality of progress and immigrant dreams fulfilled. "This is not history, but a vision of hopes realized, of dreams come true."[55]

The churches defined the community and acted as centers of family and community rituals and sociability, drawing together large numbers of people from within and beyond the neighborhood served by the church. Certainly this was true by 1916, when Anderson wrote his description of the dedication of the Elk Creek Lutheran Church. Congregations continued to invest their money and their time in their churches and affiliated activities and institutions. The rapid growth of the United Synod congregations may be explained in part by its more aggressive and creative role in organizing the social activities of the local community and giving them a religious focus. This included finding new institutional roles for women and youth, thereby making the church more inclusive of the entire commu-

The Evangelical Lutheran Church of Pigeon Creek, built in 1876, in 1915. Photo courtesy of University of Wisconsin–La Crosse, Murphy Library.

nity. In 1884 the dissenting lower church organized the first Ladies Aid Society and followed this with the Young People's League and a choir in 1892. The low church's encouragement of lay activity eventually led the upper church to follow its example, but the latter delayed doing so for several years. There the Ladies Aid did not appear until 1890, but the upper church was quicker to follow the United Synod's example in the creation of a Young People's League in 1895. In Whitehall the Lutheran churches followed the same pattern, with the United Synod's followers organizing a Ladies Aid in 1888 and the other church forming one six years later. Church-affiliated groups long provided an important focus for the sociability of women and the young. They would also do much of the fundraising for their own church activities and synodical commitments.[56]

Like the Puritans before them, the Norwegian clerics and their congregations put a high priority on religious education. One of the major expenses they incurred was the parochial schools, which all the Norwegian Lutheran congregations sponsored. These ran for one or two months in the summer and were taught by either the pastors or other educated men from Norway or from the denominational colleges that sprang up in the Midwest as creations of the competing Norwegian Lutheran synods. As one of the local pastors explained in 1916:

> The Lutheran church has always maintained that parochial schools were a necessity. Neglect of the child spells the gradual disintegration of the church. . . . Inestimable good has been accomplished by supplementing the secular training received in the common school with the systematic, intelligent religious training of the parochial school.[57]

While the leadership of the Norwegian Synod initially wanted private schools under the church's supervision to educate the young at every level, insufficient support for this position among the membership prevented these schools from becoming a reality. The United Synod, somewhat less alarmed than the Norwegian Synod at the prospect of "Americanization" by the public schools, accepted the public schools with few reservations. The arguments for the public schools were largely utilitarian: learning the English language was necessary to get on in American society, and the schools did not represent a threat to the Lutheran religion. The summer parochial schools provided a compromise with which most were comfortable.[58] From the 1880s until the mid-1930s these schools were conducted in Norwegian and instructed the young not only in church doctrine but also in Norwegian history and culture, including reading and writing Norwegian. These parochial schools no doubt were crucial to the long persistence of the Norwegian language in the area.[59] Although one- and two-week summer parochial schools continued in the postdepression years, they ceased to be an institution committed to the transmission of Norwegian culture. Instead the emphasis was exclusively on religious concerns.

These cultural and religious commitments on occasion meant conflict between the diverse ethnic groups in the communities and among the Norwegians as well. At a time when control of the common schools centered largely in the local community, old-stock Americans like J. D. Olds were deeply disturbed in 1882 when his Norwegian-American neighbors shortened the school term to allow time for the parochial schools of the Lutheran churches.[60] Similarly, in 1889 when one of the local country schools held two months of classes in the summer devoted to the Norwegian language and culture, one disapproving resident expressed his views on the matter in the *Whitehall Times:* "Such a sentiment is almost as dangerous to our institutions as the gentlemen of the Haymarket affair."[61] No doubt attitudes like these and the lack of local control by the old-stock Americans spurred the passage of Wisconsin's 1889 Bennett Law, which outlawed the use of any language except English in Wisconsin public schools. While it is not known what J. D. Olds thought of the Bennett Law, there is little question of its unpopularity among the Norwegian Americans in Pigeon and elsewhere. Governor William Dempster Hoard, an aggressive supporter of the legislation, found himself soundly defeated in the 1890 elections. In Pigeon the 1890 election brought one of the few Republican defeats before the decade of the 1930s. Voters in this solidly Republican township generally either stayed home or voted Democratic in that election.[62]

In the one-room country schools that dotted the countryside of Lincoln and Pigeon, the issue of public schools was less of a concern. Because of the ethnic clustering in the countryside the students were generally a homogeneous group. In addition, the local school boards of these schools did their own hiring of teachers and thus had a good deal of control over the education of their children. These local school boards hired Norwegian Americans such as Hans Anderson, or Anderson's daughter Rose, or Lena Ekern, Peder Ekern's niece.[63] In Whitehall the less homogeneous population, however, led to the creation of a Lutheran graded school.[64]

The Polish Americans, who steadily expanded their numbers in Lincoln, turned to the nearby village of Independence in the township of Burnside for their social, economic, educational, and religious life. There they established their own churches, schools, and businesses as the Norwegians did in Pigeon and Lincoln. By 1886 they had begun a private elementary school, and by 1916 about a third of the children of the families of the St. Peter and St. Paul Parish in Independence attended this Catholic school. From the perspective of one of the local Catholic priests: "On account of distances many children are obliged to attend the nearby public schools." Less comfortable with the public schools than the Norwegian Lutherans, the Polish Americans more successfully maintained their private Catholic elementary schools. As the minority confronting a Norwegian and Protestant majority in the county, Polish immigrants commanded less control of the local public schools. As Catholics, they found public school education, controlled by Protestants, less palatable than did the Norwegians. The village of Independence in Burnside Township remained the center of the religious and educational institutions of the Polish in Lincoln.[65]

By the end of the frontier years each ethnic group had its own religious institutions, including in some instances schools. Both the Norwegian Lutherans and the Polish Catholics established their own private schools, but that of the former was short-lived, whereas the private Catholic school of the St. Peter and St. Paul Parish has persisted in Independence into the present. The immigrant churches remained strong in the postfrontier years, keeping within the fold almost all community members. Even in the third stage of the community's history, after 1945, local loyalty to the established churches remained strong. In Pigeon, for example, in 1964 local residents listed on the plat maps with few exceptions were members of one of the Pigeon congregations. The few exceptions typically possessed Polish names. Thus, through most of Pigeon's history, church membership closely corresponded to those who lived in the area. A recent pastor of Pigeon, however, has commented that this correspondence has declined somewhat in recent years.[66]

The churches of the old-stock Americans in the nineteenth century were not as strong as those of the immigrants. In 1881 the *Whitehall Times* editor commented on the concluding exercises of the parochial school of the Methodist Episcopal Church, which featured readings, recitations, and vocal and instrumental music. "Nearly all of the young ladies" participated, yet "we regret to say but few of the boys."[67] The nineteenth century had brought, in Ann Douglas's words, the "feminization of American culture," particularly in regard to religion. While men may well have been involved in the frontier revivals, it seems that by 1881 old-stock American men and boys in Whitehall were not exceptions to the pattern of leaving religion to the women.[68]

A similar pattern did not soon surface among the Norwegian Lutherans. The local Lutheran churches have been notably successful in maintaining the loyalty and participation of entire families, not only the women. Although the Norwegian American churches did broaden the role of women, leadership in church—ministers, deacons, trustees, and officers—remained exclusively in the hands of men until well after World War II. Rather than gender differentiation, generational differences in loyalty to the church were a primary concern to Norwegian American Lutherans.

The young who left the rural communities were more prone to abandon the church, and most of the young did leave.[69]

Many, of course, did remain as the statistics on persistence indicate, often following the occupations of their parents, providing stability and continuity over the years. One second-generation Norwegian American who did so was Emmanuel Christophersen's son. Einar B. Christophersen followed his father in 1910, after Emmanuel's death, as the pastor of the upper church in Pigeon and of the other churches in his father's district, and he remained in that position until his death in 1963. Having grown up in Pigeon and attended the local schools until he went to Luther College at the age of 15, the social distance between Einar B. Christophersen and his parishioners was perhaps less than it had been for his father. He became an active community leader, furthering the economic and political goals of the farmers in the cooperative movement, the Farmers Union, and the Progressive and Democratic political parties. Seemingly Norway's peasants better preserved their politics and their culture on the American frontier than did the elites.[70]

The most lasting impact of the Norwegian elite's leadership can be found in the communities' strong musical traditions which developed in the churches and schools. In Whitehall, where the high-church tradition dominated, residents today still pride themselves on long and strong musical traditions.[71] In the 1880s there were men's choirs in both Whitehall and Pigeon Falls and numerous orchestras and bands; every week brought secular and religious occasions which included performances of the works of Norwegian composers and in some instances folk music. Year after year performers from St. Olaf College, Luther College, and even from Norway made their appearances in the community. The denominational colleges attended by men like Einar B. Christophersen were particularly important in nurturing the musical traditions of the high church. Musical talent has been a source of prestige in the area.[72]

Churches drew strength from the fact that ethnic identity was closely tied to religion among immigrants, and eventually the class hostilities brought from Norway and expressed in the doctrinal battles faded in importance. The result was a distinct weaving of traditions of both the Norwegian peasant culture and the Norwegian elites in the American environment, a process which posed pressures and opportunities of its own. The church was the central place in which the social and cultural tensions were distilled into the distinct patterns of the community.

The churches and the diverse affiliated organizations, although not as active and as important to community members' lives today as they once were, continue to be among the strongest institutions which maintain the sense of community identity that remains in the rural neighborhoods. A majority of the families in the Pigeon churches in 1964 were the progeny of those nineteenth-century immigrants who first created the congregations. In 1985 the two Lutheran churches of tiny Pigeon Falls stood about two blocks apart. The strength of historical and community identity tied to the two Lutheran churches is partly revealed in the fact that they remain separate congregations. The upper and lower churches divided in 1885 over theological issues. Since 1917 the two synods with which the churches were allied have been merged into a single synod, and today the upper and lower churches share a common minister. Despite years of pressure from their successive ministers and the synod, these two churches maintain separate institutional identities. Though the doctrinal and social issues that troubled their ancestors have long been forgotten, the members' of the two congregations refuse to merge into one church because they continue to feel differentiated within the community and loyal to the institutions assembled by their predecessors. In 1917 Einar Christophersen, the pastor of the two churches in Pigeon, expressed the opinion that although "locally the two congregations continue as two separate organizations . . . the future will undoubtedly see them united in one congregation." The present minister continues to hope for that unification.[73]

The explanation for this continued inefficient arrangement can be found in the historical role that the churches played in this highly stable community and in the churches' role as "sacred places" for many people who continue to live in the community. Since frontier times the churches have been a primary agency defining a group's identity and the status of the family and individual in that group. Many who did not involve themselves in local politics often were active church members. They worked initially in harmony with the family to re-create and maintain their vision of the traditional culture and language of Norway. Not until the 1930s did they cease to teach the young of the congregation about the language and culture of Norway. Not until that decade did they cease to keep the churches' records in the Norwegian language. In the 1940s sermons still were often if not always given in Norwegian. The upper church's building is the same one that was first constructed in 1876 and is associated not only with individual lifetime memories but also with the generations that preceded them. From the beginning the churches included entire families as they do today.[74]

The churches were the context in which these families and communities honored the important turning points in the life cycle of an individual and of a family. Since frontier times rituals and rites of passage affirmed the solidarity of kin and community networks. Involved were the ceremonies of birth (baptism), adolescence (confirmation), the creation of new families (weddings), and death (funerals). Each of these ritualized rites of passage involved and affirmed the community and kin networks of each individual and family. The religious ceremonies were always followed by visits to the families by much of the community and nearby and distant kin, frequently including hundreds of people. Not only did these rituals acknowledge the significant events in life but they were also an important component in the organization of social life for the community. These occasions regularly brought together neighbors and former residents of the community. All members of a family's neighborhood and extended kin network within commutable range were expected to be present. Not to be invited or not to appear without very justifiable excuses could cause comment, hurt feelings, and a sense of insult. Such actions could violate an individual's or a family's perception of the boundaries of community.[75]

The rituals of the church defined for each family and individual the community of which they were a part. Few were born in the area who did not participate in these community and family rituals: baptism, church weddings, golden wedding anniversary celebrations (these became semireligious events usually held in the church), and burial in the church cemetery. Confirmation, which occurred at the age of 14 or 15, signaled the beginning of adulthood and full church membership. It also marked a new freedom from the discipline of the family and the beginning of youthful independence. In the nineteenth and early twentieth centuries in this country as in Norway, before high school became a common experience for the rural young, confirmation was often followed by a departure from the family hearth for work or education. Since the 1940s high school graduation ceremonies have taken the leading position as the ritual recognizing the transition from adolescence to autonomy.[76]

This shift in the relative importance of the sacred rituals of the church and the secular rituals of the education system is paralleled by a striking change in the social life of the young in the community. When asked about their courtships and social life, those who grew up before World War II invariably mention Young People's Luther Leagues. By 1900 all the Lutheran churches in Lincoln and Pigeon had young people's organizations, and in 1897 the Young People's League built a hall of their own for their activities, which remained an important social center until 1949. Newspapers, letters, diaries, and interviews indicate the centrality of these church organizations in structuring the social activities of the young. "Don't get the idea that we were so religious," explained one woman who grew up in Pigeon. "It was the games that were so much fun, especially the Norwegian ones." The "games" which followed the obligatory religious program apparently were often accompanied by singing and in some instances what would be called folk dances today. The Norwegian peasant games and the dances of the immigrants continued to be an important source of entertainment and recreation until the organized activities of the high schools replaced the Young People's Luther Leagues as the important focus of the social life of the young.[77]

Another semireligious occasion often noted in the *Whitehall Times* after 1900 was the golden wedding anniversary, honoring 50 years of marriage. Not exactly a rite of passage, it celebrated and honored a couple's life, particularly its family life, as it approached the end of a cycle in its history. These occasions invariably included a formal program at the church, with music, speakers, prayer, and perhaps some form of entertainment, followed by a meal; then in the home of the couple there was a gathering of those closest to them in the neighborhood and family. Like weddings, they could be huge inclusive events of hundreds. Hans Anderson, who became one of the most frequently called upon and popular public speakers, wrote numerous celebratory speeches for such occasions. He invariably made it an opportunity to pay tribute to the challenges and achievements of a lifetime and to recall the historical context in which they occurred, the history of not only a family but also a community. These too were ritualized events affirming the history and solidarity of the family and community.[78]

By 1900, among both the migrant Americans and the immigrants, the intense pietism of the frontier churches had receded in importance. The institutional creativity of the years of settlement spawned the institutions and associations which permanently structured community life. The common pietistic orientation of both Norwegian Americans and old-stock Americans shaped their politics and the ways in which they adapted to the frontier environment. During the postfrontier years, the churches were primary sources of stability and continuity in the life of the family and community, binding people together in a continual cycle of ritual and sociability. Every year brought numerous baptisms, confirmations, marriages, funerals, and social events, in which the community and families celebrated life and grieved its passing. All brought together family and community—affirming again and again their solidarity over the years. The depression decade saw a clear decline in the emphasis on the Norwegian identity of local Lutheran churches: sermons increasingly were in English, the teaching of reading and writing in Norwegian in the summer schools ceased, and the church hierarchy shifted to an emphasis on a doctrinal rather than an ethnic identity. While in recent years the churches faced challenges to their preeminent position as a community institution, their fundamental role in defining community remains.

6
Work: The Ethic and the Reality

The story of Mrs. Steig's life is the story with variations, of course, of hundreds of pioneer immigrant women. . . . There was always work, hard work, and there was always a determination that things should be better. It was to the future, the future of their children and their children's children that these pioneers looked. It was so then just as it is today. They sought a way of life—the way of life that we struggle today to preserve.

Hans Anderson, "Mrs. Gilbert Steig"

By 1916, when Hans Anderson dedicated the Elk Creek Lutheran Church, it represented "a vision of hopes realized, of dreams come true."[1] From Anderson's point of view and that of many of his contemporaries, their families and communities had reached a high level of cultural and economic achievement. The harsh trials of the frontier were far behind and the farms and villages were flourishing. In 1912, in an address before the Trempealeau County Historical Society, a local minister, Charles Freeman, commented on the foundations of the "wealth and culture of what is perhaps the most beautiful and prosperous county in the United States. . . . We have churches, schools, steamheated houses, big red barns and neither millionaires nor paupers. . . ."[2] Between 1890 and 1920, residents replaced their first log cabins with comfortable and spacious farm houses that continue today to house their progeny. They constructed the barns and creameries that served as the local agricultural infrastructure of the communities for a half century and longer.[3] And in the villages, little additional construction occurred on main street until the post–World War II years. By 1912 many, including Anderson, would have agreed with J. D. Olds's assessment that their communities had achieved a "position of wealth and comfort." The communities of Trempealeau that Olds helped to build, in his view, stood at the forefront of civilization. The pioneers' hard work produced ". . . school houses, churches, villages, hotels, stores, grist mills, saw mills and all kinds of public improvements . . . thus changing a land that was once the home of the Indian and wild beasts of the forest to land that now stands on the highest pinnacle of American civilization."[4] Ironically by 1910 when the leaders of the Country Life movement began to despair of the conditions of rural America, the residents of Lincoln and

Pigeon expressed extraordinary pride and complacency in their communities and way of life.[5]

Thirty years later, however, the transformations in the economy and a decade of depression had created a sense of discomfort which an aging Anderson articulated in his obituary of Mrs. Gilbert Steig in 1940, when he stated that the pioneers had "sought a way of life—the way of life that we struggle today to preserve." The vision and the dream as well as the reality appeared fragile. The better way of life that the immigrants had worked so hard to create appeared to be threatened. In fact, Anderson was prescient; his death in 1942 coincided with the beginning of the third stage in the communities' history. This last period changed many aspects of the culture and way of life with which his generation had been so pleased. Thirty years after Anderson expressed his concern for preserving what the work of the immigrants had created, many dimensions of that way of life had been transformed or disappeared.

Anderson had little doubt about what had made this vision of a better way of life a reality. It was the years of hard work and the community spirit of the people who came. Whatever source the historian examines concerning the history of Lincoln and Pigeon or even of the Norwegian immigrants more generally, one finds few things valued more than hard work and the hard worker. Productive work, in the minds of these people, was tied to the virtues of family and community responsibility and integrity in social relationships. After 1945 the organization of work in the community and in the household was transformed in fundamental ways, altering attitudes toward work and family and community life, and perhaps changing individual character itself.

In the organization of community and household economies and in attitudes toward work, the immigrant Norwegian and the Yankee farmer had much in common. During the frontier years the near-subsistence household economy was the primary economic organization. It depended upon the cooperative work of all members of the family. In addition, the diaries of New England migrant Dave Wood reveal an almost daily cooperation and exchange with neighbors and kin involving everything from rye seed to rutabagas.[6] Most Norwegian immigrants, like Hans Anderson, who arrived in Pigeon in 1867, had grown up in largely self-sufficient peasant communities, as owners, laborers, or crofters on the small, semicommunally organized, subsistence-oriented farms. They were similarly well prepared for the demands of the frontier subsistence economy by their cooperative traditions and skills. As Hans Anderson described it, "Life in Norway on the west coast at the time was a constant struggle for mere support." There were few indeed who "escaped the necessity of work in this struggle." Adults, "even old people whose support was provided for at a partial consideration, here had to labor as long as they were able . . . nor were children old enough to work, left much time to play." As in Norway, immigrant farm families on the frontier continued to depend on the work of the entire family to provide most of their needs. Children and women carried the same responsibilities for household production as they had in Norway.[7]

The capacity for hard steady work was not only highly valued but also a necessity for survival in the subsistence peasant communities from which the immigrants came and perhaps even more so on the American frontier. As Hans Anderson suggested, the goal of the years of backbreaking effort and hardship was a better way of life for the pioneers and their children. In the hundreds of speeches, histories, and obituaries which Anderson wrote, he assessed the success and failure of his neighbors in creating that better way of life. Whether he wrote of men or women, invariably the first item on his agenda in his descriptions was their capacity and commitment to and the quality of their work. When writing about the old or deceased he often recounted their youthful strength, energy, and beauty. Physical strength and productive labor were both held in high regard, even if strenuous effort was not well repaid. Material rewards interested Anderson less than the way the life was lived, the effort that was made.

Generally Anderson reserved his greatest admiration for the men and women of Pigeon and Lincoln who tilled the soil undaunted by the hardships that it imposed. He expressed contempt for anyone who shied away from the rigorous labor that his generation had faced in their struggles to make a place for themselves. Although Anderson did not always echo his neighbors' opinions, in his high regard for the strong, enduring hard worker, he no doubt expressed a widely shared attitude. Perhaps no one had a better claim than Hans Anderson to be the spokesman of the values and morality of Lincoln and Pigeon. From the time he was a young man and a struggling school teacher in the 1870s until he was an old, retired county judge, he was called upon to speak at every sort of religious and secular occasion from funerals to Fourth of July celebrations.

This high regard for strength and hard work preceded the demands of frontier farming and remained preeminent in the mentalité of rural folk. Anderson's accounts of the history of his family in Norway and of the folklore of that country illustrate this. Of his mother's kin in Norway, he wrote, "For toughness and endurance, few if any people, excelled them." In the oral traditions of Anderson's family, most carefully preserved were accounts of strong and able men and women, what they endured, and their distinct feats of strength. Whether the context was the "rough and tumble fights" which frequently occurred at "one of those old-fashioned weddings, which lasted from three days to a week, where strong ale and stronger brandy were always freely dispensed," or the fishing boats at sea, the admiration of the Anderson family for strength and endurance was deep.[8] Such attitudes should not be surprising in a family that for centuries had been peasants in the mountains of Norway. Hard work, strength, endurance, and persistence were qualities necessary to the peasant— perhaps the most important requirements for survival.

But though peasants may have long been aware of the necessity of hard work and the value of strength, developments in the nineteenth century were changing both the conditions of work and the thinking about it. One tale recounted by Anderson about his great uncle Storviken indicates some of the conflicting attitudes. The tales about Storviken indicate that in some instances individuals of great physical strength and endurance could violate the entire configuration of values associated with the "Protestant work ethic" and still become something of folk heroes.

According to the story, Storviken spent most of his life like other peasants, working hard and achieving some success as a respectable farmer-fisherman. However, at the age of 50, after the death of his first wife in childbirth, Storviken married a young and beautiful woman "with an all together pleasing and attractive personality." But this young beauty became Storviken's undoing. Insanely suspicious and jealous of her, Storviken "took to solitary drinking and rambling." Soon he lost his business, farm, and family and became a "nationwide tramp" who "gained fame by wonderful feats of strength. . . . He gained a mythic and poetic fame" and became "a secondary hero in Norwegian novels."

Storviken reverted to the "beliefs and expression of his ancient forefathers" about "natural phenomena and fairy folks." Invariably Storviken's great feats of strength originated in his pursuit of alcohol at wedding feasts or from merchants, although sometimes, as with any good folk hero, he acted in the interest of the weak or exploited. Storviken's stature as a folk hero exposed a nostalgia for the superstitious, rowdy, hard-drinking, and profligate ways that were under seige in the nineteenth century. Demographic pressure, economic change, and religious revivals brought calls for temperance, hard work, self-discipline, and social improvement. Storviken defied the pietistic ideals with impunity. "Certain it is," wrote Anderson, that "while many kings who have ruled over Norway are unknown to most of the Norwegian peasantry, Storviken is known to most of them. . . . And the strange part of it is . . . [he] never performed anything great or very useful." Protestant pietism increasingly bound the peasant's strength and hard effort to performing "useful" tasks such as building farms in a wilderness, rather than to Storviken's indulgence in passion, drinking, dancing, and the self-display of purposeless competition and feats of strength.[9]

The attitude toward work that Anderson articulated goes well beyond the traditional peasant acceptance of the reality of "a man's got to work" and admiration of physical prowess. Work defined life's purpose, measured character, and was the essence of one's identity. Of the life of one Pigeon woman, Helen Christianson, Anderson wrote:

> The life of Mrs. Chirstianson was as uneventful as are the lives of the average toilers who find their places in the world's workshop and stick to their tasks. . . . System and order became a part of her life within and around her home. . . . She and her husband had hoped, planned and worked to gain that independence from debts and poverty which every true man and woman ought to aspire to.[10]

Or of another friend, Anderson commented, "He set to work in his steady constant way and the years brought constant gain in the building of a home. . . . He slowly pushed his way to financial independence."[11] In terms of the high regard in which work was held, the Norwegian immigrants perhaps took their biggest step toward modernity. The goal of systematic work, however, remained the traditional one of becoming independent on one's own land, which could be passed on to another generation.

Molding Anderson's and his neighbors' attitudes were the religious revivals of Norway, which did much to shape the politics of the peasants there as well as the church schism among Norwegian immigrants in the United States. Since the early nineteenth century, Norwegian peasants had been influenced by the pietistic religious revivals, which ascribed to work the sacred status of a calling—a means of worshiping God—and demanded of them a new daily discipline. The sanctification of work by an emphasis on calling originated with Martin Luther in Germany in the sixteenth century, was subsequently elaborated rigorously by John Calvin in Geneva, but did not achieve its greatest impact on Norwegian peasants until the religious revivals of the nineteenth century. The revivals of Hans Nielson Hauge and other pietists in Norway laid the basis for a Protestant asceticism among many peasants which resembled that of New England's saints of the seventeenth century. The consequences of Norwegian pietism, according to one scholar of this movement, Christen Jonassen, paralleled that of the earlier impact of Calvinism elsewhere as Max Weber has analyzed it. The result was "the creation of a worldly asceticism whose task was to free the individual from irrational impulses, to destroy spontaneous and impulsive enjoyment, and bring systematic and rigorous order in individuals' lives."[12]

Unlike the New England Puritans, the Norwegian revivalists did not call for hard work and at the same time expect people to be content in their station. As the Puritans would discover, their hard work and diligence often changed their station and thus created a contradictory situation. On the contrary, the Protestant ethic of thrift, hard work, and diligence was urged on peasants as a means of taking advantage of economic opportunities in an increasingly commercialized agriculture and as a peasant weapon in class struggle. Hans Nielson Hauge, the first and most influential revival leader in Norway and himself born a peasant, urged peasants to create businesses and cooperatives for the purpose of improving their economic and social position as a class. From the beginning of the peasant political movement, which began in the religious revivals, class hostility and the determination not to be exploited by the educated bureaucratic and merchant elite motivated Hauge and his followers. Hauge was himself a diligent businessman. Thus the rewards for hard work, diligence, and thrift offered not only the promise of salvation but improvement in this world as well. It remained to the high, or traditional, church leadership to worry about the consequences of the ambitions of the peasantry on the social order.[13]

No doubt, these religious ideals of Hauge added to the attraction and acceptability of emigration that would drain away a third of Norway's population. As has frequently been documented, the most powerful motivation behind the migration of the nineteenth century was economic—the reality of worsening conditions at home and the expectation of better opportunities elsewhere, especially in the United States—but no doubt the social ideals of the low-church, or pietistic, leaders, who urged the peasants toward self- and social improvement, reduced the resistance to emigration. Einar Haugen concluded that Norwegian peasants had "learned to be dissatisfied," though in reality their conditions were better than those of many Europeans.[14]

Nonetheless, at the time when revivalists encouraged hopes of improvement in social and economic status, the circumstances of many were declining in Norway. The population expansion in the nineteenth century had resulted in subdivision of the peasant farms to sizes as small as two or three acres and in a rapidly growing class of landless crofters, or life tenants, and day laborers. Agriculture became more intensive, but remained unmechanized, requiring considerable labor. But despite greater efforts to make the land more productive, downward mobility was the reality of a large number of peasants, who descended from freeholder in one generation to landless crofter (tenant) or laborer in the next. Between 1800 and 1850 the number of freehold peasants increased by 50 percent as families divided their land into smaller parcels and previously uncultivated land was claimed. Despite these efforts, the number of rural landless people doubled.[15] Over and over, Hans Anderson and other Norwegian immigrants and their children emphasized the economic opportunities in America and the lack of them in Norway as the reason for emigration.

While the hard work of the peasant in Norway produced declining returns, this was not true on the American frontier. In this new environment the immigrant often claimed that the physical demands were even greater than they had been in the old country. But from the perspective of the land-hungry peasant who measured success in traditional terms of numbers of acres, animals, and buildings, so too were the rewards. The motivation for pressing oneself harder was great in the United States, and Protestant asceticism served the immigrant well. On the American frontier even the smallest farms of 40 acres were larger than the biggest farms in Norway. The landless crofters who left Norway could with effort often acquire farms, and most were far larger than 40 acres. Even if they spent "twenty winters in the woods" or several years working on the farms of others to achieve the status of landowner, by the standards of immigrant peasants, the work and perseverance paid well. So the motivation to work hard intensified. Success in achieving the traditional goal of landownership was a powerful ambition among the immigrants and their children.[16] The pietistic emphasis on sobriety, hard work, and thrift not only taught Norwegians to use their current hard conditions as a training ground for character, but also motivated them to hope for a better life in the future.[17]

What these immigrant pioneers apparently valued most highly in themselves and others was what Thorstein Veblen, the son of a Norwegian immigrant, would describe as the "instinct of workmanship," the natural human desire to work hard and do one's work carefully and well. In writing about one of the Norwegian immigrants who through years of rigorous effort had become a skilled locksmith in Norway, Anderson explained: "No handicraft or trade in those days was insignificant. To attain perfection was the goal in every calling, and the reward hoped for was an ever widening reputation for excellent workmanship." On the creations of such craftsmen, Anderson noted, "All were made to last, not for a season or two but for generations."[18]

This perspective on work led to critical judgments of the ways of old-stock Americans. In describing one of the Yankees for whom he had worked in his youth, Hans Anderson noted, "He had too much of the American habit of 'slicking' things over and letting it go at that."[19] Similarly, one 93-year-old woman, a daughter of a prosperous immigrant farmer, commented, "Oh those Yankees, they never amounted to anything. They never liked to work."[20] However accurate or inaccurate these perceptions may have been (the work ethic appeared equally alive and well among the Woods, who were Yankees), these ideals of work provided a basis by which the Norwegians distinguished themselves as a group. In the quality of their workmanship and in their willingness to work, the Norwegian immigrants supposed themselves distinct from typical Americans. In many ways, they assessed their neighbors and themselves with the same values and standards that Thorstein Veblen applied to American society more generally.

But while the emphasis was on hard work for independence and social improvement, neither the pietist leaders nor a secularized Anderson sanctioned an overly individualistic ethic. As discussed earlier, those who did achieve a relative degree of wealth in the community legitimized it in the eyes of community members only by social services. Social approbrium fell on those whose individual ambitions clearly were at the expense of others. Anderson wrote critically of a pair of Pigeon pioneers, Cisten Kolbeinson and his son, who maintained the doctrine "we have to help ourselves to the utmost though our efforts may infringe on the effort and right of others." The son was a "thorough believer in his father's doctrine that only fools wait to let the other fellow get the first inning." The son, Andreas, was:

> a hustler and hard worker, who in company with others did not hesitate to take the lighter end of the work when possible. . . . Both father and son possessed the characteristic of frankness that concealed the natural avarice of their nature. . . . Their measure of men was always financial success.

If not "immoral," Anderson wrote, such individuals are "deficient in appreciation of the ethical worth of man."[21]

Anderson expressed a common criticism made of old-stock Americans by the Norwegian leadership. They perceived among Americans a crude materialism they feared would affect the immigrants. Rolvaag's novel *Pure Gold* illustrated the potentially all-consuming corruption that could result when financial gain became the only goal in life. Pursuit of the dollar had the potential to squeeze out every aspect of life that provided meaning, destroying commitments to family, community, and culture. It destroyed first the soul and ultimately life itself.[22] Anderson echoed such a judgment in a speech at Gale College in the 1920s on the theme that "only labor conquers." The wealth available in America represented a potential snare: "Opportunity begets desire, and as no other people ever had such legitimate opportunities to acquire wealth, it is but natural that our desires keep pace with our chances for acquisition." But there was a problem: "Wealth as an ideal or final object of life, like the desert mirage, draws its pursuer ever and ever onward with an increasing thirst, never to be satisfied."[23]

Hard work for financial success alone and not bound to a larger human community was not respected. "True riches," Anderson insisted, "are the abilities we acquire and the characters that we build." If an undue and selfish ambition for wealth was distrusted, even worse was the man or woman who did not do their share:

> The idle drifting man is a greater menace to the peace, prosperity and happiness of the world than the positive scoundrel. He palsies industry, impedes progress, discourages economy, and consumes the results of honest labor. He supports no schools, builds no churches, endows no charities, contributes nothing to the state, has no hope, no faith, no home and dies without a country.[24]

High valuation of work, the connection between work and character, and the emphasis on responsibility to community expressed by Anderson reveal an affinity between Norwegian-American's attitudes and those of nineteenth-century Americans. Nonetheless, this is not simply an indication of assimilation. The Norwegian pietistic and peasant origins of Anderson's views cannot be overlooked. This is also true in regard to the actual organization of work in Pigeon and Lincoln in the frontier years and after.

In Norway, the peasants long practiced traditions of communal work. Someone who "took the lighter end of the work" would have been conspicuous and little appreciated. At the same time, communal ownership and communal work had long discouraged excessively individualistic ambitions and effort. The industrial revolution and the mechanization of agriculture came late to Norway, profoundly changing traditional peasant society only in the second half of the nineteenth century and then only after large-scale intervention by the government in a series of increasingly restrictive enclosure acts. Lands which had once been held in common and rotated among families were divided into separate family farms. Initial legislation had encouraged peasants to do this voluntarily, but finally legislation mandated the shift in ownership. The state's goal was a more commercially oriented and productive agriculture. Norway, unlike other European countries, had never developed a feudal system; a landowning peasantry had managed the agriculture of the country. Thus, nineteenth-century Norway lacked a landed nobility, which in other countries initiated the enclosure movement in the interest of a more commercialized agriculture. The elite in Norway was a bureaucratic and commercial one, based on education, office, and wealth rather than a titled nobility of feudal origins. Norwegian peasants, long in control of the land, were reluctant to change the communal structures that had shaped their lives. A Norwegian scholar has described the nineteenth-century peasant community as tied "together by social intercourse and voluntary communal work with a high degree of co-operation."[25] The subsistence-oriented peasant communities were characterized by a "communitarian fellowship . . . based on strongly egalitarian norms. . . ." The term *dug-nag* was applied to this institution and to principles of work organized communally by the peasants unmediated by money.[26]

In many respects the immigrants transported their custom of collective help—*dugnag*—with them to the frontier and in subsequent years adapted its principles to the changing economic circumstances. Although the immigrant farmers no longer held land in common, they did continue to exhibit the cooperative sense of responsibility and the custom of collective work and reciprocal obligations. In doing so, the Norwegian immigrants' behavior on the frontier differed little from that of their Yankee counterparts. Neighbors and families not only built and maintained their churches and schools together but also joined in putting up their homes and barns, transporting their products to market, and harvesting their wheat. They borrowed each other's equipment, animals, and children, and bartered with each other to provide for a wide variety of needs.

Helping out neighbors in times of need or distress due to ilness or disaster was not simply frontier generosity created out of the exigencies of the circumstances, as Curti concluded.[27] Such mutual helpfulness was a long-established tradition by which peasant communities had insured their survival in the face of precarious circumstances. Peasants from subsistence-oriented communities in Norway brought to the frontier not only the physical skills but also the social traditions necessary to survive and ultimately to thrive. It is of little surprise that Hans Anderson and his neighbors would look skeptically upon those who "did not hesitate to take the lighter end of the work."[28]

In Trempealeau County, farmers cooperated in a wide range of activities. Dave Wood's diaries indicate that the Yankee farmers often organized their work in cooperation with their kin and neighbors. Wood regularly mentions "trading work" with several individuals primarily in his kin network, and his son Ralph seems to have relied as much on neighbors as he did kin. In addition, tools, equipment, animals, and almost any item related to farm production were shared between Dave and his father, sons, brothers-in-law, and cousins. Success or failure on the frontier and in farming may well have depended upon the availability of these kin and community networks.[29]

When money was scarce, which it was much of the time during the early years, even it was treated as a community resource. One early immigrant described a situation that occurred in January of 1869. His family was utterly without either cash or flour for the next day's food. The one merchant known to have any flour available refused to extend credit. Through word of mouth the hapless man was told that Deacon Alvah Wood might have some cash; indeed he did, and the loan was given. Dave

Wood's diaries reveal how the farmers got on before banks were organized locally and when little cash was available. Whoever had cash at any time became a resource, a source of credit. Wood made hundreds of small loans to numerous people and similarly borrowed at little or no interest from others when the occasion required. Sometimes repayment was made in cash; many times it was not. For the individual facing hard times, small debts such as these neighbors owed each other could be long delayed in repayment or dismissed.[30] Jim Wood, while a young man in the business of pressing hay, crossed out bills on occasion with the explanation that the "hard times" of the men in question were the reason for canceling them. No doubt large debts were handled differently.[31]

As Pigeon and Lincoln moved beyond the frontier stage in their history, the cooperative strategies continued. In the postfrontier years, as the big barns were completed, the land cleared, and some of the tasks of farming mechanized, occasions of collective work efforts declined. In addition, as the farmers became more dependent on the market economy, they developed more formal institutional strategies to render their circumstances more secure. These took the form of local cooperatives. Despite

Harvesting on Dave Wood's Farm, ca. ?1890–1910. Photo courtesy of Dave Wood, Minneapolis.

An early threshing crew, ca. 1890–1910. Photo by Charles Van Schaick. Van Schaick Collection. Photo courtesy of State Historical Society of Wisconsin, WHi (X3) 25782.

such changes, the principles and practice of *dugnag* did not entirely disappear. Even after World War II, something of the older traditions persisted. While many farmers often had either children or one or two hired men to assist them, any work that required a large crew invariably was organized by neighborhoods. Every year between 1880 and at least 1950, there were many occasions that required crews of eight or more men. As in Norway much of the labor was arranged by "exchange work" unmediated by money.[32]

Threshing was perhaps the biggest and, in retrospect to many involved, the most memorable of the tasks undertaken by these neighborhood crews. Perhaps at no time of the year did the entire community work harder than during the threshing season. Of the many things that have recently been left behind, nothing is remembered with greater nostalgia. The process in many respects remained the same from 1880 until combines became common in the 1960s. Reapers cut and tied bundles of grain, which were then stacked by hand in shocks. This first stage of the harvesting process itself required the work of several people but was usually handled by the farmer, his family, and sometimes hired help. It was the threshing that required neighborhood crews of 10–20 men. Threshing required stacking the bundles on wagons and hauling the loads to the location of the threshing machine, where they had to be unloaded again into the thresher. After the threshing machine separated the grain from the straw, the grain had to be transported to a grainery and the straw properly stacked so that it would resist water. Men arrived early in the morning accompanied by teams, wagons, children who could work, and hired men. Children as young as 9 and 10 years of age could assist with the horses. In the 1950s, when tractors became more common, children often drove those. Men, women, and children worked from dawn until dusk in the hot August sun to complete the process.[33]

The tradition of *dugnag* was carried into domestic work as well. Women too depended upon traditions of collective work, and threshing was one of the many occasions when women joined together to meet the demands of farm production. The harvest often brought extra people to the farm homes to assist. Inside the houses women worked as hard as the men in the fields, cooking on the wood stoves the noon dinner and evening supper as well as preparing the lunches of sandwiches, cookies, cake, and coffee that were expected in the fields at midmorning and midafternoon. To prepare the hearty meals of meat, vegetables, and potatoes, and to bake the breads, pies, cakes, and cookies which were the traditional cuisine of the community were no small tasks. A crew was often needed to handle the preparation and cleanup of meals for from 20 to 40 people. Threshing lasted from two weeks to a month, and the crews were on any one place one to four days, depending on the size of the farm, the weather, and the equipment. Sisters, daughters, mothers, and other female kin and friends joined in helping when the crews came. Sometimes relatives and friends no longer living in the community came to help and to enjoy the sociability associated with threshing.

When tractors replaced horses, the combine soon followed, and that machine brought an end to the annual events of the threshing season. However, not until the decade of the 1960s did combines become common on Lincoln and Pigeon farms. From 1880 until the decade of the 1950s, the neighborhoods threshed their grains together each summer. Day after day these neighbors worked side by side, ate their meals together, and often ended the long effort with a celebration of drink and dance. Members of 10–12 families worked together and depended upon each other for several weeks every year to complete this crucial stage of the annual harvest. Today it is remembered as a time of hard work, camaraderie, and good fun.

Threshing and the harvest season were not the only occasion that brought together neighbors to complete a common task. Ironically, the new technology and mechanization in the first half of the twentieth century actually promoted the extension of *dugnag* and cooperative traditions. Like the threshing machine, other technological innovations brought neighbors together as crews. After 1910, when silos became a common sight on the farms, October and November brought silo-filling crews to the farms, similarly organized by "exchange work."

Also, during the winter months farmers worked together as crews in the woods that remained on their steep hillsides.[34] Wood cutting for Wisconsin's long winters demanded hours of labor, particularly after the farmers replaced their log cabins with sizable farm houses. For cooking and for heat, most depended for fuel upon wood, which they cut and stacked during the winter months. In 1940 over 94 percent of the farm homes and 67 percent of the nonfarm homes in Trempealeau County used wood as the primary fuel for cooking.[35] J. D. Olds and Dave Wood may have worked alone with axes during the frontier years to supply wood for cooking and heating, but Wood's son Jim became one of the enterprising owners of a power saw.[36] Such "saw rigs" were rented, and a neighborhood crew was organized to do the work.

Butchering animals on the farms was another occasion during which neighbors or kin worked together. The winter months also brought crews of men together to work on the lakes and ponds, cutting the ice that would be used the next summer in the household and dairy. In the 1930s Pigeon

Silo filling, 1895. This was one of the many tasks requiring community cooperation as new technologies were introduced. Photo by Harvey J. Perkins. W.A. Henry Collection. Courtesy of State Historical Society of Wisconsin, WHi (H43) 120.

farmers organized a cooperative for the purpose of providing ice for their farms and creamery.[37]

In the frontier and postfrontier phases of the communities' history, mechanization on the farm did not alter the patterns of collective work. In some instances when technological innovations did appear, the new equipment was cooperatively owned or rented by groups of farmers, as was the case with threshing machines and silo-filling equipment. Farmers who purchased "saw rigs," threshing machines, or hay presses supplemented their own income by going from farm to farm with the equipment, or they traded the use of equipment for labor, produce, animals, or other goods.[38] This spread around the costs and benefits of expensive equipment. The 1895 Wisconsin State Census of Agriculture reveals how scarce some of the basic implements of farming were.

But the agricultural censuses are not necessarily an accurate guide concerning the degree to which farmers were reaping the benefits of mechanization. The enterprising Woods experimented over the years with a variety of farm implements including saws, hay presses, and threshing machines. The census may indicate that a majority did not own various equipment, but this did not necessarily mean that those without particular kinds of equipment did not have access to them. (See Table 6.1.) Wood and his relatives and neighbors regularly borrowed equipment from each other.

Table 6.1. Numerical Distribution of Various Farm Implements, by Township, 1895

	Pigeon (N = 192)	Lincoln (N = 139)
Mowers	114	72
Hay loaders	2	1
Hay rakes	85	68
Self binders	79	59
Threshing machines	3	2
Wagons	194	152
Carriages	42	77
Plows	176	155
Drills	97	73
Corn planters	0	5
Corn cultivators	95	100

Source: Wisconsin Department of State, *Tabular Statements of the Census Enumeration and the Agricultural, Minerals and Manufacturing Interests of Wisconsin* (Madison: State Printer, 1895) pp. 674–677.

N represents the total number of farms.

Large pieces of equipment such as the saw rigs and threshing machines were rented out. Here the entrepreneurial spirit and communal traditions comfortably coexisted to meet the needs of many. The tradition of *dugnag* continued not only in the form of cooperative work but also in the sharing of capital goods. The farmers who purchased equipment by borrowing money could help pay the loan installments by renting out the equipment when they themselves were not using it.

The cooperative work and interdependence of farmers in these seasons no doubt were a force for solidarity and harmony in the community. Alienating one's neighbors would have been expensive to the farmer who could not afford to hire a crew or buy the equipment to provide alternative help; very few would have ever been in a position to do so in these communities. Arlene Arneson, who attended high school in the 1930s, recalled having to accept an undesirable date with a neighbor boy because her father feared a refusal would mean he would not get help from the young man's family for silo-filling. Potential hostilities remained carefully repressed in light of the mutual dependence of these neighbors.[39]

Mechanization and technological innovations related to farming proceeded through stages. Initially, cooperative traditions facilitated the introduction of new machinery and seemingly added to community interdependence and solidarity. After World War II, in the third stage of the area's history, however, the further extension of technological innovations and commercialization had a different effect. Tractors and other more powerful machines then replaced both man and beast on the farms. Statistics tell part of the story of the transformation in work in Trempealeau County and the decline of *dugnag*. Tractors began replacing the work horse by 1930, but even in 1940 only slightly over a quarter of the farmers owned tractors, so necessary to the expensive and high powered machines of the 1980s (see Table 6.2). Machines such as a combine made it possible for one man to do alone what had once required the collective effort of the neighborhood.

Ultimately the new mahcines left each farm family independent of neighbors and dependent on the corporations which supplied the equipment and on creditors who helped arrange payment for it. As one woman responded when asked if the community in which she lived still organized any of this work by neighborhoods: "No, you don't help anyone anymore. Everyone is independent."[40] Individually owned combines have replaced the threshing crews, more sophisticated equipment has replaced the silo-filling crews, and electric stoves and oil and gas furnaces have stilled the saw rigs and ended the winter afternoons in the woods. By 1960 only 12 percent of the households still depended upon wood for cooking and only 13 percent for heat.[41] Refrigerators and freezers have

Table 6.2. Number of Farms, Workers, Horses, and Tractors in Trempealeau County, 1870–1970

Year	Farms	Persons Employed in Farming	Horses	Tractors	% Owning Tractors
1870	—	—	2,784	—	—
1880	2,459	—	6,002	—	—
1890	2,676	—	8,138	—	—
1900	3,138	—	10,701	—	—
1910	3,008	—	12,145	—	—
1920	3,138	—	14,700	—	—
1930	3,051	5,329	11,825	557	18
1940	3,040	5,130	10,987	841	27
1950	2,889	4,713	6,579	2,216	45
1960	2,423	3,298	1,666	3,465	83
1970	1,908	2,211	256	4,028	90

Sources: See appendix C.

eliminated the need for the ice cooperative organized to cut and store ice in Pigeon in the 1930s. After 1945 the farm families and the villagers modernized their homes and mechanized their farms. The structure of work has radically changed, and with that change so too has family and community life been transformed.

The number of occasions that neighbors see each other has most surely declined, and rare indeed is the occasion one of need rather than only social. Like the suburbanite, today the farmer and his family need not ever cross the road or field to neighbors. Thirty years ago they were in each other's fields, woods, barns, and homes several times a year and were intimately aware of each other's farm operations; indeed, they were a necessary part of the productive process of their neighbors' farms. Like the members within the farm family itself, neighbors cooperated and put up with each other to complete their common tasks and assure their common survival. They compared their crops, animals, equipment, and work habits and competed with each other to get the best output per acre and the most production per cow, and to finish their chores earlier than the neighbor across the field. They had ample opportunities to judge each other's strengths, efficiency, skill, dependability, and temperament. And because of their mutual dependence then, these were not unimportant matters. They ate at each other's tables, were well acquainted with each other's spouses and children, and particularly with what kind of worker everyone was. They knew what kind of cooks and housekeepers the women were and how much their husbands could depend upon them to accomplish outside of the house. They knew on which farms they would get the best food and from which ones they should hurry home in the evening to avoid a tasteless supper.[42]

Today each farmer depends upon his own equipment, in which he has invested many thousands of dollars and faces alone the risks of the fluctuating market and the fluctuating governmental support of farm prices. The cushion that the community, the locally organized economy, and the somewhat self-sufficient farm households once provided is gone or is at best a very pale shadow of its former self. The market's determining power over the lives of rural folk is greater than ever. Unlike horses, tractors do not reproduce themselves, nor do they depend upon hay and oats for fuel. According to a former farmer in Pigeon, "Farmers have a weakness for big machinery and they aren't afraid to go into debt to get it."[43] And into debt they have gone, and with the debt and big machines has gone the cushion of community cooperation which allowed most of the local farmers to survive the earlier fluctuations in the market, even the economic collapse of the 1930s. Farmers now look to the federal government as the determinant of their security and the quality of their lives.

Technology and the complete integration of the farm household into the market have eliminated the functional interdependence of these communities which once characterized their work and social environment. The former intimacy associated with the tradition of *dugnag* has disappeared, and the rhythm and texture of work is now structured not by the human landscape of families and communities but by the machines which have replaced the rigs and community crews. Interaction between neighbors has declined as their interdependence declined.

But it would take almost a century for the so-called independent yeoman farmer of the frontier actually to be able to do work on his farm alone with his family and to be independent of his neighbors in Lincoln and Pigeon. From the earliest days of the frontier, farmers depended upon the generosity and hospitality of their neighbors. Within their social creed, Curti found, they made those qualities the most fundamental virtues of their social code.[44] However, those values were not just the creation of the exigencies of the frontier; they were also based on centuries of tradition by which peasants had learned to survive and to sustain their own rich culture. The Norwegian immigrants clearly brought their ideals and tradition of collective work with them, but they were not alone in practicing these precepts. The diaries of Dave Wood reveal a similar pattern of interdependence and shared work among the migrant New Yorkers and New Englanders who, over generations, followed the frontier line westward. Such traditions provided the basis for organizing work and a social ethic which continued to be vital until the second half of the twentieth century.

7
Woman's Place, Woman's Work

Marie cleaned the barn, Harry helped me bake cookies and doughnuts.
Ella Hanson diary, March 30, 1932

The history of rural women, like that of rural folk in general, has been neglected by scholars and subject to stereotypes. On the one hand, research on the history of American women has tended to focus on middle-class urban women, particularly in the postcolonial period; on the other hand, studies seem to regard the frontier and the farm as a particularly masculine domain. But women trekked the overland trail, shared in building homes and communities, and lived and worked on the farms as surely as men did. In 1920 almost a third of American families still lived on farms, though by that time rural women were fleeing the farms even more rapidly than the men were.

Recent research on frontier and farm women is beginning to provide a more realistic and complete picture of women's lives on the frontier.[1] At issue are questions about the nature of women's work, the ways in which gender systems structured relationships, roles, and the power of women in the family and community. The recent research raises questions of fact and interpretation. To what extent were rural and frontier women involved in "outside work" or in taking responsibilities traditionally regarded as men's? Did the frontier break down the gender-based division of labor? Did women exclusively do the household work of child care, food preparation, and other tasks usually regarded as women's tasks in the home? How did women regard the divisions of labor, and how were women's prestige and power in the family related to their productive work? Were women unrecognized, exploited, undervalued, and disadvantaged as farm workers?[2] Or did women practice partnership and perceive their status as equal? Did rural households sustain the kind of symmetry that had "occurred earlier in the household mode of production of preindustrial economies in an agrarian past"?[3]

Another concern to historians is the question of what happens to women's work and status as the shift is made from a subsistence-oriented household economy based on land to production for the market. Does Trempealeau offer evidence for Karl Marx's conclusion that women were

157

relegated to a reproductive role and their other labor devalued in a capitalistic economy? At least some historians conclude that "the devaluation of women's work that is common in advanced capitalist societies . . . occurred in the rural economy in the early twentieth century."[4] Others studying the transition to commercial agricultural production concluded that a common gendered pattern of reorganizing work occurs; men take over responsibility for farm production which is oriented to the market, and women do those tasks which maintain the family—production for the household. In this context, though women worked hard and contributed to their families' well-being, their status and power declined as farm men immersed themselves in the mentality of money and the market.[5]

In terms of Trempealeau's history these theories and debates suggest questions. Did immigrant women give up traditional outside work on the American frontier when their husbands adopted the cash crop of wheat and new production technologies? If they did, what impact did it have on their self-concept and status? Did farm women embrace the theory and practice of the ideology of domesticity—an ideology which discounted the value of women as productive workers but lauded their virtues as moral guardians of the home and society? In the view of some analysts, as production moved out of the household, women lost more than just their work: women's status and power in the family declined as well.[6] Others argue that removing production from the household and women from the barn was actually a liberating choice for women—an assertion of autonomy from men's oversight.[7] And, after all, who could object to giving up shoveling manure?

The economic changes of the nineteenth century which transformed family life and women's work produced a potent ideology of domesticity. As an expanding economy progressively shifted production out of the household, the ideology of separate spheres differentiated ever more sharply not only the work but also the natures of men and women. This ideology elaborated traditional gender prescriptions and adapted them to a changing economic environment. According to the nineteenth-century separate-spheres doctrine, men were to provide income and take care of public affairs. Women were to manage homes which provided a haven of comfort, cheer, and morality for men, who had to cope with the heavy pressures of the competitive marketplace and the world beyond the home. Men claimed the world as their province, and women nurtured the domestic domain. The ideal of womanhood became the leisured lady who cultivated social graces and decorative "accomplishments" such as piano playing and embroidery. Nature created women morally superior to men and especially equipped them for domestic and nurturing roles. Women's proper sphere was the home and the care of those who resided there.

Motherhood represented their primary responsibility—shaping the character of children and thereby acting as the moral guardians of society. This ideology of the "cult of true womanhood" prescribed the special virtues of women to be piety, purity, domesticity, and submission.

Although the doctrine of separate spheres underwent many challenges, changes, and adaptations, nonetheless it had a twentieth-century successor, which Betty Friedan defined and labeled in 1963 as "the feminine mystique." True women continued to be expected to define themselves primarily as wives and mothers and to find fulfillment in domesticity and submission. Sigmund Freud provided the scientific rationale for the twentieth-century variation of the separate-spheres doctrine. "Anatomy is destiny," Freud declared, and for women that meant a perpetuation of many of the traditional notions about women's nature, status, and work. Physiology was the basis of identity, and theirs suited women to domestic tasks and a subordinate status.[8]

No doubt, few farm folk in Pigeon read Freud, and even if they had, the realities of the lives of many women made the achievement of middle-class ideals of womanhood problematic. Though rural women were cognizant of ideals of femininity, they would not or could not conform easily to all the precepts of those ideals. Family life on the farm made rural women's situation anomalous, not only during the frontier stage, but in the postfrontier years as well. Farm families did not undergo many of the changes confronted by urban middle- and working-class families.

On the farm, the work place and the home were one; however, historians have concluded that the separation of work from the household most conspicuously contributed to the shaping of nineteenth-century family ideals. Unlike most of their urban counterparts, farm families in Trempealeau continued to own the place and means of their production for both the market and their own subsistence. Women shared with men many of the tasks which produced their income and sustained their families. From frontier days until after World War II, many of the families in Pigeon and Lincoln produced a large share of their daily necessities. In that context, women and children played central roles as producers. Thus the structure of daily life of farm women differed strikingly from the context that gave birth to the middle-class family ideals. Not until the last stage in the county's history, after World War II, did women's experience on the farm begin to lose its exceptional character.

In rural Trempealeau, ideals of womanhood and the nature of women's work were influenced by the backgrounds of the migrants and immigrants and by the opportunities and challenges of the frontier and farm community. Hans Anderson's voluminous accounts of his neighbors'

lives provide one source for discovering local perceptions and expectations. He carefully observed and recorded the conditions and work of
women in his homeland of Norway, on the frontier, and during the years of
settled community life. Throughout his long life in Trempealeau, the doings of women held his attention as surely as did those of men.

Garrison Keillor's inversion of gender expectations, expressed in the
weekly epilogue of his radio show, "A Prairie Home Companion," satiriz-
ing the Norwegian Americans in the Minnesota small town of Lake
Wobegon, "where all the women are strong and all the men good looking,"
resembles Anderson's descriptions. When it came to assessing character,
sharp gender distinctions dissolved. Anderson admired and praised the
strong, able, hospitable, and hardworking men of Trempealeau and he
seemingly held the strong, able, hospitable, and hardworking women in
equally high regard. He admired beauty, strength, and intelligence in
women as he did in men. True beauty in both men and women required
intelligence; true character required integrity, honesty, and generosity of
spirit. Hard work was expected of all. By his lights, men were to be judged
as parents as surely as were women. Irresponsibility to the family and to
the community was a characteristic no less undesirable in men than in
women. Both men and women could be wise or foolish, strong or weak,
able or ineffectual, and kind or cruel.[9]

Nineteenth-century ideals of womanhood may have been inclined to
place women on a pedestal, lauding their superior morality, but the peasant
culture of Norway and of immigrants in Trempealeau had little inclination
to do so. In the diverse descriptions of people found in county records or in
the Norwegian folklore which locals recounted, vice and virtue seem about
equally distributed between men and women.[10] In one description of an
early pioneer couple, Hans Anderson wrote:

> His wife was short, stout and redheaded. She was a hard working woman,
> whose shadow seldom was still—neither was her tongue. She met the storms
> of life with tempest of her own. She died in middle age and her husband found
> a more genial atmosphere in his home when he took widow Otter Oliver for
> his second wife.[11]

When Wisconsin's last lynching occurred in Trempealeau County in
1889, Anderson as the county's district attorney prosecuted the case. He
concluded the culprit in the story was the victim's wife, who ably manipu-
lated leading members of the community to achieve her purpose of ridding
herself of her husband. Anderson successfully prosecuted her for murder
along with several others. Years later Anderson would write, "The primary
cause was undoubtedly Olson's wife, who poisoned his neighbors with her
stories." In other instances, Anderson wrote accounts of women who were

victims of bad marriages or circumstances. Women, like men, wielded a good deal of power and handled it with varying degrees of success and responsibility.[12]

Just as Anderson failed to be impressed with notions of women's superior morality, he and his neighbors were not inclined quickly to adopt the middle-class conception of woman's place as leisured and protected in the home. No conception of feminine delicacy, excluding women from full participation in the productive process, had penetrated the Norwegian peasant communities like Alvaren, Anderson's birthplace in Norway.

In Norway, as in other preindustrial contexts, women worked alongside men in the fields and barns. Historian Louise Tilly noted that, in preindustrial France, married women contributed to "all aspects of family life and thus fulfilled several roles within their households. They engaged in production for exchange and production for household consumption, both of which contributed to the families' economic well being."[13] Peasant households could not get along without a housekeeper. A French peasant saying applied equally to the Scandinavian peasant household and very likely to the American frontier homestead: "No wife, no cow, hence no milk, no cheese, neither hens, nor chicks, nor eggs. . . ."[14] Failure on the frontier or in farming could be explained by the premature death or incapacity of a wife.

The rhythm of the seasons and the strength and capacities of each person dictated the work of individuals in peasant communities. Anderson's account of life in Norway was not exceptional:

> There was no work about the farm that women did not perform on an equal footing with men. In fact men had the easier part, for they rarely helped women in their housework. Men frequently rested while the women attended to household duties, but when the hour came for work in the fields men and women went out working to their appointed tasks. Many women were superior to their husbands and brothers in the labors on the farm.[15]

When describing the situation in Norway, Anderson emphasized the wide range of work that men and women shared on the peasant farms. Women, he suggested, could and did work as hard and at many of the same kinds of tasks as men did.

In Norway, a division of labor based upon gender paralleled that of other peasant societies. Animal husbandry and the preparation of food and clothing were clearly women's work, while men took responsibility for forestry, fishing, and building. They shared the work of the fields, though this was somewhat more connected to men than to women, and they cooperated in a variety of other responsibilities within their subsistence economy.[16]

Frequently women migrating westward from eastern states in the nineteenth century felt less than pleased when the demands of the frontier broke down gender distinctions related to work. After leaving their homes in the East, these women as rapidly as possible sought to reestablish the principle of separate spheres in the work of men and women. According to Christiane Fischer, a historian of frontier women:

> The way in which they adjusted seemed to depend much on the kind of life they had known before their departure: the more "genteel" their background and education, the more repelled they were by their new environment. . . . If I had to point out one single factor which made the adaptation of women in the West so difficult, I would say it was the prevalent ideology centering on women's place in the home.[17]

Peasant immigrant women departing from communities in Norway and Poland and migrant American women who had grown up on farms may have been less alarmed by the experience of the frontier. The demands of the earliest years on the frontier, while perhaps more exacting, were not different in kind from what they had experienced in the past. Women worked much as they had in the subsistence communities they had left behind, "where there was no work on the farm that women did not per- form on an equal footing with men."[18] For many immigrant women, there were no discomforting pressures to depart from traditional gender-specific work roles.

In Ole Rolvaag's *Giants in the Earth,* Beret seemingly shared the despair of many eastern women in the dissolution of civilization, as she conceived it, on the frontier. But accounts of Trempealeau women's experi- ence of immigration and frontier farming did not consistently follow Be- ret's pattern. Women in some instances were as eager to make the move as men, conscious of the opportunities the frontier offered. Unlike Beret, Anderson's mother, Berthe Gunderson, initiated the decision that the fam- ily would emigrate:

> Alvaren had a very pleasant situation. But it was full of hills, rocks and sloughs. I had lived there eleven years and debts had grown heavier all the time. I had five children and liable to have more. I didn't worry about myself but I couldn't see any decent future on Alvaren for my children. After receiv- ing Knudtson's letter and thinking of the future for my children, I decided to go to America as soon as possible.[19]

The uniquely hard times of the first years after arriving were usually recognized by women to be temporary, and many proved capable of the extra effort this period demanded. On arrival in Pigeon in 1867, Berthe Gunderson worked alongside her husband in the fields of a Norwegian farmer in Pigeon, and they were paid the same salary. In Anderson's account, she surpassed her husband in efficiency and endurance: "There were few kinds of work that mother did not excel my stepfather in performing. The natural result was a strong healthy woman with almost incredible capacity for endurance."[20]

Berthe Gunderson's youth and womanhood in Norway reveal a history of work that the demands of the frontier rarely surpassed. From the time her mother had died when Berthe was still young until she reached the age of 20, she served as "maid and mistress" of her father's household. She then, in the typical fashion of peasant youth, "worked out" for many years before her marriage. Even after her marriage and the birth of two children, she continued to work separated from her husband while the children's grandparents tended to their needs.[21] Her father had once attempted to arrange a marriage for her with a man of greater wealth; however, like Beret she married a man with less hopeful prospects but more to her liking.[22]

When after four years of marriage she and her husband did manage to make a down payment on a small mountaintop farm, her work continued at an equally rigorous pace. Her husband died within six weeks of the purchase of the farm, and Berthe alone faced the responsibility for her children, the farm, and the old couple from whom the farm had been purchased. One memorable summer Berthe and her second husband were too "hard up" to hire a girl to take care of the cattle in the *stolen,* or mountain pasture. It was common practice for animals to be allowed to graze in high mountain pastures during the summer months and to be tended by young women. "Mother resolved to perform duties at the 'stolen' and also at home." Everyday that summer, Berthe Gunderson walked over rocky mountain trails to and from the *stolen,* located seven miles from their home. "Every evening and morning she stabled and milked six cows, and turned them out to pasture, made cheese and butter, walked home every morning after her chores were done carrying from eight to sixteen quarts of milk." Once home she did her housework and then "took her place beside her husband in the out of doors work until 6 p.m." She then again walked the seven miles to the *stolen* to tend the animals.[23] Women like Berthe Gunderson arrived in Trempealeau County with the will, stamina, and skills required on the frontier farms. No doubt, homesteading in Wisconsin presented few challenges to such a woman's sense of identity as a woman and her conceptions of woman's proper place.

On the frontier, women continued to work on the farms as they had in Norway. When necessary they could and did run the farms alone. In both countries, men often spent winters in the "woods," leaving the farms to women. When widowed, women continued farming alone or often remarried, as Berthe Gunderson did as a young woman with small children in Norway and again as an aging woman in Wisconsin. At the age of 70, again widowed but still independent, Berthe bought a farm, after briefly living with one of her children, and soon thereafter took a third husband. She lived and worked on her farm until the age of 88, when, according to Anderson, "feeling the weight of her advanced age, she decided to quit farming." Anderson's mother, like other women about whom he wrote, frequently chose to continue to work when options for greater leisure were available to them.[24]

When they came to the American frontier, women such as Berthe Gunderson expected to work hard and did throughout their lives. That labor and the strong character of the women provided the basis for a certain amount of power in the household. Men clearly held privileged positions legally in public institutions and in their control of property. This was true both in Norway and in the United States. Nonetheless, the distribution of power in the household followed less closely the structure of the public realm. As Louise Tilly found in French peasant society: "Within the households of the popular classes there seem to have been not just one, but several sources of power. Men did not monopolize all of them."[25] The work that women did in supplying many of the basic needs of the family provided an area of autonomy and authority for women.

In local accounts the distribution of power in the household had much to do with the personality and character of the individual. In one description of a Norwegian couple provided by an aging woman of the community, the husband was described as a:

> ... mild innocuous sort of man. ... He took the good things in life without enthusiasm and met ills and reverses with quiet resignation. ... Gunda was different. Her dominant trait was a practical optimism, backed by a restless energy and an ambition to go forward. ... Her life exemplified the old Norse saying: "If I find no way I will make a way." Physically, both Thor and Gunda were splendidly equipped for the toil and hardships they shared as husband and wife for nearly seventy years.

Of the social relationships in the peasant community in which Gunda and Thor resided, where "the tongue became the principal weapon of offense and defense," in the many contests "Gunda had several rivals, but no peer. For more than fifty years, especially during the absence of the men, this little community was literally a logocracy and Gunda was its distinguished ruler. ... She excelled in grace of person, swiftness of action, cutting irony, and polished wit." On the day of her death at the age of 90, she had been giving orders "about everything" as always. Her last words, "in a voice that seemed to have lost none of its commanding power," were, "Don't let the potatoes cook to pieces."[26] If all women did not conform to the models of womanhood represented by descriptions of Gunda and Berthe, accounts such as these nonetheless do reveal that among the immigrant generation women recognized diverse sources of authority available to them as women.

Inheritance patterns provide some indication of women's status. Scandinavian countries in some instances appear to diverge from patriarchal European patterns. In Norway in 1854, the recently politicized peasantry achieved one of its early goals, the passage of legislation protecting a woman's right to inherit property equally with men.[27] In a study of inheritance in Swedish peasant communities between 1700 and 1740, Swedish scholar Bengt Ankarloo found that "wives and daughters were almost as important as sons in the transmission of property."[28] In Pigeon and Lincoln, although initially few of the immigrant farmers wrote wills, when they did, except for those with notable wealth, they generally made their wives the executors and left their farms and stock to them as well. In some instances, the wills also arranged for equal division among the children after the wife's death. In the wills, the often-used phrase for describing this division was "share and share alike." Of 20 wills recorded between 1895 and 1910 by Pigeon and Lincoln men whose wives were still alive, only two left significant portions of their estate to anyone other than the wife. The two exceptions were Peter Ekern and John Melby. In matters of inheritance, patriarchy in Pigeon and Lincoln appears to have been the prerogative of a small elite.[29]

This does not mean that a large amount of property fell into the hands of women. When widowed women did sometimes own and manage farms themselves, they did so with the assistance of children and hired labor. As was discussed earlier, frequently farms were transferred to the next generation before the death of parents. Women cooperated with their husbands in keeping the home place in the family. Studies of inheritance indicate that *inter vivos* transfers were the preferred strategy among Norwegian American farmers, as they were among peasants in Norway. As in Norway, aging couples or widowed individuals often remained on their farms with one of their children's families after the transfer of the farm.[30]

The work of the households of the farmers and villagers in Trempealeau changed after the frontier years when the local economy shifted from wheat production to dairying and animal husbandry. But on the farms, one continuity in the experience of all the members of a family, including women, was that everyone worked hard and played an essential role in the productivity and success of the household.

Some historians have argued that immigrant families quickly adopted American bourgeois notions of women's work and women's place, rapidly rejecting the traditional peasant division of labor found in Norway. In Norway, Jon Gjerde found that "women performed all work in the cattle barns, including shoveling manure, milking, and carrying water for all the animals. In the fall they clipped the sheep and during the slaughter took care of the blood and entrails." In addition women had responsibility for food preparation and clothing.[31] Women had also worked in the fields in Norway, although grain production was traditionally somewhat more associated with men and animal husbandry with women. But peasants, Gjerde argued, soon became farmers in the American environment: the shift to production of cash crops, such as wheat, for the market and the increased mechanization resulted in a stronger identification of grain production with men, generally edging women from the fields. Gjerde concluded that on the frontier as elsewhere, when Norwegian peasants became involved in production for the market the traditional distribution of work became unsettled: work necessary to sustain the family became more exclusively associated with women, and production for the market became associated with men. Thus, when dairying later became commercially important, most American women were then edged from the barns as well. "Not only did the occupation of milkmaid vanish, but traditional duties of animal care were abandoned by women as housework and child care proved to be a heavy work burden."[32]

From frontier times until the present day, women have worked in the fields of Wisconsin farms. This scene is from 1895. Photo by Harvey J. Perkins. W.A. Henry Collection. Photo courtesy of the State Historical Society of Wisconsin, WHi (H44) 32.

Women may well have desired such a change at some point, but it was slow in coming to Pigeon and Lincoln farms. Developments there did not clearly fit the pattern which Gjerde and others have concluded is a component in the transformation of agriculture. Berthe Gunderson worked alongside her husband in the wheat fields in 1867, and in 1967 women still could be found on the huge machines that have replaced the crews of workers and animals which once plowed, planted, and harvested the land. The same was true in the barns. Trempealeau County made a rapid transition from frontier wheat production to dairying.[33] Within the county, Pigeon farmers were consistently leaders in that shift, developing herds earlier and larger than some of the neighboring townships. A critical question is, What was women's relationship to the shift to dairying and animal husbandry in Trempealeau? Did they retreat quickly and gratefully from the barns, retiring to more genteel and domestic occupations, or did they play an active role in shaping the household and local economy?

Although the development of the dairy industry has been carefully analyzed by historians, little attention has been focused on the relationship of that industry's development to the household or family economy. Like textiles, milking and tending the animals, production of butter and cheese, feeding chickens, and collecting eggs had been women's and children's work in Norway and in the United States. In Norway, women like Berthe Gunderson had kept four to seven cows and made cheese and butter for their households. Much of the diet of the Norwegian peasant was based upon dairy products.[34] Immigrant families struggled to reestablish in this country the household economy they had left behind. In doing so they relied heavily on animals, especially milk cows. Thurine Oleson's description of the importance of this is probably typical. She said that as soon as her parents could afford it: "Father bought a few cows and now mother had milk out of which she produced cheese and butter, but at first we could not afford to eat them. They were traded for necessities at the store. Best of all she had a couple of calves to love and feed as of old and a pig and some chickens to tend daily."[35] Thurine Oleson's parents recaptured their homeland routines as soon as they had the means to do so. "After they got in a little better circumstances, the folks continued to butcher as much as they had in Norway—four or five small pigs in the fall, a beef, and the lambs in the spring."[36]

Before creameries appeared in Trempealeau in the 1890s, women were responsible for the entire process of dairying, from milking the animals to churning the butter and making the cheese, as they had been in Norway. Much of this local production was used by the household, but many families supplemented their income to some extent by selling butter, as Thurine Oleson's mother did. The marketing of butter and eggs by women in European peasant communities and rural American communities was a means by which women supplemented their families' income. According to the 1880 census, each farm household in the county produced an average of 178 pounds of butter.[37]

During the frontier years, women in the villages and on the farms took responsibility for the domestic animals that provided for their households' needs. Before a notable degree of specialization in dairying developed, domestic animals continued as a part of the household economy even in the villages.[38] Pigs and cows regularly roamed the village streets making a nuisance of themselves by eating cooling pies, and bringing diatribes from the pen of the *Whitehall Times* editor against their owners, who were often fined.[39] When wheat was king on the frontier, the status of the dairy in the local economy paralleled the kitchen garden—women's responsibility, fundamental to the household economy but insignificant to the market economy.[40]

The 1895 census of agriculture indicated that by that time the farmers in Pigeon and Lincoln had acquired the means to raise home production beyond the level they had in Norway; the average farm in Pigeon included 10 cows, 3 pigs, 80 chickens, and about 8 sheep.[41] In 1915 in the town of Lincoln, long after creameries had appeared, 31,490 pounds of butter were churned in homes, but this was only a small portion—9 percent—of the 356,324 pounds produced at the local creamery.[42] In 1925, butter production on Trempealeau farms averaged 106 pounds per farm, but by that time many families no longer churned their own butter. Ten years later, in 1935, 38 percent of the county's farm families still produced butter at home, averaging 173 pounds of butter, which was close to the 1880 average per farm.[43]

The commercialization of butter production introduced critical changes for women in the postfrontier years. Beginning in the 1880s, the production of dairy items followed textiles in a series of steps out of the

Table 7.1. Butter Production on Farms in
Trempealeau County, 1900–1950

	Pounds of Butter
1900	1,128,513
1910	533,782
1920	424,133
1930	340,892
1940	72,812
1950	27,816

Sources: See appendix C.

household, and production was increasingly mechanized, rationalized, and commercialized. According to Gjerde, as dairying and sale of stock came to be the largest sources of family income, animal husbandry also should have become increasingly men's work. This, however, is not what happened.

In the 1880s, when the *Whitehall Times* reported that "most farmers conclude they will send their cream and save the labor of churning," the labor being saved was primarily that of wives and daughters. The effect of this seems to have been to free women not for other household chores but for milking larger herds of animals. Between 1880 and 1890, the average number of milk cows per farm in the county doubled, increasing from 3.1 to 6.4 (see Table 7.2). By 1920 the county average per farm was almost 10. While some clumsy milking machines had been installed by that time, most of the labor was still done by hand. As long as the cows were milked by hand, herds were small, rarely larger than 20 milk cows. By 1915 the average number of cows for the patrons of the Ekern creamery was 12. This is considerably higher than the county average of eight. Lincoln Township averaged smaller herds of around seven or eight. These local differences in the size of the herds may in part be related to the gender expectations of different ethnic groups. Pigeon women, who had long expected to handle the dairy, may have been more comfortable with larger herds than those who felt such work inappropriate to women.[44] There is abundant evidence that women in these communities carried much of the responsibility for the work in the barns. In fact, the daily demands on women's labor may have increased during the shift to dairy production and the growth in the size of the herds. The long established dependence on dairy production in Norway may explain why Pigeon, with its almost exclusively Norwegian population, took the lead in that specialization.

Table 7.2. Average Number of Milk Cows per Farm in Trempealeau County, 1880–1970

1880	3.1
1890	6.4
1900	5.6
1910	8.5
1920	9.8
1930	11.3
1940	12.6
1950	11.3
1960	15.2
1970	19.2

Sources: See appendix C.

While Hans Anderson practiced law and lived in the village of White-hall, he also owned a farm some distance from the village. There, in the first decade of the twentieth century, his wife, sons, and daughters managed the farm. His wife took primary responsibility for animal husbandry, garden-ing, and the running of a household that continued to supply a large share of the family's needs. In the letters between Anderson's daughters, Rose wrote to her sister Lily with enthusiasm about the work on the farm. The letters included news about her heifer, the chickens, and other aspects of the daily work in and outside of the house. The letters were laced with remarks such as "Ma says you can come up and milk cows and feed calves."[45] Or, as Lily wrote in 1898 to her brother: "I milked for mama this morning. It seems quite natural to go to the barn but I shouldn't like to keep it up."[46] Hans's daughter Rose supplemented her income from teach-ing by owning stock. In 1902 Rose wrote to her sister: "I bought a heifer with my first month's salary, so if I make a failure of teaching I'll go in for stock. Pa says I'll have to milk the cow next summer."[47]

Like Thurine Oleson's mother, the Andersons continued to treat their animals as pets on which they extended affection and concern rather than as simply a means to a living. As was traditional in Norway, the Andersons gave their cattle names and in letters reported on them as if they were people: "Lotty, Rose's cow, had a heifer. She prayed for a steer but it didn't do any good." In her letter, Rose noted, "My cow Lottie had a heifer calf and Tessia a steer."[48] Lily, who had grown up in the village of Whitehall, found little appeal in tending animals; however, when the family moved to a farm, her mother may well have shared the pleasure Thurine Oleson's mother felt in reestablishing the traditional household economy.

There is little indication that Hans, his wife, or daughters perceived anything inappropriate in the distribution of work which kept women in the barns milking cows, caring for chickens, and shoveling manure as they had done in Norway. Decisions of farm women like Rose with her cow Lottie may have contributed as much to the expansion of Pigeon's and Lincoln's herds as did the decisions of their husbands and fathers.

When one of the most acculturated of the immigrant families, the Andersons, who regularly socialized with the county's Yankee elite, felt no inclination to change their ways, it is hardly surprising that the ordinary farmer's family did not. The diaries for the years 1922–1945 kept by Ella Hanson, the wife of a third-generation Norwegian American on a farm near Pigeon Falls, indicate that Anderson's description of the distribution of work in the peasant household in Norway continued to hold sway. Ella Hanson and her daughters worked in the fields, milked cows, and cleaned barns regularly. Women like Ella and her daughters could hold their own as workers on the farm and were respected for doing so.[49]

Dairying, traditionally women's work, continued to be part of many women's responsibilities. Women in Pigeon who grew up on farms in the first three decades of the twentieth century uniformly recall taking their places in the dairy barns.[50] As herds expanded and dairying became a substantial source of the family's income, men did become more involved. However, it is not clear exactly when or if the milking and tending of animals became exclusively men's responsibility. This did not happen before the post–World War II years in Pigeon. Local variation in the division of labor occurred depending upon the community, ethnic group, and even particular families. Since 1950 the woman who has continued to carry primary responsibility for the animals of the farm would certainly be the exception in Pigeon and Lincoln. Less exceptional would be the farm wives who have continued to participate in the process.[51]

Fundamental changes in the work of animal care came with the arrival of electricity. The Rural Electrification Administration brought electricity to farmers of Pigeon and Lincoln in 1939. A few had had electricity from home generators earlier, but the REA brought it into widespread use on the farms. Electricity made possible the common installation and use of milking machines and barn cleaners. By 1950, 52 percent of the farmers with dairy cows had milking machines, and by 1960, 89 percent had them. The machines radically reduced the time and numbers of people involved in the process. Although a few farmers had electric milking machines in the 1920s, they did not become the norm until the postwar years. And as long as machines did not appear in the dairy, there is little doubt that women and the young did.[52]

Apparently, in some families even after mechanization, men continued to resist assuming responsibility for milking cows. One Pigeon woman remarked, "Mrs. Orvill Fremstad still does all the milking." Fremstad is a family name that has had numerous representatives in the community since frontier times.[53] Another aging woman, still tall and strong, was as proud of doing the milking all the years of her marriage as she was of being the best center on a local high school girls basketball team in the second decade of the century. Before electrical equipment appeared, milking the cows twice daily was a time-consuming task and usually involved several members of the household of various ages and both genders. Twelve-year-old Ralph Wood daily reported how many cows he milked, ranging from one to three. Ella Hanson and her daughters and son regularly shared the work. One woman recalled that four or five of the family members worked together and "we sang when we milked. That was kind of fun."[54]

Mechanization radically changed that daily ritual. The machines brought the noise of the factory into the dairy, increased production, and drastically reduced the time and the number of family members involved.

Karen Goplin (*right*) played center on a local high school girl's basketball team, and later as an adult, worked in the fields and barn. Photo courtesy of Arlene Arneson, Whitehall, Wisconsin.

Mechanization appears to have played a greater role than production for the market in redefining the dairy as the male province. Yet, while Mrs. Orvill Fremstad, who still does "all the milking," may no longer be the typical farm wife in her persistence in the traditional ways, she certainly is not the only woman who so persists in the county. At least until 1945 and on some farms still in 1980, the principle that production for the market becomes men's work did not hold true, although men very likely had made an entrance into the dairy. As Pigeon farms shifted to animal husbandry and dairying as a source of income, the work of tending animals increased. Extra hands were needed, but this did not end women's participation. Whether women worked in the barns and fields depended upon a variety of factors ranging from their own family background, the stage of the family in the life-cycle, the age and the number of sons and daughters in the household, and the extent to which the farm operation was mechanized.[55]

The diaries kept by men and women on the farms of Pigeon and Lincoln clarify the distribution of work in farm households. Ella Hanson recorded the daily round of work and sociability of her family. Young and old alike participated and contributed. The following entries made in 1932 were typical:

> Friday July 22
> Cleaned whole house, canned 1 qt. beans. I scrubbed the whole downstairs, washed windows, cleaned cupboards, etc., baked a cake and overnight cookies. Ben and Maynard cut and shocked grain. I baked bread 9 loaves and biscuits. Enola, Walter and girls came this eve [Ella's sister and family from Onalaska, which is about 50 miles south of Pigeon]. Mr. and Mrs. Sedahl, Thelma, Margaret, Lavinia, a Johnson girl [all neighbors], came for a visit in the evening. Harry rode to Pigeon on Prince to see them swim and had dinner with Josephine. [Josephine, Ella's sister-in-law, achieved some local notoriety as an eccentric and a divorcee. She was a frequent visitor at Hansons.]
>
> Saturday July 23
> Ben, Maynard, and Walter shocked. They got thru and put binder in shed. Dorothy [a daughter] baked a cake. I baked 2 pies, cleaned two hens. Enola and I picked beans, Enola and Marie [another daugher] looked for berries. Mother patched all day, made 2 new sheets. Ma, Walter, Enola, Doris, Ben, and I went to Pigeon this evening.[56]

Entries such as these tell a good deal about the work of these families and communities during the postfrontier stage from 1880 to 1945. Ella and her husband coordinated the work of a wide range of people on their farm in these two days, including themselves, five children, Ella's mother, sister, brother-in-law, and a hired hand, Maynard. In the Wood and Ella Hanson diaries, most of the work that went on around the farm was done in groups of two or more people. Ben, Maynard, and Walter shocked, while several women were in the house mending, sewing, cleaning, and baking. "Enola and Marie looked for berries." In the evening six of those staying at the household went to Pigeon Falls. While farm folk have often been thought to be isolated, they were scarcely ever alone in their fields, barns, or houses. If Bennie and Ella were not working with the assistance of a neighbor, relative, or hired laborer, then they worked together or included one of their children at their side.

The other aspect of these diary entries which should be noted is the role of the extended kin network in the work of the Hanson farm. Ella's mother, sister and brother-in-law, and their daughters were reported as staying from Friday to Sunday night.[57] Relatives came and stayed for varying lengths of time, assisting the Hanson family in every aspect of their daily and seasonal work. Bennie's mother helped with corn husking; Ella's mother made sheets, aprons, mended, and did other household work. Through the course of the year, the Hanson farm's work was shared by a wide range of people in the kin network and the community. Neighbor men worked together cutting wood, threshing, and butchering. Women worked together sewing, canning, and picking berries.

The Wood diaries reveal similar patterns, although the women of the Wood family may not have been doing the outside work that Ella Hanson and her daughters did. However, the Wood diaries were all kept by men, by Dave Wood and two of his three sons, and they record primarily their own work. In Dave Wood's household the division of labor does appear in accord with nineteenth-century ideas about women's work, but Dave had three sons to help him and no daughters who survived childhood. One woman, the grandchild of immigrants, jokingly remarked that "all of the Norwegian girls wanted to marry Yankees so they wouldn't have to work in the fields." Nonetheless, Dave Wood's diaries do reveal the same pattern of kin and neighborhood work. Martha Wood, Ralph Wood's Scandinavian wife, and her sister, Gusta Pederson, visited with each other and assisted each other with sewing, canning, cooking, butchering, and cleaning.[58]

Some degree of specialization existed among the women within kin networks and neighborhoods. Kin relied upon Martha Wood to do sewing for special occasions. Gusta Pederson was always on hand to assist when the Woods butchered animals and canned the meat. Ella Hanson had the reputation of being an extraordinary cook. The women took a good deal of pride in their various skills, and their reputations continue even now after their deaths. Community and family members possessed an intimate knowledge of what the varying capabilities and talents of individuals were. That knowledge structured the division of responsibilities in the many cooperative activities which organized the work and social life of the community and family.[59]

Not until the post–World War II years did the work of the rural household change notably. Most of the food of the farm family, and much of that of the villagers as well, was produced and processed in their own households and gardens or on nearby farms. Between 1922 and 1945 the household economy changed little if at all on the Hanson farm, and that farm differed little from that of the Wood households in 1890. Every year Ella picked and canned hundreds of quarts of blueberries, blackberries, raspberries, and strawberries. Apples, cherries, plums, and cranberries were taken from one's own or a local orchard. Every sort of fruit and vegetable was grown and canned or stored for the winter months. Typical of the productivity of the Hanson household in the summer and early fall months were 11 days in August of 1928. In her diary Ella recorded having canned the following:

3	quarts watermellon pickles
2	quarts beets
11	quarts beans
16½	quarts sweet pickles
16	quarts dill pickles
4	quarts sliced pickles
5	quarts apple pickles
4	quarts blackberries
2½	quarts juice
29	glasses jelly (blackberry, apple, crabapple, elderberry)
[illegible]	cherry plums

Besides the canning, Ella also attended to the rest of the daily and seasonal work. The wheat grown on local farms was ground at the local mills, and women baked their own breads, cakes, cookies, and pies. Ella's diary entries indicate that she baked three or four days a week. In the first week of March in 1932 she baked 2 cakes, 2 pies, 14 loaves of bread, rolls (twice), doughnuts, and cookies.[60] When relatives such as Ella's mother and sister visited, they too rolled out cookies and baked cakes or pies.[61] Meat was butchered on the farms and smoked, canned, or stored in Pigeon's icehouse and later in a freezer owned by the P. Ekern Company. Although Ella Hanson apparently did not make her own butter, many women in the area did as late as 1932. Though creameries had become common by 1890, many women still made their own butter for home consumption and sale. What foodstuffs families such as the Hansons needed to purchase from beyond the local market were quite limited.

Like Hans Anderson's mother, there were few things around the farm that Ella and her daughters did not do. Rigid conceptions of what was proper for men and women to do had no place in this busy farm household. Besides the housework of making, mending, and washing clothes, scrubbing, varnishing, and painting the house, canning and baking, Ella regularly reports doing "chores," which included the daily care of the animals and the milking of the cows. She assisted in the fields, putting up the hay, and as she phrased it, "helped mow away hay," which meant she distributed the hay dropped inside the hay barns so it was stacked evenly—a hot and heavy job. She and her daughters shoveled manure and chopped wood, as her diary noted on one typical occasion: "Dorothy, Eleanor, and Anna cleaned up the barn. Marie and I cut up some pine." According to Ella's diary, her husband and son at times assisted with what usually was regarded as women's work. On occasion, Harry baked cakes and Bennie helped with the wash and with peeling potatoes. Between 1922 and 1945 the household production of Bennie and Ella Hanson changed in no apparent way except for the regular addition and eventual integration into the work of the household of eight children, six of whom were daughters.[62]

Surveys of farm households by rural sociologists indicate that the Hanson household did not differ radically from other farm families. Surveys done in the 1920s, 1930s, and 1950s reveal continuities over time. Labor was divided along gender lines: women did the cooking, cleaning, and domestic tasks; men contributed only about two hours a week to such work. Women spent 10 hours a week on outside work, including milking, gardening, tending poultry, and, less frequently, working in the fields. Field work appeared to be optional to women—women who did field work did it by choice.[63]

While the evidence is clear that women made important contributions to the work of the farm, historians and sociologists have also raised questions about the implications of women's work to their power and status in the farm family. One of the studies concluded, "There is no evidence in the data that women worked under the economic leadership or domination of their husbands." Instead, "men and women had autonomous and interdependent spheres."[64] Decision-making studies have been used by rural sociologists as guides to determining women's status. A 1937 study of New York farm families revealed a "tendency toward democratic decision making. . . . Many decisions, especially about borrowing money, were made jointly by husbands and wives."[65] More recent studies of Wisconsin farm women indicate a persisting pattern of egalitarian decision-making on farms. A 1969 study revealed men and women to be automonous in their decision-making in areas where each concentrated his or her labor.[66] Nonetheless, men and women shared in making important decisions about financing and the allocation of farm resources, furnishing and maintaining the home, and the socialization of children.[67] A few of the studies found an exception in the egalitarian pattern among those farm families on the largest and highest-income-producing farms. At those levels, women were less likely to share in management and financial decisions. As in other aspects of farm life, perhaps in decision-making, patriarchy was an elite prerogative.[68]

Women's work on the farm differed from that of nonfarm women. On a daily basis farm women shared the work and often the decisions of the farm operation. As long as the young grew up largely in the context of homogeneous neighborhoods like those in Pigeon, available records do not indicate discontent with the family's organization of work. However, for that generation of women and men who first went to high school in significant numbers in the 1930s and who first grew up after the mass media of film and radio penetrated rural communities with models of womanhood quite different from that of their strong and busy mothers, tensions did develop between generations about women's proper place. By the 1940s new attitudes were taking shape that may have contributed to the transformation of the farm in the third stage of Trempealeau's history.

Although women still worked outside the house in the barns and fields, an ambivalence, feelings of embarrassment, and a new self-consciousness developed about such work which Lily and Rose Anderson and Ella Hanson had not experienced. Several women, including Eleanor Ackley, daughter of Ella Hanson, recalled that among their high school friends and particularly in relationship to young men courting them, she and her sisters carefully concealed the nature of their daily work on the farm. A date who arrived early could create a real crisis for the young woman who was still cleaning barn gutters or feeding pigs. The first of Ella Hanson's daughters to attend Whitehall High School, Eleanor felt herself blessed to have an allergy that prevented her from working in the barn.[69] The practice of hiding their responsibilities on the farm from their more leisured village girl friends and boy friends continued for at least another generation.[70]

Observers of these more recently learned attitudes may have projected them wrongly into the past and thus concluded that farmers early adopted middle-class gender work-role definitions. Harold Tomter, one of those Pigeon farm youths who attended high school in the 1930s, when asked if his wife worked outside of the house, responded yes, but was quick to point out that most of the time she worked in the house. He made clear that he had little interest in elaborating on his wife's assistance.[71] Another woman, who had always worked outside as a youth and wife, was told by her son to leave the barn and not come back. Like Tomter, the son had attended high school in the 1930s and obviously returned to the farm with ideas of women's work that were different from those his father's generation had had. However, he did not extend to his sisters this new privilege. He disapproved of his father's expectations of some women, if not all. By 1945, while in practice little may have changed, in perceptions a new discomfort about women's work on the farm had arisen among both men and women.[72]

This shift in perception scarcely improved the situation of rural women, especially when it brought a devaluation of their contributions. In 1950 the U.S. Census of Agriculture recorded 549 women as agricultural laborers in Trempealeau County, 91 percent of whom were unpaid family members. At the same time, there were 1,381 male agricultural laborers, 37 percent of whom were unpaid family workers.[73]

This tension between generations and new self-consciousness about women's work manifested itself at a time when the work of women on the farm became sharply differentiated from the work and lifestyles of the women in the villages. Until at least 1900, the lives of women in the villages mirrored those of farm women. They too had cows, chickens, pigs, and kitchen gardens which provided a large share of the needs of the household. They produced and processed their own foods, made their own clothes, and tended animals as did farm women. However, between 1920 and 1950 a gap developed. In the villages, homes were modernized and oriented toward a national market of consumer goods much earlier than those of farm women. Electricity and the many conveniences it afforded became common in the village by the 1920s.

Contrasts between country and town stood out in a host of areas which dictated distinctly different work lives. In 1940, 88 percent of the village homes had electricity while only 44 percent of the farm homes did. Twenty-nine percent of the village households had mechanical refrigeration while only 9 percent of the farm households did. In 1930, only 33 percent of the farm homes had running water inside; in 1950, 61 percent had this amenity compared with 79 percent in the villages. In 1940, 60

Table 7.3. Number of Farm and Nonfarm Households in Trempealeau County, 1930–1950

	Nonfarm	Farm
1930	2,482	3,114
1940	2,944	3,456
1950	3,503	3,087

Source: See appendix C.

percent of the village homes had private baths, while in the farm homes of Lincoln only 11 percent had bathrooms in their houses.[74]

By 1920, pigs and cows were no longer running loose on the streets and attracting the caustic comments of the newspaper editor. By that time, village women were more likely to have electricity, electrical appliances, indoor plumbing, and bathrooms. Village women, always more leisured then farm wives, became even more so. Local advertisers of household products regularly emphasized and idealized leisure time for women so they could golf, visit, read, and play bridge.[75] Like middle-class women elsewhere, village women defined themselves as homemakers whose habits of consumption and leisure-time pursuits determined status. Meanwhile, rural women and their daughters continued to work as producers as their mothers had. As a result, an increase in tension developed within individual women, within families, and between women as they looked in different directions for their primary source of self-definition and personal satisfaction.[76]

As the way of life of the farm women departed ever more dramatically from that of town women, farm families and farm wives shrank in numbers, becoming a minority even in Trempealeau. Nonfarm families expanded in number while the number of farm families declined. Sometime between 1940 and 1950, the majority of households in the county located themselves in the villages rather than on the farms. From frontier times until the decade of the 1940s, the majority of the population shared a common way of life. The demographic shift in population to the towns may have accentuated the sense of deviance from the norm for farm women.

Demographic statistics offer further evidence of some women's discontent with farm life. From frontier years until 1970, Trempealeau County experienced a consistent imbalance in the gender ratio. Young women left the county at younger ages and in larger numbers than their male counterparts. No doubt the greater demand for male laborers on the farm accounts for some of this differential. But the peak decade in the imbalance coincided with those years when farm work for women increasingly embarrassed the young (see Table 7.4). This was also the generation of women who first attended high school in significant numbers. By 1950 about 79 percent of the 16- and 17-year-olds were in high school. The expanding educational system and the mass media's growing presence introduced new conceptions of womanhood, challenging local and ethnic traditions of the past.

Among the young, the imbalance in the gender ratio was even greater than the overall gender-ratio statistics suggest. The consequence of the flight of the women from Trempealeau is most visible among the age group 30–44 in 1940, when there was a total of 123 men for every 100 women

Table 7.4. Gender Ratios in Trempealeau County, 1880–1980

	Males	Females	Ratio of Males to Females
1880	9,022	8,167	110.5
1890	9,883	9,037	109.4
1900	12,058	11,056	109.1
1910	11,886	11,042	107.6
1920	12,860	11,646	110.4
1930	11,373	10,085	112.8
1940	12,963	11,418	113.5
1950	12,490	11,240	111.1
1960	12,050	11,327	106.4
1970	11,832	11,512	102.7
1980	13,138	13,020	100.9

Sources: See appendix C.

Table 7.5. Number of Males per 100 Females in Trempealeau County, by Age Group, 1930–1970

	1930	1940	1950	1960	1970
0–14	109	102	104	103	107
15–29	115	114	110	105	103
30–44	113	123	119	108	101
45–64	123	117	116	115	106
≥65	119	118	110	100	92

Sources: See appendix C.

(see Table 7.5). The long-established differential in the county's gender ratio narrowed for several reasons: young family workers on the farm, male and female, were steadily replaced by machines and by farm wives in the barns and fields; the differences between male and female educational levels decreased; the gap in life styles on the farm and in the village lessened; and most families became villagers rather than farmers.

Village women may have been more leisured than farm women throughout the history of these communities. The statistics available indicate that it is a long-standing pattern for village households to average 1.0–2.0 fewer people then farm households. In 1905 the average household size in the village of Whitehall was 5.58, while those of Pigeon and Lincoln townships were 6.38 and 6.48, respectively. In 1930, the median farm household size was 4.87, while the village average was 3.98. In 1960 the pattern continued: households in the villages of Pigeon Falls and Whitehall included 2.9 people compared with 3.8 for both Pigeon and Lincoln townships. Both village and farm households reduced their size, but the differential remained. Within the county as a whole the mean household size dropped every decade after 1890, which no doubt eased women's responsibilities. (See Table 7.6.)

The declining size of the household reflects another critical change for both village and farm women: the fall in the birthrate. After 1900 the birthrate began to decline in Trempealeau County, but the rate remained above the national average for white women. In 1900, married women between the ages of 35 and 44 who had children in the two townships and villages averaged 6.11 births. The cohort 10 years older, who had completed their childbearing, averaged 6.74 births. In 1910, for Pigeon women between the ages of 45 and 54, the average number of births was 7.3, with 6.2 of those children still living. Only 18 percent of the women had four or fewer children, while 41 percent had nine or more, and another 41 percent had from five to eight children. Like Ella Hanson, who had one stillborn child, exactly half of the women between the ages of 45 and 54 had lost one or more children before the 1910 census. A total of 15.8 percent of the children born to those women did not survive to that year.[77]

Table 7.6. Mean Household Size in
Trempealeau County, 1890–1970

1890	5.38
1900	5.23
1910	4.97
1920	4.75
1930	3.68[a]
1940	3.93
1950	3.54
1960	3.50
1970	3.20

Sources: See appendix C.
[a]The statistic for 1930 represents
family size rather than household size.

Table 7.7. Fertility Ratio in Trempealeau County, 1910–1970 (Children Aged 0–9 per 1,000 Women Aged 15–44)

	1910	1920	1930	1940	1950	1960	1970
Women 15–44	—	4,448	4,811	4,900	4,288	3,778	3,799
Children 0–9	5,328	5,460	4,675	4,102	4,694	4,768	4,334
Ratio		1,228[a]	972	837	1,095	1,262	1,141

Sources: See appendix C.
[a]Based on women aged 18–44 instead of 15–44.

Ella Hanson, of a later generation of women than those in the 1910 census, married in 1916 at the age of 17 and had nine children, eight of whom grew to maturity. Her family and her work were similar in structure and organization to the nineteenth-century family. In 1930, Ella was still not a notable exception in Lincoln and Pigeon. While the twentieth century did bring a decline in family size to rural areas, in 1930 the farm families were still surprisingly large. While manuscript censuses are not yet available to provide a precise picture of birthrates in 1930, the farmer's directory of that year lists the names of the children in the households. Seventy-seven percent of the farm households in Pigeon included offspring of the head, and the average number of children in each was 4.2. In Lincoln the average was even higher. There, 84 percent of the households included children of the head, and the average was 5.92. These statistics include families at every stage of the life cycle, those beginning their families and those who had completed them. Nonetheless, they do indicate that families continued to be large.[78]

Precise data on the townships are not available after 1910, although

Ella Hanson (diarist) and her husband Adolph Benard "Bennie" Hanson and their children, ca. 1940–1950. *Back row:* Anna Ruth, Harry, Eleanor; *center row:* Phyllis, Arthur, Lloyd; *front row:* Dorothy, Ella, "Bennie," Marie. Photo courtesy of Eleanor Ackley, Pigeon Falls, Wisconsin.

Table 7.8. Number of Children Ever Born per 1,000
Married White Women Aged 35–44, in Trempealeau
County and the United States

	Trempealeau County	United States
1960 census	3,432	2,572
1970 census	3,742	3,049

Sources: See appendix C.

published census information for the county clarifies trends. In 1970, the village women had somewhat fewer children than farm women of the county as a whole. The number per 1,000 village women was 3,674, while that of farm women was 3,845.[79]

Since 1950 the physical differences between the homes of farm families and villagers have disappeared. All have the same modernized homes. While many women continue to be important to farm operations, their work has lost whatever stigma it had briefly acquired, because women everywhere in the United States have entered the work force in employment not traditionally regarded as women's work. Those women who are not working with their husbands on farms today are employed outside the home in growing numbers. In 1940, only 16 percent of the females over the age of 14 were in the work force, but by 1960 over 32 percent were included.[80]

One Pigeon farm woman recently commented that more women seem to be out working with their husbands in the fields and barns than once had been true. This may well be the case.[81] Their productive and reproductive responsibilities within the household have declined significantly in the second half of this century, because family size has declined. Other factors are also important. The technological revolution transformed housework in modernized homes, and farm families decided to purchase rather than produce most of the foods of the household.

This shift away from production for the household can be tracked in the decline in diversification on the farms. Animals and products once essential to the household economy and the daily and seasonal rhythms of work disappeared on many farms. The numbers of farmers reported in the census as owning poultry, lambs, and pigs decreased. In 1925, 94 percent of the farmers kept chickens, which women used for eggs and regularly slaughtered for meals. Gathering eggs and feeding chickens traditionally had been the responsibility of women and children. Women sold extra eggs for small sums, but usually chickens were not of major importance to the family income. Their primary role was within the household economy. In 1945, 89 percent of the farmers owned chickens, but 20 years later only 34 percent did so. Thus, eggs and chickens as food in a farmer's home now were purchased rather than produced on the farm. A similar pattern appears with pigs. In 1925, 76 percent of the farmers owned pigs; in 1965, only 19 percent did. Pork and poultry became consumer items for which farm women depended upon the supermarket almost as much as urban families did.[82]

Besides reducing diversification the transition from producer to consumer undercut traditional skills and activities. Instead of the homemade loaves of bread that Ella Hanson baked every week, her daughter relies on the grocery store. "Store-bought" bread and "store-bought" clothes became the mark of prestige, and "homemade" became associated with poverty and old-fashioned ways, a situation which deeply offended many women who had long prided themselves on their skills and hard work. Regardless of the periodic revivals of popularity of natural and homemade products, a generation of women saw their traditional skills and work devalued as consumption instead of production became symbols of status.[83]

The work associated with supplying the needs of the family has been reduced now that farm women meet those needs primarily as consumers rather than producers. Women on farms, however, have not become more leisured. Even as the numbers of farm workers declined, as labor costs increased, and as consumption standards changed, women have continued to be farm workers. One woman who lives on a large, highly mechanized farm commented that men and women seem to have less leisure time than in the past. She assists her husband in all phases of farming. But, she noted, her children participate far less than children did when she was young because of the constant round of school activities. A reduction in the work of child rearing and the household has provided the extra time for many women to replace other workers on the farm. A survey done of Wisconsin farm women in 1978 indicated that women still spent many hours in farm work. Twelve percent worked 30 or more hours a week doing farm chores, almost half reported spending some time in the fields, and 6 percent worked in the fields 60 or more days a year. In Michigan, women contributed 25 percent of all the hours of labor in farm work. Thus, women continue to play a fundamental role in the productive work of farming, however radically that work has changed in the last 30 years.[84]

Farm wives, it seems, have long faced the dilemma of the second shift of the dual-career women. Berthe Gunderson as a Norwegian peasant wife carried this double burden; not only did she work with her husband in the barn and fields, but she then did the housework as well.[85] But just as women today use their economic earning power to negotiate relationships, so too did peasant and farm women often use their fundamental role as producers to set the terms of life in their households. One Pigeon woman, now retired from farming, told how she convinced her husband of the necessity of a dishwasher. Doris Estenson, whose husband's family name is laced through the local community's past and present records, from the beginning of her marriage worked in the barn and fields with her husband. She eventually noted the injustice of her role in returning to the house at the end of the day and having to do dishes while her husband relaxed. "When your day is done, so is mine," she announced, and the dirty dishes were left regularly overnight until the desired dishwasher appeared.[86]

From frontier times until the present, fundamental to the rural woman's experience and identity has been her role as worker. Whether women worked in or outside the house, they were, and perceived themselves to be, primarily productive workers essential to their family and household economy. They took pride, as Anderson noted concerning his mother and other women, in the fact that they were equal to the challenges and tasks they faced, and they took considerable pride in their skills.

While the evidence is mixed, many farm women who shared the work on the farm may have also claimed responsibility and power within the farm household. Women from frontier times until the present participated in the critical decisions, management, hard work, and hard times of the life. In doing so, many have looked askance at middle-class ideals of women's work and place. Soon after the precepts of the "feminine mystique" made inroads in the local mentalité in the 1940s, such conceptions were about to be challenged by American women generally. This challenge may have come as a great relief to rural women, although for rather different reasons from those of the middle-class urban woman. Recent redefinitions of women's work and place seem primarily to have had the effect of eliminating the stigma that for a time accrued to the work of farm women. Women's work no longer is expected to be distinct, be it factory or farm. As one Pigeon woman put it when discussing the call of the women's movement for women's equality in the work place, "We always were liberated."[87]

8
The Country Visitor:
Patterns of Rural Hospitality

Anyone spending time perusing the *Whitehall Times* of the late nineteenth and early twentieth centuries will notice that a portion of the front page set off in bold type is devoted to the social doings of local community members. Accounts not unlike the following frequently fill much of the newspaper:[1]

> Mrs. Herman Ekern departed today for a three-week visit to the home of her parents at Long Lake, Wisconsin.

> Mrs. Anderson departed today for an extended visit with relatives and friends in Northfield, Minnesota.

> Miss Chrystal Abbott returned today after a month-long stay at the home of her sister, Mrs. William Swan.

Week after week, year after year, the newspaper recorded the visits to and fro of large numbers of residents. The length of the visits varied from a few hours between trains to several months. The distances traveled ranged from a few miles to neighboring communities to thousands of miles to distant states and other countries.

Historians, understandably, rarely pay attention to such local news of this sort. Seemingly, this kind of news could be of interest only to local residents of the time. However, careful attention to apparently trivial bits of information may prove valuable to social historians interested in family and community. A host of questions come to mind. How widespread and frequent were these country visits and receptions? Why were they reported so prominently? Whose visits and receptions were most frequently reported? These data, when systematically analyzed, are illuminating about age, gender, kinship, community, and class relations. Were visits an age- or gender-specific activity? What are the relationships between the families and the individuals involved? What are the purposes of the visits in relation-

186

ship to the social and economic life of the family and the community? What, if anything, might these visits reveal about kin networks and other social groupings?

Visiting patterns potentially provide guides to the social and emotional lives of people. The round of visiting in which individuals and families engage may suggest social status and the strategies by which social classes define or consolidate their positions. The creation and sustenance of distinctive cultures, too, often depend upon visiting. The functions of class and kinship in social relationships are better understood when the structure of sociability is delineated.[2]

To uncover visiting patterns, social historians have relied primarily on diaries, journals, and letters. The habits of families and individuals may be found in such sources. Local diarists in Lincoln and Pigeon reveal two basic concerns: the work they did and the visiting that occurred. Ella Hanson and the three Wood diarists recorded their daily labors and their visits and visitors. The letters of Herman Ekern's family members similarly elucidate their social activities.

While these sources may provide insight into particular family and individual behavior, local newspaper accounts, when systematically examined, can also suggest patterns of behavior of entire communities. Lincoln and Pigeon provide excellent sources with which to examine the phenomenon of the country visitor. Michael Lesy and Merle Curti both relied heavily upon local newspaper accounts to analyze the social experience of rural Wisconsin, although each formulated sharply contrasting conceptions of frontier life despite the similarity of sources. In *Wisconsin Death Trip,* Michael Lesy presented the social life of nearby Black River Falls between 1880 and 1900 as characterized by isolation.

Merle Curti on the other hand found an informal, simple, and democratically based round of social activities in Trempealeau. "The people of Trempealeau," he noted, "took it for granted that the need for and value of fun were easily and simply met within the circle of family, church, and neighborhood." In the social activities of the neighborhoods, "the democratic overtones were usually apparent. . . . Everyone, judging from accounts we have, was welcome. . . ." Hospitality and generosity came to be the most valued virtues of the frontier social code, values which Curti believed the frontier nurtured and which became the frontier legacy to America.[3]

As the people of Trempealeau faced the postfrontier world, habits of sociability established earlier persisted despite changes within and beyond their communities. The first 50 years of the twentieth century were years of extraordinary transformations in American society. The majority of Americans ceased to live and to make their living on farms and in small towns.

Rural communities across the nation sent hundreds of thousands of their sons and daughters into the urban frontier when land ceased to be available on the western frontier. The opportunities of expansive cities attracted rural youth. By 1900 these recently pioneered communities were making people their primary export.[4] However, they did not necessarily flee their small-town and country homes to escape deprivation, horrors, or simply tedium—Sinclair Lewis, Hamlin Garland, and Michael Lesy notwithstanding. Nor did they immediately become cosmopolitan urbanites. Among other things they became frequent "country visitors."

Examining visiting patterns in the countryside dispels the myths about the isolation of families in rural communities. The most pronounced characteristic of the country visitors was that they were ubiquitous. In her autobiographical account of her Norwegian-immigrant family's experiences in rural Wisconsin, Thurine Oleson described the social life of her family:

> We had so much company in those early days that mother had to spend a great deal of her time cooking. She had to be prepared at all times for a visitor and no one ever went away without a meal or a treat of some sort. . . . It's hard to beat the Scandinavian for hospitality. Not only did the young folks have parties, but the old folks too. They used any old excuse for a party. When there was work attached it was called a bee, and there were many of these— plowing bees, husking bees, quilting bees. After these affairs, in the evening, the young folks would dance and have a big time. Of course, it was not a right good time until they had a few drinks. Just enough to make them feel good, as they worded it, but with some it was a little more. Newcomers were the ones who had the biggest time of all.[5]

One gets the impression from Oleson and from the newspapers, journals, and letters of the people in the village of Whitehall and the surrounding area that they devoted the greater share of their energies and time to visiting and being visited or preparing to do one or the other.

Was this a Scandinavian trait? Hardly. The diaries of David Wood and his two sons, Ralph and Jim, which span the years from the 1860s, the earliest frontier period, to 1927, reveal that Yankees too could be quite hospitable. On any day of the week the Wood farm might receive or send out from three to five people for a short visit; almost any week could bring guests who stayed for hours, overnight, or longer. There were times, indeed, when a visitor spent months at this farm.[6] The Woods, like Thurine Oleson's mother, "had to be prepared at all times for a visitor."

Newspapers and diaries reveal the truth of Thurine Oleson's statement, "They used any old excuse for a party." Holidays such as the Fourth of July or special occasions could bring as many as 40 or 50 "surprise" visitors to the Wood farm for a picnic. The *Whitehall Times* reveals that "surprise parties" occurred regularly for a number of reasons—a birthday, an anniversary, or to raise money for someone who had recently experienced some misfortune. These parties could include up to 400–500 people. Such events could involve gifts, speeches, and various kinds of entertainment. The *Whitehall Times* regularly announced, in addition to "surprises," barn dances, basket socials, coffees, ice cream socials, weddings, house warmings, and a variety of other events to which "all" were welcome. Local residents also regularly attended similar occasions at the homes of people in nearby villages and townships. Food was always plentiful at such occasions, and, depending on the preferences of the hosting family, so too might the drinks have been plentiful. The inclusive character of social activities of frontier times, which Curti noted, continued to typify most local social events reported in the *Whitehall Times*.[7]

The Wood family, like most of the people in these communities, went to church twice on Sunday and to prayer meetings one night during the week at the home of one of the members, much as their Puritan forefathers had done in New England. Sunday noon dinners invariably brought guests who would stay until the evening service, held at the home of a congregation member. In the 1870s and the 1880s a typical week such as the one recorded in January of 1879 included the following round of visiting: On Sunday the Woods went to church in the morning and in the evening. In the afternoon E. F. Wade (a local resident), John Hart of "Modena," and Amos Parsons arrived. Amos left with Wade to pay the Wade family a visit. John Hart stayed until Tuesday. The next day Dave and Hart went to town to "see E. F. Wade off." They then "came home for dinner and . . . chatted the rest of the day." That evening Dave's son Archie went to a debating club. On Tuesday Dave accompanied Hart and another relative, Charlie Sherwood, on a visit to the home of Dewey Parsons, Dave's step-brother. That evening Elder Barbour arrived and spent the night. On Wednesday, Dave recorded: "Drew two loads of wood for self and went to town and took Eld. Barbour up and things. He goes to Reedsburg. J. Hart home tonight and A. L. Sherwood also." Sometime during the day Wood managed to purchase 60 bushels of wheat from another farmer. Thursday found Dave drawing wood for his father, whose farm was located about two miles from Dave's place. In the evening he accompanied his father to a neighbor's home for a prayer meeting. Friday brought a visit by Charlie Sherwood and his wife. As a result of this visit, Dave wrote, "I staid [*sic*] home all day and went to town in the evening." He may have spent the night at his father's, which he often did, because the next day he would "once again draw wood" for his father and attend a lyceum with him in the evening.[8]

While Dave's diaries clearly reveal a man constantly on the go, constantly interacting with his kin, neighbors, and friends, one might well ask, What about the women and other members of the Wood household? Hamlin Garland and Michael Lesy, among many others, portrayed rural women in the Midwest as living lives of hard work, isolation, and despair. In no sense did Dave Wood account for all the comings and goings at the Wood household. Nonetheless, in 1872 he reported that his wife, Mary, spent 68 days with friends, relatives, and neighbors and participating in functions outside of her home.[9]

The later journals of Ralph and Jim, the sons of Dave and Mary, demonstrate that Dave mentioned only those visitors with whom he was most concerned. In his diaries, Ralph, the youngest son, who was 12 years old in 1891, was especially conscientious in noting the women and younger visitors to and from the Wood farm. A typical week in 1891, as disclosed by the three diaries, included the following: On Sunday, March 22, 1891, Ralph reported, "Andrew and his girl came down." This is probably Andrew Sherwood, Mary's uncle and a frequent caller at the Wood farm. As usual, the Woods attended church in the morning and evening. Andrew and "his girl" would spend the night. On Monday Dave and his son Jim "loaded oats in town." On Tuesday Dave was once again in town, and Ralph reported, "Pa, Jim, Andrew, Emma, and I go to the basket social." Andrew and his girl Emma were still at the Wood's. The next day Ralph "went over to the Rebarchicks to see the boys" and also noted that "Mrs. Hankey and her sister came over to see us." Thursday evening the Woods were at a surprise party for Mr. Wright. On Friday Ralph was again off to the Rebarchicks along with another neighbor boy, Lewis. Also that day, a Mrs. Holmes arrived to visit Mary, Dave's wife. She would stay until April 6—a week and a half. Lydia Holmes and her son Earnie made regular appearances in these diaries. Mary too visited the Holmes household in nearby Hixton for extended periods. On Saturday, March 28, the "Rebarchick boys came over, Lydia staid," and Archie, Dave's eldest son, arrived with his wife, Jessie, and "babies." Jim went to a caucus, Dave did business in town, and Jessie and the babies spent the night.

The next week continued with a similar rhythm. Young Ralph recorded that Matt and Bernie came down, that Ruby, Mrs. Hankey, and Lydia "staid," that Ruby went home, and Fanny and Amy came to stay, that Mrs. Holmes went home, that Andrew went home (had Andrew been there all that time?), that Uncle Dewey and family came for a visit, and that Frank Breed was there. Dave's diaries indicate that he was an active and hospitable man; his son's diaries suggest that the same was true of other members of the Wood household. Later, when Mary's widowed mother moved in with them, she too kept up an active round of visiting.[10]

In the Wood household men and women, young and old, all participated in an active round of visiting. A tabulation of overnight visitors to and from the Ralph Wood household in the year of 1920 reveals that on 113 nights of the year some member of the Wood household had gone visiting, or someone was visiting the Wood household. This does not include the coming and goings of hired laborers or domestics. One or both of Ralph's children were absent 53 nights of that year. Hanson's diaries reveal a similar round of visiting through the depression and years of World War II.[11]

One need not linger long in such diaries, however sparse the entries, before concluding that, whatever else one can say about life on Dave and Ralph Wood's farm or on that of Ella and Bennie Hanson, these were not lonely or isolated people. These diaries as well as other sources suggest that women and their children may have been even more actively engaged than men in the sociability of these communities and kin networks.

Other sources confirm the active habits of the country visitor. The large number of visits reported in the columns of the *Whitehall Times* suggests that the Woods' and Hansons' constant round of visiting differed little from the activities of others in the countryside and villages in that area. In the 1880s and 1890s, the *Whitehall Times* weekly itemized 20–50 visits in and out of the community. By 1910 the *Times* typically reported from 60 to 100 or more.[12] It would seem highly unlikely that the *Times* provided anything approaching complete coverage. The letters of various members of two Norwegian-immigrant families, those of Herman Ekern and Hans Anderson, yield similar conclusions. Over the years these families were in and out of Whitehall and Pigeon Falls, and some of their members would become dispersed around the state and nation like those of other families. Yet, these families would maintain important kin and community ties by correspondence and regular and extended visits.[13]

Besides appearing with extraordinary frequency and often unannounced, the country visitor's second most characteristic feature is perhaps already clear. Visiting patterns bear testimony to the centrality of kin relationships in these people's lives. Until his father's death in 1884, Dave Wood alluded to some kind of contact with his father on almost a daily basis. Indeed, their lives were interconnected in every way—financially, religiously, and socially.

Similarly, in the 1890s when Dave's sons began to marry and establish their own households, a similar pattern of interdependence emerged. His sons and their wives and children frequently visited Dave's household, as did sisters, aunts, uncles, cousins, nieces, and nephews. Those who appeared a few times a week lived in the immediate vicinity. Mary's brother and family, Dave's sister and husband, "Shub" Breed, and children, cousin Frank Breed, Uncle Andrew Sherwood (Mary's uncle), and cousin Charlie, all make regular appearances in the diaries week after week, year after year.[14]

A sampling of those conspicuous front-page social items in the *Whitehall Times* between 1880 and 1923 verifies the preeminence of kin in the frequent visits. The following statistics were garnered from a sample based upon all the items listed for one week of each month in the *Whitehall Times* for four different years—1890, 1910, 1914, and 1922. In the earliest sample year, 39 percent specifically state that the visit was with a relative. In 1910 the proportion was 41 percent; in 1914, over 55 percent; and in 1922, about 38 percent. Because newspaper reports did not always clarify the relationships of visitors and their hosts, it is likely that even higher proportions visited relatives.

Besides visits described as between relatives, the *Whitehall Times* had numerous entries such as the following: "F. E. Beach of Ettrick is a guest in the home of Mr. and Mrs. Dan Camp"; "Mrs. Clark Getts spent the week visiting in Galesville"; and "Ruby Sherwood left today to visit friends in La Crosse."[15] No doubt many such visits were with relatives. Mrs. Getts, for example, had a daughter in Galesville whom she frequently visited.

In 1922, descriptions of visits with friends occurred more frequently than ones specifically mentioning relatives. Forty percent of all visits were between friends. In 1914 they represented 27 percent of the total, and in the earlier samples, about 20 percent. The 1922 figure may simply reflect a change in reporting habits, or it might signal a trend away from the dominance of the kin network in the social and economic lives of these country folk.[16]

While the *Whitehall Times* did not always inform its readers of the exact relationship of the visitor to the individual or family visited, in about half to three-fourths of the cases it did. Although some variation occurred based on the gender of the visitor and on the year of the sample, the inclusion of an identifying label of the relationship indicates who was visited within the kin network. In all the years sampled, parents topped the list. In 1890, in all those cases in which the nature of the kin relationship was mentioned, 69 percent visited parents. In 1900 the figure totaled 62 percent, in 1914, 38 percent visited parents, and in 1922 about half involved parents.

An apparent disinclination to visit parents-in-law existed in both women and men. Although parents were the most likely targets for a visit, married couples rarely visited together. In 1890, only 6.6 percent of the mentioned visits included couples; in 1900, only 3 percent were such. The sample from the year of 1914 produced an unusually high proportion of husband-wife visits to a parent—20 percent. This did not presage a new trend in family relations; in 1922 the earlier pattern was reestablished, when only 4 percent of the total included couples visiting parents.

Parents visited their offspring far less often than children visited parents. The number never totaled more than 14 percent of all the visits between relatives.

Following parents, the most likely candidate for a visit was a sibling. In 1914 they competed with parents in popularity at just over a third of the total. In 1900 and in 1922 of all the visits to relatives where the relationship was specified, visits between siblings totaled 28 percent of the total. In 1890, when parents received 69 percent, siblings reached a low proportion of 13 percent.

In all this visiting between kinfolk, women consistently outnumbered men as visitors. Whether this is because women visited more frequently or because women reported their doings more aggressively is unclear. In 1890 they represented two-thirds of the total. In 1900 and 1914 the differences in reported visits of men and women to kin were slight; women represented

Women were active and independent country visitors, ca. 1890–1910. Photo by Charles Van Schaick. Van Schaick Collection. Photo courtesy of State Historical Society of Wisconsin, WHi (V2) 309.

Table 8.1. Numerical Distribution of Visits to and from Trempealeau County, by Relationship/Purpose, 1890–1922

	1890		1900		1914		1922	
	Male	Female	Male	Female	Male	Female	Male	Female
Relative	31	59	56	61	120	169	98	154
Friend	24	24	30	26	59	83	88	169
Pleasure	20	9	4	6	16	9	31	26
Business or political	58	5	88	17	47	18	58	26
Total	133	97	178	110	242	279	275	375

Source: The *Times* samples.

over half at 52 and 53 percent, respectively. In 1922, 61 percent of all visits to relatives were made by women.

In addition, women and men appeared to prefer to visit their female kin over their male kin. Women especially preferred to visit their sisters, daughters, and aunts. In 1914, for example, 52 sisters were paid visits but only 21 brothers. Parents visited only 8 of their sons but 21 of their daughters, and aunts were mentioned twice as often as uncles. it was not just women who visited women; men, too, indulged in this partiality for their female kin. In the 1914 sample, men visited only 8 of their brothers but 18 of their sisters. Much of the responsibility for maintaining the bonds of kinship rested on relationships with and between women.

In the 1890 and 1900 samples of the *Whitehall Times*, men outnumbered women in the total number of visits mentioned in the paper, constituting 58 and 57 percent, respectively. By 1914 the situation had reversed itself, with women making up 53 percent of the total. By 1922 their number had increased to 58 percent. The increased proportion of women reported among the visitors was accompanied by a decreased number of reported visits involving political, professional, and educational purposes. Such visits, with the exception of education, were almost exclusively the province of men. They peaked in the attention of the press in 1900, when their number reached 37 percent of the total, up from the 28 percent of 1890; after 1914, they amounted to only 13 percent or fewer.

Newspapers, letters, and diaries all yield the same conclusion: kinship was the most frequent relationship between visitors within the community and between visitors coming from and going to communities beyond the Whitehall and Pigeon Falls area. If the time spent visiting is a guide to the emotional bonds between people, there is no doubt that for members of these communities until well into the twentieth century it was the extended family, not simply a nuclear family, that gave their lives structure and meaning.

A third pronounced feature of the country visitor is that, whether male or female, the visitor tended to act quite independently of the opposite gender. Whether they were married or single they usually did their visiting alone or with some member of their own gender. These rural women were far from being dependent on their husbands to prevent isolation on the farm. Women such as Mary Wood and her many female friends and relatives were active and independent in their socializing. Dave, while ever in motion, rarely mentioned including Mary on his visits, though no doubt she did accompany him on many occasions.

The *Whitehall Times* and the letters of the Anderson and Ekern families also bear witness to the homosocial visiting patterns in rural Wisconsin. Among all the samples from the *Whitehall Times,* women were accompanied by husbands in about 25–30 percent of the visits. For men the range was somewhat greater. Until 1900, men were reported as visiting in the company of their wives in only a fifth of the cases; however, by 1914 the proportion had doubled.

Single women, if they did not make their visits alone, which they did not do in three out of five instances, traveled and visited almost exclusively in the company of female friends and relatives. In 1914, male relatives or friends accompanied single females in only 6 percent of the visits. If single females had a companion on their visits, 40 percent of the time it was their mothers. Sisters followed mothers in popularity, accompanying single females on about a quarter of their visits, and female friends went along on 18 percent of the visits. The remaining 13 percent involved the companionship of female cousins, aunts, and nieces.

Not only did single women and girls visit in the company of other women, but also it was generally female friends and relatives whom they visited. Sisters and female friends topped the list of those whom a single female would visit. Fifty percent of the time a female relative or friend was identified as the person being visited, and in only 10 percent of the cases was a male specifically mentioned, and then only brothers and uncles.

Married women did not operate in so exclusively a homosocial world, but in many respects their visiting reflected similar patterns. In 1890, 79 percent of the visits of married women reported in the *Whitehall Times* were made without their husbands. If they did not go about their visiting alone, they did so in the company of a female relative or friend. In 1900 and 1914 the number of married women visiting without their husbands declined to about half of the total, and then increased slightly to 57 percent in the 1922 sample. In 1914, married women visiting without their husbands made their visits alone 49 percent of the time. Seventeen percent of the time they were accompanied by other couples or a brother or son. In the remaining 34 percent of the cases female friends, children, and relatives were with them.

A homosocial culture typified nineteenth-century middle-class America, but it shows some signs of having diminished in rural Wisconsin after 1890. Part of the explanation for this may be related to the departure from the community of the old-stock Americans. In 1890, 78 percent of those visits reported involved the Yankee members of the community. By 1900, they represented 54 percent of those visits reported, and by 1914, 70 percent of the visitors had Scandinavian surnames. In their sociability as in their work habits the Norwegian-immigrant families may have separated women and men less then their Yankee neighbors.

The country visitor was not a particularly "modern" character in several respects. Certainly, the modern sense of time appears to be lacking, and so also does something of the modern's regard for the privatized nuclear family. The length of time and the occasion which the country visitor found to be appropriate for a stay with relatives and friends varied more with the sun and the seasons than it did with the hands of the clock. Mud, snow, sunshine, or rain might be far more important in determining the length or time of a visit than any prearranged schedule.

Visitors often arrived unannounced with vague notions about how long they might stay. The *Whitehall Times* abounds with visits that are described as extended or indefinite in duration. Visitors arrived expecting to stay a few nights, a week or two, even months with surprising frequency. The *Whitehall Times* provided information about the length of a visit in about a third to half of those reported. In 1890, in about three out of four instances where the length of the visit was observed the visit lasted less than a week and usually only a day or two. Sunday stood out as the day most frequently mentioned for short visits between relatives and friends, but it was by no means the only time. Visits that extended over several months or were of an "indefinite" or "extended" duration totaled 16 percent, and those ranging from a week to a month in length were 11 percent of the total. By 1914 the longer stay had become more common. Fifty-three percent stayed a week or less, 30 percent a week to a month, 17 percent would stay for the "summer," for "some time," or for an "extended" visit.

In 1890 men and women were about equally likely to go on the longer visits, but by 1914 women would do so far more often than men. In that sample, women constituted 68 percent of those making visits that extended for over a month or an indefinite period of time and 60 percent of those visits lasting a week to a month. Of the visitors staying for extended

Table 8.2. Visits in Which Length of Time was Specified, 1914 *Whitehall Times* Sample

	Males		Females			
	Single and Married Without Spouse	Married With Spouse	Married With Spouse	Married Without Spouse	Single	Total
Length of Visit						
A day	15	13	13	6	9	56
2–6 days	11	4	4	5	9	33
1–4 weeks	5	6	6	2	13	32
≥1 month	7	2	2	4	13	28
Total	38	25	25	17	44	149

periods of time, single females were most common. Married and single women made week- to month-long visits in about equal numbers.

Mary Wood had married women and their children as well as single women staying with her nearly every month for varying periods of time. Many of those mentioned by Ralph in 1891 (Aunt Harriet, Aunt Ida, Mrs. Holmes and Ernie, Emma, Maggie, and others) would stay a few days or a little over a week. Others like "Alice and her baby staid" from February 15 to March 4. After Ralph married his Swedish-American wife, Martha, in 1907, she was, if anything, even more on the go than Ralph's mother.[17]

At the center of the pervasive homosocial female culture of the nineteenth century was an intimate mother-daughter relationship and close lifelong friendships between sisters and other female relatives and friends; visits served to reinforce their bonds. Evidence of the continued existence of this homosocial female culture can be found in the visiting patterns of women in Trempealeau County into the 1890s. The extended visit was an important means by which rural mobile women sustained primary emotional bonds.

The women from Norwegian-immigrant families behaved in a fashion quite similar to those of middle-class American backgrounds, but appear to have been less exclusive in separating men's and women's worlds on the farm and in the community. The visiting over short and long distances in which these women participated allowed them to maintain lifelong relationships and laid the basis for such relationships among their daughters.[18]

Although the *Whitehall Times* only occasionally reported on the visits of children except when they accompanied their mothers or parents, children and adolescents too made brief and extended visits. As a child and adolescent, Ralph rarely spent a week without a youthful companion. If he did not have a visitor of his own age, he often was off to neighbors and relatives on a visit. Mary and Dave's nieces, nephews, and grandchildren regularly turned up for a few days' visit or longer. Ralph and Martha's children also spent several weeks of the year staying with families of friends and relatives. Lily Ekern's children spent weeks at a time away from the parental eye with Lily's parents and sisters.

Rather than tying women to the kitchen and home to attend to numerous children, the large families that many rural women continued to produce throughout these years appeared to have interfered little with and may have even added to the freedom of both men and women to go visiting. Young children accompanied parents, and older children frequently assumed the responsibilities of a parent when one was absent from home. In the cases of the Wood, Anderson, and Ekern families, a variety of relatives could be depended upon to help out if someone were absent. If not a member of the household, then someone from within the kin network was available. The Ekerns' and Andersons' kin networks, while more dispersed than the Woods', nonetheless were highly integrated, interdependent, and emotionally meaningful.

In the homes of these families the size of the household was quite flexible. Women's and children's place may well have been defined as in the home, but they did not seem to be overly particular about which home. They acted independently of their nuclear families and moved about regularly among a variety of hearths. Being confined to the "domestic sphere" in this context may well not have been notably confining.[19]

Apparently this regular round of visiting and the hospitality were welcomed by almost everyone. The visiting expanded the perimeters of the community in which people were active. When they went visiting they participated in the community life of their hosts. The young, like Ralph Wood's and Lily Ekern's children, enjoyed the additional playmates, the exploring of different communities and households, and, like the adults, the relationships they established and maintained. Men and women had the companionship and assistance of their parents, siblings, other relatives, and friends. Lily Ekern and her husband, Herman, eagerly urged family members to visit and were similarly pressed to visit. Many expressions of disappointment can be found when desires were not obliged. Lily's sister Rose Anderson, an especially valued and frequent guest, spent much of her life with the Ekerns. She tended eventually to follow wherever Herman Ekern's career took Lily.[20]

Certainly not all met the welcome that the fun-loving and witty Rose did. In 1892, a series of letters between Herman, his sister Lena, and their sister-in-law Belle Ekern make clear that Lena had overstayed her welcome at Belle's home in Whitehall. Belle protested revealingly to Herman. Lena, she insisted, had always been treated very hospitably and would ever be welcome, however long she chose to stay and whatever burden her visits might impose on Belle. Expectations of hospitality could cause tensions, but there appears to have been a widely accepted social injunction to be open to a variety of people, especially within the kin network.[21]

The country visitor and the people of Whitehall and Pigeon Falls in the years between 1880 and 1925 do not seem to have developed the modern's high regard for the clear divisions between the public and the private. In all this movement between homes of people of all different ages, there seemed to be little concern for the privacy of the individual and the nuclear family. Besides operating on the basis of a premodern sense of time, the country visitor appeared to have grown up among and to continue to depend upon extended families.

A final issue that needs to be considered about the country visitor, and which in some respects further illustrates the traditionalism of these communities, is the question of the purposes and functions of all this visiting. Beyond the obvious fact that humans are social beings in need of fellowship, the reasons for visiting ranged widely.

That much of this visiting between relatives, neighbors, and friends constituted an important part of the economic life of the community is clear. Dave Wood's diaries demonstrate the considerable interdependence of himself and his relatives and neighbors. If American "rugged" individualism is rooted in the frontier experience it was not obviously so in the town of Lincoln. These farmers swapped labor, animals, equipment, every kind of agricultural product, and every conceivable item related to farm production. They depended upon each other in building barns and houses, in marketing their products, and in planting and harvesting their crops.

Their mutual interdependence manifested itself on a daily basis particularly in the early years before the market economy was highly developed. Dave's diaries leave the impression that few of the male relatives and neighbors that stopped at the Wood farm left without making arrangements for some type of exchange, and such visiting occurred on almost a daily basis. Dave Wood kept careful records of all he owed to or was owed by his father, sons, step-brothers, and neighbors. He even recorded how much a neighbor paid him for attempting to track down a horse thief. Dave may have diverged from frontier practice in his careful keeping of accounts, or perhaps his accounts reflect "the spirit of capitalism" that followed in the wake of the Puritan revolution of his forefathers. Perhaps Dave's records reflect the growing commercial ethos in the countryside, or perhaps they simply reflect a long-standing expectation that generosity, hospitality, and helpfulness were supposed to be reciprocated, if in no other way than by cash payments. One of the conspicuous reasons for visiting, then, had to do with the economic and productive needs of the people.[22]

In the past, the worlds of work and leisure were not so sharply differentiated as in our own times. It is thus hard to distinguish the purely social visit from the visit that had a financial or economic purpose. Visitors of all different ages participated in the daily routines of the farm and household, sharing the work and the pleasures of their hosts. When work was particularly heavy, as in the harvest season, or when there were special occasions such as weddings and holidays such as Christmas, men and women on the farm and in the village depended upon daughters, sons, nieces, nephews, siblings, and others to assist them. They came from neighboring towns and distant cities to share the work and good times of such seasons. As was previously mentioned, the butchering of an animal at Ralph Wood's farm invariably brought Martha's sister for a several-day stay to help. Martha frequently spent days in the homes of family members when sewing needed to be done. Among both men and women the work of the individual farms and households was shared by a variety of people. Such shared work was the occasion for conviviality and many good times. As Thurine Oleson put it, these people "used any old excuse for a party," from husking corn, to building barns, making quilts, and picking blueberries.[23]

In times of crisis, misfortune, and tragedy one could find many a country visitor. One of the reasons often given for an extended visit in the *Whitehall Times* was to care for an ill friend or relative. Men and women would return to the household of a parent to nurse them during an illness, and vice versa. The *Times* reported on women staying with their sisters and daughters at the time of a birth of a child and then remaining to assist the new mother. For the extremely ill, physically or psychologically, relatives and neighbors took turns as "watchers," as the *Whitehall Times* described those who attended the very ill.

Individuals and families faced few of life's triumphs or tragedies alone. Michael Lesy portrayed life in rural Wisconsin as one in which people lost their children to disease and disaster with tragic frequency (the Woods lost two children in one epidemic of diphtheria), and as one in which individuals often suffered harsh fates that could drive some to madness and suicide. But whatever tragedies individuals and families may have faced, and they were many, both the extended family and the community did much to ameliorate such events. People did not suffer those fates alone and unnoticed. Invariably, they found a country visitor at their side, a visitor who very likely made sure that the mad and the suicidal were quite uncommon.[24]

Neighbors and kin depended upon each other to assist with work and finances in times of crisis as well. In 1879 when Dave's step-brother's house burned, the unfortunate family stayed with the Woods and other relatives. Dave and his kinfolk took it upon themselves to find a way to finance the construction of a new home. Many of the surprise parties that so frequently occurred were for the purpose of raising money for someone who had recently faced such a misfortune.[25]

The mutual interdependence maintained by visits was complex and served a variety of functions. Besides assistance in times of need, visits could also shape future opportunities. Visits between relatives and friends, whether involving neighboring towns or distant cities and states, provided children and adults, men and women, with experiences with a host of different environments beyond those of their own village and community. Whitehall and the countryside around it may leave the impression of being a very small world "in the middle of nowhere," as one historian has described Trempealeau County, but residents rarely restricted themselves entirely to these communities.[26]

The visits of both the young and the old with relatives and friends dispersed across the state and nation could result in the discovery of information and opportunities, the establishing of relationships, and the pursuit of interests that could broaden and shape the lives of the country visitor. For children and the young who lived on farms, visits to villages or cities changed the rhythm of their lives and familiarized them with places they might very well someday make their homes. Children from urban environments with country cousins were not uncommon visitors to the countryside. A stay on an uncle's or a grandparent's farm brought children into contact with a different way of life.

Before high school, college, and other institutions and enterprises brought the young together, the visiting in kin and community networks offered many of the opportunities for employment, recreation, and courtship beyond the girl or guy next door. Jim Wood courted and married a young woman from Chicago. Her family had been one-time residents of Whitehall, but like so many others they followed the main chance to the city. Nonetheless, Olive Tull and her family regularly visited Whitehall and the Wood household. Similarly, their Chicago home welcomed their friends from Whitehall.[27] The results of such visits often appeared in the newspaper in items like the following: "Blanche Johnson, who has been staying with her brother Oliver in Suton, North Dakota, for the past eighteen months assisting him in his business, was married on January 2 to John McWetby of that place."[28]

The visits of adults could familiarize them with conditions and opportunities elsewhere and thereby provide the knowledge and contacts necessary for a move. In 1889 the *Whitehall Times* editor himself announced that he would soon follow another former Whitehall resident and friend who was visiting in town to the mines of Colorado. In the 1880s former Whitehall residents returned to sell shares in their mining operation and to convince others to join them.

Educational opportunities too could derive from kin and former residents.[29] In 1903, Lena Ekern once again depended upon the hospitality of others. In that year she studied art in Minneapolis while staying with former Pigeon Falls residents.[30] Similarly, when two sons of friends of Dave Wood wanted to go to high school they stayed at the Wood household after Dave had moved into the village in the later years of his life. Many of the rural youth depended upon kin to continue their education beyond what their one-room country school could provide.[31]

An examination of where visitors went and from where they came as recorded in the *Whitehall Times* provides a rather rough guide to the networks of kin and community. In the 1880s and 1890s visitors traveling long distances were likely to be going to or coming from small communities in Wisconsin, Minnesota, and the Dakotas. Depleted soil from wheat cultivation, economic depression, and other difficulties for farmers in the Midwest propelled many westward in search of greener pastures; thus western Canada, Oregon, Montana, Washington, and California appear in the *Times* as well. Merle Curti noted that the early residents of Trempea-

Table 8.3. Numerical Distribution of Male and Female Country Visitors to and from Trempealeau County, 1900 and 1914, by Area of Origin/Destination

| | Males (N = 245) | | | | Females (N = 322) | | | | | | Total (N = 525) | |
| | Single and Married Without Spouse | | Married With Spouse | | Married With Spouse | | Married Without Spouse | | Single | | | |
Area	To	From	To	From	To	From	To	From	To	From	To	From
Nearby	36	23	8	18	8	18	14	18	17	20	83	97
In state	15	16	9	15	9	15	7	8	24	31	64	85
Cities	15	22	8	8	8	8	8	18	22	22	61	78
Other countries or states	14	17	12	9	12	9	9	2	6	9	53	46
Total	80	78	37	50	37	50	38	46	69	82	261	306

Source: The *Times* samples, 1900 and 1914.

leau associated the West with "progress" and opportunity, and their visiting patterns confirm their confidence in it.[32]

By 1900, however, the destinations of visits of local residents indicate that they had discovered that the traditional frontier no longer existed. Cities within the state and beyond its borders increasingly grew in importance for visits. In 1914, 28 percent of all the visits reported were to or from urban areas. By 1922 the proportion had increased to 32 percent. In 1900, two-thirds of the visits to urban areas were made by men, frequently for business purposes; by 1914, women represented 60 percent of the total of such visits, and they retained this dominance in 1922. Every week the paper reported on several men and women who were pursuing educations, jobs, or careers in urban areas, returning for weekends, weeks, or more extended stays. In addition, an equal or even greater number were visiting friends and relatives in the cities.[33]

This visiting reveals something about the process by which Americans became an urban people by 1920 and about the strategies that individuals and families used for making the transition. Americans did not become an urban people overnight or on the day they moved to the city. Fortunately, those who grew up and left Whitehall and Pigeon Falls, as the majority would do, usually did not depart entirely ignorant of the world beyond their rural villages and country hamlets. They did not simply pack their bags and set out alone to distant states or strange cities where nobody knew their names. They did not often in isolation try to make sense of an alien environment.

Rather, the visiting patterns indicate that they depended upon extended kin and community networks for information, opportunities, and assistance. Once they left, they did not simply leave their childhood country homes forever. For many, the kin network and the home communities continued to play an important role in their emotional, social, and economic lives. If they should feel as if they were becoming nameless persons in a crowd, an interchangeable part in a huge impersonal machine, they could join the ranks of the many country visitors. They could go for a few days or longer where their activities and arrival would be regarded as newsworthy events that would come to the attention of hundreds.

A country visitor today who can regularly be found in Whitehall, the later Dave Wood, explains his extended visits this way: ". . . we go back for the calm regularity of small-town life and for the people I've known since I was a kid, people who actually know my name, my wife's name, know my parents, my grandparents, and even my great-grandparents. What's more they care about us and we care about them."[34]

In addition, if someone lost a job, went bankrupt, became ill, or faced some similar difficulty that so abounded in the growing cities, one could, as many did, take one's family and go visiting until the economy, one's health, or opportunities improved. Country folk and country communities extended their traditions of hospitality and generosity beyond their localities, and in doing so did much to ease the difficulties of Americans as they entered into a different kind of world.

9

From Peasant Pleasures
to Victorian Virtues

Late one September evening in 1862, many families of Trempealeau awoke to the sound of gunshots, human cries, and a chaos of bizarre sounds. Their awareness of an Indian uprising along the Minnesota frontier convinced them that one of their worst fears was being realized. Pioneers worked through the night to prepare themselves for an attack. That September evening provided a memorable event in local history, but not because of an Indian attack. In 1923, Hans Anderson recorded a detailed account as it was told to him by Knudt Olson Storley, one of the "old-timers" of the community:

> We had been threshing for Jacob Tenneson, who then lived on the farm now occupied by Elmer Thursten. After supper someone suggested that we ought to shiverie Peder Tenneson, who at the time was living on the farm now owned by Alvert Tenneson. Peder was a widower and had for his housekeeper Dorthea Gulbranson, a twin-sister of Mrs. Syver Johnson.
>
> The suggestion met with instant and unanimous approval and most of the men immediately went to their homes to get such noise-producing instruments as they could find in a hurry. Torger Gjorke got a drum which had been brought from Norway. Nels Halverson brought a string of sleighbells; two brought guns; others brought cow-bells, boilers, dishpans—in short, anything that would make the loudest noise. This preparation took time, so it was late before we silently marched to the place where Peder lived. When we got there, we found no one in the house. Suspecting that Peder and Dorthea had got wise to our coming, and were hiding somewhere around the premises, I ordered the boys in a loud voice to go home and then quietly I asked a couple of the boys to hide close by. We then noisily marched up the road, but in a short time one of our spies came running and told us that Peder and Dorthea had returned to the house, laughing over our disappointment. Then back to the house we all went and when we got there we sure did make some noise. Before long Peder came out with whiskey and for every drink there were "Skaals" and "hurrahs" that could be heard for miles. Guns were fired, the drum furnished us with "time," bells jingled, tinware rattled and jolly voices

grew louder with each drink that passed around. So liberally did Peder treat us
that some of the men did not get home that night. But while we were as happy
as we could be, across the river and up the valley, clear to Hixton many were in
deadly fear.

It was not an Indian attack that caused a night of terror in
Trempealeau, but a noisy "shiverie," or charivari. This particular charivari
coincided with a fear of an Indian uprising and thus became a long-
remembered event. Upon hearing the noise of the charivari in progress,
neighbors concluded that Indians were on the warpath and mobilized the
entire area for defense.[1]

Charivari parties—or shiverie parties, as local Norwegian Americans
spelled the word—were common in peasant society throughout northern
Europe. The charivari described by Storley well illustrates the form and the
function of this peasant tradition. In Norway, the custom was referred to as
bjolleleik and was organized by the community, particularly the male
youth, on the occasion of a marriage or when people thought a marriage
was in order.[2] The Norwegian immigrants brought their country's variation of this custom to the Trempealeau frontier where it lasted into the
postfrontier years. Charivari parties, as Anderson noted, had been "both
common and popular" at one time. Although Anderson believed the custom had declined when he wrote about it in 1923, some informants today
insist the charivari was still celebrated in the 1940s when couples did not
provide the community with a wedding dance to celebrate their marriage.
This traditional peasant celebration acknowledging or dictating the beginning of a marriage appeared in the earliest years of the frontier. Although
variations occurred in the nature and focus of the charivari, it had a long
life in Lincoln and Pigeon. The gradual transformation and ultimate demise of the charivari paralleled changes in traditional patterns of courtship
and sociability among the immigrants and their children.[3]

The charivari recalled by Storley indicated that this traditional expression of community control over marriage was being reasserted on the
American frontier. Whatever the future plans of Peder and Dorthea may
have been, the noisy demonstration that brought a night of terror to the
countryside clearly seemed to have persuaded them that a marriage should
take place. Of note is the fact that the charivari of Peder and Dorthea, who
was euphemistically described as his housekeeper, preceded the marriage
though the couple had already begun to live together. According to Anderson, "the official record shows that Peder Tenneson and Dorthea Gulbranson were married by Syver Johnson on Oct. 2, 1862," but the charivari had
occurred in September.[4]

Charivaris such as the one for Peder and Dorthea were a long-established form of conviviality and also a mechanism of community control of sexual behavior in peasant communities. It was not unusual for couples to begin a sexual liaison before marriage. However, the peasant community was careful to regulate such relations. Marriages were expected to follow the establishment of these relations, especially if a pregnancy occurred. In Norway the establishment of a sexual liaison before marriage had been most common among the class of peasants who had little or no land. Women and men of this class were often on their own, working without parental supervision from an early age. Since they had to rely on their own earnings rather than an inheritance for their futures, they could more freely regulate their own behavior. It was not unusual, in fact it was very common, for women to be pregnant or even to have had a child before marriage took place. Studies done of the landless cotters in one parish in Norway indicate that rates of illegitimacy and prenuptial conception ranged between 76.5 and 90.1 percent between 1820 and 1869. In Denmark, similarly, between 1650 and 1880, 50 percent of the first births among the peasant classes occurred within the first nine months of marriage. Illegitimate births even among the landowning peasants were often as high as 10 and even 20 percent of the first births. Among the peasant classes, marriage often became a serious prospect only after a sexual relationship had been established and a pregnancy had occurred.[5]

The premarital pregnancy rate of the Norwegian immigrants in Pigeon by 1886 was not nearly as high as in Norway, although it was notably higher than was typical of other American communities. Between 1886 and 1898, 16 percent of the marriages at the Evangelical Lutheran Church of Pigeon Falls were followed in less than six months by a birth and baptism. In one instance in the 1890s, the first birth preceded the marriage. The baptism and the marriage took place on the same day. Another 12 percent were followed by births in less than nine months but more than six.[6] The total of 28 percent of the marriages being followed by the birth of a first child in less than nine months is considerably higher than figures of approximately 11–15 percent which demographers of the early twentieth century have found.[7] This high rate of premarital pregnancy may even underestimate the numbers, because those couples who left the community after marriage and before the birth of a first child were not in local records. Of the 25 marriages recorded by the church between 1886 and 1898, 4 were preceded or followed by the birth of a first child in less than six months and 3 in more than six but less than nine months. The high rates of premarital pregnancy no doubt reflect the continuation of Norwegian peasant habits of courtship and mating.[8]

In 1862, Peder Tenneson and Dorthea Gulbranson cohabited without wedlock and began their lives together as many Norwegian peasants had done for centuries. Their neighbors responded to their arrangements as they would have in the past. To the extent that they had absorbed middle-class ideals of sexual morality, local Yankees and immigrants might have been more than a little scandalized by Peder and Dorthea's arrangements. By 1886, those who began their marriages expecting a child may well have been feeling considerable ambivalence. Middle-class reformers in both Norway and the United States pressed upon their contemporaries different views of sexual morality and courtship from those that were traditional to Norwegian communities.[9] Replacing the community controls on sexuality that the charivari represented was an emphasis on individual internal restraints. The individual, not the community, was to take responsibility for regulating sexual behavior. Such a transformation would render the charivari obsolete.

Control of sexuality became something of a preoccupation in middle-class families in the nineteenth century, and it was expressed in a new sexual ideology. Female "passionlessness," or purity, became a defining feature of the Victorian sexual ideology.[10] Between the years of 1770 and 1870 middle-class Americans embraced an ever more restrictive sexual code. Ellen Rothman discovered that "middle-class courting couples in the New Republic felt comfortable with a wide range of sexual activities, a range that narrowed as the nineteenth century went on." Before 1820, "sexual boundaries between unmarried men and women were loosely drawn and crossed with relative ease." In contrast with an earlier emphasis on women as particularly sexual beings, nineteenth-century thinking asserted that women had both the inclination and the responsibility to control sexuality.[11] By midcentury a new prescriptive literature proliferated, asserting women's lack of or limited sexuality.[12]

While the connection between behavior and the new ideology is subject to debate, behavior appeared to follow ideology in at least one respect: the second quarter of the nineteenth century brought a decline in premarital pregnancies. While it is uncertain how deeply down the social structure the "Victorian sexual ideology" penetrated, Trempealeau County farm families, immigrant and old-stock, did not remain untouched by the ideology.[13]

As influential as anyone in challenging traditional patterns of courtship and sociability in Pigeon and Lincoln was Hans Anderson himself, who as a devoted historian of the county recorded the 1862 charivari. Under the influence of first the pietistic Lutheran Hauge's Synod and then the Seventh-day Adventists, he shared those groups' revulsion toward the morality that the charivari exposed.[14] Elling Eilsen, the low-church leader of Norwegian Americans, had no intention of leaving "the miserable people to tumble about in their unresurrected lives" amid "drunkenness, cursing, swearing, dancing and fiddling and other noisy pleasures."[15] Anderson shared the pietistic determination to root out the ribald ways of the Norwegian peasants typified by the charivari of 1862.

Under the leadership of Hans Anderson, peasant customs were subjected to scrutiny and judged by the standards common to pietistic reformers and many other Americans. Customary courtship patterns, the sexual morality of the young, and general styles of sociability became issues of public debate in Pigeon at Anderson's initiative. Anderson apparently early absorbed the Victorian sexual ideology and its preoccupation with purity. As a result, with all the fervor of a convert and missionary, he set himself adamantly against the traditions of his countrymen. In 1876 he began a crusade to improve the morals of his community and to curb drinking, dancing, and the grievous "social evil" of "night running," referred to as *nattefrieri*, or night courtship, by the Norwegians. Night running was, as Anderson described it:

> . . . the custom of single men on Saturday and Sunday nights of getting together and then going from house to house, wherever there were young unmarried women, and visiting them in their bedrooms. Perhaps in most instances the young men had no intention of debauching the females, but in many instances it led to illicit relations. This custom was unknown in that part of Norway where I came from, but I regret to say in other localities it had existed from time immemorial, so that parents had come to regard it as a settled thing that their daughters would be visited in this manner as soon as old enough to regard the opposite sex as more than mere playmates.[16]

Contrary to Anderson, many of his neighbors would not regard their traditional ways as debauchery. In some respects, night courtship paralleled the seventeenth- and eighteenth-century New England tradition of bundling. According to the lyrics of an eighteenth-century song about bundling, the practice "very much abounds in many parts in country town."[17] Like bundling, night courtship in Norway was a rural phenomenon particularly common among the servant and cotter classes, from which many of the immigrants came. Young servants and even the children of peasant farmers often slept in out-buildings on the *gard*, or farm, and weekend visits by young men were a long-standing practice. In addition, young women spent the summer months alone in mountain *seters* or *stolen*, where they tended the animals in mountain pastures and made dairy products. During courtship the visiting males spent the night and often began sexual relationships, as Norway's premarital pregnancy rates reveal. Once a sexual relationship began or pregnancy occurred, a marriage usually followed. Night courtship did not, any more than bundling, allow for promiscuity as Anderson implied.

According to Eilert Sundt, a nineteenth-century Norwegian scholar renowned for the study of his country's peasants, strict standards of behavior were maintained. Sundt realized that night courtship would appear "offensive and unnatural" to his middle-class readers. He noted that couples attempted to keep the night visits secret, but he qualified this:

> No doubt the situation cannot be kept secret long but it is a point of honour for fellow servants not to disclose this kind of secret and when it is found that they believe in one another and that she does not receive other boys and that he does not visit other girls, none of their acquaintances will criticize them in the slightest. For this is the custom of the country in many of our rural districts and the only way by which young people of the servant class can become "acquainted" and in many cases it is conducted in all modesty and faithfulness. This night courtship is naturally always extremely dangerous for flesh and blood. But it is a mistake to assume that all the girls who take to their lovers in this way are girls without modesty. In all classes where night courtship has its home there are rules for it which maintain a certain strictness in the ideas of how a modest girl must behave.

In the choice of mates, youths of the lower classes wielded a large degree of discretion. As long as property was not involved, little or no parental supervision and interference occurred. The peer group monitored sexual behavior to a greater extent than parents. Any woman who violated the peer group's informal rules became a marked woman in the servant class and might confront various censures: her behavior might be exposed to her employer by other servants, causing the loss of her position, or other servants might refuse to work with her and thus resign.[18]

The independence of peasant youth from parental supervision in courtship was a long-established custom in Norway. The peer group, rather than the parents, set the standards and maintained discipline. Once a sexual relationship did begin, the couple was expected to marry, particularly once pregnancy occurred. And, as even before marriage, fidelity was expected. The charivaris which preceded marriages represented a not-so-subtle form of peer pressure to make the relationship official.[19]

Parental supervision tended to be indirect and noncoercive. Knut Hamsun's novels of peasant life indicate that whom one brought into the household as a hired girl or a hired man might be carefully screened on the basis of that person's potential as a mate. Such employment also provided employers with the opportunity to determine compatability and to observe a youth's character and capacities as a worker.[20] Being a hired girl or housekeeper often was a transitional status to becoming the mistress of the household. Housekeepers and domestic servants, like Dorthea Gulbranson, often became wives in stages. While working as servants or housekeepers, relationships gradually evolved with their employer or a member of the household in which they worked. A marriage might then occur when compatability was established or a child was expected.

Similarly, hired men could become husbands of widows, or they could become sons-in-law and eventually the head of the household where no male heir appeared. Peder Ekern's clerk became his son-in-law and heir to much of Ekern's property and position of leadership in the community. Hans Anderson's law partner, Herman Ekern, married Anderson's daughter. Among peasants, businessmen, and professionals, selection of those who became part of the household or business indirectly structured marriage choices.[21]

Courtship in Norwegian peasant communities and in the Pigeon and Lincoln Norwegian American communities resembled the descriptions of late eighteenth- and early nineteenth-century American patterns: "Sexual boundaries between unmarried men and women were loosely drawn and crossed with relative ease."[22] Just as American couples faced a more restrictive atmosphere by 1850, so too did many of the immigrants to Trempealeau County by the end of the nineteenth century. In Norway, the pietistic Haugeans were pressuring peasants to change their traditional behavior, as were representatives of the high church. The conflict that surfaced relating to night running in Pigeon reflected cultural tensions brought from Norway as much as it reflected pressure to adopt American moral standards.[23] When Anderson launched his crusade against night running he had recently been converted to the pietistic religion of the Yankee households in which he worked, but earlier he had been affiliated with the Haugeans. The concern of pietists and Haugeans for sexual purity among men and women appears to have been an influential source of Anderson's perceptions. More quickly than his immigrant neighbors, Anderson accepted the Victorian sexual ideology of the middle classes.

In 1876 at a series of meetings at the local schoolhouse in Pigeon, Anderson attempted to have resolutions passed, declaring the traditional night visits to the bedrooms of young girls an exhibition of "libertinism" and homes which permitted such visits by young men "bawdy-houses." His effort to publish these resolutions in a Norwegian language paper, the *Skandinavian,* published in La Crosse and read by many in the area, caused quite a stir in the Norwegian American community. Pressure mounted until he ultimately backed down. Although Anderson reported that influential men in the community such as Peder Ekern initially supported his campaign, in the face of "severe criticism from some of the members of their respective churches, . . . they soon withdrew from the field of battle." According to Anderson, the Norwegian Synod leadership involved itself in the conflict and censured the local minister for supporting the war on traditional morality.[24]

The Norwegian immigrants and their children met Anderson's effort to redefine traditional courtship patterns as sinful with outright hostility. "My activity against night-running aroused considerable hostility against me, and at times promised to result in violence to my person." Violating conceptions of virtuous womanhood as being chaste and submissive, several of Pigeon's "more prominent" young women, in defense of their traditional ways, organized to disrupt Anderson's meetings. By laughing and causing a disturbance, the daughters of leading local families brought to a halt one of the meetings. When Anderson asked the young women to leave, the young men of the community followed them out.[25] In this and a host of other ways, these women were not easily awed by the expectations and standards of their new country or of the clerical leadership in Norway.

Similar responses surfaced in Norway when pressure was put on peasants to change courtship practices. Apparently these Norwegian peasants and immigrants had no intention of redefining traditional conceptions of sexual morality in terms of prevailing middle-class standards.[26] The lyrics of the previously mentioned satiric bundling song, penned with an eye toward reform, suggest that eighteenth-century New England women responded with a similar boldness to efforts aimed at stamping out bundling:

> Some maidens say, if through the nation,
> bundling should quite go out of fashion,
> Courtship would lose its sweets; and they
> Could have no fun till weddin day.
> It shant be so, they rage and storm,
> And country girls in clusters swarm,
> And fly and buzz, like angry bees,
> And vow they'll bundle when they please.
> Some mothers, too, will plead their cause,
> And give their daughters great applause,
> And tell them, 'tis no sin nor shame,
> For we, your mothers, did the same.[27]

Peasant pleasures were given up only with reluctance and resistance. Anderson, however, claimed eventual victory: "In a few years there was an almost unanimous sentiment against night-running."[28]

Exactly when attitudes and courtship patterns changed in Norwegian-American communities is unclear. An account in the *Whitehall Times* in September of 1883 indicates that the immigrants continued to begin living together before marriage, and that the Norwegian-American community continued to use the charivari as a source of community control over such relationships. On September 20, 1883, the *Whitehall Times* reported a charivari for a couple who the editor concluded had been secretly married in a neighboring town. The *Times* noted that several people had become convinced that a marriage had occurred, and as a result "a large delegation accompanied by the band repaired to Ole's domicile and blew them out. Ole at once acknowledged the corn and immediately ordered liquid refreshments." Two weeks later the *Times* reported on Ole and Sophia again: "Ole and Sophia reported married some weeks ago were not wedded then, but took the marriage vow before justice Knight in this village last Tuesday and the event was celebrated by a big dance and roaring good time at Scott's hall Tuesday night." Despite the *Times* editor's supposition that a secret marriage had occurred, the participants in the charivari may well have been aware that this was not the case. The decision to wed shortly after the charivari suggests that the community played a role in notifying the couple that it was time for them to do so. The *Times'* account of this incident, however, reveals that the Yankee community may have had little understanding of the immigrants' traditions or may have felt compelled to use discretion in reporting about them. Because the couple should have been married, a secret marriage was presumed or the fiction maintained.[29]

New restraints on premarital sexual activity initially appear to have been an innovation of the young as a result of exposure to American values or Lutheran pietism rather than an imposition by parents. In Pigeon, after confirmation at the age of 14 or 15, the young continued to be as independent as they had been in the past, with the peer group continuing as the important source of discipline and values. The converts to pietistic religions were often the young, and they initiated changes in the standards of their peers and later shaped those of their own children. Anderson is a good example of an initiator of such change. At one of his meetings on morality, a leading member of the Pigeon community stood up and condemned him as a presumptuous "young upstart." Whatever the source of his pietism, the 20-year-old Anderson indeed was challenging traditional leadership and attempting to assert leadership in transforming the behavior of his generation.[30]

The first generation of immigrants seems not to have been unduly impressed by the reformers' critique of courtship. Anderson recorded his own aunt, Oline Fredrickson, on the chronology of her life as follows: "On April 5, 1853, I married Gunder Fredrickson Hjelmeland. . . . By my second husband I had the following children: Andre, born May 27, 1853. . . ." The first child arrived less than two months after the marriage. In 1919 when Oline supplied specific autobiographical details about her marriage and the birth of her first child, she apparently felt no compulsion to conceal the dates, and no self-consciousness about the traditional sexual morality that those dates revealed. Oline's account also appears to belie

Anderson's own claim that night courtship did not exist in that part of Norway from which his family came.[31]

Exactly how and when attitudes changed is unclear. Surely Anderson did not single-handedly reform locals. Premarital pregnancy rates rapidly declined from the high rates of nineteenth-century Norway for a variety of reasons, not the least of which were the much-expanded economic opportunities available to the immigrants and their children. Peasant couples delayed marriages until minimal economic circumstances were achieved. This could even mean postponing a marriage until after a pregnancy and birth of children. The economic opportunities of the American frontier and expansive industrializing economy removed these restraints on marriage. Earlier marriages and lower premarital pregnancy rates appeared in the new economic environment.[32] In the 1850s, peasant women in Norway typically married during their 25th and 26th years, whereas by 1910 in Pigeon for those women between the ages of 40 and 44 the average age of marriage was 22. Fifty-six percent had married by that age.[33]

If they never entirely adopted some of the more extreme strictures of the Victorian sexual ideology, certainly by the third and fourth generations very different principles of sexual behavior from those of the immigrant generation were in place. In Pigeon and Lincoln the custom of night courtship persisted as it did in other Norwegian American communities at least through the frontier years. An interview by Einar Haugen with a third-generation Norwegian American provided the following description:

> The old Norwegians have told about how they used to go a-courting a little more boldly than they do now. They used to have a ladder, you see, and climb up through windows. And there were two or three who got one fellow fooled into climbing up the ladder and crawling in. Then they took the ladder away, so he had to hoist himself down the wall, or else he had to go down the stairs. Then it often happened that the old folks woke up and came and chased him away. There was one who got panned that way. He was up visiting the girls, and then there were some rascals who had taken his ladder, you know, and so he couldn't get out again. When he was leaving they had been in the stairway and set up a whole raft of tin cans and things, you know. When he stepped on the top of the step, the whole shebang tumbled down with a big crash and made dents in much of it. They had quit by the time I started to court.[34]

By the 1920s and 1930s, when the third generation of immigrants came of age, night courtship had disappeared, though it was not forgotten. Evidence that courtship became a troublesome area for immigrants and their children can be found in the very popular "Han Ola og han Per" cartoons created by Peter J. Rosendahl, a second-generation Norwegian

American farmer. This farmer-cartoonist's comic strips appeared in the Norwegian-language newspaper *Decorah-Posten* from 1918 to 1942 and have subsequently been reissued in the variety of forms and places. The "Han Ola og han Per" cartoons documented the many travails of the immigrant. Often the humor turned upon the failure of traditional peasant wisdom and ways in coping with the American situation. Courtship proved to be an area of particular trouble for the Norwegian bachelor farmer Per. His efforts to court women invariably resulted in misfortune. In one of the cartoon strips, "Per Goes Courting," after a long lonely day of work in the fields, Per spiffed up in his finest attire and set out to court a beautiful woman he had recently encountered. Proceeding in the traditional manner he approached the woman with a ladder to her bedroom window. Unfortunately for Per, as he ascended, the ladder snapped and Per crashed through a window into the parents' bed, and a harrowing flight followed. Rosendahl ended that cartoon with the following reflection: "When beauty now in after days / Appears on his unhappy ways, / He slyly laughs at all his pain / 'I'll never go through that again.' "[35] Seemingly this ladder-at-the-window adaptation of night courtship had little future for Per and for Norwegian Americans in general.

Although middle-class youth presumably were making a revolution in morals and manners by 1920, the youth of Trempealeau and perhaps in many rural Norwegian-American communities confronted instead a more restrictive social and sexual code of behavior than their parents or grandparents had faced. Courting couples in the early twentieth century in Pigeon and Lincoln, like their American counterparts in 1850, found that the range of sexual activity with which they were comfortable had narrowed. As noted, Haugen's informant observed that the old Norwegians "used to go a-courting a little more boldly than they do now." And Per's bold efforts quickly came to naught. Premarital sexual experimentation, cohabitation, and pregnancies, once part of a continuum toward marriage, now led to public condemnation and individual humiliation. The noisy community coercion and reconciliation which the charivari offered were displaced. Night courtship and the charivaris disappeared when responsibility for controlling sexual activity shifted from the community to the individual, particularly to women.

Indicative of the transformation are the contemporary reactions of individuals tracing their family geneology. "Shocked," "hurt," and "ashamed" are descriptions of the responses of some individuals to the discovery that grandmother's or great-grandmother's first child had arrived three months after she was married.[36] Not until the generation that grew up in the 1960s and 1970s, when the second wave of the sexual

Double wedding of Anna Ruth and Eleanor Hanson, 1946. By the time Ella and "Bennie" Hanson's daughters were married in this double wedding, peasant courtship patterns were a remote memory. Though charivaris were still common at this time, the temperance-minded Hansons avoided the traditional charivari by arranging wedding dances for some of their offspring. Photo courtesy of Eleanor Ackley, Pigeon Falls, Wisconsin.

revolution occurred, did the restrictive sexual code and the intensified double standard begin a retreat.

Courtship patterns and sexual morality were not the only aspects of traditional peasant sociability that were challenged by Norwegian American and other reformers. At the charivari of 1862, the reluctant if hospitable host liberally supplied the expected whiskey with the result that many of the celebrators did not make it home for the night.[37] Whiskey, wine, and beer accompanied most family and community events in the frontier years. Among both the Norwegian and Polish immigrants and among many of the Yankee settlers as well, from the earliest years of the county's settlement, alcohol accompanied the occasions of family and community sociability. In Pigeon, J. D. Olds was known as a hospitable man, and an important component of that hospitality was the alcohol made readily available to his guests. Among both the Yankees and the Norwegians and most certainly among the Polish, alcoholic beverages accompanied the many social occasions of the community in relationship to both work and the rituals of the seasons. As Thurine Oleson observed of the numerous dances and celebrations among the immigrant Norwegians: "Of course, it was not a right good time until they had a few drinks. Just enough to make them feel good, as they worded it, but with some it was a little more." A few drinks invariably accompanied the completion of the harvest, barn raisings, weddings, and the wide range of activities that traditionally brought the Norwegian peasants together and American farmers together.[38]

But this long-standing peasant tradition of sociability, like other peasant traditions both in this country and in Norway, fell into disrepute among pietistic reformers. Among the social evils against which Hans Anderson crusaded beginning in 1876 were the ubiquitous "whiskey parties" and dances. As in his crusade against the custom of night running, he battled to bring social odium upon the twin evils of dance and drink. Temperance like chastity he held up as essential to morality. Dancing apparently became suspect by association, because "at that time dancing and drinking went hand in hand and were fostered by many of the householders for the sake of making a little money." In Anderson's lectures and meetings organized to raise the moral standards of the community, he did not "mince words in denouncing this custom . . . the drink evil, and also dancing." Anderson apparently had less success in his crusade against alcohol than he had in his effort to transform community sentiment against night running. Gradually, he believed, "whiskey parties" became scarce, but the "drink evil" persisted and dances continued undiminished.[39]

Anderson's crusade to transform peasant customs of sociability involving alcohol and dancing found support among the Lutheran leadership. The Haugean Lutheranism, in which Anderson was confirmed before his conversion to the Seventh-day Adventist persuasion, had been attempting to transform traditional peasant culture while promoting pietism. Eventually the emphasis on personal pietism affected most of the Norwegian Lutheran leadership in the United States. Many of the local Lutheran clergy, like the Baptists in the area, became active supporters of temperance and prohibition. An aggressive prohibition movement emerged among the Norwegians and the Yankees of the community. Dave Wood, a Baptist, ran several times in local elections as a prohibition candidate, though never successfully; he "lacked political finesse," in Anderson's analysis.[40]

However, prohibition never appealed to the Catholic Polish community, which steadily expanded in the town of Lincoln during the twentieth century. Thus, while Whitehall periodically voted itself dry between 1880 and 1918 by not permitting licenses to be issued for the sale of alcohol, a few miles away Independence and Arcadia continued their customary ways.[41] Despite the enthusiasm of men like Anderson and the leaders of the church, young and old continued to resist changing their ways in regard to drinking. Yet, local residents did not comfortably violate the prescriptions of the church. A satiric poem penned by a resident of "Voss Cooley" in Pigeon Township expressed something of the conflict:

Valley of Trempe'leau's Christmas Ball

To a Christmas Ball many a youth did go,
In the beautiful Valley of Trempe'leau
Unbounded pleasure expecting to find,
As onward exulting their way they did wind.

Merrily the strain of fiddle did sound,
And cheerful and happy the voices around,
When, Lo and Behold! in walks the Priest,
More respected than others, but welcomed the least.

The older were struck with terror and shame,
And sought for their presence, sons and daughters to blame;
The youngsters who soon confirmed were to be,
And hither had come the frolic to see.

Some, in their flight, 'neath the bedstead did creep,
Others, in dismay, through the window did leap,
And for hours without in the cold did remain,
While Preacher within found his mission in vain.

Aye, behold us! (youth of this beautiful Vale)
Whose amusements and pleasures our Priest would curtail,
As though the glee of our blossoming Prime
Were a soul staining Sin and a Crime.

S . . .

Attached to this poem in the Trempealeau County Historical Society files
was the following note, written in 1910: "Later informed dance was at
Alecksons in Voss cooley. They had intoxicating liquors at dances in those
days. Rev. Hoxde went there to put a stop to it. Got into a bitter discussion
with Haakon Grandberg."[42]

Like Anderson, the church leaders faced a good deal of resistance
from their communities in their efforts to redefine traditional patterns of
sociability as sinful. Such incidents, though, also reveal the church leaders'
continued presumption of their role as moral guardians of the community.
The reality of their disestablished status did not diminish their high-
handed ways. They were more than willing to intrude aggressively on the
private lives of members of their congregations.

But the drinking and the dancing continued. Thurine Oleson, in her
youth in the late nineteenth century, shared the enthusiasm for dances held
by the Pigeon and Lincoln youth; "nothing came up to dancing" in her
estimate. After weddings "as soon as the minister leaves" the fiddler got
out his fiddle and the dance began. Thurine Oleson's husband, to her
chagrin, abandoned the ways of his Norwegian-immigrant neighbors.
"John was wild until he was nineteen," and then he became quite pious.
"He never danced again and we never had liquor in our house in all our
lives." To Thurine this was a considerable hardship, for since the age of 15,
after her confirmation, her greatest pleasure in life was the regular dances
which included the usual beer, whiskey, and wine. "Of course, not one of
the girls put any kind of drink to her lips but homemade beer." But she later
recalled that her "only salvation" was that her future husband went away
to work in lumbering in the spring and summer until they were married. "I
really had a fling when he was gone." They married halfway through her
19th year. Years later, she still felt some regret: "In order to live in peace
with him, I had to cut out the most fun I ever had in life." Thurine Oleson
advised other young women to "never marry anyone so entirely different
in disposition." Her pious hardworking husband was a good provider, but
Thurine Oleson looked back on the loss of traditional peasant conviviality
with lifelong regret.[43]

The temperance movement apparently arrived during the earliest pioneer years of the county, when former New Englanders and New Yorkers
from the "burned-over" district of New York brought their commitments
and enthusiasms with them. One of the earliest pioneer women in the

county anticipated Carrie Nation's dramatic ways with the hatchet by several years. A Mrs. Masseure won local fame as "a heroine of a crusade against saloons." She and 19 others entered a saloon and knocked the heads off the whiskey barrels and put the saloon keeper out of business. It was in the winter and the "whiskey froze in icicles under the floor of the building."[44] But while some of the women of the county were ruining the saloon business, many of the immigrant women were busy making homebrew and keeping alive their traditional conceptions of hospitality. Immigrant women and later generations as well, though to a lesser extent, made wine from the grapes and berries that thrived in the area. Beer was brewed, and blackberry, blueberry, elderberry, dandelion, as well as grape, wines were made in the homes. As Thurine Oleson recalled, "My mother made wine, as was the style everywhere, and treated friends who came to see us." Her mother was both a brewer and a vintner.[45]

Despite the efforts of reformers, the association of alcohol with hospitality and good times persisted. In 1914 Anderson was still lecturing his neighbors on the evils of drink. In an essay entitled "The Influence of Custom," he continued to try to convince the locals that their customs of drinking produced a wide array of social problems. "How many times," he opined, "I have witnessed wives and mothers, red-eyed from weeping over the failings of their sons and husbands, welcome their guests with foaming bankers and steaming bowls, filled with the same stuff that had poisoned the happiness of their homes and brought their loved ones to shame and ruin."[46] Throughout the frontier years and despite the emergence of opposition from those who favored temperance, the making and drinking of alcoholic beverages persisted.

If private whiskey parties slowly declined, as Anderson claimed, the beneficiaries may well have been the saloon keepers. In 1914, commercial establishments selling alcohol concerned Anderson as much as the private whiskey parties had worried him in 1876. One difference, however, between the saloon and the whiskey parties of the past was that saloons became more exclusively associated with adult males. They were important centers of sociability by the early twentieth century to many of the men in the community.

Moreover, the pressure to change customs may have been making greater headway among the women. Among the immigrant generation, women by all accounts felt few inhibitions about drinking their homebrew at their parties. The saloons, however, were seen as the male province, and certainly Anderson identified men with the problems associated with drinking. In "The Influence of Custom," Anderson clearly acknowledged a double standard operating in the expectations about men's and women's behavior:

Why is it that men can swear, drink, gamble and even violate the laws of chastity with apparent impunity to their standing in society? If children and women did the same things they would be outcasts and vagrants. If I meet a woman, once my intimate friend, staggering down the street, howling and cursing, as drunken men often do, I turn from her with disgust, but as I walk a little further I find one of my boyhood's chums lying in the gutter befouled by his own vomit and without a moment's hesitation I lift him up and help him to a more comfortable lodging and the next day perhaps laugh with him over the incident as if it were a joke. Custom explains.[47]

Women more than men may have found their social behavior constrained under the pressure of the standards of their American neighbors, religious leaders, and reformers like Anderson.

Despite a growth in local opinion in favor of temperance, some women clearly persisted in what would by 1900 be perceived as disreputable ways. In 1904 Herman Ekern received a desperate letter of appeal from the brother of a woman who was "getting to be a habitual drunkard." The man's father had apparently turned his farm over to sister Rosa for half of its market value on the assumption that she would provide for him there in his old age. Unfortunately in 1904 the old man's security was threatened because the irresponsible Rosa had her own plans. As J. T. Qually explained, "She is crazy to move to town which is a very poor place for her as she is getting to be a habitual drunkard."[48] The stigma against women drinking or frequenting saloons was clearly present by 1900 and persisted until the second half of the twentieth century.

In the 1870s, prohibition consistently appeared as an issue in local elections.[49] From 1880 until the passage of the prohibition amendment to the federal constitution, temperance and the issue of whether or not to license establishments for the sale of alcoholic beverages presented conspicuous and divisive political issues. Through the years it was perhaps the hottest local political issue. Dave Wood on more than one occasion ran as the prohibition party's candidate, and though that party did not win elections, voters did periodically vote the village dry. Politically the prohibition issue overshadowed almost any other. The votes that were related to the issue of licensing saloons very likely had a more immediately felt effect than votes on any other issue.

In 1914 while Anderson lectured locals on the evils of drink, Whitehall residents had again just voted the village dry. Before the election there was a good deal of discussion of what effect this would have on the business of the town. A citizen's committee even arranged to poll farmers on the question before the election.[50] Would farmers take their business elsewhere if they could not stop at one of the local saloons for a drink while doing business? That was not an unimportant issue to merchants in small

towns who faced fierce competition from other nearby towns. And certainly they all knew that while the village of Blair might vote itself dry,
nearby Independence and Arcadia with their large Polish and German
Catholic populations never would do so; thus the merchants of those
towns might gain an advantage among farmers who had a taste for combining beer and business. Any major financial arrangement such as horse
trading traditionally was completed with a few drinks at a saloon. In 1884
when Lincoln voted not to issue any licenses for the sale of alcohol, neighboring Independence had six thriving saloons. Thus such votes when they
did occur often were later rescinded.[51]

Even those Lincoln residents who presumably voted to keep liquor
outside their own community did not hesitate to take advantage of hospitality nearby, as the infuriated editor of the *Times* noted in 1884:

> Two of our citizens settled a war of words with blows in Independence the
> other day. We are so ashamed of their proceeding that we refrain from men-
> tioning their names, trusting it will teach them better manners. What is surpris-
> ing in the matter is the fact that since the last town meeting both were sup-
> posed to be rank prohibitionists.[52]

The combination of diverse ethnic traditions in a small area and the
local control over licensing made it very difficult for reformers to achieve
the social discipline they desired. While they could successfully convince
community members at least publicly to support temperance and prohibition in their own communities, Anderson was very aware that the old
custom would persist. The appeal of the saloon was too great. As Anderson
described it, the saloon represented a haven of hospitality and good cheer
that could not be found elsewhere except perhaps in the home. It appealed
to "men with instincts for sociability and comradeship." The saloon's
warm welcome and wise motto was "Make the boys feel at home." There
men could gather even when "damp, cold, hungry, dirty, shabby and tired"
and comfortably stay the hour or the day. "While the saloon is the most
destructive institution in our country, it is at the same time the most democratic providing freedom and good fellowship." The saloons had become
the center of sociability for men in the community, and despite the periodic
prohibition on selling alcohol in Lincoln, the attachment to the institution
was unlikely to change.[53]

And indeed Anderson was correct. Neighboring Independence became the center of sociability from 1880 until at least the decade of the
1960s. There the youth and adults of Pigeon and Lincoln continued their
peasant pleasures of dancing, drinking, and fighting for generations, as the
Times editor had noted that leading citizens of Lincoln were doing in 1884.

According to the younger Dave Wood, his grandfather, Ralph, and his father, Harold, had come particularly to enjoy their Polish neighbors:

> Despite their Baptist backgrounds, my grandfather and father learned to dance, to drink, etc., etc. . . . The Poles taught the latter Woods to spend their money (all of it unfortunately!) and to have a good time. I don't mean to say that Norwegians can't have a good time, but I honestly believe that Ralph and Harold enjoyed the Polish mode more. My sister Kip must have really enjoyed it, because, as they say in Whitehall, she married one.[54]

Personal pietism such as that which the Lutheran and Baptist church leaders held up as a model, although winning public deference, may have promoted the hypocrisy for which small towns are often noted. Traditional tastes for the conviviality associated with drink and dance persisted, though the center of activity was relocated from time to time.

In the frontier years the homes and barns were the locale of the whiskey dances. By 1900 the commercial establishments—saloons and dance halls in the villages—became the centers, and when villages like Whitehall proved inhospitable to such establishments, neighboring towns filled the need. The years of prohibition apparently inhibited local consumption little. The talent for making home-brew had not been lost, and local producers did a good business out of the backs of their cars and trucks parked conveniently if inconspicuously near the dance halls.[55]

In Anderson's description of the saloons of 1914, a time when at least the town of Lincoln publicly proclaimed the consumption of alcohol a violation of their moral standards, he remarked that the saloon was among the most democratic of institutions. "To enter and be entertained requires no certificate of character or social position, for there the outlaw and tramp may drink and hob-nob with the prince and the millionaire." No doubt this mixing of folk continued through the years of prohibition, when anyone wanting a drink had to find his or her way through the woods to the ambulatory saloon.

As long as the community's elites such as the Melbys, Andersons, and Ekerns publicly maintained a prohibitionist position, saloons all retained a disreputable but egalitarian tone. In the post–World War II years, the community's more prominent families led the way in making drinking an acceptable dimension of social life again. At the same time, as women took up social drinking, the institutions which provided alcohol became more socially differentiated. Age and class defined a particular place's clientele at a time when the rural communities increasingly resembled urban suburbs in the structuring of social and economic relationships. The much improved communication and transportation systems facilitated the removal of leisure-time activities from the locality to nearby cities.[56]

Traditional peasant social behavior in the areas of sexual morality, drink, and dance was subject to a new scrutiny in nineteenth-century Norway and America. In Lincoln and Pigeon these issues became a source of social conflict and division, which persisted until the post–World War II years. The division may be best described as establishment versus nonestablishment, to which individuals responded in several ways: acceptance and promotion of the standards, as was true of Dave Wood, public deference if not behavioral conformity by some, and simple rejection by others. The postfrontier youth of Trempealeau confronted a more restrictive social and sexual code of behavior than their parents or grandparents had faced.

One dimension of the changing expectations was an intensification of the double standard of sexual morality and social behavior. Established by World War I, the double standard persisted until long after World War II. Regarding both sexual behavior and alcohol consumption, pietistic reformers had the greatest impact on the social behavior expected of women. The code of behavior which replaced the authority of charivaris in the community placed a disproportionate responsibility on women for regulating sexual behavior. Traditional peasant weddings and frontier whiskey parties included men and women in the sociability of the community. Saloons, a male domain, replaced these events. What were once common social activities and responsibilities became more differentiated by gender in the twentieth century. For good or ill, since World War II, women have reclaimed their peasant prerogatives to sing, dance, and drink with their husbands, beaus, and brothers in the local pubs as they once had done at the whiskey parties and other community events.

Conclusion: Mentalité and Locality in Rural Wisconsin

It's too bad money and capitalism are so powerful in this country.
Harold Tomter interview

Frederick Jackson Turner and his frontier thesis might well have been placed among the antimodernist intellectuals examined by Jackson Lears in *No Place of Grace*. Individuals such as Turner and Henry Adams reacted to a time of crisis between 1890 and 1920, when a rural way of life and a production-oriented social ethic gave way to the urban, industrial, secular order and to consumerism. Despite their profound discomfort with and in some instances insightful critiques of the changes coming to American society, the antimodernists sought spiritual solace in looking back toward earlier ideals, traditions, and institutions. They adapted the cultural forms of the past, if not the substance, to their own needs, which allowed them to adjust fitfully to a world where it seemed that "all that is solid melts into air."[1]

In precarious times Turner found a solid base for the future in the frontier past—the source of American character, values, and institutions, which presumably had and would sustain American society as it evolved into an urban industrial society. Although scholars have rightfully criticized the Turnerian vision for many reasons, he did recognize that this country was at a vital turning point. The way of life of most Americans, based on the frontier and on the land, had long been giving way to the new social and economic forms of the expanding urban arena. Like the antimodernists, Turner believed the cultural forms, institutions, and character of the past could be sustained, although the structure which had supported them in the past was dissolving.

At the turn of the century, when an antimodernist elite was becoming self-conscious consumers of traditional culture's creations, religions, crafts, and environments, many country folk were un-self-consciously preserving and adapting the substance of theirs. As Mary Ryan discovered, those who settled Oneida County in New York in the 1790s retained the traditional patriarchal corporate household economy. By 1850 the children and grandchildren of those upstate New York pioneers were turning up in Trempealeau County. By repeatedly moving west they maintained the foundations of their traditional corporate communities. Although immigrants who appeared on the frontier differed in a variety of ways, they generally shared the experience of having come almost directly from peasant communities in Scandinavia and Europe, seeking land. Such emigration often was a conservative act.

The ambitions of most of those who came to Pigeon and Lincoln townships were modest and traditional: to establish themselves and their children on the land. To a large extent those who arrived before 1880 and remained in the community, and to a lesser extent those who arrived by 1900, fulfilled those ambitions. To the Trempealeau frontier, immigrants and migrants brought the skills and social traditions which allowed them to survive and eventually to thrive. In their economies and communities they continued their corporate and cooperative traditions, adapting them even in the postfrontier years to dairy cooperatives, the continued tradition of *dugnag,* the community organization of work.

After the frontier years the neighborhoods grew ethnically more homogeneous, and within the rural communities a distinct Norwegian-American culture survived for a much longer period of time than it did among urban immigrants. The adjustments made to a new rural environment were far fewer than many immigrants faced in American cities. People could comfortably live out their lives in places like Pigeon. As one Norwegian traveler commented when he visited some of these immigrant communities, "I had to pinch myself to remember that I was not in Norway."[2]

What rural locations offered to both migrants and immigrants was a unique opportunity to preserve aspects of their traditional cultures and values as they dissolved elsewhere. This is revealed in the long retention of the Norwegian language in families and neighborhoods, in local religious ideals and institutions, in cooperative organizations, and in the structuring of work within the family and community, particularly the long duration of the institution of *dugnag,* or communal work arrangements. The cooperative movement expressed the traditional peasants' high valuation of localism and communal responsibility. In some instances aspects of the Old World culture were sustained longer in the rural communities of the Midwest than in Norway itself, including the retention of particular regional language dialects, peasant crafts such as rosemaling, and festivities like the charivari and jule bokking ("Christmas fooling"). By the 1920s Norwegian visitors and immigrants discovered a cultural gap between themselves and the earlier immigrants and their children, not in that the latter were more Americanized, but in that they were "old fashioned."[3]

Although individualistic entrepreneurs like T. H. Earle were numerous and played an important role in the early economic development of the frontier communities, such men did not leave the deepest imprint on Pigeon and Lincoln. Earle moved on, along with many others, to places where better opportunities beckoned, carrying his individualistic spirit and entrepreneurial ambitions with him. In Trempealeau, men like Hans Anderson, John Melby, and Peder Ekern, immigrants with roots in Norwegian peasant communities, replaced him. The local economic, political, and social institutions and the local mentalité owed much to those European and Scandinavian peasant origins, and that historical background has left locals with a still meaningful legacy.

Hans Anderson in his speeches declared that the world would be much improved without those who pursued only their own interests and advancement; half a century later, Harold Tomter, schooled in Lutheran religious doctrine and Progressive and Farmers Union economics and politics, expressed similar views. In a regretful, quiet, and matter-of-fact tone, Tomter noted, "It's too bad money and capitalism are so powerful in this country." A strong supporter of cooperatives, country schools, and the Lutheran church, Tomter, like most of the local farmers, fitted the rural sociologists' description of the "traditionalist" or "refugist" farmer. His politics echoed those of the Jeffersonian Populist tradition of J. D. Olds and the Progressivism of Herman Ekern and the Norwegian immigrants who brought their peasant radicalism to the American frontier. Wisconsin's Progressivism represented the political coming of age in the state of the immigrants, and Pigeon's Herman Ekern became one of the movement's outstanding state leaders. The Farm Bureau, which had been closely allied with the agricultural infrastructure of the government and the educational system, in Tomter's view, "represented the very successful crowd and didn't have the needs of the less successful in mind. . . . I almost got the impression that they were more for hampering the less successful than for helping them." With the laboring men of the city, Tomter felt a common bond in that they too were producers; labor and farmers needed each other's support.[4]

By 1900 when La Follette and Progressivism burst on the political scene in Wisconsin, distinct communities and a distinct culture had already taken shape in rural Trempealeau. That rural culture flowered between 1900 and 1930 and, despite the blows of the Great Depression and World War II, was still recognizable two decades later. This persistence rested on the Norwegian and American backgrounds and on the distinct environment and opportunities the frontier had provided. It was a culture "between memory and reality" and, in the view of its participants, it was a rich one. By 1910 the sense of achievement in the communities was notable. Pride in local institutions was high. Community and family life drew on both Norwegian and American traditions, and that combination was a source of economic and political creativity and achievement.

Community depends upon a shared set of values, common concerns, and a context for communication. Local institutions, religious, economic, political, and social, provided an arena for achieving individual prestige as well as common goals. Rural neighborhoods developed their own standards of measurement and functioned as reference groups and audiences both for those who remained within the locality and for many of those who moved away. These standards of measurement extended across space and time. By 1900 mentalité and locality were inextricably interconnected, but the mentalité of the locale was not limited to the local residents. By that time the political culture upon which leaders such as Robert A. La Follette depended was in place.[5]

Turner and other historians concerned with the American frontier have not as a rule given much attention to women's experiences. Frontier and farm appeared to be a particularly masculine place, with a particularly masculine appeal. Statistics on rural communities do seem to indicate that women made choices to flee the farm far more often than did men. Beret Holms of Rolvaag's *Giants in the Earth* has often stood as a symbol of the meaning of the frontier to women: she was a woman driven to madness by the desolate life on the plains—by locusts, howling winter blizzards, and isolation. Michael Lesy's *Wisconsin Death Trip* and Hamlin Garland's *Daughter of the Middle Border* reinforce such a picture. In the latter, an unwilling wife is pushed to ever more ominous frontiers.

Careful study of women's choices, perceptions, and work in frontier Trempealeau and the subsequent rural communities challenges such stereotypes. Immigrant women in particular were no less accustomed to hardship and hard work than their husbands and no less capable of dealing with it. *Giants in the Earth* was the first volume in Rolvaag's trilogy. After the death of her husband, Beret became a strong-willed woman who lived to an old age, built up her farm, reared her sons, arranged for their future on the land, and became a person to be reckoned with in the community. What followed the frontier was a settled rural culture that faced challenges far different from avoiding freezing during a blizzard, building basic shelters, and planting crops which afforded survival. Beret built the big barn and helped shape local community ideals and institutions. Women such as Beret were central to the development of family farms and rural communities. From frontier times, they played an active, independent, and primary role in the productive work of the farm and community and in ordering the sociability of the neighborhood and kin. When they had to do so, like Beret, women managed the farms alone.[6]

Both the migrants and the immigrants brought a way of life deeply rooted in a very distant past, which they adapted to the opportunities and demands of the frontier and later to the twentieth century. Historians have often supposed that farmers, early dependent on the market economy particularly in the Midwest, acted as possessive individualists, approaching the land with an individualistic and entrepreneurial spirit as a resource to be exploited for personal profit. Farming became a business, a means to a living, and people lost the traditional peasant's sense of attachment to and the sacredness of the land.

In contrast with these assumptions, rural sociologists observing farm communities in the twentieth century have long distinguished between the farmers who approached farming as a means to a living, acting as historians have supposed they did, and the "traditionalists" or "refugists," who were often the majority and who dominated rural communities. The latter group perceived farming as a way of life. Unlike the risk-taking entrepreneurial farmer, they sought to insulate themselves from the hazards of the market and often successfully did so. Rather than profits, they valued security on the land, familial continuity over generations, and community prestige in local institutions for which the more venturesome farmer had little time.

The evolving rural culture in Trempealeau County was shaped by the tensions born of perpetuating a way of life and mentalité rooted in the past and of confronting challenges and exploiting the opportunities of the frontier and the market economy. Most farmers may not have been aware of the dichotomy between farming as a way of life and farming as a business or means to a living; to them, farming probably has seemed to be both and not exclusively one or the other. Their behavior, choices, and mentalité reflect an attempt to assimilate these two realities, which often of necessity are in conflict. An illustration of this tension and its impact on rural culture and behavior can be found in the response to technology. In this century and particularly since 1945, many if not most farmers eagerly introduced labor-saving machines and technological innovations that reduced labor and increased productivity. This new equipment made farmers increasingly independent of each other and more dependent on institutions outside the locality. Harold Tomter noted about himself and others of Trempealeau that "farmers have a weakness for big machines."[7] But rather than revealing the mentalité of a modern profit-maximizer seeking to reduce labor costs and increase productivity, the attraction of farmers to big machines has often been precisely what Tomter asserted it to be—a weakness. By the 1980s this attraction to big equipment expressed itself in the unseemly debt acquired by farmers, which has subsequently contributed to severe economic crisis. As one Iowa farm woman saw the problem: "Too many tractors with too much horsepower"; and as one farmer observed about the powerful four-wheeled tractors: "You can pretty much tell which farms are in trouble by whether they're a four wheel or a two wheel." Another commentator noted, "Farmers like to buy tractors, managers like to make money."[8]

When farmers have given up their peasant caution in relationship to the market economy, they have perhaps done it more as conspicuous consumers than as rational investors. It is the same mentalité that pressed Per Hansa in *Giants in the Earth* to build the biggest sod hut, plant the earliest and largest crop, and be the first to finish his tasks. The larger the estate or the herd, the better, in that more prestige was acquired, though not necessarily greater profits. In this orientation the bigger and more sophisticated equipment has provided more prestige, even if it has meant living on the verge of bankruptcy.

The introduction of new technologies, whatever the reasons farmers may have had for adopting them, has been one of the most powerful forces for change. The supposition of the isolation of all rural men and women in the past stands as one of the most striking and well-established misconceptions of rural life which the Trempealeau County sources challenge. It is a misconception which blocks an understanding of the dynamics of change in rural culture and the significance of those changes to rural communities. Technology and the supposed improvements in communications systems in the countryside have in fact created isolation on the farm. Although perhaps far more informed about the activities of presidents of the United States, farm families know considerably less about their neighbors. The innumerable reasons for which neighbors visited each other have largely been eliminated by these diverse "improvements." As one rural Methodist pastor recently noted: "Machines made you really self-reliant. People didn't realize the machines would also make you isolated. As soon as it became technologically possible to farm independently, everybody wanted that."[9]

The decline in sociability is a change that few in the countryside fail to note, and the changes in the organization of work are often recognized as the source, along with the disappearance of important local economic and educational institutions. The number of women working outside the household is another factor. Women did play the more prominent role in organizing the sociability of the kin networks and the community, and their responsibilities in this regard were a primary source of satisfaction in their lives. As they have become wage workers in growing numbers, their personal goals and roles have changed.

It cannot be argued that Pigeon and Lincoln townships and the village of Whitehall in Trempealeau County, Wisconsin, are typical American communities; perhaps they are not even typical rural midwestern communities. But an examination of their history does indicate that the rural culture and the rural social experience in America are fraught with misconceptions. The settlement of Trempealeau no doubt has much in common with that of other midwestern counties. Frontier historians have made large contributions to understanding rural America's beginnings, but they have explored only a single stage in the history of rural America. Patricia Limerick has recently castigated historians of the American West for limiting their vision to this brief stage, and she has fashioned a powerful conceptual lens for viewing the West as a place and the frontier as a process of conquest—"the contest for property and profit . . . accompanied by a contest for cultural dominance."[10]

What, if any, is the frontier legacy in Trempealeau County? It too experienced conflict and competition for property and cultural hegemony during the years of settlement. But ethnic clustering and mobility patterns produced homogeneous rural neighborhoods that allowed for local hegemony of distinctly local cultures and mentalités. By 1900 local cultures, or "little traditions," contoured the social landscape of Trempealeau. The frontier legacy of local hegemony of one ethnic or cultural group or another was a reality in a variety of rural places from Louisiana to Washington state. Not until after World War II would the pressures of another economic and cultural contest for legitimacy prevail over locality. Local cultures and economies may have been contested terrain, dynamically interconnected economically, socially, and culturally with the world beyond the neigborhood, but they maintained identities and often defined the terms of institutional and economic interaction. Rural areas did not simply become the backwaters of civilization, cut off from the mainstream of American history, places that people of sense and sensibility fled, nor were they swallowed up by remote and overwhelming forces.

Rural Lincoln and Pigeon since frontier times have been involved in a dynamic process of change. For the family and the community the most striking changes came in the post–World War II years. The sources of those changes are not mysterious, and they are similar in many rural areas across the United States. They came both from within the communities and families themselves and from the outside. Rural sociologists before and after the fact have been astute in identifying and often promoting the sources of transformation coming from outside the community: the market, the credit system, the government and educational bureaucracies, and the mass media. From within came the pressures generated by what has been referred to here as the extended kin and community networks, which prohibited country folk from isolating themselves in their localities.

These rural communities have not, however, simply been delayed in evolving toward an undifferentiated modern American community. Nor have they been developing simply a poorer and less sophisticated version of the larger urban culture. Pigeon and Lincoln may represent a typical rural experience in the local creation of distinct communities and cultures from a combination of sources. A distinct mentalité connected to the locality took shape, a mentalité rooted in the past and adapted to and influenced by a changing context. While much of that distinctive community life has recently dissolved, this is less surprising than the fact that it lasted so long.

Appendices

Notes

Bibliography

Index

Appendix A

Percentage Distribution of Voting Patterns in Gubernatorial Elections, by Township/Village, 1876–1970

	Village of Whitehall[a]			Lincoln Township			Pigeon Township[b]		
	Republican	Democrat	Other	Republican	Democrat	Other	Republican	Democrat	Other
1876				80.8	11.0	8.2	65.2	0.7	34.1
1880				79.4	15.2	5.4	93.3	6.7	0.0
1884				49.8	40.3	9.9	55.9	30.3	13.8
1886				45.3	37.8	16.9	48.5	35.6	15.9
1888				48.3	41.3	10.4	41.7	52.3	6.0
1890				52.3	34.9	12.8	39.2	53.6	7.2
1892				53.1	33.3	13.6	50.2	44.5	5.3
1894				63.5	19.9	16.6	59.3	28.7	12.0
1896				69.2	26.5	4.3	76.6	19.2	4.6
1898	69.8	20.6	9.5	63.1	25.0	11.9	76.4	17.8	5.9
1900	76.0	17.0	7.0	63.7	29.0	7.3	83.7	11.5	4.8
1902	80.1	11.5	8.4	87.0	5.6	7.4	94.4	4.9	0.7
1904	73.4	16.9	9.7	76.3	15.8	10.9	88.5	8.0	3.5
1906	84.1	7.6	8.5	62.7	31.3	6.0	94.8	4.5	0.7
1908	69.4	26.6	9.0	61.5	27.4	11.1	89.0	10.5	0.7
1910	76.5	19.9	4.4	66.7	21.3	12.0	76.6	23.4	0.0
1912	64.9	29.8	5.3	66.3	29.0	4.7	84.8	13.8	1.4
1914	40.9	26.2	32.9	48.1	31.5	20.4	56.4	26.6	17.0
1916	54.4	41.2	4.4	56.3	37.5	6.2	65.2	33.7	1.1
1918	68.8	29.6	2.4	68.8	27.1	4.1	52.1	45.8	2.1
1920	65.2	34.1	0.7	84.0	13.0	3.0	94.7	4.9	0.3
1924	55.2	43.6	1.2	86.0	11.6	2.4	91.6	7.1	1.3
1926	65.4	5.7	28.9	53.0	7.5	39.5	71.4	1.0	27.6
1928	83.4	15.8	0.8	—	—	—	65.7	33.8	0.5
1930	74.0	22.4	3.6	89.0	6.8	4.2	95.3	4.0	0.7
1932	57.3	42.3	0.4	23.0	75.5	1.5	27.8	72.2	0.0
1934	16.2	30.8	53.0	10.0	18.7	71.3	7.9	11.1	81.0
1936	33.5	4.2	45.3	9.6	7.1	83.3	16.5	7.5	76.0
1938	48.4	2.1	49.5	31.2	5.8	63.0	26.3	0.9	72.8
1940	36.7	7.5	55.8	15.3	17.2	67.4	15.1	14.2	70.7
1942	36.3	1.1	62.6	9.6	2.4	88.0	15.1	2.1	82.8
1944	73.4	14.3	12.3	61.2	25.4	13.4	55.5	14.7	29.8
1946	76.8	23.2	0.0	54.3	45.7	0.0	57.9	42.1	0.0
1948	73.1	26.9	0.0	50.3	49.7	0.0	53.2	46.8	0.0
1950	71.6	28.0	0.4	44.1	55.9	0.0	40.7	59.3	0.0
1952	82.5	17.5	0.0	55.1	44.9	0.0	84.6	15.4	0.0
1954	68.8	31.2	0.0	33.2	66.8	0.0	41.7	58.3	0.0
1956	68.6	31.4	0.0	41.6	58.4	0.0	47.2	52.8	0.0
1958	66.7	33.3	0.0	42.8	57.2	0.0	41.5	58.5	0.0

(table continued on following page)

Percentage Distribution of Voting Patterns in Gubernatorial Elections, by Township/
Village, 1876–1970 (*continued*)

	Village of Whitehall[a]			Lincoln Township			Pigeon Township[b]		
	Republican	Democrat	Other	Republican	Democrat	Other	Republican	Democrat	Other
1960	67.9	32.1	0.0	61.0	39.0	0.0	63.4	36.6	0.0
1962	69.4	30.6	0.0	44.6	55.4	0.0	35.2	64.8	0.0
1964	70.0	30.0	0.0	43.3	56.7	0.0	38.6	61.4	0.0
1966	70.2	29.8	0.0	50.0	50.0	0.0	51.6	48.4	0.0
1968	69.1	30.9	0.0	45.2	54.8	0.0	43.3	56.6	0.0
1970	55.6	44.4	0.0	35.8	64.2	0.0	35.9	64.1	0.0

Source: State of Wisconsin, *Blue Books,* 1871–1972 (Madison: State Printer).

[a]Votes for the village of Whitehall for the years 1876–1896 are included in the tallies for Lincoln Township.

[b]Votes for the village of Pigeon Falls for the years 1960–1970 are broken out of the tallies for Pigeon Township.
There was no third-party vote in Pigeon Falls. The voting pattern breaks down as:

	Republican	Democrat
1960	58.6	41.4
1962	63.4	36.6
1964	57.5	42.5
1966	69.7	30.3
1968	67.2	32.8
1970	56.4	43.6

Appendix B

Numerical and Percentage Distributions of Voting Patterns in Presidental Elections, by Township/Village, 1876–1976

		Republican		Democrat		Other	
	Total N	N	%	N	%	N	%
		PIGEON TOWNSHIP					
1876	124	123	99.1	1	0.8	0	0.0
1880	123	121	98.4	1	1.6	0	0.0
1884	192	91	47.4	70	36.5	31	16.1
1888	218	89	40.8	116	53.2	13	6.0
1892	227	113	49.8	100	44.0	14	6.2
1896	259	197	76.1	50	19.3	12	4.6
1900	227	191	84.1	26	11.5	10	4.4
1904	228	201	88.2	17	7.4	10	4.4
1908	270	252	93.3	16	5.9	2	0.8
1912	220	94	42.7	50	22.7	76	34.5
1916	182	114	62.6	64	35.2	4	2.2
1920	314	301	95.9	11	3.5	2	0.6
1924	401	67	16.7	4	1.0	330	82.3
1928	399	328	82.2	69	17.3	2	0.5
1932	429	134	31.2	289	67.4	6	0.6
1936	442	133	30.1	285	64.5	24	5.4
1940	467	183	39.2	280	60.0	4	0.8
1944	404	161	39.9	243	60.1	0	0.0
1948	362	125	34.5	232	64.0	5	1.4
1952	465	254	54.6	210	45.2	1	0.2
1956	458	223	48.7	235	51.3	0	0.0
1960	343	162	47.2	181	52.8	0	0.0
1964	317	78	24.6	239	75.4	0	0.0
1968 [a]	305	107	35.1	173	56.7	25	8.2
1972	315	135	42.9	180	57.1	0	0.0
1976	334	120	35.9	214	64.1	0	0.0
		VILLAGE OF PIGEON FALLS					
1960	131	93	71.0	38	29.0	0	0.0
1964	133	41	30.8	92	69.2	0	0.0
1968 [a]	120	72	60.0	45	37.5	3	2.5
1972	144	92	63.9	52	36.1	0	0.0
1976	156	92	59.0	64	41.0	0	0.0

(*table continued on following page*)

Numerical and Percentage Distributions of Voting Patterns in Presidental Elections, by Township/Village, 1876–1976 (*continued*)

	Total N	Republican		Democrat		Other	
		N	%	N	%	N	%
LINCOLN TOWNSHIP							
1876	182	164	90.1	18	9.9	0	0.0
1880	163	134	82.2	29	17.8	0	0.0
1884	200	82	41.0	94	47.0	24	12.0
1888	240	113	47.1	100	41.7	27	11.6
1892	227	120	52.9	77	33.9	30	13.2
1896	269	193	71.7	76	28.3	0	0.0
1904	115	87	75.6	17	14.8	11	9.6
1908	144	100	69.4	36	25.0	8	5.6
1912	108	52	48.1	30	27.8	26	24.1
1916	87	36	41.4	48	55.2	3	3.4
1920	91	80	87.9	9	9.9	2	2.2
1924	136	18	13.2	1	0.8	117	86.0
1928	204	124	60.8	80	39.2	0	0.0
1932	202	50	24.8	150	74.3	2	0.2
1936	241	53	22.0	169	70.1	19	7.9
1940	282	79	28.0	202	71.6	1	0.4
1944	232	83	35.8	149	64.2	0	0.0
1948	171	55	32.2	112	65.5	4	2.3
1952	223	94	42.2	129	57.8	0	0.0
1956	239	87	36.4	152	63.6	0	0.0
1960	269	112	41.6	157	58.4	0	0.0
1964	341	161	47.2	180	52.8	0	0.0
1968	215	95	44.2	108	50.2	12	5.6
1972	144	92	63.9	52	36.1	0	0.0
1976	327	132	40.4	195	59.6	0	0.0
VILLAGE OF WHITEHALL							
1900	360	129	35.8	219	60.8	12	3.3
1904	151	122	80.8	18	11.9	11	7.3
1908	186	145	78.0	27	14.5	14	7.5
1912	156	70	44.9	55	35.2	31	19.9
1916	189	107	56.6	75	39.7	7	3.7
1920	315	280	88.9	26	8.2	9	2.9
1924	373	134	35.9	13	3.5	226	60.6
1928	499	466	93.4	32	6.4	1	0.2
1932	478	267	55.8	205	42.9	6	1.3
1936	491	255	52.0	225	45.8	11	2.2
1940	593	335	56.5	258	43.5	0	0.0
1944	591	337	57.0	250	42.4	4	0.6
1948	578	215	37.2	357	61.8	6	1.0
1952	750	559	74.5	191	25.5	0	0.0

(*table continued on following page*)

Numerical and Percentage Distributions of Voting Patterns in Presidental Elections, by Township/Village, 1876–1976 (*continued*)

	Total N	Republican		Democrat		Other	
		N	%	N	%	N	%
		LINCOLN TOWNSHIP					
1956	719	539	75.0	180	25.0	0	0.0
1960	759	543	71.5	216	28.4	0	0.0
1964	675	348	51.6	327	48.4	0	0.0
1968	589	354	60.1	217	36.8	18	3.0
1972	795	550	69.2	238	29.9	7	0.9
1976	819	470	53.4	349	42.6	0	0.0

Source: State of Wisconsin, *Blue Books,* 1871–1977 (Madison: State Printer); Statement of Board of County Canvassers for Trempealeau County, Presidential Elections, 1924 and 1928, State Historical Society of Wisconsin, Madison.

ªAfter 1960, votes for the village of Pigeon Falls were counted separately from those of the township. Although the village was small, voters nonetheless evidenced the town-country split: a majority rather consistently voted for the Republican party.

Appendix C

Sources for Table 1.5, Table 1.6, Figure 1.1, and Table 4.8

Compendium of the Tenth Census of the United States, 1880: Part 1, *Population* (Washington, D.C.: Government Printing Office, 1883), Table 45, p. 737.

Compendium of the Eleventh Census of the United States, 1890: Vol. 5, *Report on the Statistics of Agriculture* (Washington, D.C.: Government Printing Office, 1895), Table 5, p. 196.

Twelfth Census of the United States, 1900: Agriculture, Part 1, *Farms, Livestock, and Animal Products* (Washington, D.C.: Government Printing Office, 1902), Table 10, p. 140.

Thirteenth Census of the United States, 1910: Vol. 2, *Agriculture* (Washington, D.C.: Government Printing Office, 1913), Table 1, p. 919.

Fourteenth Census of the United States, 1920: Vol. 6, *Agriculture,* Part 1, *The Northern States* (Washington, D.C.: Government Printing Office, 1922), Table 1, p. 465.

Fifteenth Census of the United States, 1930: Vol. 2, *Agriculture,* Part 1, *The Northern States* (Washington, D.C.: Government Printing Office, 1932), Table 2, p. 474.

U.S. Census of Agriculture, 1935: Vol. 2, *Report for States with Statistics for Counties and a Summary for the United States,* Part 1 (Washington, D.C.: Government Printing Office, 1936) Table 4, p. 217.

Sixteenth Census of the United States, 1940: Vol. 1, *Agriculture,* Part 1, *Statistics for Counties* (Washington, D.C.: Government Printing Office, 1942), Table 3, p. 912.

U.S. Census of Agriculture, 1954: Vol. 1, Part 7, *Wisconsin* (Washington, D.C.: Government Printing Office, 1956), County Table 1, p. 49.

U.S. Census of Agriculture, 1964: Vol. 1, Part 14, *Wisconsin* (Washington, D.C.: Government Printing Office, 1965), Table 3, p. 253.

U.S. Census of Agriculture, 1974: Vol. 1, Part 49, *Wisconsin* (Washington, D.C.: Government Printing Office, 1977), Table 1, p. 367.

Sources for Table 4.1, Table 4.3, Table 4.6, Table 7.5, Table 7.7, and Table 7.8

Fifteenth Census of the United States, 1930: Vol. 3, *Population,* Part 2, *Report by States* (Washington, D.C.: Government Printing Office, 1932), Table 13, p. 1327, Table 14, p. 1332, Table 21, p. 1363.

Sixteenth Census of the United States, 1940: Vol. 2, *Population,* Part 7, *Characteristics of Population* (Washington, D.C.: Government Printing Office, 1943), Table 22, p. 590.

U.S. Census of Population, 1950: Vol. 2, *Characteristics of Population,* Part 49, *Wisconsin* (Washington, D.C.: Government Printing Office, 1952), Table 41, p. 94.

U.S. Census of Population, 1960: Vol. 1, *Characteristics of Population,* Part 51, *Wisconsin* (Washington, D.C.: Government Printing Office, 1961), Table 27, p. 137.

U.S. Census of Population, 1970: Vol. 1, *Characteristics of Population,* Part 51, *Wisconsin* (Washington, D.C.: Government Printing Office, 1973), Table 38, p. 176.

U.S. Census of Population, 1980: Vol. 1, *Characteristics of Population,* Part 51, *Wisconsin* (Washington, D.C.: Government Printing Office, 1982), Table 52, p. 322.

Sources for Figure 4.1 and Table 7.4

Compendium of the Tenth Census of the United States, 1880: Part 1, *Population* (Washington, D.C.: Government Printing Office, 1883), p. 606.

Compendium of the Eleventh Census of the United States, 1890: Part 1, *Population* (Washington, D.C.: Government Printing Office, 1892), Table 27, p. 809.

Twelfth Census of the United States, 1900: Population, Part 1 (Washington, D.C.: Government Printing Office, 1902), Table 22, p. 608.

Thirteenth Census of the United States, 1910: Vol. 3, *Population* (Washington, D.C.: Government Printing Office, 1913), Table 1, p. 1095.

Fourteenth Census of the United States, 1920: Vol. 3, *Population* (Washington, D.C.: Government Printing Office, 1922), Table 9, p. 1130.

Fifteenth Census of the United States, 1930: Vol. 3, *Population,* Part 2, *Report by States* (Washington, D.C.: Government Printing Office, 1932), Table 13, p. 1327, Table 14, p. 1332, Table 21, p. 1363.

Sixteenth Census of the United States, 1940: Vol. 2, *Population,* Part 7, *Characteristics of Population* (Washington, D.C.: Government Printing Office, 1943), Table 22, p. 590.

U.S. Census of Population, 1950: Vol. 2, *Characteristics of Population,* Part 49, *Wisconsin* (Washington, D.C.: Government Printing Office, 1952), Table 41, p. 94.

U.S. Census of Population, 1960: Vol. 1, *Characteristics of Population,* Part 51, *Wisconsin* (Washington, D.C.: Government Printing Office, 1961), Table 27, p. 137.

U.S. Census of Population, 1970: Vol. 1, *Characteristics of Population,* Part 51,

Wisconsin (Washington, D.C.: Government Printing Office, 1973), Table 38, p. 176.

U.S. Census of Population, 1980: Vol. 1, *Characteristics of Population,* Part 51, *Wisconsin* (Washington, D.C.: Government Printing Office, 1982), Table 52, p. 322.

Sources for Table 4.7

Thirteenth Census of the United States, 1910: Vol. 3, *Population* (Washington, D.C.: Government Printing Office, 1913), Table 1, p. 1095.

Fourteenth Census of the United States, 1920: Vol. 3, *Population* (Washington, D.C.: Government Printing Office, 1922), Table 9, p. 1130.

Fifteenth Census of the United States, 1930: Vol. 3, *Population,* Part 2, *Report by States* (Washington, D.C.: Government Printing Office, 1932), Table 13, p. 1327.

Sixteenth Census of the United States, 1940: Vol. 2, *Population,* Part 7, *Characteristics of Population* (Washington, D.C.: Government Printing Office, 1943), Table 26, p. 611, Table 27, p. 616.

U.S. Census of Population, 1950: Vol. 2, *Characteristics of Population,* Part 49, *Wisconsin* (Washington, D.C.: Government Printing Office, 1952), Table 42, p. 99.

U.S. Census of Population, 1960: Vol. 1, *Characteristics of Population,* Part 51, *Wisconsin* (Washington, D.C.: Government Printing Office, 1961), Table 83, p. 255.

U.S. Census of Population, 1970: Vol. 1, *Characteristics of Population,* Part 51, *Wisconsin* (Washington, D.C.: Government Printing Office, 1973), Table 120, p. 424.

Sources for Table 6.2

Ninth Census of the United States, 1870 (Washinton, D.C.: Government Printing Office, 1872), p. 792.

Compendium of the Tenth Census of the United States, 1880: Part 1, *Population* (Washington, D.C.: Government Printing Office, 1883), Table 49, pp. 922–923.

Compendium of the Eleventh Census of the United States, 1890: Vol. 5, *Report on the Statistics of Agriculture* (Washington, D.C.: Government Printing Office, 1895), Table 12, p. 354.

Twelfth Census of the United States, 1900: Agriculture, Part 1, *Farms, Livestock, and Animal Products* (Washington, D.C.: Government Printing Office, 1902), Table 35, p. 495.

Thirteenth Census of the United States, 1910: Vol. 2, *Agriculture* (Washington, D.C.: Government Printing Office, 1913), Table 2, p. 927.

Fourteenth Census of the United States, 1920: Vol. 6, *Agriculture,* Part 1, *The Northern States* (Washington, D.C.: Government Printing Office, 1922), Table 11, p. 473.

Fifteenth Census of the United States, 1930: Vol. 2, *Agriculture,* Part 1, *The North-*

ern States (Washington, D.C.: Government Printing Office, 1932), Table 4, p. 757, Table 12, p. 799.

Sixteenth Census of the United States, 1940: Vol. 1, *Agriculture,* Part 1, *Statistics for Counties* (Washington, D.C.: Government Printing Office, 1942), Table 4, p. 920, Table 10, p. 953.

U.S. Census of Agriculture, 1954: Vol. 1, Part 7, *Wisconsin* (Washington, D.C.: Government Printing Office, 1956), Table 5, p. 71, Table 7, p. 83.

U.S. Census of Agriculture, 1964: Vol. 1, Part 14, *Wisconsin* (Washington, D.C.: Government Printing Office, 1965), Table 3, p. 253.

U.S. Census of Agriculture, 1974: Vol. 1, Part 49, *Wisconsin* (Washington, D.C.: Government Printing Office, 1977), Table 6, p. 369, Table 8, p. 370.

Sources for Table 7.1

Twelfth Census of the United States, 1900: Agriculture, Part 1, *Farms, Livestock, and Animal Products* (Washington, D.C.: Government Printing Office, 1902), Table 35, p. 495.

Thirteenth Census of the United States, 1910: Vol. 2, *Agriculture* (Washington, D.C.: Government Printing Office, 1913), Table 2, p. 927.

Fourteenth Census of the United States, 1920: Vol. 6, *Agriculture,* Part 1, *The Northern States* (Washington, D.C.: Government Printing Office, 1922), Table 11, p. 473.

Fifteenth Census of the United States, 1930: Vol. 2, *Agriculture,* Part 1, *The Northern States* (Washington, D.C.: Government Printing Office, 1932), Table 10, p. 789.

Sixteenth Census of the United States, 1940: Vol. 1, *Agriculture,* Part 1, *Statistics for Counties* (Washington, D.C.: Government Printing Office, 1942), Table 4, p. 921.

U.S. Census of Agriculture, 1950: Vol. 1, Part 7, *Wisconsin* (Washington, D.C.: Government Printing Office, 1952), Table 4, p. 63.

Sources for Table 7.2

Compendium of the Tenth Census of the United States, 1880: Part 1, *Population* (Washington, D.C.: Government Printing Office, 1883), Table 49, pp. 922–923.

Compendium of the Eleventh Census of the United States, 1890: Vol. 5, *Report on the Statistics of Agriculture* (Washington, D.C.: Government Printing Office, 1895), Table 12, p. 354.

Twelfth Census of the United States, 1900: Agriculture, Part 1, *Farms, Livestock, and Animal Products* (Washington, D.C.: Government Printing Office, 1902), Table 35, p. 495.

Thirteenth Census of the United States, 1910: Vol. 2, *Agriculture* (Washington, D.C.: Government Printing Office, 1913), Table 2, p. 927.

Fourteenth Census of the United States, 1920: Vol. 6, *Agriculture,* Part 1, *The Northern States* (Washington, D.C.: Government Printing Office, 1922), Table 11, p. 473.

Fifteenth Census of the United States, 1930: Vol. 2, *Agriculture,* Part 1, *The North-*

ern States (Washington, D.C.: Government Printing Office, 1932), Table 9, p. 785.

Sixteenth Census of the United States, 1940: Vol. 1, *Agriculture*, Part 1, *Statistics for Counties* (Washington, D.C.: Government Printing Office, 1942), Table 4, p. 920.

U.S. Census of Agriculture, 1950: Vol. 1, Part 7, *Wisconsin* (Washington, D.C.: Government Printing Office, 1952), Table 4, p. 63.

U.S. Census of Agriculture, 1964: Vol. 1, Part 14, *Wisconsin* (Washington, D.C.: Government Printing Office, 1965), Table 3, p. 253.

U.S. Census of Agriculture, 1970: Vol. 1, Part 14, *Wisconsin* (Washington, D.C.: Government Printing Office, 1972), Table 7, p. 480.

Sources for Table 7.3

Fifteenth Census of the United States, 1930: Population, Vol. 4, *Families* (Washington, D.C.: Government Printing Office, 1932), Table 19, p. 1467.

Sixteenth Census of the United States, 1940: Vol. 2, *Housing,* Part 5, *General Characteristics* (Washington, D.C.: Government Printing Office, 1943), Table 22, p. 895.

U.S. Census of Housing, 1950: Vol. 1, *General Characteristics,* Part 6, *Texas to Wyoming* (Washington, D.C.: Government Printing Office, 1952), Table 29, p. 64, Table 32, p. 77.

Sources for Table 7.6

Compendium of the Eleventh Census of the United States, 1890: Part 1, *Population* (Washington, D.C.: Government Printing Office, 1892), Table 3, p. 877.

Twelfth Census of the United States, 1900: Vol. 2, *Population,* Part 2 (Washington, D.C.: Government Printing Office, 1902), Table 103, p. 639.

Thirteenth Census of the United States, 1910: Vol. 3, *Population* (Washington, D.C.: Government Printing Office, 1913), Table 1, p. 1095.

Fourteenth Census of the United States, 1920: Vol. 3, *Population* (Washington, D.C.: Government Printing Office, 1922), Table 9, p. 1130.

Fifteenth Census of the United States, 1930: Population, Vol. 4, *Families* (Washington, D.C.: Government Printing Office, 1932), Table 19, p. 1467.

Sixteenth Census of the United States, 1940: Vol. 2. Housing. Part 5. *General Characteristics.* (Washington, D.C.: Government Printing Office, 1943), Table 22, p. 590.

U.S. Census of Population, 1950: Vol. 2, *Characteristics of Population,* Part 49, *Wisconsin* (Washington, D.C.: Government Printing Office, 1952), Table 41, p. 99.

U.S. Census of Housing, 1960: Vol. 1, *States and Small Areas,* Part 8, *Texas–Wyoming* (Washington, D.C.: Government Printing Office, 1961), Table 29, p. 72.

U.S. Census of Housing, 1970: Vol. 1, *Housing Characteristics for States, Cities, and Counties,* Part 51, *Wisconsin* (Washington, D.C.: Government Printing Office, 1973), Table 60, p. 177.

Notes

Introduction: Looking at Rural America

1. For a comprehensive historiographic discussion regarding the social history of rural communities in the nineteenth century, see Hal Barron, *Those Who Stayed Behind: Rural Society in Nineteenth-Century New England* (New York: Cambridge University Press, 1984), pp. 1–15; also valuable are Robert Swierenga, "Towards a 'New Rural History,' " *Historical Methods Newsletter* 6 (1973): 112; Robert Swierenga, "Theoretical Perspectives on the New Rural History: From Environmentalism to Modernism," *Agricultural History* 56 (1982): 495–502; Steven Hahn and Jonathan Prude, eds., "Introduction," in *The Countryside in the Age of Capitalist Transformation: Essays in the Social History of Rural America* (Chapel Hill: University of North Carolina Preess, 1985), pp. 3–21.

2. Frederick Jackson Turner, *The Significance of the Frontier in American History*, ed. Harold P. Simonson, reprinted. (New York: Frederick Unger, 1963); Walter T. K. Nugent, *Changing Structures of American Social History* (Bloomington: Indiana University Press, 1981), p. 111.

3. For the negative images of rural life, see Hamlin Garland, *Main-Travelled Roads* (1891; reprinted New York: American Library, Inc., 1962); Sinclair Lewis, *Main Street* (New York: Harcourt, Brace and Co., 1920); Sherwood Anderson, *Winesburg, Ohio* (New York: Viking Press, 1919; reprinted, 1960).

4. For a recent assessment of historians' changing perspective on rural America, see: David B. Danbom, "The Professors and the Plowmen in American History Today," *Wisconsin Magazine of History* 69 (Winter 1985–1986): 106–128; Arthur J. Vidich and Joseph Bensman, *Small Town in Mass Society: Class, Power and Religion in a Rural Community* (Princeton: Princeton University Press, 1958). One of the primary issues that emerged from the latter study was "what techniques of personal and social adjustment enable the community members to live constructive and meaningful lives in the face of an environment which is hostile to their values, aspirations and illusions?" An earlier but much less well-known study of the "inner life" of a small town that manages to escape the critical biases of most academic observers is Albert Blumenthal, *Small Town Stuff* (Chicago: University of Chicago Press, 1932). See also Richard Hofstadter, *The Age of Reform: From Bryan to F.D.R.* (New York: Alfred A. Knopf, Inc., 1955). For a recent attempt to discern the

historical realities of small-town life, see Lewis Atherton, *Main Street on the Middle Border* (Bloomington: Indiana University Press, 1984).

5. Paul A. Carter, *The Twenties in America*, 2nd ed. (Arlington Heights, Illinois: Harlan Davidson, 1975), p. 95.

6. Michael Lesy, *Wisconsin Death Trip: 1869–1879* (New York: Pantheon–Random House, 1973).

7. Merle Curti, *The Making of an American Community: A Case Study of Democracy in a Frontier County* (Stanford, California: Stanford University Press, 1959); Turner, *The Significance of the Frontier in American History*.

8. For examples of the rejection of the Turnerian interpretation, see: Arthur M. Schlesinger, Sr., *The Rise of the City, 1878–1898* (New York: Macmillan Co., 1933); and Arthur M. Schlesinger, Sr., "The City in American History," *Mississippi Valley Historical Review* 27 (June 1940): 43–66.

9. Danbom, "The Professors and the Plowmen," pp. 126, 128.

10. John Demos, *A Little Commonwealth: Family Life in Plymouth Colony* (New York: Oxford University Press, 1970); Phillip J. Greven, Jr., *Four Generations: Population, Land, and Family in Colonial Andover, Massachusetts* (Ithaca: Cornell University Press, 1970); Kenneth Lockridge, *A New England Town: The First Hundred Years: Dedham, Massachusetts, 1636–1736* (New York: W. W. Norton and Co., 1970).

11. Thomas Bender, *Community and Social Change in America* (Baltimore: Johns Hopkins University Press, 1978), pp. 51, 58–61.

12. James Henretta, "Families and Farms: Mentalite in Pre-Industrial America," *William and Mary Quarterly*, 3rd ser., 35 (1978): 3–32. James Henretta speculated about the persistence of a traditional mentalité that flourished in the context of the colonial frontier community's farms: Ethnically and religiously homogeneous, the frontier and rural communities transmitted traditional cultural patterns and family "lineal values" which inhibited the development of individualism and an entrepreneurial orientation. For a recent effort to combine historians' understanding of rural and frontier experience with conceptions of the traditional social order, see Nugent. Borrowing on the approaches associated with the French *annales* scholars, Nugent, in an attempt to synthesize recent insights into American social history, has argued that frontier and rural America were this country's variation of the traditional social order. Like Henretta, Nugent maintained that available land in the frontier areas allowed a variant of the traditional social order to be sustained in this country. On the persistence of tradition on the frontier see also, Mary P. Ryan, *Cradle of the Middle Class: The Family in Oneida County, New York, 1790–1865* (New York: Cambridge University Press, 1981), pp. 24, 43. Ryan was careful to note that the forms of family and community were "by definition temporary, doomed to extinction probably within the space of a generation," p. 15. On the continuation of communal traditions on the frontier see: John Mack Faragher, *Sugar Creek: Life on the Illinois Prairie* (New Haven: Yale University Press, 1986); John Mack Faragher, "Open-Country Community: Sugar Creek, Illinois, 1820–1890," in Hahn and Prude, pp. 251–252. Faragher found evidence of continuities of community and family organization. He concluded that

"in important ways communal elements retained much strength in the Turnerian environment."

13. For a recent study tracing emigrants from Norway to the midwestern frontier and a careful analysis of persistence and change in social and economic behavior on the frontier, see Jon Gjerde, *From Peasants to Farmers: The Migration from Balestrand, Norway, to the Upper Middle West* (Cambridge: Cambridge University Press, 1985), pp. 236–238. Jon Gjerde carefully traced families from a mountain community in Norway to the midwestern frontier and concluded that the immigrants rapidly took up the social and economic ways of Americans, though the springboard of the change was not simply the result of "Americanization" but could be located in Norway, where peasants were also being transformed "from peasant to farmer." The transition to modern behavior, Gjerde argued, resulted from the transmitting of cultural ideals evolving in Norway to the American environment. Further evidence of continuities with the past has been discovered by those scholars examining inheritance patterns; see Kathleen Neils Conzen, "Peasant Pioneers: Generational Succession among German Farmers in Frontier Minnesota," in Hahn and Prude, p. 285. For the Swedish immigrants' story see Robert C. Ostergren, *A Community Transplanted: The Trans-Atlantic Experience of a Swedish Immigrant Settlement in the Upper Midwest, 1835–1915* (Madison: University of Wisconsin Press, 1988).

14. Bender, p. 111; Robert Wiebe, *The Search for Order, 1877–1920* (New York: Hill and Wang, 1967).

15. Bender, pp. 77, 83.

16. Vidich and Bensman, pp. 30–46, 306–307. For a contrasting view of small-town America see Herve Varenne, *Americans Together: Structured Diversity in a Midwestern Town* (New York: Teachers College Press, 1977).

17. Robert Wiebe, *The Search for Order, 1877–1920* (New York: Hill and Wang, 1967); for a study of the new professionals, see: Thomas L. Haskell, *The Emergence of Professional Social Science: The American Social Science Association and the Nineteenth-Century Crisis of Authority* (Urbana: University of Illinois Press, 1977); Lowry Nelson, *Rural Sociology: Its Origins and Growth in the United States* (Minneapolis: University of Minnesota Press, 1969), p. 101.

18. An early example of the orientation of a rural sociologist can be found in Josiah Galpin, *Rural Life* (New York: Century, 1918); Galpin is regarded as the "father of rural sociology." For an indication of Galpin's standing today, see Don Dillman, "The Social Impacts of Information Technologies in Rural North America," *Rural Sociology* 50 (Spring 1985): 4. For later examples, see: T. Lynn Smith, *The Sociology of Rural Life in the United States* (New York: Harper and Brothers, 1940; reprinted, 1953); Carl C. Taylor et al., *Rural Life in the United States* (New York: Alfred A. Knopf, 1949); Bird T. Baldwin, Eva Abigail Fillmore, and Lora Hadley, *Farm Children* (New York: D. Appleton and Co., 1930); Ezra Dwight Sanderson, "Scientific Research in Rural Sociology," *American Journal of Sociology* 33 (September 1927): 181–82. A rare voice in defense of traditional rural culture is found in Lowry Nelson, "Action Programs for the Conservation of Rural Life and Culture," *Rural Sociology* 4 (December 1939): 414–432. Rural sociolo-

gists' work that is clearly informed by modernization theory include: Charles P. Loomis, *Social Systems: Essays on Their Persistence and Change* (Princeton: Van Nostrand Co., 1960); Irwin T. Sanders, *Rural Society* (Englewood Cliffs, New Jersey: Prentice-Hall, 1977). For an assessment of the impact of rural sociologists as represented in the "Country Life" movement and their direction of government policy in the U.S. Department of Agriculture, see David B. Danbom, *The Resisted Revolution: Urban America and the Industrialization of Agriculture, 1900–1930* (Ames: Iowa State University Press, 1979). For a critical view of the traditional stance of rural sociologists and as an indicator of new directions in rural sociology see Frederick H. Buttel and Howard Newby, "Toward a Critical Rural Sociology," in *The Rural Sociology of the Advanced Societies: Critical Perspectives,* ed. Frederick H. Buttel and Howard Newby, pp. 1–35 (Montclair, New Jersey: Allanheld, Osmun and Co., 1980); this publication reveals a new self-consciousness on the part of rural sociologists about their historical and present role in determining government policy and corporate behavior. Stimulating this reflection were critical attacks such as that on the land-grant colleges for functioning as clients of corporate agribusiness; examples can be found in: Jim Hightower, *Hard Tomatoes, Hard Times: A Report of the Agribusiness Accountability Project on the Failure of America's Land Grant College Complex* (Cambridge, Massachusetts: Schenkman Publishing Co., 1973); Alain de Janvry, "Social Differentiation in Agriculture and the Ideology of Neopopulism," in Buttel and Newby, pp. 155–168. For an overview of new directions in rural sociology since the mid-1970s see, Frederick H. Buttel and Philip McMichael, "Sociology and Rural History," *Social Science History* 12 (Summer 1988): 93–120.

19. Darrett B. Rutman, "Behind the Wide Missouri" (review of *Those Who Stayed Behind: Rural Society in Nineteenth Century New England,* by Hal S. Barron), *Reviews in American History* 13 (1985): 235.

20. In addition to Curti's work on Trempealeau County, other sources on frontier agriculture are: John Giffen Thompson, *The Rise and Decline of the Wheat Growing Industry in Wisconsin,* Economic and Political Science Series (Madison: University of Wisconsin, 1909); Benjamin Horace Hibbard, *The History of Agriculture in Dane County, Wisconsin,* Economic and Political Science Series (Madison: University of Wisconsin, 1904); Allan Bogue, *From Prairie to Cornbelt: Farming on the Illinois and Iowa Prairies in the Nineteenth Century* (Chicago: Quadrangle Books, 1963); on the Norwegian adjustment to frontier agriculture, see Gjerde, pp. 168–201.

21. For descriptions of demographic trends in rural areas, see: Nugent, pp. 111–113; Robert Higgs, "Mortality in Rural America," *Explorations in Economic History* 10 (Winter 1973): 177–195.

22. John L. Shover, *First Majority—Last Minority: The Transforming of Rural Life in America* (Dekalb: Northern Illinois University Press, 1976); for a recent study of the rural South which finds the post–World War II years as bringing critical changes to rural areas, see: Jack Temple Kirby, *Rural Worlds Lost: The American South, 1920–1960* (Baton Rouge: Louisiana State University Press, 1987); Gilbert C. Fite, *American Farmers: The New Minority* (Bloomington: Indiana University Press, 1981).

Chapter 1: On Being "Left Behind"

1. Interview with Pastor Peter Sherven, Pigeon Falls, Wisconsin, November 1983. Pastor Sherven related the decline in church membership to the arrival of new people in the Pigeon area. At one time in the not-too-distant past, church membership and population in the township closely corresponded to one another.

2. For an analysis of changing demographic trends on the countryside, see: Richard A. Easterlin, "Population Change and Farm Settlement in the Northern United States," *Journal of Economic History* 36 (1976): 45–75; Richard A. Easterlin, "Factors in the Decline of Farm Fertility in the United States: Some Preliminary Research Results," *Journal of American History* 63 (1976): 600–614; Wilbur Zelinsky, "Changes in the Geographic Patterns of Rural Population in the United States, 1790–1960," *Geographic Review* 52 (1962): 492–524; Calvin L. Beale, "Rural Depopulation in the United States: Some Demographic Consequences of Agricultural Adjustments," *Demography* 1 (1964): 264–272; Calvin L. Beale and Donald J. Bogue, "Recent Population Trends in the United States and Their Causes," in *Our Changing Rural Society: Perspectives and Trends*, ed. James H. Copp (Ames: Iowa State University Press, 1964), pp. 71–126.

3. Eben Douglas Pierce, ed., *History of Trempealeau County, Wisconsin* (Chicago: H. C. Cooper, Jr., and Co., 1917), pp. 283, 686–87.

4. *Atlas of Trempealeau County, Wisconsin* (Minneapolis: Standard Atlas Co., 1964); interview with Marlene Hanson, superintendent of schools, Whitehall, Wisconsin, July 1984. In 1984 the district closed the last of the two-room elementary schools. Only the Pigeon Falls Elementary School remains outside the consolidated elementary school system in Whitehall. For a discussion of the demise of the country school as a result of the organized efforts of professional educators, see Wayne E. Fuller, *The Old Country School* (Chicago: University of Chicago Press, 1982).

5. *U.S. Census of Housing, 1950:* Vol. 1, *General Characteristics*, Part 6, *Texas to Wyoming* (Washington, D.C.: Government Printing Office, 1952), Table 33, p. 8.

6. On the religious divisions among the Norwegians, see: Clifford Nelson and Eugene L. Fevold, *The Lutheran Church among Norwegian-Americans: A History of the Evangelical Lutheran Church*, 2 vols. (Minneapolis: Augsburg Publishing, 1960); Ann M. Legreid and David Ward, "Religious Schism and the Development of Rural Immigrant Communities: Norwegian Lutherans in Western Wisconsin, 1880–1905," *Midwest History* 2 (Summer 1982): 13–28; Ingrid Semmingsen, *Norway to America: A History of Migration* (Minneapolis: University of Minnesota Press, 1978), pp. 134–137.

7. U.S. Census of Population, Manuscript Census, Pigeon and Lincoln townships, Trempealeau County, Wisconsin, 1880, State Historical Society of Wisconsin; Pigeon Falls Lutheran Parish directory, 1981, in the Pigeon Falls Lutheran Parish records, Pigeon Falls, Wisconsin.

8. U.S. Census of Population, Manuscript Censuses, 1870, 1880.

9. For an account of several of the early settlers and their genealogy, see: Dave Wood, ed., *Wisconsin Prarie Diary: 1869–1879* (Whitehall, Wisconsin: Dan

Camp Press, 1979), pp. vii–xi; Rebecca L. Taylor, *Briggs Ancestors: With Brief Sketches of Some Related Families* (Whitehall, Wisconsin: Dan Camp Press, 1979).

10. Mary P. Ryan, *Cradle of the Middle Class: The Family in Oneida County, New York, 1790–1865* (New York: Cambridge University Press, 1981).

11. U.S. Census of Population, Manuscript Census, 1870.

12. D. Wood, *Prarie Diary*, pp. vii–xi; Pierce, pp. 108, 861–862. Besides the published portion of Dave Wood's diaries, edited by his great-grandson Dave Wood, there are unpublished volumes that span the years 1869–1927. There are also several unpublished volumes of diaries kept intermittently by two of Daves's sons, Ralph and Jim, from adolescence to adulthood; these are held by the Area Research Center of the University of Wisconsin–Eau Claire.

13. Ryan, p. 21.

14. D. Wood, *Prarie Diary*, passim; Pierce, pp. 551, 643.

15. D. Wood, *Prarie Diary*, p. 11.

16. Merle Curti, *The Making of an American Community: A Case Study of Democracy in a Frontier County* (Stanford, California: Stanford University Press, 1959), pp. 115–123.

17. Hans Anderson, "J. D. Olds," typescript, Trempealeau County Historical Society; Pierce, p. 295; J. D. Olds, "Communication," *Whitehall Times*, April 1, 1881, p. 1. On the colonial and revolutionary generation's perspective, see: Bernard Bailyn, *The Ideological Origins of the American Revolution* (Cambridge, Massachusetts: Harvard University Press, 1967); Gordon S. Wood, *The Creation of the American Republic, 1776–1787* (New York: W. W. Norton and Co., 1969); Richard Bushman, *From Puritan to Yankee: Character and Social Order in Connecticut, 1690–1765* (Cambridge, Massachusetts: Harvard University Press, 1967); Michael Zuckerman, *Peaceable Kingdoms: New England Towns in the Eighteenth Century* (New York: W. W. Norton and Co., 1970). For ideological connections between the earlier republican moralism of the revolutionary ideology and the Populist movement, see Lawrence Goodwyn, *Democratic Promise: The Populist Movement in America* (New York: Oxford University Press, 1976).

18. On the morphology of the New England town, see James Henretta, *The Evolution of an American Society: 1700–1815* (Lexington, Massachusetts: D. C. Heath, 1973). For an extensive review and analysis of common findings of the early town studies, see John Murrin, "Review Essay," *History and Theory* 11 (1972): 226–275.

19. Curti, p. 138.

20. Jon Gjerde, *From Peasants to Farmers: The Migration from Balestrand, Norway, to the Upper Middle West* (Cambridge: Cambridge University Press, 1985), pp. 134–135.

21. Ibid., pp. 134–136; see also: Ingrid Semmingsen, "Nordic Research into Emigration," *Scandinavian Journal of History* 3 (1978): 49–51; Semmingsen, *Norway to America*, p. 40; Sune Akerman, "The Psychology of Migration," *American Studies in Scandinavia* 8 (1978): 49–51.

22. Mack Walker, *Germany and the Emigration, 1816–1885* (Cambridge, Massachusetts: Harvard University Press, 1964), p. 69.

23. Curti, pp. 65–73.

24. Pierce, p. 156.

25. U.S. Census of Population, Manuscript Censuses, 1870, 1880, 1910; records of the Pigeon Creek Lutheran Church and records of the Pigeon Falls Evangelical Lutheran Church, both contained in the Pigeon Falls Lutheran Parish records, Pigeon Falls, Wisconsin; *Standard Atlas of Trempealeau County, Wisconsin* (Chicago: George A. Ogle and Co., 1901); *Atlas and Farmers Directory of Trempealeau County, Wisconsin* (St. Paul, Minnesota: Webb Publishing Co., 1930); *Triennial Atlas and Plat Book, Trempealeau County, Wisconsin* (Rockford, Illinois: Rockford Map Publishers, 1954); *Atlas of Trempealeau County* (1964); *Ownership Atlas, Trempealeau County, Wisconsin* (Quincy, Illinois: Artcraft Co., 1975); Tax records, Pigeon and Lincoln townships, 1870–1930, held by the Area Research Center, University of Wisconsin–La Crosse.

26. Ibid.

27. John Demos, *A Little Commonwealth: Family Life in Plymouth Colony* (New York: Oxford University Press, 1970); Philip J. Greven, Jr., *Four Generations: Population, Land, and Family in Colonial Andover, Massachusetts* (Ithaca: Cornell University Press, 1970), pp. 212–221; Kenneth Lockridge, *A New England Town: The First Hundred Years: Dedham, Massachusetts, 1636–1736* (New York: W. W. Norton and Co., 1970), pp. 63–78.

28. *U.S. Census of Population, 1960:* Vol. 1, *Characteristics of Population,* Part 51, *Wisconsin* (Washington, D.C.: Government Printing Office, 1961), Table 91, p. 284.

29. Personal communication from Mrs. Ila Staff, November 1983.

30. D. Wood, *Prarie Diary*, pp. 197–198.

31. On patterns of land transfer, see: Sonya Salamon, "Ethnic Differences in Farm Family Land Transfer," *Rural Sociology* 45 (1980): 290–308; Kathleen Neils Conzen, "Peasant Pioneers: Generational Succession among German Farmers in Frontier Minnesota," in *The Countryside in the Age of Capitalist Transformation: Essays in the Social History of Rural America*, ed. Steven Hahn and Jonathan Prude (Chapel Hill: University of North Carolina Press, 1985), pp. 259–292; Mark Friedberger, "The Farm Family and the Inheritance Process: Evidence from the Corn Belt, 1870–1950," *Agricultural History* 57 (1983): 1–13; Robert C. Ostergren, "Land and Family in Rural Immigrant Communitites," *Annals of the Association of American Geographers* 71 (1981): 400–411.

32. Alumni records of Whitehall High School graduates, assembled in 1922 and 1938, indicate the very different mobility patterns of the young in these two decades.

Chapter 2: Between Memory and Reality

1. L. W. Boe as quoted in Clifford Nelson and Eugene L. Fevold, *The Lutheran Church among Norwegian-Americans: A History of the Evangelical Lutheran Church*, 2 vols. (Minneapolis: Augsburg Publishing, 1960), p. 240.

2. Eban Douglas Pierce, ed., *History of Trempealeau County, Wisconsin* (Chicago: H. C. Cooper, Jr., and Co., 1917), p. 817.

3. The centrality of local neighborhoods to the organization of the social life of the community is revealed year after year in the *Whitehall Times,* which reported on events and people with reference to very small units—usually associated with a school, a church, and in some instances a country store. References were to "a farmer from Monson's coulee" (November 4, 1980) and to such localities as the Big Slough, Hegge coulee, French Creek, Chimney Rock, and others. For many years the *Times* featured correspondents from these diverse rural communities who reported on events in their neighborhoods. Judge and local historian Hans Anderson attempted to write histories of each of these distinct rural communities. Rural sociologists since the beginning of this century have been evolving a conception of rural community, particularly the open-country community, and exploring the character and perimeters of such; see, for example, Warren H. Wilson, *The Evolution of the Country Community* (Boston: Pilgrim Press, 1912); John H. Kolb, *Rural Primary Groups: A Study of Agricultural Neighborhoods* (Madison: University of Wisconsin Press, 1921); Charles P. Loomis and J. Allan Beegle, *Rural Social Systems: A Textbook in Rural Sociology and Anthropology* (New York: Prentice-Hall, 1950); Irwin T. Sanders, *The Community: An Introduction to a Social System* (New York: Ronald Press Co., 1958).

4. The several plat maps record the owner's name on each property. Thus, almost at a glance, or by reference to the manuscript census, the ethnic concentration in particular townships and the divisions within townships are readily apparent: *Standard Atlas of Trempealeau County, Wisconsin* (Chicago: George A. Ogle and Co., 1901); *Atlas and Farmers Directory of Trempealeau County, Wisconsin* (St. Paul, Minnesota: Webb Publishing Co., 1930); *Triennial Atlas and Plat Book, Trempealeau County, Wisconsin* (Rockford, Illinois: Rockford Map Publishers, 1954); *Atlas of Trempealeau County, Wisconsin* (Minneapolis, Minnesota: Standard Atlas Co., 1964). This kind of concentration by ethnic groups in neighborhoods was widespread in the Midwest. Careful analysis of the place of origin indicates the organization of neighborhoods not only according to nationality but also on the basis of particular communities or sections of the home country. This kind of ethnic clustering has been noted by other historians; see Jon Gjerde, *From Peasants to Farmers: The Migration from Balestrand, Norway, to the Upper Middle West* (Cambridge: Cambridge University Press, 1985), pp. 144–150; Robert C. Ostergren, "Cultural Homogeneity and Population Stability among Swedish Immigrants in Chisago County," *Minnesota History* 47 (1973): 256; Robert C. Ostergren, "Prairie Bound: Migration Patterns to a Swedish Settlement in the Dakota Frontier," in *Ethnicity on the Great Plains,* ed. Frederick C. Luebke (Lincoln: University of Nebraska Press, 1980), pp. 73–91; John G. Rice, *Patterns of Ethnicity in a Minnesota County, 1880–1905,* University of Umea, Department of Geography, Geographical Report No. 4 (Umea, Sweden, 1973); Peter Munch, "Segregation and Assimilation of Norwegian Settlements in Wisconsin," *Norwegian-American Studies and Records* 18 (1954): pp. 102–141; David G. Vanderstel, "Dutch Immigrant Neighborhood Development in Grand Rapids, 1850–1900," in *The Dutch in America: Immigration, Settlement, and Cultural Change,* ed. Robert P. Swierenga (New Brunswick: Rutgers University Press, 1985), pp. 125–155; Rob-

ert P. Swierenga, "Settlement of the Old Northwest," *Journal of the Early Republic* 9 (Spring 1989): 73–105.

5. "St. John's Catholic Parish," in *Atlas of Trempealeau County,* 1964.

6. Interview with Arlene Arneson, November 1984, Whitehall, Wisconsin. According to local community members, many of the older members of the area speak either Norwegian or Polish in addition to English.

7. Interview with Harold Tomter, taped by Dale Treleven for the State Historical Society of Wisconsin, Madison.

8. Arneson interview.

9. The Bennett Law was a political disaster for the Republican party in power; see Robert C. Nesbit, *Wisconsin: A History* (Madison: University of Wisconsin Press, 1973), pp. 377–378. For the reaction of particular ethnic groups to the legislation, see David L. Brye, *Wisconsin Voting Patterns in the Twentieth Century, 1900–1950* (New York: Garland Publishing, Inc., 1979), pp. 171–174; Roger E. Wyman, "Wisconsin Ethnic Groups and the Election of 1890," *Wisconsin Magazine of History* 51 (Summer 1968): 269–293; Robert J. Ulrich, "The Bennett Law of 1889: Education and Politics in Wisconsin," Ph.D. dissertation, University of Wisconsin, 1965.

10. Einar Haugen, *The Norwegian Language in America: A Study in Bilingual Behavior,* 2 vols. (Philadelphia: University of Pennsylvania Press, 1953), vol. 1, pp. 3–4.

11. Pierce, pp. 283, 686; "Peder Ekern and Pigeon," typescript, Trempealeau County Historical Society; Hans Anderson, "Autobiography," manuscript, Herman Ekern Papers, Manuscript Division, State Historical Society of Wisconsin. Anderson was Herman Ekern's law partner in Whitehall and his father-in-law.

12. Haugen, p. 278.

13. Ibid., pp. 76–87, 91.

14. Hans Anderson, "J. D. Olds," typescript, Trempealeau County Historical Society.

15. Interview with Lila Pederson, Whitehall, November 1984.

16. Haugen, pp. 522–523.

17. *Whitehall Times,* September 12, 1918, p. 1.

18. Ibid., October 4, 1883, p. 1.

19. "Peder Ekern and Company," typescript, Trempealeau County Historical Society; letter from F. G. Steig to Hans Anderson, March 16, 1933, Trempealeau County Historical Society; in this letter Steig, a former resident of Lincoln and a farmer who had gone bust in the Great Depression in North Dakota, compares Melby as a banker with those of 1933: everyone had great confidence in him, he was everyone's "friend, rich or poor," direct, and honest.

20. Merle Curti, *The Making of an American Community: A Case Study of Democracy in a Frontier County* (Stanford, California: Stanford University Press, 1959); in chapter 11 of his study of Trempealeau County, Curti focuses on the functioning of the town government in Pigeon and Lincoln; see pp. 295–318.

21. Brye, *Wisconsin Voting Patterns,* pp. 179–180; Nesbit, *Wisconsin: A History,* p. 405.

22. Nesbit, *Wisconsin: A History,* pp. 436, 468; Brye, *Wisconsin Voting Patterns,* p. 179; biography of Herman Ekern, Herman Ekern Papers, Manuscript Division, State Historical Society of Wisconsin.

23. Haugen, vol. 1, pp. 281–283.

24. Ibid., p. 52.

25. Ibid., pp. 270–271.

26. Hans Anderson was the driving force behind the Trempealeau County Historical Society in 1907 and the House of Memories collection of materials on which Merle Curti depended heavily. Unfortunately, the House of Memories has since gone out of existence, and the once well-organized and extensive sources on the county are in sad disarray. Portions of Anderson's original files have been lost. *U.S. Census of Population, 1970:* Vol. 1, *Characteristics of Population,* Part 51, *Wisconsin* (Washington, D.C.: Government Printing Office, 1973), Table 119, p. 418.

27. Ralph Wood diaries, 1906–1926, passim.

28. Dave Wood, *Wisconsin Life Trip* (Whitehall, Wisconsin: Dan Camp Press, 1976), p. 56.

29. Ibid., pp. 45, 56–58.

30. Curti, pp. 105–106.

31. Arneson interview; interview with Janet Peterson, June 1982, Whitehall, Wisconsin.

32. For a systematic analysis of marriage patterns among Wisconsin ethnic groups, see Richard M. Bernard, *The Melting Pot and the Altar: Marital Assimilation in Early Twentieth Century Wisconsin* (Minneapolis: University of Minnesota Press, 1981).

33. Arneson interview.

34. Peterson interview.

35. Letter from Dave Wood to author, January 11, 1985.

36. Anderson, "Autobiography," p. 16; also on the centrality of Lutheranism to a Norwegian identity, see Peter A. Munch, "Social Adjustment among Wisconsin Norwegians," *Norwegian-American Studies and Records* 16 (1952): 785.

37. For the important role of the churches, see the Dave, James, and Ralph Wood diaries, Area Research Center, University of Wisconsin–Eau Claire, Ella Hanson's diaries, kept between 1922 and 1945, suggest the churches' continuing importance. Hanson's diaries are presently held by her daughter, Eleanor Ackley, Pigeon Falls, Wisconsin. For an assessment of family and church in another rural Wisconsin Norwegian community, see Munch, "Segregation and Assimilation of Norwegian Settlements."

38. Curti, p. 109.

39. Ibid., p. 97.

40. *Whitehall Times:* January 26, 1882, p. 1; November 29, 1987; 1880–1920; passim.

41. For this discussion of dual social structures in rural and small-town communities, see Munch, "Social Adjustment among Wisconsin Norwegians," pp. 785–786.

42. Ibid.

43. *Whitehall Times*, 1900–1906, passim; Curti, pp. 106–107.

44. Pierce, pp. 283–285, 293–294.

45. Ibid. pp. 283–285; Curti, pp. 175, 326.

46. Pierce, p. 283.

47. Ibid., p. 285.

48. Hans Anderson, "John O. Melby," typescript, Trempealeau County Historical Society.

49. *Whitehall Times:* "Disloyalty Argument Hit Hard," September 12, 1918, p. 1; "Senate Declares War Against Germany," March 5, 1917, p. 4; "Faithful to Son," May 9, 1918, p. 1; editorial comments in March 3, 1918 and October 31, 1917; "Germans Wronged Most," September 12, 1918.

50. Ibid., "Armed Neutrality," March 15, 1917, p. 5.

51. The trend toward consensus over time was true in the nineteenth-century rural community of Chelsea, Vermont, as noted in Hal Barron, *Those Who Stayed Behind: Rural Society in Nineteenth-Century New England* (New York: Cambridge University Press, 1984); the dynamics of the consensus of another small community studied in the twentieth century can be found in Arthur J. Vidich and Joseph Bensman, *Small Town in Mass Society: Class, Power and Religion in a Rural Community* (Princeton: Princeton University Press, 1958), pp. 112–133.

52. For a discussion of localism in Norwegian American communitites, see Munch, "Social Adjustment among Wisconsin Norwegians." For a consideration of peasant localism in Norway and the relationship of local communal goals to a centralizing bureaucracy and national politics, see Oyvind Osterude, *Agrarian Structure and Peasant Politics in Scandinavia: A Comparative Study of Rural Response to Economic Change* (Oslo, Norway: Universitetsforlaget, 1978), pp. 227–244; according to Osterude's description of the peasants' attempt to preserve the peasantry and peasant autonomy in the face of an increasingly obtrusive government, their situation parallels the one in early seventeenth-century England which shaped the New England colonial experience; see also Timothy H. Breen, "Presistent Localism: English Social Change and the Shaping of New England Institutions," *William and Mary Quarterly* 32 (January 1975): 3–28. To some extent there appear to be parallels between the social impact of the World War I experience on Trempealeau and the American Revolution's impact on colonial communities. Thomas Bender has argued that the American Revolution functioned as what Clifford Geertz has described as an "integrative revolution" fostering identities beyond the local ones of the colonial period. World War I appears to me to have functioned in a similar way in Pigeon and Lincoln. See Thomas Bender, *Community and Social Change in America*, (Baltimore: Johns Hopkins University Press, 1978), pp. 78–82.

53. *Whitehall Times*, "Call for Volunteers to Buy Liberty Bonds," October 11, 1917, p. 1.

54. *Whitehall Times:* "Lutheran Drive Is a Big Success," March 7, 1918, p. 1; "Whitehall and Lincoln Go over the Top," May 2, 1918; "Liberty Loan Drive in County Meets with Success, October 18, 1917.

55. Curti, pp. 296–297, 303–304.

56. Ibid., p. 443.

57. Ibid., p. 448.

58. Ingrid Semmingson, *Norway to America: A History of Migration* (Minneapolis: University of Minnesota Press, 1978), pp. 89–90; for a discussion of Norwegian peasants' acquisition of local political power in the early nineteenth century, see Osterude, pp. 227–243; for Pigeon and Lincoln township governments' responsibilities and the early political career of Ekern, see Curti, pp. 310–319.

59. Seemingsen, *Norway to America*, pp. 148–151; see also: Odd S. Lovoll, *The Promise of American Life: A History of the Norwegian-American People* (Minneapolis: University of Minnesota Press, 1983), pp. 128–131; Jon Wefald, *A Voice of Protest: Norwegians in American Politics, 1890–1917* (Northfield, Minnesota: Norwegian-American Historical Association, 1971); Carl H. Chrislock, "The Norwegian-American Impact on Minnesota Politics: How Far 'Left of Center'?" In *Norwegian Influence on the Upper Midwest*, ed. Harald S. Naess, pp. 106–116 (Duluth: University of Minnesota Press, 1976).

60. *Whitehall Times:* "State News," February 17, 1881, p. 3; July 13, 1922, p. 1; biography of Herman Ekern, Herman Ekern Papers, Manuscript Division, State Historical Society of Wisconsin.

61. Osterude, p. 55.

62. Ibid., pp. 185–186.

63. See chapters 3 and 6 on cooperative traditions.

64. Return trips to Norway were regularly reported in the *Whitehall Times;* there are also references to return trips in the Ekern Papers. On the Norwegian-language press in the Midwest, see: Semmingsen, *Norway to America*, pp. 84–84, 138–40; Odd S. Lovoll, "*Decorah-Posten:* The Story of an Immigrant Newspaper," *Norwegian-American Studies* 27 (1977): 77–100; Agnes M. Larson, "The Editorial Policy of *Skandinaven*, 1900–1903," *Norwegian-American Studies and Records* 8 (1934): 112–135.

65. Brye, *Wisconsin Voting Patterns*, p. 178. See also David L. Brye, "Wisconsin Scandinavians and Progressivism, 1900–1950," *Norwegian-American Studies* 27 (1977): 163–193; Richard Jensen, *The Winning of the Midwest: Social and Political Conflict, 1888–1896* (Chicago: University of Chicago Press, 1971), pp. 122–148; Paul Kleppner, *The Cross of Culture: A Social Analysis of Midwestern Politics, 1850–1900* (New York: Free Press, 1970), pp. 158–171.

66. Brye, *Wisconsin Voting Patterns*, p. 180.

67. Ibid., pp. 174–178, 377–386.

68. Nesbit, *Wisconsin: A History*, p. 405.

69. Ibid., p. 468.

70. Ibid., pp. 486–490.

Chapter 3: The Men and Mentality of Main Street

1. Thorstein Veblen, "The Country Town," in *The Portable Veblen*, ed. Max Lerner (New York: Viking Press, 1948), p. 407; chapter excerpted from Thorstein

Veblen, *Absentee Ownership and Business Enterprise in Recent Times* (1923; reprinted, New York: A. M. Kelly, 1964), pp. 142–165.

2. "Coral City," typescript, Trempealeau County Historical Society.

3. Merle Curti, *The Making of an American Community: A Cast Study of Democracy in a Frontier County* (Stanford, California: Stanford University Press, 1959), p. 37.

4. Dave Wood, ed., *Wisconsin Prarie Diary: 1869–1879* (Whitehall, Wisconsin: Dan Camp Press, 1979), p. 7.

5. Curti, p. 299.

6. *Whitehall Times,* November 12, 1884.

7. For descriptions of the persistence of the ideal of a moral economy, see: Lawrence Goodwyn, *Democratic Promise: The Populist Movement in America* (New York: Oxford University Press, 1976); David Montgomery, *Workers' Control in America: Studies in the History of Work, Technology, and Labor Struggles* (New York: Cambridge University Press, 1979); Christopher Clark, *The Roots of Rural Capitalism: Western Massachusetts, 1780–1860* (Ithaca: Cornell University Press, 1990).

8. "Roll Call of Departed Pioneers," typescript, Trempealeau County Historical Society; Eben Douglas Pierce, ed., *History of Trempealeau County, Wisconsin* (Chicago: H. C. Cooper, Jr., and Co., 1917), pp. 236–238; Curti, p. 23.

9. "Roll Call."

10. Curti, pp. 373–377.

11. "T. H. Earle," typescript, Trempealeau County Historical Society.

12. "Coral City."

13. D. Wood, *Prarie Diary,* pp. 73–74.

14. Curti, p. 244.

15. "T. H. Earle"; "Roll Call."

16. *Whitehall Times,* "Exchange Gleanings": June 8, 1881, June 1, 1882, July 30, 1885.

17. Hans Anderson, "Autobiography," p. 33, Herman Ekern Papers, Manuscript Division, State Historical Society of Wisconsin; Wood, *Prarie Diary,* pp. 145–146; Curti, pp. 170–174.

18. Wisconsin Department of State, *Tabular Statements of the Census Enumeration and the Agricultural, Minerals and Manufacturing Interests of Wisconsin* (Madison: State Printer, 1886), pp. 545–546; Wisconsin Department of State, *Tabular Statements of the Census Enumeration and the Agricultural, Minerals and Manufacturing Interests of Wisconsin* (Madison: State Printer, 1895), pp. 68–69.

19. *Whitehall Times,* "Exchange Gleanings": June 1 and June 6, 1882, March 27, 1884.

20. Hans Anderson, "J. D. Olds," typescript, Trempealeau County Historical Society.

21. U.S. Census of Population, Manuscript Censuses, Lincoln and Pigeon townships, Trempealeau County, Wisconsin, 1870, 1880, 1900, 1910, State Historical Society of Wisconsin.

22. Ibid.

23. Ibid.

24. Anderson, "Autobiography," pp. 1–10, quotation found on p. 10.

25. Ibid., pp. 11–13.

26. Ibid., pp. 14–15, 19–20; the arrival of several friends and relatives to homes of Mads Knudtson and of Anderson's parents is typical of the "chain migration" patterns noted by scholars of Scandinavian migration. See Jon Gjerde, *From Peasants to Farmers: The Migration from Balestrand, Norway, to the Upper Middle West* (Cambridge: Cambridge University Press, 1985), chapter 3, footnote 4.

27. Anderson, "Autobiography," pp. 33, 36–37.

28. Ibid., p. 39.

29. Extensive front-page obituaries were common in the years during which the pioneering generation was dying. Of 28 such obituaries found in the *Whitehall Times* between 1914 and 1925, 15 mentioned that their subjects spent some period of time in another community after immigration and before arriving in the Lincoln and Pigeon area. The obituaries of six immigrants specifically mentioned two places of residence before arrival in the area, and the obituary of an unusually mobile man listed three. Four persons were reported as spending some years working in the lumber industry. Only one immigrant came directly from Norway to the Lincoln and Pigeon area. All except two stayed in the area for 40 years or more after these initial moves. Half of these immigrants located in the community in less than five years after immigration, and eight did between five and nine years after immigration. For one immigrant the number of years was uncertain, and the remaining four took over 10 years to find their way to Trempealeau. These initial moves that immigrants made in their first decade in the United States and then the stability that followed may explain the patterns of mobility of the frontier and the period that followed it. High mobility occurred while communities formed through a process of self-selection, which resulted in the more stable, harmonious, and homogeneous communities that followed.

30. *Whitehall Times,* November 21, 1889. See also the *Times:* February 10, 1881, January 27, 1887, January 19, 1888, and October 24, 1889.

31. Ibid.: January 19, 1880, January 27, 1887.

32. Ibid., February 10, 1881.

33. Anderson, "J. D. Olds."

34. *Whitehall Times:* May 9, 1880, May 32, 1880. For an analysis of the free-labor ideology, see Eric Foner, *Free Labor, Free Soil, Free Men: Ideology of the Republican Party before the Civil Wart* (New York: Oxford University Press: 1970); for the application of these ideas in post–Civil War years, see Goodwyn.

35. Thurine Oleson, *Wisconsin, My Home,* as told to Erna Oleson Xan (Madison: University of Wisconsin Press, 1950), p. 124.

36. "Peder Simonson," typescript, Trempealeau County Historical Society.

37. Pierce, p. 283.

38. Veblen, p. 407. For an analysis of the tension between an ethics of local exchange—"moral economy"—and the growth of the market economy and ethics in Massachusetts, see Clark, *The Roots of Rural Capitalism,* pp. 195–227.

39. Hans Anderson, "Melby Park," Trempealeau County Historical Society; Letter from F. G. Steig to Hans Anderson, March 16, 1933, Trempealeau County Historical Society; George M. Foster, "Introduction: What Is a Peasant?" in *Peasant Society: A Reader*, ed. Jack M. Potter, May N. Diaz, George M. Foster (Boston: Little, Brown and Co., 1967), pp. 8–9; Robert Redfield, *Peasant Society and Culture: An Anthropological Approach to Civilization* (Chicago: University of Chicago Press, 1956), pp. 44–54.

40. Hans Anderson, "John O. Melby," typescript, Trempealeau County Historical Society.

41. Anderson, "Melby Park."

42. Peder Ekern's name as well as his rapid acquisition of property suggest that he came from a relatively privileged background in Norway. Peasants in Norway did not have surnames passed from one generation to another; the Ekern's family name was passed on to him. Also, according to Norwegian scholar Aslaug Nesset in a conversation at Luther College in May 1985, Ekern is a name associated with the Danish Norwegian elite. For the quotation in the text and other community perceptions of Ekern, see "Peder Ekern and Company," typescript, Trempealeau County Historical Society. For Ekern's political career, see Curti, pp. 316–318; for biographical information on Ekern, see Pierce, p. 686.

43. Wills of John Melby and Peder Ekern, in the Trempealeau County Records, Trempealeau County Courthouse, Whitehall, Wisconsin; "H. E. Getts," typescript, Trempealeau County Historical Society; interview with Arlene Arneson, November 1984, Whitehall, Wisconsin.

44. Curti, p. 296.

45. Foster, p. 8.

46. Peter A. Munch, "Social Adjustment among Wisconsin Norwegians," *Norwegian-American Studies and Records* 16 (1952): 785–786.

47. Oyvind Osterude, *Agrarian Structure and Peasant Politics in Scandinavia: A Comparative Study of Rural Response to Economic Change* (Oslo, Norway: Universitetsforlaget, 1978), pp. 180–184; according to Osterude: "The cooperative associations involved economic coalitions between local peasant groups. These were thus socially horizontal without control by superior outsiders and basically oriented to well-defined single interest purposes" (p. 185).

48. Eric E. Lampard, *The Rise of the Dairy Industry in Wisconsin: A Study in Agricultural Change, 1820–1920* (Madison: State Historical Society of Wisconsin, 1963), p. 45; John Rice, "The Role of Culture and Community in Frontier Prairie Farming," *Journal of Historical Geography* 3 (1977): 165.

49. For a detailed description of the patterns of organization and production of the Norwegian *gard* and the ways in which those patterns adapt to the frontier in communities of the Midwest, see Gjerde, pp. 27–45; on the Norwegian peasant community, see Peter A. Munch, " 'Gard,' the Norwegian Farm," *Rural Sociology* 12 (1947): 357–358; Andreas Holmsen, "The Old Norwegian Peasant Community: General Survey and Historical Introduction," *Scandinavian Economic Review* 4 (1956): 25–29; Halvard Bjorkvik, "The Old Norwegian Peasant Community: The Farm Territories," *Scandinavian Economic Review* 4 (1956): 33–35.

Other historians have found a reassertion of ethnocultural behavior after the frontier; see Terry G. Jordan, *German Seed in Texas Soil: Immigrant Farmers in Nineteenth-Century Texas* (Austin: University of Texas Press, 1966), p. 199; Bradley H. Baltensperger, "Agricultural Change among Nebraska Immigrants, 1880–1900," in *Ethnicity on the Great Plains*, ed. Frederick C. Luebke (Lincoln: University of Nebraska Press, 1980), pp. 170–189; Robert P. Swierenga, "Ethnicity and American Agriculture," *Ohio History* 89 (Summer 1980): 323–344.

50. *Whitehall Times,* January 14, 1880, p. 1.

51. Ibid., April 20, 1880, p. 1.

52. Ibid., June 15, 1884, p. 1.

53. Ibid.: February 21, 1884, p. 1; March 6, 1884, p. 3.

54. Lampard, pp. 271–272.

55. Pierce, p. 672; Curti, pp. 236–237.

56. *Whitehall Times:* June 15, 1882, p. 1; July 20, 1882, p. 1.

57. Ibid.: March 16, 1882, p. 1; November 1, 1883, p. 1.

58. Ibid., June 11, 1885. See also: February 2, 1882, p. 1; June 15, 1882, p. 1; July 20, 1882, p. 1; November 1, 1883; and October 28, 1886.

59. Wisconsin Department of State, *Tabular Statements of the Census Enumeration,* 1886, p. 551; Wisconsin Department of State, *Tublar Statements of the Census Enumeration,* 1895, p. 676, 815; Wisconsin Department of State, *Tabular Statements of Census Enumeration and the Agricultural, Dairying and Manufacturing Interest of Wisconsin* (Madison: State Printer, 1906), pp. 378, 395, 400.

60. Pierce, pp. 811–812; *Compendium of the Tenth Census of the United States: 1880,* Part 1, *Population* (Washington, D.C.: Government Printing Office, 1883), Table 49, pp. 922–923; Wisconsin Department of State, *Tabular Statements of Census Enumeration,* 1905, pp. 378–379.

61. *Compendium of the Tenth Census of the United States: 1880,* Part 1, *Population,* p. 923.

62. Oleson, p. 35.

63. Pierce, p. 811.

64. *U.S. Census of Agriculture: 1925,* Part 1, *The Northern States* (Washington, D.C.: Government Printing Office, 1927), Table 3, p. 690; *Sixteenth Census of the United States, 1940:* Vol. 1, *Agriculture,* Part 1, *Statistics for Counties* (Washington, D.C.: Government Printing Office, 1942), Table 4, p. 921.

65. *Compendium of the Tenth Census of the United States: 1880,* Part 1, *Population,* Table 49, p. 922; *Sixteenth Census of the United States, 1940:* Vol. 1, *Agriculture,* Part 1, *Statistics for Counties,* Table 4, p. 921.

66. Pierce, pp. 812–816; Osterude, pp. 180–184.

67. Curti, pp. 172–175.

68. Lampard, pp. 271–272.

69. *Whitehall Times,* February 7, 1884, p. 1. This is but one example of the alarm felt over the growing competition of the immigrants. In that same year the *Times* proposed monopoly as a solution: "J. B. Ingalls, the jeweler is closing up shop. Too many other stores sell his kind of wares. Thus he is moving. It's too bad

something couldn't be worked out giving Ingalls sole control so the town wouldn't lose him" (August 14, p. 1).

70. John Allen, "Fifty Years of Service, 1918–1968: Early History of the Pigeon Falls Cooperative Creamery," typescript, Trempealeau County Historical Society.

71. *Whitehall Times,* March 9, 1882, p. 1.

72. Ibid.: March 9, 1882; April 25, 1882; March 24, 1916; March 2, 1923.

73. Ibid., February 9, 1882, p. 1.

74. Wisconsin Department of State, *Tabular Statements of Census Enumeration,* 1905, p. 319.

75. Ibid.

76. Robert C. Nesbit, *Wisconsin: A History* (Madison: University of Wisconsin Press, 1973), pp. 293–294.

77. "Miscellaneous" volumes 1–10, in the Trempealeau County Records, Trempealeau County Courthouse, Whitehall, Wisconsin; Pierce, pp. 269, 812–816.

78. *Whitehall Times,* "A Warning to Dairymen," January 24, 1929, p. 3.

79. Allen "Pigeon Creamery"; for a discussion of the role of the local Farmers Union, see Harold Tomter, taped interview by State Historical Society of Wisconsin.

80. Trempealeau County Records, Trempealeau County Courthouse, Whitehall, Wisconsin: Lincoln Telephone Cooperative, Miscellaneous, vol. 2 (the "Miscellaneous" volumes include articles of incorporation), number 433; Pigeon Valley Farmer Telephone Cooperative, Miscellaneous, vol. 3, number 264, and vol. 29, number 637; for annual meetings and reports on finances, see the *Whitehall Times:* January 25, 1917, February 14, 1918, January 8, 1925, January 22, 1924, January 24, 1927.

81. *Whitehall Times,* "Farm Relief Sometimes Relieves the Wrong Way," February 21, 1929, p. 1.

82. Pigeon Mutual Fire Insurance Company, Miscellaneous: vol. 1, number 24, vol. 3, number 264, and vol. 24, number 149, Trempealeau County Records, Trempealeau County Courthouse, Whitehall, Wisconsin; *Whitehall Times:* May 18, 1882, p. 1; January 29, 1885, p. 1; January 26, 1898, p. 1; January 21, 1915, p. 4; January 8, 1925, p. 5.

83. Trempealeau County Records, Trempealeau County Courthouse, Whitehall, Wisconsin: Whitehall and Pigeon Trading Association, Miscellaneous, vol. 1, number 79; Pigeon Grain and Stock Cooperative, vol. 5, number 48; Cooperative Oil Company, vol. 9, number 338.

84. Allen, "Pigeon Creamery."

85. Interview with Trempealeau County Agent Edward Austerude, June 1982.

86. Allen, "Pigeon Creamery"; for other assessments of the equalitarian, even leveling, orientation in small towns, see Arthur J. Vidich and Joseph Bensman, *Small Town in Mass Society: Class, Power, and Religion in a Rural Community* (Princeton: Princeton University Press, 1958), pp. 37–42; Albert Blumenthal, *Small Town Stuff* (Chicago: University of Chicago Press, 1932), pp. 55–57, 105.

87. *Whitehall Times:* March 4, 1886, p. 1; January 21, 1915; November 18,

1915; February 3, 1916, p. 1; January 8, 1926, p. 1; E. L. Luther, "Farmers' Institutes in Wisconsin, 1885–1933," *Wisconsin Magazine of History* 30 (September 1946): 59–68.

88. *Whitehall Times,* February 24, 1887, p. 1.

89. Ibid., March 6, 1884.

Chapter 4: The Home Town and the Home Place: To Leave or Stay?

1. *Farm Youth: Proceedings of the Ninth National Country Life Conference* (Chicago: University of Chicago Press, 1926). Few aspects of the experience of rural youth were left unexamined by rural sociologists at the University of Wisconsin–Madison and elsewhere; see, for example: A. F. Wileden, *What Douglas County Young People Want and What They Are Doing about It,* Special Circular, Wisconsin Agricultural College, Extension Service, Madison (December 1935); Barnard D. Joy, *Organizations and Programs for Rural Young People* State Extension Service Circular No. 248 (1935), Madison, Wisconsin; E. L. Kirkpatrick and Agnes M. Doynton, *Interests and Needs of the Rural Youth in Wood County, Wisconsin,* Special Circular, Wisconsin Agricultural College, Extension Service (January 1938), Madison; Edmund S. Brunner, "Working with Rural Youth," prepared for the American Youth Commission, Washington, D.C., American Council on Education (1942); Lee G. Burchinal, "Rural Youth in Crisis: Facts, Myths, and Social Change," prepared for the National Commission for Children and Youth, Washington, D.C., U.S. Department of Health, Education and Welfare, Welfare Administration, 1965.

2. Thurine Oleson, *Wisconsin, My Home,* as told to Erna Oleson Xan (Madison: University of Wisconsin Press, 1950), pp. 94–95.

3. For a recent analysis of midwestern farmers' commitment to keeping the home place in the family, see Kathleen Neils Conzen, "Peasant Pioneers: Generational Succession among German Farmers in Frontier Minnesota," in *The Countryside in the Age of Capitalist Transformation: Essays in the Social History of Rural America,* ed. Steven Hahn and Jonathan Prude, (Chapel Hill: University of North Carolina Press, 1985), pp. 259–292.

4. Ole Semb, as quoted by Hans Anderson, "Ole O. Semb," 1914, typescript, Trempealeau County Historical Society.

5. The Whitehall High School Alumni Records include information about the locations and occupations of the graduates in 1922 and 1938. In addition, the records indicate whether the women were married or not by mentioning the maiden names.

6. See chapter 6.

7. *Whitehall Times,* "Raymond K. Warner," September 20, 1919.

8. Eben Douglas Pierce, ed., *History of Trempealeau County, Wisconsin* (Chicago: H. C. Cooper, Jr., and Co., 1917), pp. 283–285.

9. *Whitehall Times,* February 22, 1917.

10. Pigeon Falls Evangelical Lutheran Church, "Centennial Anniversary, Pigeon Falls Evangelical Lutheran Church: 1878–1978," Pigeon Falls, Wisconsin,

1978; Pigeon Creek Evangelical Lutheran Church, "Centennial Anniversary, Pigeon Creek Evangelical Lutheran Church: 1866–1966," Pigeon Falls, Wisconsin, 1966. The passing of a clerical position from father to son was very common in Norway, where such positions were highly attractive, state-supported appointments commanding considerable prestige, financial security, and power.

11. *Whitehall Times,* November 11, 1916. See also January 3, 1914.

12. Ibid., June 1, 1882.

13. Ibid.

14. Merle Curti, *The Making of an American Community: A Case Study of Democracy in a Frontier County* (Stanford, California: Stanford University Press, 1959), p. 316; Peder Ekern, Will, file 1339, Trempealeau County Courthouse; Tomter interview.

15. "Ludwig L. Solsrud," 1941, typescript, Trempealeau County Historical Society.

16. Letter from Gus E. Low to Herman Ekern, March 1898; letter from Herman Ekern to Lena Ekern, March 2, 1891; both in the Herman Ekern Papers, Manuscript Division, State Historical Society of Wisconsin. Like her brother, Lena Ekern was eager to return to Whitehall or Pigeon to teach after pursuing an education in Superior, Wisconsin, a Great Lakes shipping center. Lena pressed her brother to help her find a position in Whitehall, while disparaging "the class of people we have in the country around here" (letter from Lena Ekern to Herman Ekern, June 21, 1897, Herman Erkern Papers). Later she expressed her relief when Herman found a job for her, because in Whitehall she knew she "would be among civilized people," and it would be "more pleasant to be with nice people" (letter from Lena Ekern to Herman Ekern, June 27, 1897, Herman Ekern Papers).

17. Hans Anderson, "J. D. Olds," typescript, Trempealeau County Historical Society.

18. "Hans Anderson Fremstad," June 29, 1933, typescript, file 220, Trempealeau County Historical Society.

19. Interview with Eleanor Ackley, November 1984, Pigeon Falls, Wisconsin.

20. *Whitehall Times,* January 3, 1929.

21. Hans Anderson, "Nels Nelson," 1931, typescript, file 476, Trempealeau County Historical Society.

22. Letter from Michael Feuling to Hans Anderson, March 13, 1919, file 207, Trempealeau County Historical Society.

23. Dave Wood, ed., *Wisconsin Prarie Diary: 1869–1879* (Whitehall, Wisconsin: Dan Camp Press, 1979), pp. 197–198.

24. Letter from Feuling to Anderson.

25. Interview with Harold Tomter, taped by Dale Treleven for the State Historical Society of Wisconsin. For a moving autobiographical account of a tenant-farmer family's desperate and life-long quest for landownership, see Clark Mallam, "Other Farms, Other Places," part of an unpublished manuscript, Decorah, Iowa.

26. Tomter interview; tenancy was often a family strategy for the transition of

land between generations. In 1930, for example, when tenancy peaked, 22.0 percent of Lincoln's farmers were tenants, and 18.6 percent of Pigeon's were. Of these tenants, 33.3 percent of Lincoln's had the same surnames as the individuals from whom they rented, and 50.0 percent of Pigeon's did.

27. Dave Wood diaries, 1890, Area Research Center, University of Wisconsin–Eau Claire.

28. U.S. Census of Population, Manuscript Census, Pigeon and Lincoln townships, Trempealeau County, Wisconsin, 1900, State Historical Society of Wisconsin.

29. Hans Anderson, "Autobiography," p. 7, manuscript, Herman Ekern Papers, Manuscript Division, State Historical Society of Wisconsin.

30. Oleson, pp. 127, 133, 159.

31. U.S. Census of Population, Manuscript Census, Pigeon and Lincoln townships, Trempealeau County, Wisconsin, 1900.

32. Ibid., 1910.

33. Important sources of information concerning the location of Whitehall and Pigeon youth can be found in the obituaries of the *Whitehall Times;* see note 3 above.

34. As reported in Odd S. Lovoll, *The Promise of American Life: A History of the Norwegian-American People* (Minneapolis: University of Minnesota Press, 1983), p. 73.

35. Letter from Leslie Stratton to Hans Anderson, October 15, 1931, as well as other materials in file 640, Trempealeau County Historical Society.

36. "Ludwig L. Solsrud;" "Longevity Is Inherited in the Pederson Family," January 16, 1941, typescript, file 518, Trempealeau County Historical Society.

37. Anderson, "Autobiography," pp. 5–7. Kin networks functioned in the process of immigration and migration across the country and into the cities. The functioning of kin networks in rural Trempealeau appears to have followed the premodern patterns described in Tamara K. Hareven, "The Dynamics of Kin in an Industrial Community," in *Turning Points: Historical and Sociological Essays on the Family,* ed. John Demos and Sarane Spence Boocock, pp. 151–182. (Chicago: University of Chicago Press, 1978).

38. Robert Ostergren, "Prairie Bound: Migration Patterns to a Swedish Settlement on the Dakota Frontier," in *Ethnicity on the Great Plains,* ed. Frederick C. Luebke (Lincoln: University of Nebraska Press, 1980), p. 91.

39. *Whitehall Times:* January 6, 1881. See also September 20, 1917.

40. Ibid., April 28, 1881.

41. Ibid., September 13, 1883.

42. Ibid., October 14, 1884.

43. Ibid., June 3, 1886.

44. Ibid., September 22, 1887.

45. Ibid., October 3, 1918.

46. Manuscript Census, 1880, 1900.

47. *Whitehall Times,* June 6, 1916.

48. Ibid., January 29, 1917.

49. Ibid.

Chapter 5: Salvation and Social Rituals of Community

1. Einar Haugen, *The Norwegian Language in America: A Study in Bilingual Behavior*, 2 vols. (Philadelphia: University of Pennsylvania Press, 1953), vol. 1, p. 44.

2. Timothy L. Smith, "Religion and Ethnicity in America," *American Historican Review* 83 (1978): 1161.

3. Merle Curti, *The Making of an American Community: A Case Study of Democracy in a Frontier County* (Stanford, California: Stanford University Press, 1959), pp. 128–130; Ingrid Semmingsen, *Norway to America: A History of Migration* (Minneapolis: University of Minnesota Press, 1978), p. 80.

4. Eben Douglas Pierce, ed., *History of Trempealeau County, Wisconsin* (Chicago: H. C. Cooper, Jr., and Co., 1917), pp. 817–842, 857–863.

5. Ibid., pp. 857–863; *Atlas of Trempealeau County, Wisconsin* (Minneapolis: Standard Atlas Company, 1964).

6. Dave Wood, ed., *Wisconsin Prarie Diary: 1869–1879* (Whitehall, Wisconsin: Dan Camp Press, 1978), passim.

7. Pierce, pp. 846–848.

8. Ibid., pp. 857–862; *Atlas of Trempealeau County*, pp. 8, 16–17; Semmingsen, *Norway to America*, pp. 134–35; Curti, p. 97.

9. Semmingsen, *Norway to America*, p. 80.

10. Clifford Nelson and Eugene L. Fevold, *The Lutheran Church among Norwegian-Americans: A History of the Evangelical Lutheran Church*, 2 vols. (Minneapolis: Augsburg Publishing, 1960), vol. 1, p. 113; for an analysis of the tensions between Puritan practice and ideals of social order, see Stephen Foster, *Their Solitary Way: The Puritan Social Ethic in the First Century of Settlement in New England* (New Haven: Yale University Press, 1971).

11. Ann M. Legreid and David Ward, "Religious Schism and the Development of Rural Immigrant Communities: Norwegian Lutherans in Western Wisconsin, 1880–1905," *Midwest History* 2 (Summer 1982): 13–28; Peter A. Munch, "Authority and Freedom: Controversy in Norwegian-American Congregations," *Norwegian-American Studies* 28 (1979): 3–34.

12. Nelson and Fevold, pp. 16–18; Semmingsen, *Norway to America*, pp. 134–135.

13. Semmingsen, *Norway to America*, p. 8.

14. Christen T. Jonassen, "The Protestant Ethic and the Spirit of Capitalism in Norway," *American Sociological Review* 12 (December 1947): 681.

15. Michael Walzer, *The Revolution of the Saints: A Study in the Origins of Radical Politics* (New York: Atheneum, 1976). On conditions in Norway, see Jon Gjerde, *From Peasants to Farmers: The Migration from Balestrand, Norway, to the Upper Middle West* (Cambridge: Cambridge University Press, 1985); Michael Drake, *Population and Society in Norway, 1735–1865* (Cambridge: Cambridge University Press, 1969).

16. Elling Eilsen as quoted in Semmingsen, *Norway to America*, p. 80.

17. Nelson and Fevold, pp. 20–22.

18. Semmingsen, *Norway to America,* p. 136; Pierce, pp. 817–842.

19. Pierce, pp. 822–833; Pigeon Falls Evangelical Lutheran Church, "Centennial Anniversary, Pigeon Falls Evangelical Lutheran Church: 1878–1978," Pigeon Falls, Wisconsin, 1978, pp. 7–8; Pigeon Creek Evangelical Lutheran Church, "Centennial Anniversary, Pigeon Creek Evangelical Lutheran Church: 1866–1966," Pigeon Falls, Wisconsin, 1966.

20. Pierce, pp. 174–115, 780.

21. Ibid., pp. 817–833.

22. Nelson and Fevold, pp. 185–187, 271–298; Semmingsen, *Norway to America,* p. 137.

23. Pierce, p. 686; interview with Martha Meade, assistant director of admissions at Luther College, Decorah, Iowa, January 1985; interview with Marlene Hanson, superintendent of schools, Whitehall, Wisconsin, July 1984.

24. Curti, p. 409.

25. Pierce, pp. 822–833; Pigeon Falls Evangelical Lutheran Church, "Centennial Anniversary," pp. 7–8; Pigeon Creek Evangelical Lutheran Church, "Centennial Anniversary."

26. Records of Pigeon Falls Evangelical Lutheran Church, 1866–1920, in the Pigeon Falls Lutheran Parish Records, Pigeon Falls, Wisconsin; on changing naming practices, see Haugen, pp. 192–205.

27. Nelson and Fevold, pp. 37, 182–192.

28. Ibid., pp. 221, 230–236.

29. Ibid., pp. 115–116, 169–179.

30. For a detailed discussion of the union of 1917, see ibid., pp. 184–225. The *Whitehall Times* regularly reported on local involvement in the synods' meetings; see *Whitehall Times:* November 11, 1914, October 15, 1914, November 5, 1914, May 27, 1915, September 2, 1916. On local unification efforts, see: ibid., January 31, 1918; Pigeon Falls Evangelical Lutheran Church, "Centennial Anniversary"; Pigeon Falls Lutheran Parish, *The Ambassador* 5, no. 6 (June 1983); Pigeon Creek Evangelical Lutheran Church, "Centennial Anniversary."

31. Smith, p. 1181.

32. O. E. Rolvaag, *Giants in the Earth* (Olso, Norway: H. Ashehoug and Co., 1924; New York: Harper and Row, Publishers, 1955).

33. Jonassen, p. 681.

34. Rolvaag, *Giants in the Earth,* pp. 432–452.

35. Besides *Giants in the Earth,* two other novels form the trilogy which continues the story of Beret as an immigrant pioneer until her death as an old woman: O. E. Rolvaag, *Peder Victorious,* trans. Nora O. Solum (New York: Harper and Brothers, 1929); and O. E. Rolvaag, *Their Father's God,* trans. Trygue M. Ager (New York: Harper and Brothers, 1931). Semmingsen, *Norway to America,* p. 137.

36. Nelson and Fevold, p. 23.

37. Ann Douglas, *The Feminization of American Culture* (New York: Alfred A. Knopf, 1977).

38. Interview with Arlene Arneson, November 1984, Whitehall, Wisconsin; interview with Harold Tomter, taped by the State Hisotrical Society of Wisconsin.

39. Hans Anderson, "Autobiography," pp. 1–2, 22–24, manuscript in Herman Ekern Papers, Manuscript Division, State Historical Society of Wisconsin.

40. Ibid., pp. 23–24; for a description of the importance of the pietistic religions to midwestern politics in the nineteenth century, see Paul Kleppner, *The Cross of Culture: A Social Analysis of Midwestern Politics, 1850–1900* (New York: Free Press, 1970), pp. 35–91.

41. Letter from Lily Ekern to Fanny, March 6, 1904, Herman Ekern Papers, Manuscript Division, State Historical Society of Wisconsin.

42. *Whitehall Times*, June 16, 1881; for additional examples, see ibid.: October 13, 1881, June 8, 1882, December 5, 1889.

43. Ibid., September 22, 1881.

44. Ibid., September 29, 1881.

45. Hamlin Garland, "A Day of Grace," in *Other Main-Traveled Roads* (New York: Harper and Brothers, 1910), pp. 65–68.

46. Anderson, "Autobiography," pp. 22–23.

47. Letter from Lena Ekern to Herman Ekern, October 1900, Herman Ekern Papers.

48. Letter from Lena Ekern to Herman Ekern, December 1900, Herman Ekern Papers. Rolvaag includes a similar crisis for Beret in the third novel of his trilogy when Peder Victorious married an Irish Catholic woman; see Rolvaag, *Their Father's God.*

49. Biography of Herman Ekern, Herman Ekern Papers, State Historial Society of Wisconsin; *Whitehall Times*, "Ekern Is President of Lutheran Brotherhood," March 7, 1929.

50. Semingsen, *Norway to America*, pp. 80–81.

51. *Atlas of Trempealeau County;* Pigeon Falls Evangelical Lutheran Church, "Centennial Anniversary"; Pigeon Creek Evangelical Lutheran Church, "Centennial Anniversary."

52. Arneson interview; interview with Eleanor Ackley, November 1984, Pigeon Falls, Wisconsin.

53. Rolvaag, *Peder Victorious.*

54. Thurine Oleson, *Wisconsin, My Home,* as told to Erna Oleson Xan (Madison: University of Wisconsin Press, 1950), pp. 101–102.

55. Hans Anderson, "Church Dedicated," *Whitehall Times*, June 22, 1916.

56. Pierce, pp. 817–842; Pigeon Falls Evangelical Lutheran Church, "Centennial Anniversary."

57. Pierce, pp. 832–833.

58. On the controversy related to education, see: Nelson and Fevold, pp. 183–187, 284–289; Frank C. Nelson, "The School Controversy among Norwegian Immigrants," *Norwegian-American Studies* 26 (1974): 206–209; James Hamre, "Norwegian Immigrants Respond to the 'Common' School: A Case Study of American Values and the Lutheran Tradition," *Church History* 50 (1981): 305–315; James Hamre, "Three Spokesmen for Norwegian Lutheran Academies: Schools for Church, Heritage, Society," *Norwegian-American Studies* 30 (1985): 221–246.

59. Pierce, pp. 306, 832–843; Tomter interview.

60. *Whitehall Times*, June 15, 1882.

61. Ibid., December 12, 1889.

62. Robert C. Nesbit, *Wisconsin: A History* (Madison: University of Wisconsin Press, 1973), pp. 377–378, 395–396.

63. Anderson, "Autobiography," pp. 30–33; letter from Lena Ekern to Herman Ekern, May 10, 1898, Herman Ekern Papers; letter from Rose Anderson to Lily Ekern, September 5, 1902, Herman Ekern Papers.

64. *Atlas of Trempealeau County.*

65. Pierce, pp. 846–848.

66. Records of the Pigeon Falls Evangelical Lutheran Church and the Pigeon Creek Lutheran Church, both in the Pigeon Falls Lutheran Parish Records, Pigeon Falls, Wisconsin; interview with Pastor Peter Sherven, February 1984, Pigeon Falls, Wisconsin.

67. *Whitehall Times,* June 15, 1881.

68. For an analysis of the adjustment of American Protestant churches to losing their position as established state churches, see Douglas, pp. 17–49.

69. See the records of the Pigeon Creek Lutheran Church and the Pigeon Falls Evangelical Lutheran Church, in the Pigeon Falls Lutheran Parish records, Pigeon Falls, Wisconsin.

70. Tomter interview; Pierce, pp. 714–715; Pigeon Falls Evangelical Lutheran Church, "Centennial Anniversary."

71. Hanson and Arneson interviews *Whitehall Times,* 1880–1980, passim.

72. On musical traditions, see Gerhard M. Cartford, "Music in the Norwegian Lutheran Church: A Study of Its Development in Norway and Its Transfer to America, 1825–1917," Ph.D. dissertation, University of Minnesota, 1961.

73. Einar B. Christophersen as quoted in the *Whitehall Times,* December 12, 1917.

74. Tomter interview.

75. Oleson, pp. 61–78; interview with Dorothy Rongstad, December 1984, Osseo, Wisconsin; Arneson interview.

76. Tomter interview; Pigeon Creek Evangelical Lutheran Church, "Centennial Anniversary"; Pigeon Falls Evangelical Lutheran Church, "Centennial Anniversary."

77. Ackley interview.

78. "Anderson Golden Wedding," typescript, Trempealeau County Historical Society.

Chapter 6: Work: The Ethic and the Reality

1. Hans Anderson, "Dedication of the Elk Creek Lutheran Church Sunday," address reprinted in the *Whitehall Times,* June 22, 1916.

2. Charles Freeman, "Address," 1912, typescript, Trempealeau County Historical Society.

3. *U.S. Census of Housing, 1960:* Vol. 1, *States and Small Areas,* Part 8, *Texas–Wyoming* (Washington, D.C.: Government Printing Office, 1961), Table 29, p. 72.

4. Letter from J. D. Olds to Hans Anderson, February 17, 1912, typescript, file 498, Trempealeau County Historical Society.

5. For the perspective of the Country Life movement, see David B. Danbom, *The Resisted Revolution: Urban America and the Industrialization of Agriculture, 1900–1930* (Ames: Iowa State University Press, 1979), pp. 23–50.

6. Dave Wood, ed., *Wisconsin Prarie Diary: 1869–1879* (Whitehall, Wisconsin: Dan Camp Press, 1979).

7. Hans Anderson, "Autobiography," p. 1, manuscript, Herman Ekern Papers, Manuscript Division, State Historical Society of Wisconsin.

8. Hans Anderson, "Storviken," typescript, Trempealeau County Historical Society.

9. Ibid.

10. Hans Anderson, "Helen Christianson," December 16, 1924, typescript, file 116, Trempealeau County Historical Society.

11. Hans Anderson, "Halvor Hanson," October 15, 1929, typescript, Trempealeau County Historical Society.

12. Christen T. Jonassen, "The Protestant Ethic and the Spirit of Capitalism in Norway," *American Sociological Review* 12 (December 1947): 682. Jonassen argued that Norwegian pietism had the same kind of impact that Max Weber described as resulting from Calvinism: "Asceticism turned with all its force against one thing: the spontaneous enjoyment of life and all it had to offer." Weber noted the tendency of pietism to bring "ascetic conduct into the non-Calvinistic denominations." Pietism, he concluded, "worked out ideas which, in a way essentially similar to Calvinism, though milder, established an aristocracy of the elect resting on God's especial grace, with all the psychological results pointed out above"; Max Weber, *The Protestant Ethic and the Spirit of Capitalism: The Relationships between Religion and the Economic and Social Life in Modern Culture, trans. Talcott Parsons* (1904–1905; New York: Charles Scribner's Sons, 1958), pp. 132–133, 166.

13. Clifford Nelson and Eugene L. Fevold, *The Lutheran Church among Norwegian-Americans: A History of the Evangelical Lutheran Church*, 2 vols. (Minneapolis: Augsburg Publishing, 1960), vol. 1, pp. 13–24.

14. Einar Haugen, *The Norwegian Language in America: A Study in Bilingual Behavior*, 2 vols. (Philadelphia: University of Pennsylvania Press, 1953), vol. 1, p. 22.

15. Oyvind Osterude, *Agrarian Structure and Peasant Politics in Scandinavia: A Comparative Study of Rural Response to Economic Change* (Oslo, Norway: Universitetsforlaget, 1978), pp. 114–124; Michael Drake, *Population and Society in Norway, 1735–1865* (Cambridge: Cambridge University Press, 1969), pp. 41–74.

16. Drake, pp. 18–23; Jon Gjerde, *From Peasants to Farmers: The Migration from Balestrand, Norway, to the Upper Middle West* (Cambridge: Cambridge University Press, 1985), pp. 119–128.

17. See the epigraph at the beginning of this chapter: Hans Anderson, "Mrs. Gilbert Steig," February 12, 1940, tpyescript, Trempealeau County Historical Society.

18. Hans Anderson, "Mads Evenson," 1926, typescript, file 198, Trempealeau County Historical Society; for a recent analysis of Thorstein Veblen's views,

see John Diggins, *Bard of Savagery: Thorstein Veblen and Modern Social Theory* (New York: Seabury Press, 1978).

19. Anderson, "Autobiography," p. 16.

20. Interview with Lila Pederson, May, 1984, Osseo, Wisconsin.

21. Hans Anderson, "Some Characteristics of Big Slough Men," February 3, 1916, typescript, Trempealeau County Historical Society.

22. Ole Rolvaag, *Pure Gold*, trans. Sivert Erdahl (New York: Harper and Brothers, 1930).

23. Hans Anderson, "Address at Gale College," undated but appears to be around 1915, typescript, Trempealeau County Historical Society.

24. Ibid.

25. Osterude, p. 111.

26. Ibid., p. 192.

27. See, for example, Wood, *Prarie Diary,* for the year 1875, pp. 124–134; Merle Curti, *The Making of an American Community: A Case Study of Democracy in a Frontier County* (Stanford, California: Stanford University Press, 1959), pp. 114–116; Anderson, "Big Slough Men"; interview with Harold Tomter, taped by Dale Treleven for the State Historical Society of Wisconsin.

28. Anderson, "Big Slough Men."

29. Wood, *Prarie Diary,* p. 2.

30. Ibid., pp. 1–2, January 1869; for a description of colonial rural economies similar to that of early Trempealeau County, see Mike Merrill, "Cash Is Good to Eat: Self-Sufficiency and Exchange in the Rural Economy of the United States," *Radical History Review* 3 (1977); 42–71; Christopher Clark, *The Roots of Rural Capitalism: Western Massachusetts, 1780–1860* (Ithaca: Cornell University Press, 1990), pp. 121–155.

31. James Wood diary, March 8, 1891, Area Research Center, University of Wisconsin–Eau Claire.

32. Tomter interview; interview with Arlene Arneson, November 1984, Whitehall, Wisconsin. Excellent sources on the work of farm households and rural communities are the diaries of Ella Hanson, the wife of a third-generation Norwegian American. She was herself Dutch in background but spent her life in Norwegian communities and, according to her daughter, that cultural background was the most influential. See Hanson's diaries from 1922 to 1945.

33. See the Wood diaries and Hanson diaries for the months of August and September during almost any year; for a description of the process and of children's participation, see Thurine Oleson, *Wisconsin, My Home,* as told to Erna Oleson Xan (Madison: University of Wisconsin Press, 1950), pp. 36–37; see also the autobiographical account of Ben Logan, *The Land Remembers: The Story of a Farm and Its People* (New York: Viking Press, 1975), pp. 127–144.

34. Tomter interview; interview with a Laila Pederson, June 1984, Osseo, Wisconsin.

35. *Sixteenth Census of the United States, 1940:* Vol. 2, *Housing,* Part 5, *General Characteristics* (Washington, D.C.: Government Printing Office, 1943), Table 23, p. 914.

36. James Wood diary, 1893.

37. Laila Pederson interview; Tomter interview.

38. Wisconsin Department of State, *Tabular Statements of Census Enumeration and the Agricultural, Minerals and Manufacturing Interest of Wisconsin* (Madison: State Printer, 1895), pp. 674–675.

39. Arneson interview.

40. Laila Pederson interview.

41. *U.S. Census of Housing, 1960:* Vol. 1, *States and Small Areas,* Part 8, *Texas–Wyoming* (Washington, D.C.: Government Printing Office, 1961), Table 29, p. 72.

42. Logan, p. 138.

43. Tomter interview.

44. Curti, pp. 114–116.

Chapter 7: Woman's Place, Woman's Work

1. Recent studies of women's work and reactions to the frontier are becoming quite numerous; see, for example: Sandra L. Myers, *Westering Women: The Frontier Experience, 1800–1915* (Albuquerque: University of New Mexico Press, 1982); John Mack Faragher, *Women and Men on the Overland Trail* (New Haven: Yale University Press, 1979); Christiane Fischer, ed., *Let Them Speak for Themselves: Women in the American West, 1849–1900* (Hamden, Connecticut: Shoe String Press, 1977); Glenda Riley, *Frontierswomen: The Iowa Experience* (Ames: Iowa State University Press, 1981); Julie Roy Jeffrey, *Frontier Women: The Trans-Mississippi West, 1840–1880* (New York: Hill and Wang, 1979).

2. Joan M. Jensen, *With These Hands: Women Working on the Land* (Old Westbury, new York: Feminist Press, 1981); Joan M. Jensen, *Loosening the Bonds: Mid-Atlantic Farm Women, 1750–1850* (New Haven: Yale University Press, 1986); Joan M. Jensen, *Promises to the Land: Essays on Rural Women* (Albuquerque: University of New Mexico Press, 1991); Carolyn E. Sachs, *The Invisible Farmer: Women in Agricultural Production* (Totowa, New Jersey: Rowman and Allanheld, 1983); Sonya Salamon and Ann Mackey Keim, "Land Ownership and Women's Power in a Midwestern Farming Community," *Journal of Marriage and the Family* 41 (February 1979): 109–119; Nancy Grey Osterud, "Strategies of Mutuality: Relations among Women and Men in an Agricultural Community," Ph.D. dissertation, Brown University, 1984; Nancy Grey Osterud, *The Bonds of Community: The Lives of Farm Women in Nineteenth Century New York* (Ithaca: Cornell University Press, 1990); Wava Haney and Jane B. Knowles, eds., *Women and Farming: Changing Roles, Changing Structures* (Boulder, Colorado: Westview Press, 1988); Mary Neth, "Gender and the Family Labor System: Defining Work in the Rural Midwest," paper presented at the Social Science History Association meeting, Minneapolis, November 1990. For a review of scholarship on rural women see *Agricultural and Human Values* 2 (Winter 1985).

3. Joann Vanek, "Work, Leisure, and Family Roles: Farm Households in the United States, 1920–1955," *Journal of Family History* 5 (Spring 1980); 423.

Vaneck, reviewing several surveys by sociologists of farm families spanning the years 1920–1955, found that the relationships of farm wives and their husbands was one of "symmetry," or partnership.

4. Nancy Grey Osterud, "The Valuation of Women's and Men's Work: Gender, Kinship and the Market in an Upstate New York Dairy Farming Community during the Late Nineteenth Century," paper presented at the annual convention of the Social Science History Association, Chicago, November 1985. Osterud found that distinct gender-based systems of valuation emerged in New York farm communities as farmers increased their market orientation.

5. Jon Gjerde, *From Peasants to Farmers: The Migration from Balestrand, Norway, to the Upper Middle West* (Cambridge: Cambridge University Press, 1985), p. 67. Jon Gjerde found that immigrant Norwegian women who had long worked in the fields and barns rather quickly and happily gave up outside work on the American frontier when their husbands adopted the cash crop wheat and new production technologies. Also see Bengt Ankarloo, "Agriculture and Women's Work: Directions of Change in the West, 1700–1900," *Journal of Family History* 4, no. 2 (1979): 111–121.

6. Louise Tilly and Joan Scott, *Women, Work, and Family* (New York: Holt, Rinehart, and Winston, 1978), pp. 54–55. According to Louise Tilly, women's important role in production in the preindustrial households of peasants and craftsmen gave them "a certain power in the household."

7. Sachs, *Invisible Farmer*, pp. 12–14. Carolyn Sachs suggested that that women in the nineteenth century withdrew from the work of the fields and barns as a way of escaping the authority of men.

8. The ideology of separate spheres has been examined by several historians beginning with Barbara Welter, "The Cult of True Womanhood: 1820–1860," *American Quarterly* 18 (Summer 1966): 151–174. The post–World War II variety of the concept of separate spheres was identified and given a label by Betty Friedan in the title of her book *The Feminine Mystique* (New York: W. W. Norton and Co., 1963). Since these publications, several historians have expanded our understanding of the precepts and practice of the ideology of separate spheres; see: Kathryn Kish Sklar, *Catharine Beecher: A Study in American Domesticity* (New York: W. W. Norton and Co., 1973); Nancy F. Cott, *The Bonds of Womanhood: "Women's Sphere" in New England, 1780–1835* (New Haven: Yale University Press, 1977); Carroll Smith-Rosenberg, "The Female World of Love and Ritual: Relations between Women in Nineteenth-Century America," *Signs* 1 (Autumn 1975): 1–29; Mary P. Ryan, *Cradle of the Middle Class: The Family in Oneida County, New York, 1790–1865* (New York: Cambridge University Press, 1981). For a description of conceptions of womanhood in an earlier period, see Laurel Thatcher Ulrich, *Good Wives: Image and Reality in the Lives of Women in Northern New England, 1650–1750* (New York: Oxford University Press, 1980).

9. Hans Anderson, "A Ballad to a Well Known Pioneer," typescript, Trempealeau County Historical Society.

10. Hans Anderson, "Autobiography," manuscript, Herman Ekern Papers, Manuscript Division, State Historical Society of Wisconsin.

11. Hans Anderson, "Memories of Big Slough," typescript, file 54, Trempealeau County Historical Society.

12. Letter from Hans Anderson to Duane Mowry, September 30, 1908, file 503, Trempealeau County Historical Society.

13. Tilly and Scott, pp. 43–44.

14. Ibid., p. 45.

15. Hans Anderson, "Autobiography," pp. 3–4.

16. Ibid., pp. 3–6; see also Gjerde, pp. 66–69.

17. Fischer, p. 13; Jeffrey, pp. 10–11; Myers, pp. 160–165. A striking exception to the rule, Fischer suggests, can be found in David T. Nelson, ed. and trans., *The Diary of Elisabeth Koren, 1853–1855* (Northfield, Minnesota: Norwegian-American Historical Association, 1955). Koren was from a family of Norway's elites and arrived on the Iowa frontier as the wife of a minister. She confronted the hardships of the frontier with exuberance, curiosity, a sense of humor, and purpose. For an excellent description of the actual work of frontier women, see Riley, pp. 29–87.

18. Anderson, "Autobiography," p. 4.

19. Hans Anderson, "Berthe Benson," typescript, file 49, Trempealeau County Historical Society.

20. Hans Anderson, "Autobiography," p. 7.

21. Anderson, "Berthe Benson."

22. Anderson, "Berthe Benson."

23. Anderson, "Autobiography," p. 7.

24. Anderson, "Berthe Benson."

25. Louise A. Tilly and Joan W. Scott, *Women, Work, and Family* (New York: Holt, Rinehart and Winston, 1978), pp. 54–55.

26. Hans Anderson, "The Red-Haired Norwegian," typescript, Trempealeau County Historical Society. This is the account of Gunda and Thor as described to Anderson by an aging woman of the community, much regarded for her talent in the folk art of story-telling.

27. Oyvind Osterude, *Agrarian Structure and Peasant Politics in Scandinavia: A Comparative Study of Rural Response to Economic Change* (Oslo, Norway: Universitetsforlaget, 1978), p. 239.

28. Ankarloo, p. 113.

29. A thorough examination of wills and inheritance in these townships remains to be completed. Unfortunately, the records have been stored in a disorganized fashion in a dark basement room of the Trempealeau County Court House. This study is based on a careful examination of the recorded wills only for the years 1895–1910.

30. Knut Hamsun, *Growth of the Soil,* trans. W. W. Worster (New York: Alfred A. Knopf, 1921). Hamsun provides a sensitive description of the passage of a peasant's lands and household from one generation to the next. See also: Mark W. Friedberger, "Handing Down the Home Place: Farm Inheritance Strategies in Iowa, 1870–1945," *Annals of Iowa* 8 (November 1981): 518–536; Kenneth H. Parsons and Eliot O. Waples, *Keeping the Farm in the Family,* Wisconsin Agricul-

tural Experiment Station Bulletin 157, pp. 4–14; Sonya Salamon, "Ethnic Differences in Farm Family Land Transfer," *Rural Sociology* 45 (1980): 290–308; Robert Ostergren, "Land and Family in Rural Immigrant Communities," *Annals of the Association of American Geographers* 71 (1981): 400–411.

31. Gjerde, p. 67. See also Ester Boserup, *Woman's Role in Economic Development* (London: Allen and Unwin, 1970), pp. 32–33; Ankarloo, pp. 111–120. For a detailed description of women's work in Norway as provided by the daughter of Norwegian immigrants to Wisconsin, see Thurine Oleson, *Wisconsin, My Home,* as told to Erna Oleson Xan (Madison: University of Wisconsin Press, 1950), pp. 6–16.

32. Gjerde, pp. 194–195.

33. Eric E. Lampard, *The Rise of the Dairy Industry in Wisconsin: A Study of Agricultural Change, 1820–1920* (Madison: State Historical Society of Wisconsin, 1963), pp. 271–272; see also John G. Rice, "The Role of Culture and Community in Frontier Prairie Farming," *Journal of Historical Geography* 3 (1977): 165.

34. Anderson, "Autobiography," pp. 6–7; Gjerde, pp. 34–37. For a detailed description of the kinds of foods typically produced in a Norwegian immigrant farm household, see Oleson, pp. 8–12, 49–58.

35. Oleson, p. 35.

36. Ibid., p. 52.

37. *Compendium of the Tenth Census of the United States, 1880: Part 1, Population* (Washington, D.C.: Government Printing Office, 1883).

38. Eben Douglas Pierce, ed., *History of Trempealeau County, Wisconsin* (Chicago: H. C. Cooper, Jr., and Co., 1917), pp. 811–812; regarding Norwegian immigrants on the frontier, also see Gjerde, pp. 194–195.

39. *Whitehall Times,* June 10, 1881.

40. Pierce, p. 811.

41. Wisconsin Department of State, *Tabular Statements of the Census Enumeration and the Agricultural, Minerals and Manufacturing Interests of Wisconsin* (Madison: State Printer, 1895), pp. 666–669.

42. Pierce, p. 816.

43. *Fourteenth Census of the United States, 1920:* Vol. 6, *Agriculture,* Part 1, *The Northern States* (Washington, D.C.: Government Printing Office, 1922), Table 11, p. 473; *Fifteenth Census of the United States, 1930:* Vol. 2, *Agriculture,* Part 1, *The Northern States* (Washington, D.C.: Government Printing Office, 1932), Table 10, p. 789; *Sixteenth Census of the United States, 1940:* Vol. 1, *Agriculture,* Part 1, *Statistics for Counties* (Washington, D.C.: Government Printing Office, 1942), Table 4, p. 921.

44. Pierce, pp. 812–816.

45. Letters from Rose Anderson to Lily Ekern, March 23 and April 27, 1902, Herman Ekern Papers, Manuscript Division, State Historical Society of Wisconsin.

46. Letter from Lily Anderson to Emil Anderson, December 12, 1898, Herman Ekern Papers.

47. Letter from Rose Anderson to Lily Ekern, February 6, 1902, Herman Ekern Papers.

48. Letter from Olive and Rose Anderson to Lily Ekern, January 11, 1902, Herman Ekern Papers.

49. Ella Hanson diaries, 1922–1945, passim, privately held.

50. Interviews: Doris Estenson, November 1983, Pigeon Falls, Wisconsin; Eleanor Ackley, November 1983, Pigeon Falls, Wisconsin; and Arlene Arneson, November 1984, Whitehall, Wisconsin.

51. Surveys by rural sociologists indicate women have continued to participate, particularly in milking; see Vanek, pp. 425–426; Ruth M. Clark and Greta Grey, *The Routine and Seasonal Work of Nebraska Farm Women,* Nebraska Experiment Station Bulletin No. 237 (Lincoln: University of Nebraska Press, 1930). A recent study of Wisconsin farm women indicated that 12 percent spent 30 or more hours a week doing farm work; as many as 48 percent worked in the fields some of the time, and 6 percent did so at least during 60 days; see Eugene A. Wilkening, *Farm Husbands and Wives in Wisconsin: Work Roles, Decisionmaking and Satisfaction, 1962 and 1978* (Madison: University of Wisconsin Press, 1981). For a recent survey of the work of rural sociologists, see Peggy J. Ross, "A Commentary on Research on American Farm Women," *Agriculture and Human Values* 2 (Winter 1985): 19–30.

52. *Sixteenth Census of the United States, 1940:* Vol. 1, *Agriculture,* Part 1, *Statistics for Counties,* p. 953; *U.S. Census of Agriculture, 1950:* Vol. 1, Part 7, *Wisconsin* (Washington, D.C.: Government Printing Office, 1952), Table 3, p. 55; *U.S. Census of Agriculture, 1964:* Vol. 1, Part 14, *Wisconsin* (Washington, D.C.: Government Printing Office, 1965), Table 8, p. 289. For a description of the introduction of electricity to rural Lincoln and Pigeon, see the interview with Harold Tomter, taped by the State Historical Society of Wisconsin. Recent work on farm women in Denmark indicates a pattern of development similar to that of Pigeon's Norwegian-American women. It was the introduction of the milking machine rather than commercial production which redefined animal husbandry as men's work; see Birthe Friis, "Changes in Furniture, Housekeeping, and Diet among Danish Peasants, 1850–1900," paper presented at the Scandinavian Immigration Conference, Decorah, Iowa, October 1985.

53. Ackley interview.

54. Interview with Karen Goplin, May 1984, Pigeon Falls, Wisconsin; personal communication from Dorothea Tomter, November 1984, Pigeon Falls, Wisconsin.

55. Osterud found a similar distribution of work on New York farms: "The gender division of labor, to the extent that one existed at all, was highly variable and flexible; the dairy process was the least gender-marked of any farm and household operations" ("Valuation of Women's and Men's Work," p. 3).

56. Ella Hanson diary, July 22–23, 1932.

57. For more on visiting, see chapter eight.

58. Ralph Wood diaries, 1909–1921, Area Research Center, University of Wisconsin–EauClaire; Arneson interview.

59. Ackley interview.

60. Ella Hanson diary, August 1928, March 1932.

61. Ibid., March 30, 1932.

62. Ella Hanson diary, November 6, 1933.

63. Vanek, pp. 425–426.

64. Ibid., p. 426.

65. Howard Beers, "A Portrait of the Farm Family in Central New York State," *American Sociological Review* 2 (October 1937): 591–600.

66. Ross, p. 21.

67. Frederick H. Buttel and Gilbert W. Gillespie, "The Study of the Structure of On-Farm and Off-Farm Labor Allocation among Farm Men and Women," *Rural Sociology* 49 (Summer 1984): 183–209; Robert O. Blood and Donald M. Wolfe, *Husbands and Wives* (New York: Free Press, 1960); Lee G. Burchinal and Ward W. Bauder, *Family Decision-making Patterns among Iowa Farm and Non-Farm Families,* Research Bulletin 528 (Ames: Iowa Agricultural Experiment Station, 1965).

68. Eugene A. Wilkening, "Joint Decision-making in Farm Families as a Function of Status and Role," *American Sociological Review* 23 (April 1958): 187–192; Wilkening, *Farm Husbands and Wives in Wisconsin.*

69. Ackley interview.

70. Interview with Irene Hanson, Pigeon Falls, Wisconsin, November 1983.

71. Tomter interview.

72. Arneson interview.

73. *U.S. Census of Population, 1950:* Vol. 2, *Characteristics of Population,* Part 49, *Wisconsin* (Washington, D.C.: Government Printing Office, 1952), Table 48, p. 119.

74. *Fifteenth Census of the United States, 1930:* Vol. 2, *Agriculture,* Part 1, *The Northern States,* Table 12, p. 799; *Sixteenth Census of the United States, 1940:* Vol. 2, *Housing,* Part 5, *General Characteristics* (Washington, D.C.: Government Printing Office, 1943), Table 6, p. 784, Table 23, p. 914, Table 29, p. 943; *U.S. Census of Housing, 1950:* Vol. 1, *General Characteristics,* Part 6, *Texas to Wyoming* (Washington, D.C.: Government Printing Office, 1952), Table 30, p. 68, Table 33, p. 82.

75. *Whitehall Times,* April 11, 1929, p. 4.

76. That the tensions between and within women related to this shift from a producer to a consumer ethic is revealed when local women are asked about changes in sociability as well as consumption. As Ila Staff commented when comparing the past and present, "We all had it the same then"; this was a reference to contrasting styles and levels of consumption that have created a greater self-consciousness and which have perhaps contributed to the decline in neighborliness that many note.

77. U.S. Census of Population, Manuscript Censuses, Lincoln and Pigeon township, Trempealeau County, Wisconsin, 1900, 1910, State Historical Society of Wisconsin.

78. Ackley interview; *Atlas and Farmer's Directory of Trempealeau County, Wisconsin* (St. Paul, Minnesota: Webb Publishing Company, 1930).

79. *U.S. Census of Population, 1970:* Vol. 1, *Characteristics of Population,* Part 51, *Wisconsin* (Washington, D.C.: Government Printing Office, 1973), Table 38, p. 176.

80. *Sixteenth Census of the United States, 1940:* Vol. 2, *Population,* Part 7, *Characteristics of Population* (Washington, D.C.: Government Printing Office, 1943), Table 23, p. 600; *U.S. Census of Population, 1960:* Vol. 1, *Characteristics of Population,* Part 51, *Wisconsin* (Washington, D.C.: Government Printing Office, 1961), Table 91, p. 284; Katherine Jellison, " 'Tractorettes' Go to War: Midwestern Farm Women in World War II," paper presented at the Newberry Seminar in Rural History, Newberry Library, February 1991.

81. Personal communication from Barbara Staff, Pigeon Falls, Wisconsin, November 1983.

82. *U.S. Census of Agriculture: 1925,* Part 1, *The Northern States* (Washington, D.C.: Government Printing Office, 1927), Table 6, p. 718; *U.S. Census of Agriculture, 1950:* Vol. 1, Part 7, *Wisconsin* (Washington, D.C.: Government Printing Office, 1952), Table 4, p. 69; *U.S. Census of Agriculture, 1964:* Vol. 1, Part 14, *Wisconsin* (Washington, D.C.: Government Printing Office, 1965), Table 9, p. 297.

83. One incident recounted by Lila Pederson and her daughter illustrates the attitudes and household economy: During the depression this woman's daughter was elected prom queen at the local high school, an important event for both parents and daughter. Mrs. Pederson recounted her desperate efforts to collect enough eggs to sell to pay for gowns for her daughter and herself. During the difficult years of the depression, her husband thought such purchases an extravagance. They usually made all their own clothes, but for this occasion "store bought" gowns seemed mandatory. Normally extra cash from the sale of eggs was not so aggressively pursued.

84. Ross, p. 22.

85. Anderson, "Autobiography," pp. 3–4.

86. Estenson interview.

87. Ibid.

Chapter 8: The Country Visitor: Patterns of Rural Hospitality

1. *Whitehall Times,* 1880–1925, passim.

2. Alan Macfarlane, *The Family Life of Ralph Josselin: A Seventeenth-Century Clergyman* (Cambridge: Cambridge University Press, 1970); Michael Zuckerman, "William Byrd's Family," *Perspectives in American History* 12 (1979): 253–312. Zuckerman noted the regularity with which southern aristocrats engaged in a constant round of visiting. Zuckerman connected this southern style of hospitality to the persistence of traditional interactions among family and community members, which in turn served to consolidate the Virginia elite's social position. In "The Female World of Love and Ritual: Relations between Women in Nineteenth-Century America" (*Signs* 1 [Autumn 1975]: 1–29); Carroll Smith-Rosenberg found that visiting was essential to the creation and maintenance of a distinctive female culture. Nancy Tomes ("The Quaker Connection: Visiting Patterns among Women in the Philadelphia Society of Friends, 1750–1800," in *Friends and Neighbors: Group Life in America's First Plural Society,* ed. Michael Zuckerman [Philadelphia: Temple University Press, 1982], pp. 174–195) explored

the visiting patterns of women of Philadelphia's Quaker elite between 1750 and 1800 and discovered that they offered important clues to the function of kinship and class-inherited status as Americans left behind traditional social relationships and attitudes.

3. Michael Lesy, *Wisconsin Death Trip* (New York: Pantheon-Random House, 1973); Merle Curti, *The Making of An American Community: A Case Study of Democracy in a Frontier Society* (Stanford, California: Stanford University Press, 1959), pp. 115, 124.

4. State of Wisconsin: *Blue Book,* 1882, p. 370; *Blue Book,* 1921, p. 484; *Blue Book,* 1931, p. 623 (Madison: State Printer).

5. Thurine Oleson, *Wisconsin, My Home,* as told to Erna Oleson Xan (Madison: University of Wisconsin Press, 1950), p. 49.

6. Dave Wood, ed., *Wisconsin Prarie Diary: 1869–1879* (Whitehall, Wisconsin: Dan Camp Press, 1979).

7. Dave Wood diary, July 4, 1879 (the unpublished diaries of Dave, James, and Ralph Woods are held by the Area Research Center, University of Wisconsin–Eau Claire); *Whitehall Times,* 1880–1925, passim; for examples, see: June 12, 1884, p. 1; February 16, 1882; March 4, 1916, p. 5.

8. Dave Wood diary, January 12–19, 1879.

9. Ibid., 1872, passim.

10. Dave, Ralph, and James Wood diaries, March 22–29, 1891. In the 1920s the Wood families' visiting continued at a similar pace.

11. Ralph Wood diary, 1920, passim. The diaries begun in 1922 by Ella Hanson, a woman who spent most of her married life on a farm in Pigeon, suggest the continuation of similar patterns of visiting into the 1950s, as do interviews with individuals who grew up in the community (interviews with Eleanor Ackley, Doris Estenson, and Arlene Arneson undertaken in January, February, and November of 1984, Pigeon Falls and Whitehall).

12. *Whitehall Times,* 1880–1925, passim.

13. Letters of the Ekern family, Herman Ekern Papers, Manuscript Division, State Historical Society of Wisconsin; letters of the Anderson family, Trempealeau County Historical Society.

14. Dave, Ralph, and James, Wood diaries, 1889, 1891, 1918, 1922, passim.

15. The *Times* samples included intercommunity visits reported during 15 weeks of 13 months from November of 1889 to December of 1890. Visits totaled 368: 164 going from the community, and 204 visiting it. The 1900 and the 1914 samples involved visits reported in one week of every month of the year. They totaled 315 and 525, respectively. In 1900, 184 of the visitors were from the community, and 131 visited from outside the area. In 1914, 280 were going from the community, and 245 were coming to it. The 1922 sample included one week of every month from September 1921 to July 1922. There were 635 visits reported in those weeks: 341 leaving the community for a visit, and 267 entering. Data from these samples will hereafter be referred to as the *Times* samples.

16. *Times* samples.

17. Ralph Wood diaries, February–March 1891, May–July 1922.

18. Smith-Rosenberg, pp. 1–29.

19. Ralph Wood diary, 1920, passim; letters of Lily Ekern and her sisters illustrate the frequency of visits by children: Rose Anderson to Lily Ekern, May 30, 1902; Myrtle Anderson to Lily Ekern, July 2, July 8, August 4, 1902; Lily Ekern to mother and family, April 3, 1903; all in the Herman Ekern Papers.

20. Ekern letters: Lily Ekern to mother and family, March 6, 1903; Lily Ekern to Rose Anderson, January 27, 1903.

21. Lena Ekern to Herman Ekern, April 2, 1892; Belle Ekern to Herman, April 8, 1892; Herman Ekern Papers.

22. Dave Wood diaries, June 29–30, 1874; and 1879–1900, passim.

23. Oleson, p. 49; interviews with Karen Goplin, Juanita Passo, Arlene Arneson, December 1983 and January 1984, Whitehall, Wisconsin; Ralph Wood diary, February 22–28, April 12–16, and June 15–17, 1920.

24. Dave Wood diaries, December 25–29, 1874, September–October 1877; *Whitehall Times:* February 23, 1882, August 6, 1914, January 7, 1914, also 1880–1925, passim.

25. Dave Wood diary, December 25–29, 1874.

26. Quote from a lecture by historian Richard Jensen at the Newberry Library, Chicago, June 1979.

27. James Wood diaries, January 15–17, 1888, June –November 1888, and May 16, June 8–21, August 29–31, 1892.

28. *Whitehall Times,* January 11, 1917.

29. Ibid.: January 6, 1881, April 4, 1881, December 4, 1890, October 3, 1918.

30. Letter from Lena Ekern to Lily Ekern, January 27, 1903, Herman Ekern Papers.

31. Ralph Wood diary, June–July 1922; Arneson and Ackley interviews.

32. Curti, p. 115.

33. *Times* samples.

34. Dave Wood, *Wisconsin Life Trip* (Whitehall, Wisconsin: Dan Camp Press, 1976), p. 99.

Chapter 9: From Peasant Pleasures to Victorian Virtues

1. Knudt Olson Storley, "A Memorable Charivari Party," as told to Hans Anderson, 1923, file 111, Trempealeau County Historical Society.

2. Jon Gjerde, *From Peasants to Farmers: The Migration from Balestrand, Norway, to the Upper Middle West* (Cambridge: Cambridge University Press, 1985), pp. 90–91; Natalie Z. Davis, "The Reasons of Misrule: Youth Groups and Charivaris in Sixteenth-Century France," *Past and Present* 50 (1971): 41–75; Edward P. Thompson, " 'Rough Music': Le Charivari anglais," *Annales: ESC* 29 (1974): 693–704.

3. Storley, "Charivari."

4. Ibid.

5. Gjerde, p. 105; Joan Rockwell, "Concepts and Terms: 'Mand,' " *Journal of Peasant Studies* 1, no. 3 (April 1974): 387; Fredrick Barth, "Family Life in a

Central Norwegian Mountain Community," in *Norway's Families: Trends, Problems, Programs,* ed. Thomas D. Eliot, Arthur Hillman, et al. (Philadelphia: University of Pennsylvania Press, 1960), p. 97; Michael Drake, *Population and Society in Norway, 1735–1865* (London: Cambridge University Press, 1969), pp. 145–147.

6. Pigeon Creek Evangelical Lutheran Church records, 1886–1898, contained in the Pigeon Falls Lutheran Parish Records, Pigeon Falls, Wisconsin; Gjerde, pp. 213–214. Gjerde has attributed the rapid decline in premarital pregnancy of Norwegian immigrants to the expanded economic opportunities available to immigrants in the American environment.

7. Daniel Scott Smith and Michael S. Hindus, "Premarital Pregnancy in America, 1640–1971: An Overview and Interpretation," *Journal of Interdisciplinary History* 4 (Spring 1975): 537–570.

8. Pigeon Creek Evangelical Lutheran Church records, 1886–1898.

9. Hans Anderson, "Autobiography," p. 29, manuscript Herman Ekern Papers, Manuscript Division, State Historical Society of Wisconsin.

10. Nancy F. Cott, "Passionlessness: An Interpretation of Victorian Sexual Ideology, 1790–1850," in *A Heritage of Her Own: Toward a New Social History of American Women,* ed. Nancy F. Cott and Elizabeth H. Pleck (New York: Simon and Schuster, 1979), p. 163; Cott's chapter is reprinted from *Signs: A Journal of Women in Culture and Society* 4 (1978): 219–236.

11. Ellen K. Rothman, "Sex and Self-Control: Middle-Class Courtship in America, 1770–1870," in *The American Family in Social-Historical Perspective,* ed. Michael Gordon, 3rd ed. (New York: St. Martin's Press, 1983), p. 398; Rothman's chapter is reprinted from the *Journal of Social History* 15 (Spring 1982): 409–425. Edward Shorter has argued that the Victorian sexual ideology had little impact on behavior. He posited that the apparently higher levels of sexual activity revealed by increased illegitimacy and premarital pregnancy which occurred after 1750 continued into the twentieth century, but that this sexual behavior was masked by contraception, which reduced the rates of premarital pregnancy and illegitimacy. See Edward Shorter, *The Making of the Modern Family* (New York: Basic Books, Inc., 1975), pp. 80–85.

12. Carl Degler, *At Odds: Women and the Family in America from the Revolution to the Present* (New York: Oxford University Press, 1980), p. 253.

13. Rothman, pp. 398–399.

14. Anderson, "Autobiography," pp. 27–29.

15. Elling Eilsen as quoted in Ingrid Semmingsen, *Norway to America: A History of Migration* (Minneapolis: University of Minnesota Press, 1978), p. 80.

16. Anderson, "Autobiography," pp. 28–29.

17. "A New Bundling Song," in Donald M. Scott and Bernard Wishy, *America's Families: A Documentary History* (New York: Harper and Row, Publishers, 1982), pp. 65–67; song reprinted from Henry Stiles, *Bundling, Its Origin, Progress, and Decline in America* (Albany, 1884), pp. 70–71.

18. Eilert Sundt as quoted by Drake, pp. 138, 144–146; Barth, p. 97; Eliot, Hillman, et al., p. 40; Gjerde, pp. 85–115; Orvar Lofgren, "Family and Household among Scandinavian Peasants: An Exploratory Essay," *Ethnological Scandinavica*

4 (1974): 31. For a Norwegian novelist's account of peasant courtship and marriage, see Knut Hamsun, *Growth of the Soil,* trans. W. W. Worster (New York: Alfred A. Knopf, Inc., 1921).

19. Gjerde, pp. 91, 105–107; Rockwell, p. 387; Drake, pp. 144–145.

20. Hamsun, chapters 15 and 18.

21. Eben Douglas Pierce, ed., *History of Trempealeau County, Wisconsin* (Chicago: H. C. Cooper, Jr., and Co., 1917), pp. 686–687.

22. Rothman, p. 398.

23. Gjerde, pp. 94–95; Eliot, Hillman, et al., p. 40.

24. Anderson, "Autobiography," pp. 27–29.

25. Ibid., p. 28.

26. Gjerde, pp. 91, 105–107; Rockwell, p. 387; Drake, pp. 144–145.

27. "New Bundling Song" in Scott and Wishy.

28. Anderson, "Autobiography," p. 29.

29. *Whitehall Times:* September 20, 1883, October 4, 1883.

30. Anderson, "Autobiography," p. 29.

31. Hans Anderson, "Oline Frederickson," typescript, 1919, file 217, Trempealeau County Historical Society.

32. For comparative statistics on premarital conception in Norway and the United States, see Gjerde, pp. 214–220. During the frontier years premarital conception rates in Spring Grove, Wisconsin approximated those of Norway. For example, between 1860 and 1864 in Spring Grove, 54.5 percent of all first births were conceived before marriages. By 1900 the ratio was 18.8 percent. Highest rates of illegitimacy in Norway and among immigrants were connected to the cotter class, or the landless peasants, who depended upon their own earnings to support themselves and their families. Gjerde argued that the decline in illegitimacy and prenuptial conceptions resulted from a decline in traditional courtship patterns (night courtship) and the success of the moral reformers in the "development of strong moral constraints against premarital sex." Gjerde's work, like that of Ellen Rothman (see n. 11 above), contradicts the conclusions of Edward Shorter, who asserted that contraception, not new restraints on behavior, brought down the prenuptial pregnancy rates in the nineteenth century. For another interpretation of American attitudes which emphasizes growing restraints on sexuality, see Howard Gadlin, "Private Lives and Public Order: A Critical View of the History of Intimate Relations in the United States," *Massachusetts Review* 17 (1976): 304–330.

33. Drake, p. 78; U.S. Census of Population, Manuscript Census, 1910, Pigeon and Lincoln townships Trempealeau County, Wisconsin, State Historical Society of Wisconsin.

34. Einar Haugen, *The Norwegian Language in America: A Study in Bilingual Behavior,* 2 vols. (Philadelphia: University of Pennsylvania Press, 1953), vol. 2, pp. 543–544.

35. Peter J. Rosendahl, *Han Ola og han Per: A Norwegian-American Comic Strip,* ed. Joan N. Buckley and Einar Haugen (Oslo: Universitetsforlaget, 1984), p. 44.

36. In April of 1986 after I delivered a lecture on the topic of night courtship to the local chapter of the American Association of University Women in Decorah, Iowa, several members of the audience noted the contemporary reactions of individuals to discovering prenuptial pregnancies while tracing family records. Two women in particular, both wives of Lutheran ministers, had had wide experience with the issue, because their husbands regularly assisted people in using church records.

37. Storley, "Charivari."

38. Ibid, p. 28; Thurine Oleson, *Wisconsin, My Home,* as told to Erna Oleson Xan (Madison: University of Wisconsin Press, 1950), p. 101.

39. Anderson, "Autobiography," p. 29.

40. Anderson as quoted in Dave Wood, ed., "*Wisconsin Prarie Diary: 1869–1879* (Whitehall, Wisconsin: Dan Camp Press), p. 189.

41. *Whitehall Times:* August 4, 1887, May 23, 1914, October 16, 1919.

42. "Valley of Trempe'leau's Christmas Ball," introduction by Hans Anderson, typescript, 1910, Trempealeau County Historical Society; when and by whom the poem was written is unknown.

43. Oleson, p. 146; interview with Dorothy Rongstad, July 1985, Osseo, Wisconsin. Rongstad grew up in the town of Pigeon and recalled attending barn dances as late as the decade of the 1930s.

44. George Y. Freeman, "Pioneer Women of Trempealeau County Prominent in the Home, Field and Forum," typescript, November 12, 1912, file 551, Trempealeau County Historical Society.

45. Oleson, pp. 19, 82.

46. Hans Anderson, "The Influence of Custom," typescript, 1914, file 513, Trempealeau County Historical Society.

47. Ibid.

48. Letter from J. T. Qually to Herman Ekern, November 6, 1904, Herman Ekern Papers.

49. Merle Curti, *The Making of an American Community: A Case Study of Democracy in a Frontier County* (Stanford, California: Stanford University Press, 1959), p. 325.

50. *Whitehall Times:* March 19 and April 9, 1914, October 16, 1919.

51. Ibid.: April 3, 1884, April 24, 1884.

52. Ibid., July 3, 1884.

53. Anderson, "Influence of Custom."

54. Letter from Dave Wood to author, February 11, 1985.

55. Arneson and Rongstad interviews.

56. Ibid.; Anderson, "Influence of Custom"; interview with Marlene Hanson, July 1984, Whitehall, Wisconsin.

Conclusion: Mentalité and Locality in Rural Wisconsin

1. Karl Marx as quoted by T. J. Jackson Lears, *No Place of Grace: Antimodernism and the Transformation of American Culture* (New York: Pantheon Books, 1981), p. 41.

2. Quoted in Ingrid Semmingsen, *Norway to American: A History of the Migration* (Minneapolis: University of Minnesota Press, 1978).

3. Odd S. Lovoll, *The Promise of American Life: A History of the Norwegian-American People* (Minneapolis: University of Minnesota Press, 1983), p. 212.

4. Tomter interview.

5. Robert C. Nesbit, *Wisconsin: A History,* (Madison: University of Wisconsin Press, 1973), p. 405; David L. Brye, "Wisconsin Scandinavians and Progressivism, 1900–1950," *Norwegian-American Studies* 27 (1977): 163–193.

6. For Beret's entire life story see the trilogy of novels by O. E. Rolvaag: *Giants in the Earth,* trans. Lincoln Coleord (New York: Harper and Brothers, 1927); *Peder Victorious,* trans. Nora O. Solum (New York: Harper and Brothers, 1929); *Their Father's God,* trans. Sivert Erdahl (New York: Harper and Row, Publishers, 1931).

7. Tomter interview.

8. Quoted in Gregg Easterbrook, "Making Sense of Agriculture: A Revisionist Look at Farm Policy," *Atlantic Monthly,* July 1985, p. 74.

9. Quote, ibid., p. 74.

10. Patricia Nelson Limerick, *The Legacy of Conquest: The Unbroken Past of the American West* (New York: W. W. Norton and Co., 1987), p. 27.

Bibliography

Primary Sources

Trempealeau County Historical Society, Galesville, Wisconsin

The collections of the Trempealeau County Historical Society are considerable, varied, and valuable, but they are in a very disordered condition. Several moves since the time when Merle Curti used the House of Memories records in Whitehall have led to disorganization and losses. Most of the sources I consulted there are contained in the Hans Alfred Anderson Papers.

Allen, John. "Fifty Years of Service, 1918–1968: Early History of the Pigeon Falls Cooperative Creamery," typescript.
"Anderson Golden Wedding," typescript.
Anderson, Hans Alfred. Papers.
Anderson, Hans. "Address at Gale College," ca. 1915?, typescript.
Anderson, Hans "A Ballad to a Well Known Pioneer," typescript.
Anderson, Hans. "Berthe Benson," typescript, file 49.
Anderson, Hans. "Halvor Hanson," October 15, 1929, typescript.
Anderson, Hans. "Hanna Smith," typescript, file 619.
Anderson, Hans. "Hans Nelson," 1931, typescript, file 476.
Anderson, Hans. "Helen Christianson," December 16, 1924, typescript, file 116.
Anderson, Hans. "The Influence of Custom," 1914, file 513.
Anderson, Hans. "J. D. Olds," typescript.
Anderson, Hans. "John O. Melby," typescript.
Anderson, Hans. "Mads Evenson," 1926, typescript.
Anderson, Hans. "Memories of Big Slough," typescript, file 54.
Anderson, Hans. "Ole O. Semb," 1914, typescript.
Anderson, Hans. "Oline Frederickson," 1919, file 217.
Anderson, Hans. "The Red-Haired Norwegian," typescript.
Anderson, Hans. "Some Characteristics of Big Slough Men," February 3, 1916, typescript.
Anderson, Hans. "Storviken," typescript. "Coral City," typescript.
Freeman, Charles. "Address," 1912, typescript.

Freeman, George Y. "Pioneer Women of Trempealeau County Prominent in the Home, Field and Forum," November 12, 1912, file 551.

"Hans Anderson Fremstad," June 29, 1933, typescript.

"H. D. Getts," typescript.

"Longevity Is Inherited in the Pederson Family," typescript, file 518.

"Ludwig L. Solsrud," 1941, typescript.

"Mrs. Gilbert Steig," February 12, 1940, typescript.

"Peder Ekern and Company," typescript.

"Peder Ekern and Pigeon," typescript.

"Peder Simonson," typescript.

Pierce, Eben. Papers.

"Roll Call of Departed Pioneers," typescript.

Storley, Knudt Olson. "A Memorable Charivari Party," as told to Hans Anderson, 1923, file 111.

"T. H. Earle," typescript.

"Valley of Trempe'leau's Christmas Ball," with an introduction by Hans Anderson written in 1910.

State Historical Society of Wisconsin, Madison

Anderson, Hans. "Autobiography," manuscript, Herman Ekern Papers, Manuscript Division.

Biography of Herman Ekern, Herman Ekern Papers, Manuscript Divison.

Ekern, Herman. Papers. Containing, among other things, various letters written to and from members of the Ekern family. Manuscript Division.

Statement of Board of County Canvassers for Trempealeau County. Presidential Elections. 1924 and 1928.

Area Research Centers, University of Wisconsin, La Crosse and Eau Claire

Real and Personal Property Tax Rolls for Trempealeau County. County Treasurer's Records. 1870, 1880, 1890, 1900, 1910, 1920, 1930. University of Wisconsin–La Crosse.

Tax Records for Pigeon and Lincoln Townships. 1870–1930. University of Wisconsin–La Crosse.

Woods, Dave, James, and Ralph. Diaries. 1869–1927. University of Wisconsin–Eau Claire.

Other Personal and Public Records

Hanson, Ella. Diaries. 1922–1945. In the possession of her daughter, Eleanor Ackley, of Pigeon Falls, Wisconsin.

Pigeon Creek Evangelical Lutheran Church. "Centennial Anniversary, Pigeon Creek Evangelical Lutheran Church: 1866–1966." Pigeon Falls, Wisconsin, 1966.

Pigeon Falls Evangelical Lutheran Church. "Centennial Anniversary, Pigeon Falls Evangelical Lutheran Church: 1878–1978." Pigeon Falls, Wisconsin, 1978.

Pigeon Falls Lutheran Parish Records. Containing the records of the Pigeon Falls Evangelical Lutheran Church and the records of the Pigeon Creek Lutheran Church. Pigeon Falls, Wisconsin.

Trempealeau County Records. 1870–1970. Miscellaneous, including wills, affidavits, judgment decrees, articles of incorporation, and marriage records. Trempealeau County Records Office, Trempealeau County Courthouse, Whitehall, Wisconsin.

Whitehall High School Alumni Records. 1904–1938. Located at the Office of the Superintendent of Schools, Whitehall, Wisconsin. Compiled in 1922 and 1938.

Interviews

Between 1982 and 1985, the following individuals, who grew up in or are presently living in the area of Pigeon and Lincoln townships, were interviewed:
Eleanor Ackley
Arlene Arneson
Edward Austerude
Janet Broderick
Doris Estenson
Karen Goplin
Irene Hanson
Marlene Hanson
Marie Johnson
Sharon Lehtinen
Martha Meade
Juanita Passo
Laila Pederson
Lila Pederson
Janet Peterson
Dorothy Rongstad
Pastor Peter Sherven
Tomter, Harold. Interview taped by Dale Treleven for the State Historical Society of Wisconsin. Madison, Wisconsin. 1978.

Government Census Sources

Federal Sources

Censuses of Population

U.S. Census of Population, Manuscript Censuses, Lincoln and Pigeon townships, Trempealeau County, Wisconsin. State Historical Society of Wisconsin, Madison. 1880, 1890, 1900, 1910.

1870

Ninth Census of the United States, 1870. Washington, D.C.: Government Printing Office, 1872.

1880
Compendium of the Tenth Census of the United States, 1880: Part 1. *Population.* Washington, D.C.: Government Printing Office, 1883.

1890
Compendium of the Eleventh Census of the United States, 1890: Part 1. *Population.* Washington, D.C.: Government Printing Office, 1892.

1900
Twelfth Census of the United States, 1900 Vol. 2, *Population,* Parts 1 and 2. Washington, D.C.: Government Printing Office, 1902.

1910
Thirteenth Census of the United States, 1910: Vol. 3. *Population.* Washington, D.C.: Government Printing Office, 1913.

1920
Fourteenth Census of the United States, 1920: Vol. 3. *Population.* Washington, D.C.: Government Printing Office, 1922.

1930
Fifteenth Census of the United States, 1930: Vol. 3. *Population.* Part 2. *Report by States.* Washington, D.C.: Government Printing Office, 1932.
Fifteenth Census of the United States, 1930: Population. Vol. 4. *Families.* Washington, D.C.: Government Printing Office, 1932.

1940
Sixteenth Census of the United States, 1940: Vol. 2. *Population.* Part 7. *Characteristics of Population.* Washington, D.C.: Government Printing Office, 1943.

1950
U.S. Census of Population, 1950: Vol. 2. *Characteristics of Population.* Part 49. *Wisconsin.* Washington, D.C.: Government Printing Office, 1952.

1960
U.S. Census of Population, 1960: Vol. 1. *Characteristics of Population.* Part 51. *Wisconsin.* Washington, D.C.: Government Printing Office, 1961.

1970
U.S. Census of Population, 1970: Vol. 1. *Characteristics of Population.* Part 51. *Wisconsin.* Washington, D.C.: Government Printing Office, 1973.

1980
U.S. Census of Population, 1980: Vol. 1. *Characteristics of Population.* Part 51. *Wisconsin.* Washington, D.C.: Government Printing Office, 1982.

Censuses of Housing

1940

Sixteenth Census of the United States, 1940: Vol. 2. *Housing.* Part 5. *General Characteristics.* Washington, D.C.: Government Printing Office, 1943.

1950

U.S. Census of Housing, 1950: Vol. 1. *General Characteristics.* Part 6. *Texas to Wyoming.* Washington, D.C.: Government Printing Office, 1952.

1960

U.S. Census of Housing, 1960: Vol. 1. *States and Small Areas.* Part 8. *Texas–Wyoming.* Washington, D.C.: Government Printing Office, 1961.

1970

U.S. Census of Housing, 1970: Vol. 1. *Housing Characteristics for States, Cities, and Counties.* Part 51. *Wisconsin.* Washington, D.C.: Government Printing Office, 1973.

Censuses of Agriculture

1890

Compendium of the Eleventh Census of the United States, 1890: Vol. 5. *Report on the Statistics of Agriculture.* Washington, D.C.: Government Printing Office, 1895.

1900

Twelfth Census of the United States, 1900: Agriculture, Part 1. *Farms, Livestock, and Animal Products.* Washington, D.C.: Government Printing Office, 1902.

1910

Thirteenth Census of the United States, 1910: Vol. 2. *Agriculture.* Washington, D.C.: Government Printing Office, 1913.

1920

Fourteenth Census of the United States, 1920: Vol. 6. *Agriculture.* Part 1. *The Northern States.* Washington, D.C.: Government Printing Office, 1922.
U.S. Census of Agriculture: 1925. Part 1. *The Northern States.* Washington, D.C.: Government Printing Office, 1927.

1930

Fifteenth Census of the United States, 1930: Vol. 2. *Agriculture.* Part 1. *The Northern States.* Washington, D.C.: Government Printing Office, 1932.
U.S. Census of Agriculture, 1935: Vol. 2. *Report for States with Statistics for Counties and a Summary for the United States.* Part 1. Washington, D.C.: Government Printing Office, 1936.

1940

Sixteenth Census of the United States, 1940: Vol. 1. *Agriculture.* Part 1. *Statistics for Counties.* Washington, D.C.: Government Printing Office, 1942.

1950

U.S. *Census of Agriculture, 1950:* Vol. 1. Part 7. *Wisconsin.* Washington, D.C.: Government Printing Office, 1952.
U.S. *Census of Agriculture, 1954:* Vol. 1. Part 7. *Wisconsin.* Washington, D.C.: Government Printing Office, 1956.

1960

U.S. *Census of Agriculture, 1960:* Vol. 1. Part 7. *Wisconsin.* Washington, D.C.: Government Printing Office, 1961.
U.S. *Census of Agriculture, 1964:* Vol. 1. Part 14. *Wisconsin.* Washington, D.C.: Government Printing Office, 1965.

1970

U.S. *Census of Agriculture, 1970:* Vol. 1. Part 14. *Wisconsin.* Washington, D.C.: Government Printing Office, 1972.
U.S. *Census of Agriculture, 1974:* Vol. 1. Part 49. *Wisconsin.* Washington, D.C.: Government Printing Office, 1977.

State Sources

State of Wisconsin. *Blue Book.* Madison: State Printer, 1871–1977.
Wisconsin State Census, Manuscript Censuses, Lincoln and Pigeon townships, Trempealeau County, Wisconsin. 1885, 1895, 1905.
Wisconsin Department of State. *Tabular Statements of the Census Enumeration and the Agricultural, Minerals and Manufacturing Interests of Wisconsin.* Madison: State Printer, 1886.
Wisconsin Department of State. *Tabular Statements of the Census Enumeration and the Agricultural, Minerals and Manufacturing Interests of Wisconsin.* Madison: State Printer, 1895.
Wisconsin Department of State. *Tabular Statements of Census Enumeration and the Agricultural, Dairying and Manufacturing Interests of Wisconsin.* Madison: State Printer, 1906.

Other Sources

Akerman, Sune. "The Psychology of Migration." *American Studies in Scandinavia* 8 (1978): 47–56.
Anderson, Arlow W. *The Norwegian Americans.* New York: Twayne, 1975.
Anderson, Sherwood. *Winesburg, Ohio.* New York: Viking Press, 1919; reprinted 1960.
Ankarloo, Bengt. "Agriculture and Women's Work: Directions of Change in the West, 1700–1900." *Journal of Family History* 4, no. 2 (1979): 111–121.

Atack, Jeremy, and Fred Bateman. *To Their Own Soil: Agriculture in the Antebellum North*. Ames: Iowa State University Press, 1987.

Atherton, Lewis. *Main Street on the Middle Border*. Bloomington: Indiana University Press, 1984.

Atkeson, Mary Weeks. "Women in Rural Life and Rural Economy." *In America through Woman's Eyes*, ed. Mary Ritter Beard, pp. 398–407. New York: Macmillan Co., 1933.

Atlas and Farmer's Directory of Trempealeau County, Wisconsin. St. Paul, Minnesota: Webb Publishing Co., 1930.

Atlas of Trempealeau County, Wisconsin. Minneapolis: Standard Atlas Co., 1964.

Bailey, Illena, and Melissa F. Snyder. "A Survey of Farm Houses." *Journal of Home Economics* 13 (1921): 346–356.

Bailyn, Bernard. *Ideological Origins of American Revolution*. Cambridge, Massachusetts: Harvard University Press, 1967.

Baldwin, Bird T., Eva Abigail Fillmore, and Lora Hadley. *Farm Children*. New York: D. Appleton and Co., 1930.

Baltensperger, Bradley H. "Agricultural Change among Nebraska Immigrants, 1880–1900." In *Ethnicity on The Great Plains*, ed. Frederick C. Luebke, pp. 170–189. Lincoln: University of Nebraska Press, 1980.

Barker-Benfield, G. J. *The Horrors of the Half-Known Life: Male Attitudes toward Women and Sexuality in Nineteenth-Century America*. New York: Harper and Row, Publishers, 1976.

Barron, Hal. *Those Who Stayed Behind: Rural Society in Nineteenth-Century New England*. New York: Cambridge University Press, 1984.

Barth, Fredrick. "Family Life in a Central Norwegian Mountain Community." In *Norway's Families: Trends, Problems, Programs,* ed. Thomas D. Eliot, Arthur Hillman, et al., pp. 81–107. Philadelphia: University of Pennsylvania Press, 1960.

Beale, Calvin L. "Rural Depopulation in the United States: Some Demographic Consequences of Agricultural Adjustments." *Demography* 1 (1964): 264–272.

Beale, Calvin L., and Donald J. Bogue. "Recent Population Trends in the United States and Their Causes." In *Our Changing Rural Society: Perspectives and Trends,* ed. James H. Copp, pp. 71–126. Ames: Iowa State University Press, 1964.

Beers, Howard. "A Portrait of the Farm Family in Central New York State." *American Sociological Review* 2 (October 1937): 591–600.

Bender, Thomas. *Community and Social Change in America*. Baltimore: Johns Hopkins University Press, 1978.

Berkner, Lutz K. "The Stem family and the Developmental Cycle of the Present Household: An Eighteenth-Century Austrian Example." *The American Historical Review* 77 (April 1972): 398–418.

Bernard, Richard M. *The Melting Pot and the Altar: Marital Assimilation in Early Twentieth Century Wisconsin*. Minneapolis: University of Minnesota Press, 1981.

Bjork, Kenneth O. "A Covenant Folk, with Scandinavian Colorings." *Norwegian-American Studies* 21 (1962): 212–251.

Bjorkvik, Halvard. "The Old Norwegian Peasant Community: The Farm Territories." *Skandinavian Economic History Review* 4 (1956): 17–81.

Blegen, Theodore C., ed. *Land of Their Choice: The Immigrants Write Home.* Minneapolis: University of Minnesota Press, 1955.

Blegen, Theodore C. *Norwegian Migration: The American Transition.* Northfield, Minnesota: Norwegian-American Historical Association, 1940.

Blood, Robert O., and Donald M. Wolfe. *Husbands and Wives.* New York: Free Press, 1960.

Blumenthal, Albert. *Small Town Stuff.* Chicago: University of Chicago Press, 1932.

Bogue, Allan. *From Prairie to Cornbelt: Farming on the Illinois and Iowa Prairies in the Nineteenth Century.* Chicago: Quadrangle Books, 1963.

Boserup, Ester. *Woman's Role in Economic Development.* London: Allen and Unwin, 1970.

Breen, Timothy H. "Persistent Localism: English Social Change and the Shaping of New England Institutions." *William and Mary Quarterly* 32 (January 1975): 3–28.

Briggs, Doris Haugh. *From There to Here.* Decorah, Iowa: Amundsen Publishing Co., 1980.

Brinkley, Alan. *Voices of Protest: Huey Long, Father Coughlin, and the Great Depression.* New York: Alfred A. Knopf, 1982.

Brunner, Edmund S. "Working with Rural Youth." Prepared for the American Youth Commission, Washington, D.C., American Council on Education, 1942.

Brye, David L. "Wisconsin Scandinavians and Progressivism, 1900–1950." *Norwegian-American Studies* 27 (1977): 163–193.

Brye, David L. *Wisconsin Voting Patterns in the Twentieth Century, 1900–1950.* New York: Garland Publishing, Inc., 1979.

Burchinal, Lee G. "Rural Youth in Crisis: Facts, Myths, and Social Change." Prepared for the National Commission for Children and Youth, Washington, D.C., U.S. Department of Health, Education and Welfare, Welfare Administration, 1965.

Burchinal, Lee G., and Ward W. Bauder. *Family Decision-making Patterns among Iowa Farm and Non-Farm Families.* Research Bulletin 528, Ames: Iowa Agricultural Experiment Station, 1965.

Buttel, Frederick H., and Gilbert W. Gillespie. "The Study of the Structure of On-Farm and Off-Farm Labor Allocation among Farm Men and Women." *Rural Sociology* 49 (Summer 1984): 183–209.

Buttel, Frederick H., and Philip McMichael. "Sociology and Rural History." *Social Science History* 12 (Summer 1988): 93–120.

Buttel, Frederick H., and Howard Newby. "Toward a Critical Rural Sociology." In *The Rural Sociology of the Advanced Societies: Critical Perspectives,* ed. Buttel and Newby, pp. 1–35. Montclair, New Jersey: Allanheld, Osmun and Co., 1980.

Buttel, Frederick H., and Howard Newby, eds. *The Rural Sociology of the Advanced Societies: Critical Perspectives.* Montclair, New Jersey: Allanheld, Osmun and Co., 1980.

Bushman, Richard. *From Puritan to Yankee: Character and Social Order in Connecticut, 1690–1765.* Cambridge, Massachusetts: Harvard University Press, 1967.

Carroll, Edward V., and Sonya Salamon. "Inheritance Patterns in Two Illinois Farm Communities." Paper prepared for the Tenth Annual Meeting of the Social Science History Association, Chicago, Illinois, 1985.

Carter, Paul. *The Twenties in America.* 2nd ed. Arlington Heights, Illinois: Harland Davidson, 1975.

Cartford, Gerhard M. "Music in the Norwegian Lutheran Church: A Study of Its Development in Norway and Its Transfer to America, 1825–1917." Ph.D. dissertation, University of Minnesota, 1961.

Chrislock, Carl H. "The Norwegian-American Impact on Minnesota Politics: How Far 'Left of Center'?" In *Norwegian Influence on the Upper Midwest,* ed. Harald S. Naess, pp. 106–116. Duluth: University of Minnesota Press, 1976.

Clark, Christopher. "The Household Economy, Market Exchange and the Rise of Capitalism in the Connecticut Valley, 1800–1860." *Radical History Review* 4 (1977): 166–171.

Clark, Christopher. *The Roots of Rural Capitalism: Western Massachusetts, 1780–1860.* Ithaca: Cornell University Press, 1990.

Clark, Ruth M. and Greta Grey. *The Routine and Seasonal Work of Nebraska Farm Women.* Nebraska Experiment Station Bulletin No. 237. Lincoln: University of Nebraska Press, 1930.

Conzen, Kathleen Neils. "Community Studies, Urban History and American Local History." In *The Past Before Us: Contemporary Historical Writing in the United States,* ed. Michael Kammen, pp. 270–291. Ithaca, New York: Cornell University Press, 1980.

Conzen, Kathleen Neils. "Peasant Pioneers: Generational Succession among German Farmers in Frontier Minnesota." In *The Countryside in the Age of Capitalist Transformation: Essays in the Social History of Rural America,* ed. Steven Hahn and Jonathan Prude, pp. 259–292. Chapel Hill: University of North Carolina Press, 1985.

Conzen, Michael P. *Frontier Farming in an Urban Shadow; The Influence of Madison's Proximity on the Agricultural Development of Blooming Grove, Wisconsin.* Madison: State Historical Society of Wisconsin, 1971.

Copp, James H., ed. *Our Changing Rural Society: Perspectives and Trends.* Ames: Iowa State University Press, 1964.

Cott, Nancy F. *The Bonds of Womanhood: "Woman's Sphere" in New England, 1780–1835.* New Haven: Yale University Press, 1977.

Cott, Nancy F. "Passionlessness: An Interpretation of Victorian Sexual Ideology, 1790–1850." In *A Heritage of Her Own: Toward a New Social History of American Women,* ed. Nancy F. Cott and Elizabeth H. Pleck, pp. 162–181. New York: Simon and Schuster, 1979. Chapter reprinted from *Signs: a Journal of Women in Culture and Society* 4 (1978): 219–236.

Curti, Merle. *The Making of an American Community: A Case Study of Democracy in a Frontier County.* Stanford, California: Stanford University Press, 1959.

Danbom, David B. "The Professors and the Plowmen in American History Today." *Wisconsin Magazine of History* 69 (Winter 1985–1986): 106–128.

Danbom, David B. *The Resisted Revolution: Urban American and the Industrialization of Agriculture, 1900–1930.* Ames: Iowa State University Press, 1979.

Danhof, Clarence H. *Change in Agriculture: The Northern United States, 1820–1870.* Cambridge, Massachusetts: Harvard University Press, 1969.

Davis, Natalie Z. "The Reasons of Misrule: Youth Groups and Charivaris in Sixteenth-Century France." *Past and Present* 50 (1971): 41–75.

Degler, Carl N. *At Odds: Women and the Family in America from the Revolution to the Present.* New York: Oxford University Press, 1980.

Degler, Carl N. "What Ought to Be and What Was: Women's Sexuality in the Nineteenth Century." *American Historical Review* 79 (December 1974): 1467–1490.

Demos, John. *A Little Commonwealth: Family Life in Plymouth Colony.* New York: Oxford University Press, 1970.

Demos, John. *Past, Present, and Personal: The Family and the Life Course in American History.* New York: Oxford University Press, 1986.

Diggins, John. *Bard of Savagery: Thorstein Veblen and Modern Social Theory.* New York: Seabury Press, 1970.

Dillman, Don. "The Social Impacts of Information Technologies in Rural North America." *Rural Sociology* 50 (Spring 1985): 1–26

Douglas, Ann. *The Feminization of American Culture.* New York: Alfred A. Knopf, 1977.

Doyle, Dan Harrison. *The Social Order of a Frontier Community: Jacksonville, Illinois, 1825–1870.* Urbana: University of Illinois Press, 1978.

Drake, Michael. *Population and Society in Norway, 1735–1865.* Cambridge: Cambridge University Press, 1969.

Easterbrook, Gregg. "Making Sense of Agriculture: A Revisionist Look at Farm Policy." *Atlantic Monthly,* July 1985, pp. 63–80.

Easterlin, Richard A. "Factors in the Decline of Farm Family Fertility in the United States: Some Preliminary Research Results." *Journal of American History* 36 (1976): 600–614.

Easterlin, Richard A. "Population Change and Farm Settlement in the Northern United States." *Journal of Economic History* 63 (1976): 45–75.

Easterlin, Richard A., George Alter, and Gretchen A. Condran. "Farms and Farm Families in Old and New Areas: The Northern States in 1860." In *Family and Population in the Nineteenth-Century America,* ed. Tamara K. Hareven and Maris A. Vinovskis, pp. 22–84. Princeton, New Jersey: Princeton University Press, 1978.

Eliot, Thomas D., Arthur Hillman, et al., eds. *Norway's Families: Trends, Problems, Programs.* Philadelphia: University of Philadelphia Press, 1960.

Elkins, Frank. "Norwegian Influence on American Skiing." *American-Scandanavian Review* (December 1947): 335–341.

Elkins, Stanley, and Eric McKitrick. "A Meaning for Turner's Frontier: Democracy in the Old Northwest." *Political Science Quarterly* 69 (November 1954): 321–353.

Fairbanks, Carol. *Prairie Women, Images in American and Canadian Fiction.* New Haven: Yale University Press, 1986.

Faragher, John Mack. "History from the Inside-Out: Writing the History of Women in Rural America." *American Quarterly* 33 (1981): 537–557.

Faragher, John Mack. "Open-Country Community: Sugar Creek, Illinois, 1820–1890." In *The Countryside in the Age of Capitalist Transformation: Essays in the Social History of Rural America*, ed. Steven Hahn and Jonathan Prude, pp. 233–258. Chapel Hill: University of North Carolina Press, 1985.

Faragher, John Mack. *Sugar Creek: Life on the Illinois Prairie*. New Haven: Yale University Press, 1986.

Faragher, John Mack. *Women and Men on the Overland Trail*. New Haven: Yale University Press, 1979.

Farm Youth: Proceedings of the Ninth National Country Life Conference. Chicago: University of Chicago Press, 1926.

Fass, Paula. *The Damned and the Beautiful: American Youth in the 1920s*. New York: Oxford University Press, 1977.

Fevold, Eugene L. "The Norwegian Immigrant and His Church." *Norwegian-American Studies* 23 (1967): 335–341.

Fink, Deborah. *Open Country, Iowa: Rural Women, Tradition and Change*. Albany: State University Press of New York, 1986.

Fischer, Christiane, ed. *Let Them Speak for Themselves: Women in the American West, 1849–1900*. Hamden, Connecticut: Shoe String Press, 1977.

Fishman, Joshua A. *Language Loyalty in the United States: The Maintenance and Perpetutation of Non-English Mother Tongues by American Ethnic and Religious Groups*. The Hague: Mouton, 1966.

Fite, Gilbert C. *American Farmers: The New Minority*. Bloomington: Indiana University Press, 1981.

Flora, Cornelia B. "Women and Agriculture." *Agriculture and Human Values* 1 (Winter 1985): 5–12.

Foner, Eric. *Free Soil, Free Labor, Free Men: Ideology of the Republican Party before the Civil War*. New York: Oxford University Press, 1970.

Foster, George M. "Introduction: What Is a Peasant?" In *Peasant Society: A Reader*, ed. Jack M. Potter, May N. Diaz, and George M. Foster, pp. 2–14. Boston: Little Brown and Co., 1967.

Friedan, Betty. *The Feminine Mystique*. New York: W. W. Norton and Co., 1963.

Friedberger, Mark W. *Farm Families and Change in 20th-Century America*. Lexington: University Press of Kentucky, 1988.

Friedberger, Mark W. "The Farm Family and the Inheritance Process: Evidence from the Corn Belt, 1870–1950." *Agricultural History* 57 (1983): 1–13.

Friedberger, Mark W. "Handing Down the Home Place: Farm Inheritance Strategies in Iowa, 1870–1945." *Annals of Iowa* 8 (November 1981): 518–536.

Friis, Brithe. "Changes in Furniture, Housekeeping, and Diet among Danish Peasants, 1850–1900." Paper presented at the Scandanavian Immigration Conference, Decorah, Iowa, October 1985.

Fuller, Wayne E. *The Old Country School*. Chicago: University of Chicago Press, 1982.

Gadlin, Howard. "Private Lives and Public Order: A Critical View of the History of Intimate Relations in the United States." *Massachusetts Review* 17 (1976): 304–330.

Galpin, Charles Josiah. *Rural Life.* New York: Century Co., 1918.

Galpin, Charles Josiah. *Rural Social Problems.* New York: Century Co., 1924.

Garland, Hamlin. *A Daughter of the Middle Border.* New York: Macmillan Co., 1921.

Garland, Hamlin. *Main-Travelled Roads.* New York: Harper and Brothers, 1891.

Garland, Hamlin. *Other Main-Traveled Roads.* New York: Harper and Brothers, 1910.

Gjerde, Jon. *From Peasants to Farmers: The Migration from Balestrand, Norway, to the Upper Middle West.* Cambridge: Cambridge University Press, 1985.

Goodwyn, Lawrence. *Democratic Promise: The Populist Movement in America.* New York: Oxford University Press, 1976.

Goody, Jack, Joan Thirsk, and E. P. Thompson, eds. *Family and Inheritance: Rural Society in Western Europe, 1200–1800.* Cambridge: Cambridge University Press, 1976.

Greven, Philip J., Jr. *Four Generations: Population, Land, and Family in Colonial Andover, Massachusetts.* Ithaca: Cornell University Press, 1970.

Greven, Philip J., Jr. *The Protestant Temperament: Patterns of Child Rearing, Religious Experience, and the Self in Early America.* New York: Alfred A. Knopf, Inc., 1977.

Griffen, Clyde. "Making It in America: Social Mobility in Mid Nineteenth-Century Poughkeepsie." *New York History* 51 (1970): 479–499.

Hagood, Margaret Jarman. *Mothers of the South: Portraiture of the White Tenant Farm Woman.* New York: W. W. Norton and Co., 1977.

Hahn, Steven. *The Roots of Southern Populism: Yeoman Farmers and the Transformation of the Georgia Upcountry, 1850–1890.* New York: Oxford University Press, 1983.

Hahn, Steven, and Jonathan Prude, eds. *The Countryside in the Age of Capitalist Transformation: Essays in the Social History of Rural America.* Chapel Hill: University of North Carolina Press, 1985.

Hamre, James. "Norwegian Immigrants Respond to the 'Common' School: A Case Study of American Values and the Lutheran Tradition." *Church History* 50 (1981): 305–315.

Hamre, James. "Three Spokesmen for Norwegian Lutheran Academies: Schools for Church, Heritage, Society." *Norwegian-American Studies* 30 (1985): 221–246.

Hamsun, Knut. *Growth of the Soil,* trans. W. W. Worster New York: Alfred A. Knopf, Inc., 1921.

Haney, Wava, and Jane B. Knowles, eds. *Women and Farming: Changing Roles, Changing Structures.* Boulder, Colorado: Westview Press, 1988.

Hanson, Marcus L. "Immigration and Puritanism." *Norwegian-American Studies and Records* 9 (1936): 1–28.

Hareven, Tamara K., ed. *Anonymous Americans: Explorations in Nineteenth-Century Social History.* Englewood Cliffs, New Jersey: Prentice-Hall, 1971.

Hareven, Tamara K. "The Dynamics of Kin in an Industrial Community." In

Turning Points: Historical and Sociological Essays on the Family, ed. John Demos and Sarane Spence Boocock, pp. 151–182. Chicago: University of Chicago Press, 1978. Supplement to the *American Journal of Sociology* 84.

Haskell, Thomas L. *The Emergence of Professional Social Science: The American Social Science Association and the Nineteenth-Century Crisis of Authority.* Urbana: University of Illinois Press, 1977.

Haugen, Einar. *The Norwegian Language in America: A Study in Bilingual Behavior.* 2 vols. Philadelphia: University of Pennsylvania Press, 1953.

Henretta, James A. *The Evolution of an American Society: 1700–1815.* Lexington, Massachusetts: D. C. Heath, 1973.

Henretta, James A. "Families and Farms: Mentalité in Pre-Industrial America." *William and Mary Quarterly,* 3rd ser., 35 (1978): 3–32.

Hibbard, Benjamin Horace. *The History of Agriculture in Dane County, Wisconsin.* Economic and Political Science Series. Madison: University of Wisconsin, 1904.

Higgs, Robert. "Mortality in Rural America." *Explorations in Economic History* 10 (Winter 1973): 177–195.

Hightower, Jim. *Hard Tomatoes, Hard Times: A Report of the Agribusiness Accountability Project on the Failure of America's Land Grant College Complex.* Cambridge, Massachusetts: Schenkman Publishing Co., 1973.

Hine, Robert C. *Community on the American Frontier: Separate but Not Alone.* Norman: University of Oklahoma Press, 1980.

Hofstadter, Richard. *The Age of Reform: From Bryan to F.D.R.* New York: Alfred A. Knopf, Inc. 1955.

Hofstadter, Richard, and Seymour Martin Lipset, eds. *Turner and the Sociology of the Frontier.* New York: Basic Books, Inc., 1968.

Hollingshead, A. B. *Elmstown's Youth and Elmtown Revisited.* New York: John Wiley, 1975.

Holmsen, Andreas. "The Old Norwegian Peasant Community: General Survey and Historical Introduction." *Scandinavian Economic Review* 4 (1956): 25–29.

Hudson, John C. *Plains Country Towns.* Minneapolis: University of Minnesota Press, 1985.

Jackson Lears, T. J. *No Place of Grace: Antimodernism and the Transformation of American Culture,* New York: Pantheon Books, 1981.

Janvry, Alain de. "Social Differentiation in Agriculture and the Ideology of Neopopulism." In *Rural Sociology of the Advanced Societies: Critical Perspectives,* ed. Frederick H. Buttel and Howard Newby, pp. 155–168. Montclair, New Jersey: Allanheld, Osmun and Co., 1980.

Jeffery, Julie Roy. *Frontier Women: The Trans-Mississippi West, 1840–1880.* New York: Hill and Wang, 1979.

Jellison, Katherine. " 'Tractorettes' Go to War: Midwestern Farm Women in World War II." Paper presented at the Newberry Seminar in Rural History. Newberry Library, Chicago, February 1991.

Jensen, Joan M. *Loosening the Bonds: Mid-Atlantic Farm Women, 1750–1850.* New Haven: Yale University Press, 1986.

Jensen, Joan M. *Promise to the Land: Essays on Rural Women.* Albuquerque: University of New Mexico Press, 1991.

Jensen, Joan M. "The Role of Farm Women in American History: Areas for Additional Research." *Agriculture and Human Values* 2 (Winter 1985): 13–17.

Jensen, Joan M. *With These Hands: Women Working on the Land.* Old Westbury, New York: Feminist Press, 1981.

Jensen, Richard. *The Winning of the Midwest: Social and Political Conflict, 1888–1896.* Chicago: University of Chicago Press, 1971.

Jonassen, Christen T. "The Protestant Ethic and the Spirit of Capitalism in Norway." *American Sociological Review* 12 (December 1947): 676–686.

Jones, Calvin, and Rachel A. Rosenfeld. *American Farm Women: Findings from a National Survey.* National Opinion Research Center Report No. 130. Chicago, 1981.

Jordan, Terry G. *German Seed in Texas Soil: Immigrant Farmers in Nineteenth-Century Texas.* Austin: University of Texas Press, 1966.

Joy, Barnard D. *Organizations and Programs for Rural Young People.* State Extension Service Circular No. 248. Madison, Wisconsin, 1935.

Katz, Michael B. *The People of Hamilton, Canada West: Family and Class in a Mid Nineteenth-Century City.* Cambridge, Massachsetts: Harvard University Press, 1975.

Katz, Michael B., J. Doucet, and Mark J. Stein. "Migration and Social Order in Erie County, New York: 1855." *Journal of Interdisciplinary History* 8 (1978): 669–701.

Kirby, Jack Temple. *Rural Worlds Lost: The American South, 1920–1960.* Baton Rouge: Louisiana State University Press, 1987.

Kirkpatrick, Ellis L. *The Farmer's Standard of Living.* New York: Century Co., 1929.

Kirkpatrick, Ellis L., and Agnes M. Doynton. *Interests and Needs of the Rural Youth in Wood County, Wisconsin.* Special Circular, Wisconsin Agricultural Extension Service. Madison, January 1938.

Kleppner, Paul. *The Cross of Culture: A Social Analysis of Midwestern Politics, 1850–1900.* New York: Free Press, 1970.

Kleppner, Paul. *The Third Electoral System, 1853–1892.* Chapel Hill: University of North Carolina Press, 1979.

Knights, Peter R. *The Plain People of Boston, 1830–1860: A Study in City Growth.* New York: Oxford University Press, 1971.

Kohl, Seena B. "The Making of a Community: The Role of Women in an Agricultural Setting." In *Kin and Communities: Families in America,* ed. Allan J. Lichtman and Joan R. Challinor, pp. 175–186. Washington, D.C.: Smithsonian Institution Press, 1979.

Kohn, Howard. *The Last Farmer: An American Memoir.* New York: Harper and Row, Publishers, 1988.

Kolb, John H. *Rural Primary Groups: A Study of Agricultural Neighborhoods.* Madison: University of Wisconsin Press, 1921.

Lampard, Eric E. *The Rise of the Dairy Industry in Wisconsin: A Study in Agricul-*

tural Change, 1820–1920. Madison: State Historical Society of Wisconsin, 1963.

Larson, Agnes M. "The Editorial Policy of *Skandinaven,* 1900–1903." *Norwegian-American Studies and Records* 8 (1934): 112–135.

Legreid, Ann M., and David Ward. "Religious Schism and the Development of Rural Immigrant Communities: Norwegian Lutherans in Western Wisconsin, 1880–1905." *Midwest History* 2 (Summer 1982): 13–28.

Lesy, Michael. *Wisconsin Death Trip, 1869–1879.* New York: Pantheon–Random House, 1973.

Lewis, Sinclair. *Main Street.* New York: Harcourt, Brace and Co., 1920.

Limerick, Patricia Nelson. *The Legacy of Conquest: The Unbroken Past of the American West.* New York: W. W. Norton and Co., 1987.

Lindberg, Duane Rodell. *Men of the Cloth and the Social Fabric of the Norwegian Ethnic Community in North Dakota.* New York: Arno Press, 1980.

Lindberg, Duane Rodell. "Pastors, Prohibition and Politics: The Role of Norwegian Clergy in the North Dakota Abstinence Movement, 1880–1920." *North Dakota Quarterly* (Autumn 1981).

Lockridge, Kenneth. *A New England Town: The First Hundred Years: Dedham, Massachusetts, 1636–1736.* New York: W. W. Norton and Co., 1970.

Lofgren, Orvar. "Family and Household among Scandinavian Peasants: An Exploratory Essay." *Ethnological Scandinavica* 4 (1974): 2–52.

Logan, Ben. *The Land Remembers: The Story of a Farm and Its People.* New York: Viking Press, 1975.

Loomis, Charles P. *Social Systems: Essays on Their Persistence and Change.* Princeton: Van Nostrand Co., 1960.

Loomis, Charles P., and J. Allan Beegle. *Rural Social Systems: A Textbook in Rural Sociology and Anthropology.* New York: Prentice-Hall, 1950.

Lovoll, Odd S. "*Decorah-Posten:* The Story of an Immigrant Newspaper." *Norwegian-American Studies* 27 (1977): 77–100.

Lovoll, Odd S. *A Folk Epic: The Bygdelag in America.* Boston: Twayne Publishers, 1975.

Lovoll, Odd S. *The Promise of American Life: A History of the Norwegian-American People.* Minneapolis: University of Minnesota Press, 1983.

Luebke, Frederick C., ed. *Ethnicity on the Great Plains.* Lincoln: University of Nebraska Press, 1980.

Luther, E. L. "Farmers' Institutes in Wisconsin, 1885–1933." *Wisconsin Magazine of History* 30 (September 1946): 59–68.

Macfarlane, Alan. *The Family Life of Ralph Josselin: A Seventeenth-Century Clergyman.* Cambridge: Cambridge University Press, 1970.

Merrill, Michael. "Cash Is Good to Eat: Self-Sufficiency and Exchange in the Rural Economy of the United States." *Radical History Review* 3 (1977): 42–71.

Montgomery, David. *Workers' Control in America: Studies in the History of Work, Technology, and Labor Struggles.* New York: Cambridge University Press, 1979.

Munch, Peter A. "Authority and Freedom: Controversy in Norwegian-American Congregations." *Norwegian-American Studies* 28 (1979): 3–34.

Munch, Peter A. " 'Gard," The Norwegian Farm." *Rural Sociology* 12 (1947): 356–367.

Munch, Peter A. "Segregation and Assimilation of Norwegian Settlements in Wisconsin." *Norwegian-American Studies and Records* 18 (1954): 102–141.

Munch, Peter A. "Social Adjustment among Wisconsin Norwegians." *Norwegian-American Studies and Records* 16 (1952): 780–787.

Murrin, John. "Review Essay." *History and Theory* 11 (1972): 226–275.

Myers, Sandra L. *Westering Women: The Frontier Experience, 1800–1915*. Albuquerque: University of New Mexico Press, 1982.

Naess, Harald S., ed. *The Norwegian Influence in the Upper Midwest*. Duluth: University of Minnesota Press, 1976.

Nelson, Clifford, and Eugene L. Fevold. *The Lutheran Church among Norwegian-Americans: A History of the Evangelical Lutheran Church*. 2 vols. Minneapolis: Augsburg Publishing, 1960.

Nelson, David T., ed. and trans. *The Diary of Elisabeth Koren, 1853–1855*. Northfield, Minnesota: Norwegian-American Historical Association, 1955.

Nelson, Frank C. "The School Controversy among Norwegian Immigrants." *Norwegian-American Studies* 26 (1974): 206–209.

Nelson, Lowry. "Action Programs for the Conservation of Rural Life and Culture." *Rural Sociology* 4 (December 1939): 414–432.

Nelson, Lowry. *Rural Sociology: Its Origins and Growth in the United States*. Minneapolis: University of Minnesota Press, 1969.

Nesbit, Robert C. *The History of Wisconsin: Urbanization and Industrialization, 1873–1893*, vol. 3. Madison: State Historical Society of Wisconsin, 1985.

Nesbit, Robert C. *Wisconsin: A History*. Madison: University of Wisconsin Press, 1973.

Neth, Mary. "Gender and the Family Labor System: Defining Work in the Rural Midwest." Paper presented at the Social Science History Association meeting, Minneapolis, November 1990.

Nugent, Walter, T. K. *Changing Structures of American Social History*. Bloomington: Indiana University Press, 1981.

Oleson, Thurine. *Wisconsin, My Home*. As told to Erna Oleson Xan. Madison: University of Wisconsin Press, 1950.

Ostergren, Robert C. *A Community Transplanted: The Trans-Atlantic Experience of Swedish Immigrant Settlement in the Upper Midwest, 1835–1915*. Madison: University of Wisconsin Press, 1988.

Ostergren, Robert C. "Cultural Homogeneity and Population Stability among Swedish Immigrants in Chicago County." *Minnesota History* 47 (1973): 255–269.

Ostergren, Robert C. "Land and Family in Rural Immigrant Communities." *Annals of the Association of American Geographers* 71 (1981): 400–411.

Ostergren, Robert C. "Prairie Bound: Migration Patterns to a Swedish Settlement in the Dakota Frontier." In *Ethnicity on the Great Plains*, ed. Frederick C. Luebke, pp. 73–91. Lincoln: University of Nebraska, 1980.

Osterud, Nancy Grey. *The Bonds of Community: The Lives of Farm Women in Nineteenth Century New York*. Ithaca: Cornell University Press, 1990.

Osterud, Nancy Grey. "Strategies of Mutuality: Relations among Women and Men in an Agricultural Community." Ph.D. dissertation, Brown University, 1984.

Osterud, Nancy Grey. "The Valuation of Women's and Men's Work: Gender, Kinship and Market in an Upstate New York Dairy Farming Community during the Late Nineteenth Century." Paper presented at the annual convention of the Social Science History Association, Chicago, November 1985.

Osterude, Oyvind. *Agrarian Structure and Peasant Politics in Scandanavia: A Comparative Study of Rural Response to Economic Change.* Oslo, Norway: Universitetsforlaget, 1978.

Ownership Atlas, Trempealeau County, Wisconsin. Quincy, Illinois: Artcraft Co., 1975.

Parsons, Kenneth H., and Eliot O. Waples. *Keeping the Farm in the Family,* Wisconsin Agricultural Experiment Station Bulletin 157, September 1945.

Pierce, Eben Douglas, ed. *History of Trempealeau County, Wisconsin.* Chicago: H. C. Cooper, Jr., and Co., 1917.

Pigeon Falls Lutheran Church Parish. *The Ambassador* 5, no. 6 (June 1983).

Potter, Jack M., May N. Diaz, and George M. Foster. *Peasant Society: A Reader,* Boston: Little Brown and Co., 1967.

Redfield, Robert. *Peasant Society and Culture: An Anthropological Approach to Civilization.* Chicago: University of Chicago Press, 1956.

Rice, John G. *Patterns of Ethnicity in a Minnesota County, 1880–1905.* University of Umea, Department of Geography, Geographical Report No. 4, Umea, Sweden, 1973.

Rice, John G. "The Role of Culture and Community in Frontier Prairie Farming." *Journal of Historical Geography* 3 (1977): 156–176.

Riley, Glenda. *Frontierswomen: The Iowa Experience.* Ames: Iowa State University Press, 1981.

Rockwell, Joan. "Concepts and Terms: 'Mand.' " *Journal of Peasant Studies* 1, no. 3 (April 1974): 387–389.

Rolvaag, O. E. *Giants on the Earth.* Oslo, Norway: H. Ashehoug and Co., 1924; New York: Harper and Row Publishers, 1955.

Rolvaag, O. E. *Peder Victorious.* Translated by Nora O. Solum. New York: Harper and Brothers, 1929.

Rolvaag, O. E. *Pure Gold.* Translated by Sivert Erdahl. New York: Harper and Brothers, 1931.

Rolvaag, O. E. *Their Father's God.* Translated by Trygue M. Ager. New York: Harper and Brothers, 1931.

Rosendahl, Peter J. *Han Ola og han Per: A Norwegian-American Comic Strip.* Edited by Joan N. Buckley and Einar Haugen. Oslo, Norway: Universitetsforlaget, 1984.

Ross, Peggy J. "A Commentary on Research on American Farm Women." *Agriculture and Human Values* 2 (Winter 1985): 19–30.

Rothman, Ellen K. "Sex and Self-Control: Middle-Classs Courtship in America, 1770–1870." In *The American Family in Social-Historical Perspective,* ed. Michael Gordon, 3rd ed. New York: St. Martin's Press, 1983. Chapter reprinted from *Journal of Social History* 15 (Spring 1982): 409–425.

Russo, David J. *Families and Communities: A New View of American History.* Nashville: American Association for State and Local History, 1974.

Rutman, Darrett B. "Behind the Wide Missouri." (Review of *Those Whoe Stayed Behind: Rural Society in Nineteenth Century New England,* by Hal S. Barron.) *Reviews in American History* 13 (1985): 230–235.

Ryan, Mary P. *Cradle of the Middle Class: The Family in Oneida County, New York, 1790–1865.* New York: Cambridge University Press, 1981.

Sachs, Carolyn E. *The Invisible Farmer: Women In Agricultural Production.* Totawa, New Jersey: Rowman and Allanheld, 1983.

Sachs, Carolyn E. "Women's Work in the U.S.: Variations by Regions." *Agriculture and Human Values* 2 (Winter 1985): 31–39.

Salamon, Sonya. "Ethnic Differences in Farm Family Land Transfer." *Rural Sociology* 45 (1980): 290–308.

Salamon, Sonya, and Ann Mackey Keim. "Land Ownership and Women's Power in a Midwestern Farming Community." *Journal of Marriage and the Family* 41 (1979): 109–119.

Sanders, Irwin T. *The Community: An Introduction to a Social System.* New York: Ronald Press Co., 1958.

Sanders, Irwin T. *Rural Society.* Englewood Cliffs, New Jersey: Prentice-Hall, 1977.

Sanderson, Ezra Dwight. "Scientific Reserach in Rural Sociology." *American Journal of Sociology* 33 (September 1927): 177–221.

Sawer, Barbara. "Predictors of the Farm Wife's Involvement in General Management and Adoption Decisions." *Rural Sociology* 38 (Winter 1983): 412–426.

Schlesinger, Arthur, Sr. "The City in American History." *Mississippi Valley Historical Review* 27 (June 1940): 43–66.

Schlesinger, Arthur, Sr. *The Rise of the City, 1878–1898.* New York: Macmillan Co., 1933.

Schob, David E. *Hired Hands and Plowboys: Farm Labor in the Midwest, 1815–60.* Urbana: University of Illinois Press, 1975.

Scott, Donald M., and Bernard Wishy. *America's Families: A Documentary History.* New York: Harper and Row, Publishers, 1982.

Semmingsen, Ingrid. "Nordic Research into Emigration." *Scandinavian Journal of History* 3 (1978): 49–51.

Semmingsen, Ingrid. *Norway to America A History of Migration.* Minneapolis: University of Minnesota Press, 1978.

Shannon, Fred A. *The Farmer's Last Frontier: Agriculture, 1860–1897.* New York: Farrar and Rinehart, Inc., 1945.

Shorter, Edward. *The Making of the Modern Family.* New York: Basic Books, Inc., 1975.

Shover, John L. *First Majority—Last Minority: The Transforming of Rural Life in America.* DeKalb: Northern Illinois University Press, 1976.

Sklar, Kathryn Kish. *Catharine Beecher: A Study in American Domesticity.* New York: W. W. Norton and Co., 1973.

Smith, Daniel Scott, and Michael S. Hindus. "Premarital Pregnancy in America, 1640–1971: An Overview and Interpretation." *Journal of Interdisciplinary History* 4 (Spring 1975): 537–570.

Smith, Timothy L. "Religion and Ethnicity in America." *American Historical Review* 83 (1978): 1155–1185.

Smith, T. Lynn. *The Sociology of Rural Life in the United States.* New York: Harper and Brothers, 1940; reprinted, 1953.

Smith-Rosenberg, Carroll. "The Female World of Love and Ritual: Relations between Women in Nineteenth-Century America." *Signs* 1 (Autumn 1975): 1–29.

Standard Atlas of Trempealeau County, Wisconsin. Chicago: George A. Ogle and Co., 1901.

Stone, Lawrence. *The Family, Sex, and Marriage in England, 1500–1800.* New York: Harper and Row, Publishers, 1977.

Sutter, Ruth. *The Next Place You Come To: The Town in North America.* Englewood Cliffs, New Jersey: Prentice Hall, 1973.

Swierenga, Robert P. *The Dutch in America: Immigration, Settlement and Cultural Change.* New Burnswick, New Jersey: Rutgers University Press, 1985.

Swierenga, Robert P. "Ethnicity and American Agriculture." *Ohio History* 89 (Summer 1980): 323–344.

Swierenga, Robert P. "Settlement of the Old Northwest." *Journal of the Early Republic* 9 (Spring 1989): 73–105.

Swierenga, Robert P. "Theoretical Perspectives on the New Rural History: From Environmentalism to Modernism." *Agricultural History* 56 (1982): 495–502.

Swierenga, Robert P. "Towards a 'New Rural History.' " *Historical Methods Newsletter* 6 (June 1973): 111–121.

Taylor, Carl C., et al. *Rural Life in the United States.* New York: Alfred A. Knopf, Inc., 1949.

Taylor, Rebecca L. *Briggs Ancestors: With Brief Sketches of Some Related Families.* Whitehall, Wisconsin: Dan Camp Press, 1979.

Thernstrom, Stephen. *The Other Bostonians: Poverty and Progress in the American Metropolis, 1880–1897.* Cambridge, Massachusetts: Harvard University Press, 1971.

Thompson, Edward P. " 'Rough Music': Le Charivari anglais." *Annales: ESC* 29 (1974): 693–704.

Thompson, John Giffen. *The Rise and Decline of the Wheat Growing Industry in Wisconsin.* Economic and Political Science Series. Madison: University of Wisconsin, 1909.

Tilly, Louise, and Joan Scott. *Women, Work, and Family.* New York: Holt, Rinehart, and Winston, 1978.

Tomes, Nancy. "The Quaker Connection: Visiting Patterns among Women in the Philadelphia Society of Friends, 1750–1800." In *Friends and Neighbors: Group Life in America's First Plural Society,* ed. Michael Zuckerman, pp. 174–195. Philadelphia: Temple University Press, 1982.

Triennial Atlas and Plat Book, Trempealeau County, Wisconsin. Rockford, Illinois: Rockford Map Publishers, 1954.

Turner, Frederick Jackson. *The Significance of the Frontier in American History,* ed. Harold P. Simonson, reprint ed. New York: Frederick Unger, 1963.

Ulrich, Laurel Thatcher. *Good Wives: Image and Reality in the Lives of Women in Northern New England, 1650–1750.* New York: Oxford University Press, 1980.

Ulrich, Robert J. "The Bennett Law of 1889: Education and Politics in Wisconsin." Ph.D. dissertation, University of Wisconsin, 1965.

Vanderstel, David G. "Dutch Immigrant Neighborhood Development in Grand Rapids, 1850–1900." In *The Dutch in America: Immigration, Settlement, and Cultural Change,* ed. Robert P. Swierenga, pp. 125–155. New Brunswick: Rutgers University Press, 1985.

Vanek, Joann. "Work, Leisure, and Family Roles: Farm Households in the United States, 1920–1955." *Journal of Family History* 5 (Spring 1980): 423.

Varenne, Herve. *Americans Together: Structured Diversity in a Midwestern Town.* New York: Teachers College Press, 1977.

Veblen, Thorstein. *Absentee Ownership and Business Enterprise in Recent Times.* 1923; reprint, New York: A. M. Kelly, 1964.

Vidich, Arthur J., and Joseph Bensman. *Small Town in Mass Society: Class, Power and Religion in a Rural Community.* Princeton: Princeton University Press, 1958.

Walker, Mack. *Germany and the Emigration, 1816–1885.* Cambridge, Massachusetts: Harvard University Press, 1964.

Wallace, Anthony F. C. *Rockdale: The Growth of an American Village in the Early Industrial Revolution.* New York: Alfred A. Knopf, Inc., 1978.

Waller, Altina L. *Feud: Hatfields, McCoys, and Social Change in Appalachia, 1860–1900.* Chapel Hill: University of North Carolina Press, 1988.

Walzer, Michael. *The Revolution of the Saints: A Study in the Origins of Radical Politics.* New York: Atheneum, 1976.

Waples, Eliot O. *Keeping the Farm in the Family.* Wisconsin Agricultural Experiment Station Bulletin 157, Madison.

Weber, Max. *The Protestant Ethic and the Spirit of Capitalism: The Relationships between Religion and the Economic and Social Life in Modern Culture.* Translated by Talcott Parsons. 1904–1905; New York: Scribner's Sons, 1958.

Wefald, Jon. *A Voice of Protest: Norwegians in American Politics, 1890–1917.* Northfield, Minnesota: Norwegian-American Historical Association, 1971.

Welter, Barbara. "The Cult of True Womanhood: 1820–1860." *American Quarterly* 18 (Summer 1966): 151–174.

Whitehall Times. 1880–1975. Whitehall, Wisconsin.

Wiebe, Robert. *The Search for Order, 1877–1920.* New York: Hill and Wang, 1967.

Wileden, A. F. *What Douglas County Young People Want and What They Are Doing about It.* Special Circular, Wisconsin Agricultural College, Extension Service. Madison, December 1935.

Wilkening, Eugene A. *Farm Husbands and Wives in Wisconsin: Work Roles, Decisionmaking and Satisfaction, 1962 and 1978.* Madison: University of Wisconsin Press, 1981.

Wilkening, Eugene A. "Joint Decision-making in Farm Families as a Function of Status and Role." *American Sociological Review* 23 (April 1958): 187–192.

Wilkening, Eugene A., and Denton Morrison. "A Comparison of Husband and Wife Responses Concerning Who Makes Farm and Home Decisions." *Journal of Marriage and the Family* 25 (August 1963): 349–351.

Williams, Raymond. *The Country and the City.* New York: Oxford University Press, 1973.

Wilson, Warren H. *The Evolution of a Country Community.* Boston: Pilgrim Press, 1912

Wood, Dave. *Wisconsin Life Trip.* Whitehall, Wisconsin: Dan Camp Press, 1976.

Wood, Dave, ed. *Wisconsin Prarie Diary: 1869–1879.* Whitehall, Wisconsin: Dan Camp Press, 1979.

Wood, Gordon S. *The Creation of the American Republic, 1776–1787.* New York: W. W. Norton and Co., 1969.

Wyman, Roger E. "Wisconsin Ethnic Groups and the Election of 1890." *Wisconsin Magazine of History* 51 (Summer 1968): 269–293.

Zelinsky, Wilbur. "Changes in the Geographic Patterns of Rural Population in the United States, 1790–1960." *Geographic Review* 52 (1962): 492–524.

Zuckerman, Michael. *New England Towns in the Eighteenth Century.* New York: W. W. Norton and Co., 1970.

Zuckerman, Michael. *Peaceable Kingdoms: New England Towns in the Eighteenth Century.* New York: W. W. Norton and Co., 1970.

Zuckerman, Michael. "William Byrd's Family." *Perspectives in American History* 12 (1979): 253–312.

Zuckerman, Michael, ed. *Friends and Neighbors: Group Life in America's First Society.* Philadelphia: Temple University Press, 1982.

Index